The Wilder House Series in
Politics, History, and Culture
is published in association with
the Wilder House Board of Editors
and the University of Chicago.

David Laitin, *Editor*
Leora Auslander, *Assistant Editor*
George Steinmetz, *Assistant Editor*

Language and Power: Exploring Political Cultures in Indonesia by
Benedict R. O'G. Anderson

Also in the series

*State and Society in Medieval Europe: Gwynedd and Languedoc
under Outside Rule* by James Given
*Reclaiming the Sacred: Lay Religion and Popular Politics in
Revolutionary France* by Suzanne Desan

Benedict R. O'G. Anderson

Language and Power

EXPLORING POLITICAL CULTURES

IN INDONESIA

Cornell University Press

ITHACA AND LONDON

First published 1990 by Cornell University Press.

International Standard Book Number (cloth) 0–8014–2354–6
International Standard Book Number (paper) 0–8014–9758–2
Library of Congress Catalog Card Number 90–55126
Printed in the United States of America
*Librarians: Library of Congress cataloging information
appears on the last page of the book.*

⊗The paper in this book meets the minimum requirements
of the American National Standard for Information Sciences—
Permanence of Paper for Printed Library Materials, ANSI Z39.48–1984.

For Jim, Amrih, Kampret, and both Claires

Contents

Language and Power

Introduction

Das war kein wahres Paradies—
Es gab dort verbotene Bäume
Heinrich Heine

One pleasant English afternoon, in early November 1956, I was sauntering idly through Cambridge when I came across a small crowd of mostly dark-skinned students listening attentively to a politely passionate Indian or Pakistani orator. He was denouncing Prime Minister Anthony Eden's decision to join with France and Israel in the invasion of the Suez Canal zone. For me, it might as well have been an open-air puppet show, and I was ready, after a few minutes, to saunter on, when a band of large, heavyset, upperclass English students appeared out of nowhere and assaulted the little assembly. The slightly built "colonials" were no match for them and put up little resistance. The scene seemed incomprehensible, and I feebly tried to get the educated louts to stop. My spectacles were smacked off my face, and so, by chance, I joined the column of the assaulted. Two things then amazed me. First, that the beaters were singing "God Save the Queen" and attempting to make everyone join the singing with them. Second, that I was almost blind with rage. I was then twenty years old and had never had a serious political thought in my life. About a year later, I sailed to America to begin thirty years of studying Indonesia and her politics.

For a youngster whose education until then had been largely confined to study of the classics, and French and English literature, the move toward Asia through America felt like an exhilarating break with the past. But looking back, it seems to me that this feeling was in part a youthful illusion. My father had been born in Penang, where his father, an officer in the imperial army, was stationed. As a young man, he had been more or less disowned by the elderly general when he failed his first-year examinations at Cambridge; so, for adventure as much as anything else, he went off to join the Imperial Maritime Customs in China. Almost three decades of work in China made him fluent in Chinese and a quizzical Sinophile. Hence, I was born in Kunming, grew up in a household filled with things Chinese, and developed eating habits very different from those of my neighboring Irish contemporaries. And there was a further link to Asia, in that Ti Hai, the *amah* my mother hired to nurse me (and who became her much loved friend), was a young Vietnamese girl who had ridden the spectacular mountain railway up from Hanoi through Lang Son to Kunming. The family photograph albums were full of pictures of colonial Vietnam and Chiang Kai-shek's dilapidated China.

Remoter family history—though I became aware of it only later— played its own role. On my English mother's side there were mainly conventional businessmen, judges, and policemen, though my great-uncle had made what in those days was a daring journey through Central Asia, and even wrote a book about it. My father's family, however, was odder, and of mixed Irish and Anglo-Irish origins. My grandmother's people, the O'Gormans, had long been active in na-tionalist politics. Her great-uncle had been imprisoned for joining the United Irishmen's rebellion of 1798. Her grandfather had joined, and later became secretary of, Daniel O'Connell's Catholic Association, fighting for Catholic emancipation. One of her cousins became a very stout member of Charles Parnell's group of Irish nationalist parlia-mentarians at Westminster. Because of all this, though I was educated in England from the age of eleven, it was difficult to imagine myself English.

Nor was America so strange. In 1941, already very ill, and foresee-ing the coming war in the Pacific, my father decided to take the family home from China via the United States. Pearl Harbor and the sub-marine warfare in the Atlantic made completion of this journey im-possible for four more years. He found work as a Chinese translator for British Intelligence, and we spent the war years in California and in Denver, where I got my initial formal schooling. There began a series of estrangements—English accent in American schools, later American accent in Irish schools, Irishisms in English schools—that made language for me beneficially problematic.

But why Indonesia? Perhaps partly because in the late 1950s China was closed to Westerners, and my father had long since died. Mainly, I now think, because in 1957–58 Indonesia was in the throes of a civil war, in which the CIA was actively involved. To a youngster only recently made aware of politics—one might say imperialist politics— Indonesia seemed both Asian and of immediate political relevance. I knew that Cornell University was then, besides Yale, the only place in the United States where Indonesia was seriously studied. But the effective reason I managed to get there was that an old friend of mine had found me a job as a teaching assistant in politics (for which I was wholly unqualified). In Ithaca, I had the opportunity to study Indonesia under George Kahin, pioneer of Indonesian studies in America, founder of the Cornell Modern Indonesia Project, and author of the inspiring classic *Nationalism and Revolution in Indonesia*. No less important for me were the people whom Kahin had gathered round him in Ithaca. There was the late John Echols, courtly Virginian master of a dozen languages from Swedish to Old Javanese, who published the first modern Indonesian-English dictionary. He introduced me to Indonesian literature, and selflessly built Cornell's Southeast Asian library into the preeminent collection that now bears his name. There was also the late Claire Holt, born to a wealthy Jewish family in Riga, who had been a dancer and dance journalist in Paris and New York before spending the 1930s in colonial Java as the colleague and lover of the iconoclastic German archaeologist Wilhelm Stutterheim. Having worked as a translator and Indonesian teacher for the American government during World War II, she left in disgust during the McCarthy years and was recruited by Kahin to teach Indonesian language and culture, though she had no formal academic qualifications. It was she, more than any one else, who gave me links to the world of preindependence Indonesia, to Javanese culture, and to the best in Dutch colonial scholarship. Like John Echols, she was devoted to Java and Indonesia, but never to the exclusion of the wider world.

In December 1961 I arrived in Jakarta to do doctoral research, and managed to stay, thanks to the Indonesian hyperinflation of those years, until April 1964. It was the sunset heyday of President Sukarno and his populist-authoritarian, conservative-radical Guided Democracy. There were few Westerners in Jakarta then, partly as a result of the country's down-spinning economy and partly because of Sukarno's generally anti-Western foreign policy. Although a conservative, ex-guerrilla military controlled the economy and much of everyday public life, the complex balance of forces between the president, the military, the Muslims, the Communists, and the secular bourgeois nationalists made for round-the-clock, unending political warfare. I had never been in a society so politicized and yet, to a young, insignificant outsider, so accessible. In September 1963 I returned from a brief trip to Kuala Lumpur to find the British Embassy, which happened to adjoin the house where I was lodging, being torched by a variety of groups supporting President Sukarno's angry response to London's establishment of the Federation of Malaysia. I had gone a bit native by then, and recall watching the burning building with a certain Irish schadenfreude, leaning over the fence in my T-shirt and sarong. One of the arsonist leaders, a former army man I knew, dropped by to tell me not to worry, I was completely safe. I had never imagined that I was in danger.

The politics of the period were absorbing, but I cannot say that I took any intelligent sides. There were a hundred reasons to dislike the corrupt and often brutal military, but a couple of the people I most respected were army officers. Sukarno's populist and anti-imperialist rhetoric was exhilarating, but I lived a stone's throw from Indonesia's first "international class" hotel, the Hotel Indonesia, which the president had ordered built to put his country, as it were, on the map. Every week some skeletal laborer, unused to working a hundred and more feet above the ground in the tropical noonday, hurtled to his death. The Communist party's leader, D. N. Aidit, regularly published the most cogent and lucid analyses of current Indonesian politics, but it was strange, following a huge Communist rally in downtown Jakarta, to find the crowd lustily singing anti-Western songs created under the auspices of the Japanese Military Occupation regime of 1942–45 (which had executed most of the then Communist leaders).

The truth is that, thanks to the example of Claire Holt and the experience of everyday life, I eventually became more interested in the society and its culture than in its politics. Indonesia was then, to a degree that astonished someone accustomed to the class hierarchies of England, Ireland, and even America, an egalitarian country. Kitty-corner from the burned-out British Embassy and across the road from my lodgings was a muddy, triangular bit of open land. In the late afternoons, little slum boys would play football there, using their youngest siblings as crawling goalposts, and distinguishing sides by wearing either shorts or nothing. It was quite easy to wangle an invitation to shadow plays put on in the presidential palace, and that, too, was an eye-opener. Sukarno would always be there, flirting with foreign female guests and politicking with members of the corps diplomatique, but so were we hoi polloi, maids and their children, shadow play aficionados of every stripe, students, veterans of the revolutionary era, and so on. One could stretch out on a flea-infested mat along with everyone else, get one's plate of cold rice and curry and a glass of warm tea, and watch the whole night through. There must have been security personnel around, but one didn't notice them.

For most of my time there, Indonesia was under martial law. When I first arrived it was thought perilous to drive by night the four hours needed to reach the cool mountain city of Bandung, because of the presence of Islamic rebels. Insurrections, or their smoking residues, were still going on in Sumatra and Sulawesi (Celebes); and West Irian was in the process of being "absorbed" into Mother Indonesia after thirteen years of bitter Dutch-Indonesian conflict. Together with the shattered economy, these events made travel outside Java very difficult, and so my first two and a half years in Indonesia were essentially spent on that island, aside from brief visits to Bali and North Sumatra.

For me, then, Indonesia became largely Java. If I thought of myself as politically on the muddled left, my social background, my classical education, my interest in literature and art, and Claire Holt all led to a sort of love affair with what I then imagined as "traditional Javanese culture"—gamelan music, folk theater, the shadow play, court dance, bandit legends, magic, and so forth. It was a good time in which so to become infatuated, since in the early 1960s power and Javanese culture were largely separated. The old royal palaces were filthy and dilapidated—and perfectly accessible in an untouristic way. The Revolution and postrevolutionary populist politics had come very close to eliminating the feudal aristocracy as a serious political force. I was lucky enough to have two remarkable elderly Javanese teachers, who were also brothers. The elder, Professor Poerbatjaraka, had as a young man been the first Dutch-trained "Javanologist" to get a doctorate at the University of Leiden. But he had a jovial contempt for much Dutch colonial scholarship, as well as for the guardians of the feudal past. His lips were often red from betel-chewing, and he much enjoyed telling anyone, Javanese or foreigner, whom he found too reverential that religion, any religion, was self-deception. His slightly younger brother, Pak Kodrat, who taught me a bit of Javanese music, was no less iconoclastic, though one of the three most accomplished classical Javanese musicians then active. Both were loyal to their tradition, but wholly sharp-eyed about it. Only much later, however, did I begin to understand, and appreciate, their stance.

I returned to America, via Holland, in the late summer of 1964, just before Lyndon Johnson's election as president and just after the passage of the Gulf of Tonkin Resolution by the American Congress. The good days were almost over. The next year was the turning point. That spring the massive American bombing of Vietnam began, and the troops soon followed in their thousands. George Kahin appeared on television in the first national teach-in on the war, and, like his other senior students, I tried to do what little I could to help. Then, in the early morning of October 1 that year, Lieutenant-Colonel Untung, an obscure battalion commander in Sukarno's Tjakrabirawa Palace Guard, went on the radio to announce that what he called the "September 30th Movement" had been launched to save the president from a "Council of Generals," which, backed by the CIA, was plotting to overthrow the regime. Within hours, Untung's "coup" had been countercouped by forces under then Major-General Suharto. It transpired that six prominent Indonesian generals had been killed by the Untung group. All nonmilitary mass media were immediately closed down, and within seventy-two hours the army was announcing that Untung was a Communist pawn, and that the party had been behind the coup and the murders. Three weeks later began massacres by the army and by civilian vigilantes, which, between October 1965 and January 1966, resulted in the deaths of at least half a million Indonesians identified, correctly or not, as being on the left. Hundreds of thousands of others were imprisoned, tortured, orphaned. In March 1966, Suharto carried out a bloodless coup against Sukarno. By March 1967 he was acting president, by March 1968 president. So he has been ever since. Sukarno died under house arrest in 1970, almost at the same time as Claire Holt. I started to write in earnest about Indonesia in the winter of 1965–66, with the sense that the Indonesia I had known and loved was gone forever.

Between January 1966 and March 1967 I wrote three texts, of which one, "The Languages of Indonesian Politics," is included in this volume. But it is of a piece with the others: my doctoral dissertation, published eventually in 1972 as *Java in a Time of Revolution;* and the hurried, provisional study of Untung's "coup," done in collaboration with Ruth McVey and Frederick Bunnell, which, leaked in the late spring of 1966, became notorious as the "Cornell Paper," and eventually became the main reason for my being barred from Indonesia for now eighteen years.

In those great times, Vietnam and Indonesia came together for me in a new way. For most Southeast Asianists, they had long been loosely linked. Sukarno and Ho Chi Minh had proclaimed their respective countries' independence within a few days of each other in August

1945. Both countries had fought bloody, and up to a point successful, wars for independence against fading European imperialist powers, unlike Burma, Malaysia, Cambodia, Thailand, or the Philippines.

The link was nationalism, and probably, deeper down, Ireland. Ireland was exemplary in its long, savage struggle for autonomy from the most powerful imperialist state of the pre—World War II era, in its extraordinary literature, its fratricides, its self-absorption, and its economic involution. One could, in those days, fully recognize all this, and still strongly feel: "She has a right to be what she is." So with Indonesia and Vietnam.

I remember rather sympathizing with Sukarno when he told incensed American officials to "go to hell with your aid." The best-meaning among them were convinced, quite correctly, that Sukarno had no coherent economic alternative in mind, and were painfully aware of the near-famine conditions that prevailed in Java in the bad harvest year of 1963. The majority, however, were imperially certain that nationalism, in Indonesia as in Vietnam, was largely a blind for communism and anti-Americanism. When I was back in Ithaca, I recall feeling angry at official Washington's lordly way of talking about the "underdeveloped nations" of Asia and Africa. The term seemed to reduce particular histories and unique cultures to a homogeneous rubble.

Perhaps it was out of an inverted Orientalism, but my sympathies, like those of many of my fellow Southeast Asianists, were then strongly with the nationalisms of the region. Vietnamese heroism in the face of the American firestorm, which I saw as a nationalist more than a socialist heroism, linked itself to Indonesia's fate. Sukarno was no Ho Chi Minh, but once he had been overthrown, by an American-supported military regime of exceptional brutality, he easily acquired the pathos of a Kossuth.

Yet it was impossible not to remember that almost all the key actors in the Indonesian catastrophe of 1965 were Indonesians, indeed Javanese: Sukarno, Suharto, Untung. Most of those massacred in 1965–66 were Javanese, and their killers were also Javanese. Nothing the Dutch imperialists had done in 350 years of depredations in the archipelago matched the speed, scale, and ferocity of Suharto's *matanza* against his own people. Claire Holt reminded me that the most loved part of Javanese mythology was an indigenized version of the Mahabharata, which culminates in an orgy of bloodshed between close kinsmen. Still, it felt like discovering that a loved one is a murderer.

It was at this juncture in my life that the questions developed that animate all the essays in this book: emotionally, how still to love a murderer; politically, how to understand what Java and Indonesia have done to each other; morally, how to conjoin human solidarity with respect for difference; and theoretically, how to link the splendors of the imagining life with the remorseless engines of global economic and technological change.

All things considered, it is rather surprising that I was permitted to return three times to Indonesia (in 1967, 1968, and 1972) after the leaking of the so-called Cornell Paper.[1] For its tentative argument—that discontented army officers rather than Communists were responsible for Untung's bloody "coup"—removed any possible justification for the massacres of 1965–66 and questioned the military government's claims to legitimacy. Perhaps the Indonesian authorities hoped that my coauthors and I would recant and repudiate the text. But on the basis of the available evidence we found this impossible to do, certainly in the terms expected of us. In any case, by 1972, the Indonesian government had had enough. Irritated to discover that, owing to confusion and rivalry among its intelligence services, I had managed to get into the country once again, it lost little time in expelling me.

Exile came at a fortunate moment. It happened just as certain Thai intellectuals, young professors, and students were beginning their campaign against the Thanom-Praphat military dictatorship and its complicity in the Vietnam War—a campaign that ultimately brought the regime down in the popular demonstrations of October 1973. A number of those involved in the campaign were close friends from Cornell. I therefore turned from Indonesia to Siam, arriving in Bangkok to study the language, culture, and politics of the country at the end of 1974. It was a good time to be there. The euphoria resulting from the restoration of basic freedoms was infectious. Reasonably free elections were held in the spring of 1975 for the first time in almost thirty years. Trade unions were legalized, peasant leagues were formed, censorship

---

[1]When completed in early January 1966, the study was circulated to a small circle of trusted specialists for their comments. While permitting them any use they cared to make of its contents, we asked them to keep the document itself strictly confidential. Given the theses of the study, and the fact that in Indonesia the massacres were still going on, we feared for the safety of friends and former students there (even though they knew nothing of our work) in the event of its becoming public. But we managed the matter amateurishly. Once leaked, the document became widely seen, in Washington and in Indonesia, as evidence of a concerted, behind-the-scenes conspiracy. To try to set the record straight, we later published the entire text, unchanged, as *A Preliminary Analysis of the October 1, 1965, Coup in Indonesia* (Ithaca, N.Y.: Cornell Modern Indonesia Project, Interim Report Series, 1971).

dwindled and came close to being abolished, and student activists pressed hard for long overdue social and economic reforms. I returned to America just before the right-wing murders of student activists, trade unionists, and peasant leaders began, at the end of 1975, which culminated in the bloody coup of October 6, 1976. But I had been there long enough, and later visited there frequently enough, to become almost as attached to Siam as I was to Indonesia. Luckily, too, for reasons too complex to describe here,[2] the terror of 1976–77 abated, and by the early 1980s a reasonably stable, reasonably open bourgeois parliamentary democracy was coming into being. A generation of brilliant students who had been imprisoned or had fled to the maquis in 1976 returned to the universities. Disillusioned by their experiences with a Communist Party of Thailand, whose leadership blindly followed Peking's Machiavellian whims, they nonetheless retained their *marxisant* traditions, their patriotism, and their critical outlook. In the early 1980s they began to produce the best scholarship on a Southeast Asian country by its own nationals. A number of them became my friends.

Two other beneficial consequences of exile were being forced to start thinking comparatively, against the friendly Orientalist grain, and to return seriously to the written word, especially literature.

Uncolonized, monarchical, Buddhist, and Sinicized, Siam offered, in the Southeast Asian region, perhaps the sheerest contrast with long-colonized, republican, Muslim and Hindu-Javanese Indonesia. Almost everything I discovered about the former raised new questions about the latter. I began to feel the need for a framework in which it would be possible to think coherently about both. At this juncture I was greatly helped by my brother Perry, who in 1974 published his *Passages from Antiquity to Feudalism* and *Lineages of the Absolutist State,* both models of sober, intricate, comparative historical enquiry. Up to this time, our lives had taken us in very different directions. While I was Orientalizing and particularizing in America, Indonesia, and Siam he had been living in London and making the *New Left Review* the most intellectually serious, comparative, and internationally oriented of English-language Marxist journals, as well as writing books on Swedish socialism and Portugal's colonial empire. I had ignored earlier gentle suggestions that Indonesians were, after all, part of the human species, and could not possibly be incomparable and

---

[2]A brief account of these changes, and the domestic and international forces that engendered them, can be found in my "Murder and Progress in Siam," *New Left Review,* Modern 181 (May–June 1990), pp. 33–48. See also the introduction to my *In the Mirror: Literature and Politics in Siam in the American Era* (Bangkok: Duang Kamol, 1985).

unique as I had nationalistically insisted. Now I was ready to see his point, and to learn substantially from *Passages* and *Lineages*. Through him, I also gradually came into closer personal and intellectual touch with the circle of the *NLR*. The journal's very pages, in which theoretical exegeses and political-historical articles on dozens of different countries comfortably jostled each other, encouraged the hope that, through a broadly Marxist optic, my Indonesia could join the world.

After 1972, on the other hand, I stopped speaking Indonesian, except with students at Cornell and occasional Indonesian visitors to the campus. It was only then that I realized how much my earlier studies had depended on constant conversations and absorption in the strange routines of everyday Indonesian life. There was now no help for it but to turn back to documents. So it was that in the mid-1970s I began to study seriously, for the first time, Indonesian and Javanese literature. Fortunately, the greatest living Southeast Asian writer, Pramoedya Ananta Toer, was both Indonesian and Javanese. I had not met him when I first went to Indonesia, and after the upheaval of October 1965 he was imprisoned, without trial, for fourteen years. To this day, though we have regularly corresponded, we have never met. But thanks to my friend and colleague Jim Siegel, who prodded me into sharing with him a graduate seminar on Pramoedya's writings and showed me novel ways of reading these texts, I began to perceive the outline of an unexpectedly new "traditional Java," fantastical, yet profoundly serious.[3] More broadly, Pramoedya gave me an inkling of how one might fruitfully link the shapes of literature with the political imagination.

The convergence of all these fortuities came in 1982. With the stimulus provided by the *NLR*'s Anthony Barnett, visiting Cornell to work on a book about Vietnam and Cambodia, and the encouragement of my brother Perry, I began writing the manuscript that in 1983 was published as *Imagined Communities: Reflections on the Origin and Spread of Nationalism*. As I look back on it now, it seems an odd book to be written by someone born in China, raised in three countries, speaking with an obsolete English accent, carrying an Irish passport, living in America, and devoted to Southeast Asia. Yet perhaps it could only be written from various exiles, and with divided loyalties.

---

[3]Siegel's three remarkable books are: *The Rope of God* (Berkeley: University of California Press, 1969); *Shadow and Sound: The Historical Thought of a Sumatran Kingdom* (Chicago: University of Chicago Press, 1979); and *Solo in the New Order: Language and Hierarchy in an Indonesian City* (Princeton, N.J.: Princeton University Press, 1986).

Such, briefly, is the background for the present book. But it was the writing of *Imagined Communities* that made it possible to look back over twenty-five years of writing about Java and Indonesia, and make some sense of a "devious-cruising" search. The friendly reader will quickly see not so much progress as a circling, back and around, of the three themes by which the eight chapters assembled here are ordered.

Part I consists of three essays, dating from 1972, 1985 and 1983, on the issue of power. The first was written directly out of my fieldwork in Java between 1961 and 1964. Its mood is indigenist and nationalist. Composed at a time when Western officialdom was cheering the elimination of Sukarno's anti-Western, Javanese "irrationalism" in favor of what was then esteemed as the pragmatic, pro-Western rationalism of the Suharto regime, it attempted to show that "traditional Javanese thought" was perfectly rational once its assumptions about the nature of power were properly understood. It also argued, against the prevailing wisdom of the time, that Suharto shared many Javanese conceptions with the man he dethroned. (When the essay was later published in the Indonesian language, all reference to this continuity was censored.) The essay concluded with some speculative paragraphs suggesting how an understanding of Javanese ideas about power might encourage a rethinking of Max Weber's concept of charisma. Chapter 2, composed in 1985 and hitherto unpublished, reconsidered the implications of the first chapter's conclusions in the context of *Imagined Communities'* comparative framework, and in light of what I had learned from the study of Pramoedya Ananta Toer. Chapter 3, published in 1983, is fully comparative, and focuses on institutions rather than cultural conceptions. Its theme is another rationality, that of the late colonial state, and a different continuity, that between the colonial regime and the one currently straddling Indonesia. Methodologically, the three essays are inconsistent with one another, and have other obvious flaws besides. I think each contains a partial truth, but have as yet been unable to see how these fragments might intelligently be linked together.

The essays in part II, published in 1966, 1978, and 1984, focus on the relationship between politics and languages in Indonesia (especially Indonesian and Javanese). The first, chapter 4, was written when I was still a graduate student, and during the time of the massacres. It is the one essay that I have tampered with in preparing this volume, not to change an argument or an outlook, but to save myself embarrassment over slovenly English and youthful extravagancies. I include it primarily for historical reasons, since it was, I think, the first study in English of how changing language-use in Indonesia reflected the decay of revolutionary impulses, the restratification of postrevolutionary society, and the increasingly visible antagonism between Indonesian and Javanese. Chapter 5 came directly out of my last brief stay in Indonesia, in 1972. My passport had been taken away for "inspection" by the immigration service and military intelligence, and I had been forbidden to conduct any interviews. I spent a good deal of my enforced leisure reading newspapers and comic books, going to movies, and walking about downtown Jakarta. The experience encouraged me to think about visual languages—what public monuments, cartoons, and mediocre popular films could tell the student about Indonesian politics if they were seen in comparative perspective. The essay also enlarged explicitly on a theme only confusedly broached in the text of 1966: the ways in which the revolutionary Indonesian nationalism of 1945–49 had been logoized, ossified, and Javanized, by memory, time, the massacres, and political artifice, into its own negation.

Chapter 6, published in 1984, was written wholly out of documents, primarily literary texts. In the late 1970s I had started to read, more seriously than before, about the pre–twentieth-century history of the archipelago, and on the singular trajectory of the Netherlands and Dutch imperialism in the context of world history. Remarkable research by Indonesian scholars like Sartono Kartodirdjo and Onghokham and younger Western scholars such as Peter Carey, Tony Day, Ann Kumar, and Jim Rush were radically changing the accepted view of nineteenth-century Java. For the first time, I began to see that Javanese tradition, as I had so long hypostasized it, was largely a twentieth-century invention, and that the old culture was tense with inner contradictions and antagonistic currents. It now became possible to circle back, gingerly, toward my youthful affections—for visible to me now were Javanese who hated much in what they had been bequeathed. The chapter thus attempts to trace a tradition of Javanese nonconformism, from the 1870s to the 1970s—naturally via the bridge of Pramoedya Ananta Toer.

Part III contains only two essays, both experimental. They deal with the difficult problem of explaining and understanding the profound changes in consciousness among certain Javanese intellectuals between the end of the eighteenth century and the first decades of the twentieth. Chapter 7, originally published in 1979, looked closely at the strange autobiography written by Dr. Soetomo, an attractive, moderately conservative Indonesian nationalist of the period 1908–38. Trained as a Western-style medical doctor, Soetomo was a member of the first, small generation of Javanese to get a good modern education. It was an education he appreciated, and which he used selflessly to serve his people, but it also created a Foucaultian break in consciousness with his immediate forebears. I tried to decipher how Soetomo understood this break, and how he attempted to negotiate a resolution between his Indonesian nationalism and his Javanese roots. Of all the essays in this volume, this is the one that is, I think, the most achieved. It is certainly the one closest to my heart today, perhaps because the old Javanese doctor was, as the Irish used to say, a "lovely man." Chapter 8, hitherto unpublished, was only finished in 1989, though it draws on an earlier paper and article. It is the essay most directly inspired by Pramoedya Ananta Toer, especially by the phantasmagoric tales he published in the 1950s.[4] But it could not have been written without the benefit of discussions with Amrih Widodo and John Pemberton. By looking at two famous (or notorious) Javanese literary texts, it tries to understand how certain nineteenth-century Javanese intellectuals struggled, within the syntax of the traditions available to them, to deal with the utter collapse of aristocratic Javanese political leadership and the final crushing subjugation of the island's population to colonial capitalism—in an era before the establishment of Western-style schools, newspapers, and so on. Whether its conclusions are sound remains to be seen, but I think it is at least methodologically novel. For it treats the two poems neither as works or art nor as decodable evidence of historical events or cultural practices, but as phantasmagoria: "political" dreams before any word for politics entered the Javanese language; "class" fantasies before the advent of class consciousness.

Only the reader can judge whether the book as a whole has an intelligible shape. If it does, it is because of the questions that haunt it. Since these questions arise from experienced life and history, they will not go away, even if the answers are always missing.

Most of the essays, when they originally appeared, contained ac-

---

[4]Especially those contained in the volumes entitled *Subuh* [Dawn] (Jakarta: Balai Pustaka, 1950); *Tjerita dari Blora* [Tales of Blora] (Jakarta: Balai Pustaka, 1952); and, my favorite, *Tjerita dari Djakarta, Sekumpulan Karikatur Keadaan dan Manusianja* [Tales of Jakarta, A Collection of Caricatures of Circumstances and Their Human Beings] (Jakarta: Grafica, 1957).

knowledgments of intellectual and other debts. I have omitted these references in the various chapters to avoid irritating repetition. It is therefore all the more appropriate to say some heartfelt thanks here:

To my much-missed mother and my aunt, who brought me up with infinite love, tolerance, encouragement, and discipline.

To George Kahin, Claire Holt, and John Echols, who with endless generosity gave me the foundations for a life's work on Southeast Asia, especially Indonesia.

To Jim Siegel, who has influenced my thinking more than anyone else, and without whose presence at Cornell for the past twenty-five years I cannot imagine how I would have seen beyond my nose.

To Charnvit Kasetsiri, who gave me a second life.

To Pramoedya Ananta Toer, a moral inspiration and a writer who has given me countless hours of pleasure and puzzlement.

To Southeast Asianist friends and colleagues, at Cornell and elsewhere, in particular Taufik Abdullah, Nidhi Aeusrivongse, Thanet Aphornsuwan, the late Harry Benda, Thak Chaloemtiarana, Anthony Day, Herbert Feith, Nancy Florida, Clifford Geertz, Vedi Hadiz, Martin Hatch, Reynaldo Ileto, Tsuyoshi Kato, Arnold Kohen, Ann Kumar, Daniel and Arlene Lev, Burhan Magenda, Ruth McVey, Rudolf Mrázek, Goenawan Mohamad, Soemarsaid Moertono, Onghokham, John Pemberton, Seksan and Chiranan Prasertkul, Vicente Rafael, Craig Reynolds, Suchart Sawatsi, Savitri Scherer, James Scott, Takashi and Saya Shiraishi, Toenggoel Siagian, John Smail, Mas Soeryono, Robert Taylor, Kasian Tejapira, Carl Trocki, Kenji Tsuchiya, Mildred Wagemann, Amrih Widodo, Thongchai Winichakul, Oliver Wolters, and many others, who gave me so many ideas, materials, insights, and criticisms.

To three Good Germans, Karl Marx, Walter Benjamin, and Eric Auerbach, who helped me to think about the modern world.

To my brother Perry, and friends now or formerly at the *New Left Review*—Anthony Barnett, Judith Herrin, Robin Blackburn, Tom Nairn, among others, who helped a frog out from under its coconut shell.

And to my students—American, Indonesian, Thai, Filipino, Malaysian, Burmese, Chinese, Japanese, English, Australian, Dutch, and French. There is no way to describe what I have learned, day by day, year by year, from them and their affectionate questioning.

PART I

POWER

CHAPTER I

The Idea of Power
in Javanese Culture

In spite of the considerable body of scholarly work that has been done on Indonesian, and especially Javanese, history and culture, few attempts have been made at a systematic analysis either of traditional political conceptions or of their powerful, continuing impact on contemporary Indonesia.[1]

The first deficiency can in part be attributed to the fact that Indonesia's classical literatures, unlike those of China and India, contain no full-fledged expositions of any indigenous "political theory." A contemporary reconstruction of such a theory has therefore to be abstracted from scattered historical sources and then synthesized with fragmentary insights drawn from field experience.

The second deficiency stems clearly from the first: The absence of a systematic exposition of a political theory in the classical literatures of Indonesia has fostered the assumption that no such theory, however implicit, exists, and thus has hindered an awareness of the actual coherence and logic of traditional political conceptions. This lack of awareness has, in turn, hampered the analysis and evaluation of the influence of such conceptions on contemporary political behavior. The tendency has been to select discrete elements from traditional

First published in 1972. C. Holt, ed., *Culture and Politics in Indonesia* (Ithaca, N.Y.: Cornell University Press, 1972), pp. 1–69. Reprinted with permission.

[1]The final form of this essay owes much to the insights and critical comments offered by Harry Benda, Lance Castles, Herbert Feith, Clifford Geertz, Claire Holt, George Kahin, Lionel Landry, Daniel Lev, Denys Lombard, Ruth McVey, Soemarsaid Moertono, Onghokham, James Siegel, John Smail, Soedjatmoko, Mildred Wagemann, and Oliver Wolters. I wish to express my deep appreciation for all this help, while taking full responsibility for the content of the text.

culture[2] and correlate them in an arbitrary and ad hoc manner with particular aspects of present-day politics. Cultural factors are typically brought in as a sort of deus ex machina when the combination of social, economic, and historical variables seems not completely to account for particular forms of political behavior. These cultural elements are thus introduced essentially to "save the phenomena." The implicit assumption of a lack of coherence in the cultural tradition has, it seems to me, inevitably led to a lack of methodological coherence in developing an overall approach to contemporary Indonesian politics.

The present essay is an effort to remedy at least the first of the two basic deficiencies that I have pointed out. By offering a systematic exposition of traditional Javanese conceptions[3] about politics and demonstrating their inner coherence, I hope to make a preliminary step toward a fuller investigation of the interrelationships between culture and social action in Indonesia.[4] Such a presentation should make it evident that traditional Javanese culture did have a political theory that offered a systematic and logical explanation of political behavior quite independent of the perspectives of modern political science and in many ways in fundamental opposition to them. In effect, the same objective political phenomena can be, and have been, interpreted in quite different but equally consistent ways by observers from within each intellectual tradition. To use a time-worn but convenient simile, the two traditions provide strikingly different lenses for viewing the political landscape.

My intention, then, is to describe the picture of social and political life seen through traditional Javanese lenses, and to draw explicit contrasts with the pictures seen through the lenses of modern social science. Yet these lenses obviously not only structure the perceptions (and thus the interpretations) of those who wear them but, in so doing, influence their behavior. The pictures that filter through the

[2]In this essay the terms *tradition, cultural tradition,* and *traditional culture* are used interchangeably.

[3]My focus throughout is on Javanese tradition, partly for reasons of economy and clarity, but also because of my greater ignorance of the political traditions of other Indonesian ethnic groups.

[4]In many respects this essay tries to follow the program for the development of a "scientific phenomenology of culture" suggested by Geertz in his brilliant analysis of Balinese cultural tradition. See Clifford Geertz, *Person, Time, and Conduct in Bali: An Essay in Cultural Analysis,* Southeast Asia Studies, Cultural Report Series no. 14 (New Haven: Yale University, 1966), p. 7. The second chapter of his study gives an excellent outline of the reasons why such a program is urgently required and the intellectual problems involved in its implementation.

lenses are, after all, approximately what Weber called the subjective meanings attached to social action by its participants, meanings that, as he amply demonstrated, are essential for any full understanding of such action by an observer.[5] Only a deciphering of the meaning attached by traditional (and partly detraditionalized) Javanese to such objective phenomena as sexual activity or the accumulation of wealth will open the way to a general comprehension of the workings of politics in both traditional and present-day Java. But I cannot undertake here a detailed analysis of the complex interplay of meaning and action within either traditional or contemporary Javanese society; for ideas must be systematically presented before their practical influence on objective phenomena can be studied in an orderly fashion.

I should also stress at the outset that I in no way assume that Javanese conceptions about politics are, in their separate elements, peculiarly Javanese—although I do believe that, in their totality, they form a unique amalgam. Many of these elements derive historically from the influence of Indic civilization; others have parallels in a wide range of Asian and non-Asian traditional cultures.[6] If an unwarranted uniqueness seems to be attributed here to Javanese conceptions, this stems mainly from the wish to avoid constant, irritating qualifications. Indeed, the similarities between Javanese and other traditional conceptions of politics are so integral a part of the assumptions behind this exposition that they form the basis of its theoretical conclusion: the possibility of a useful simplification and revision of the conventional concept of charisma and its historical emergence.[7]

Concepts of Power

Study of classical Javanese literature and present-day political behavior suggests that one key to understanding the Javanese theory of politics may be the traditional interpretation of what social science refers to as *power*.[8] For the Javanese conception differs radically from

[5]See the discussion of Weber's use of the term *Sinn* as a key theoretical concept in Reinhard Bendix, *Max Weber: An Intellectual Portrait* (Garden City, N.Y.: Doubleday Anchor, 1962), p. 474.

[6]Compare, for example, the excellent discussion of comparable Japanese concepts in Masao Maruyama, *Thought and Behaviour in Modern Japanese Politics* (London: Oxford University Press, 1963), chap. 1.

[7]See the conclusion to this essay.

[8]It is important to bring out from the start an inherent linguistic and conceptual problem in the analysis that I am about to develop. Because this essay is written in English, by a native English-speaker, primarily for native English-speakers, and also because my own

the concept of power that has evolved in the West since the Middle Ages, and from this difference there logically follow contrasting views of the workings of politics and history.[9]

It is perhaps useful to recall that the concept of power became an explicit problem for Western political thinkers only after the waning of the Middle Ages. The first philosophers to devote serious and extended attention to it were Machiavelli and Hobbes. The fact that, particularly since the time of Hobbes, the nature, sources, and use of power have been a major concern of Western political thinkers is surely no historical accident: It parallels more or less directly the tide of secularization that has swept over Europe since the Renaissance and

---

intellectual perspective is irremediably Western, I see no choice but to use words and concepts like *power,* which are drawn from a Western analytical and interpretative framework, in dealing with the problem of contrasting that framework with the Javanese. There is clearly a fundamental bias inherent in such a method of work. But without a superordinate language and conceptual framework in which to place both Western and Javanese terms and concepts, all that one can do is to recognize and remain constantly aware of this bias. When I say that the Javanese have a radically different idea of power from that which obtains in the contemporary West, properly speaking this statement is meaningless, since the Javanese have no equivalent word or concept. Conversely, speaking from within the Javanese framework, one could say that the West has a concept of *kasektèn* radically different from that of the Javanese, while in fact modern English does not really have such a concept at all. (The old usage of the word *power,* which survives in such phrases as "The Great Powers" or "Power had gone out of him" [Gospel according to St. Mark, 5:30] approximates the Javanese idea, but by no means coincides with it.) Thus in strict intellectual principle the whole discussion of differing concepts of power in the ensuing section should be accompanied by a parallel discussion of differing Western concepts of kasektèn, as seen from the Javanese viewpoint. This parallel discussion might begin: "Westerners have a concept of kasektèn quite different from ours: they divide it up into concepts like power, legitimacy, and charisma." A full development of this line of analysis is indispensable in principle, but for the reasons given above I have not attempted here more than a pointer as to how it should be approached. Probably only a Javanese could do it effectively.

[9]In the ensuing discussion of Javanese political ideas, I am attempting to map out a pure model for analytical purposes. Traditional Javanese political culture was an extremely complex phenomenon, in which, as in any other culture, it would be naive to try to discern complete consistency. In that traditional culture an indigenous matrix was imperfectly compounded with heterogeneous Brahmanic, Buddhist, and Islamic elements. Nonetheless, the slow process of absorption and synthesis over the centuries prior to the "coming of the West" permitted the crystallization of a relatively high degree of internal consistency. The model I am trying to delineate is thus an "ideal type" of precolonial Javanese political thought, deliberately simplified and exaggerated, which should not be taken as a historical reality.

Java's subjection to Western political, economic, and cultural domination has, particularly in the past hundred years, set in motion an irremediable process of decrystallization. Contemporary Javanese political culture is therefore a heterogeneous, disjunctive, and internally contradictory complex of traditional and Western elements, with a lower degree of internal logic and coherence than in the past. A start at understanding this complex requires a preliminary model of the pre-Western framework of reference—a model this essay tries to provide.

the Reformation. The contemporary concept of power arose historically from the need to interpret politics in a secular world.

Clarification of the Javanese idea of power may be facilitated by a schematic contrast with the more significant aspects of the modern European concept, which can be summarized under four main headings:[10]

1. *Power is abstract.* Strictly speaking, it does not "exist." *Power* is a word used commonly to describe a relationship or relationships. Like the words *authority* or *legitimacy,* it is an abstraction, a formula for certain observed patterns of social interaction. Thus, we normally infer the existence of power in a wide variety of situations in which some men appear to obey, willingly or unwillingly, the wishes of others. We do not usually assert that a particular individual or group has power except by demonstrating the causal linkage between an order, explicit or implicit, and its execution.

2. *The sources of power are heterogeneous.* Since power is ascribed to or inferred from certain patterns of behavior and certain social relationships, a great deal of Western political thought has been devoted to the classification and analysis of these patterns and relationships, and thereby to the distinguishing of different sources of power. Thus, we have come to accept such various sources of power as wealth, social status, formal office, organization, weapons, population, and so forth. Though in practice each of these sources of power may be, indeed usually is, linked with others, in everyday political analysis they are treated as separate variables influencing behavior.

3. *The accumulation of power has no inherent limits.* Since power is simply an abstraction describing certain human relationships, it is not inherently self-limiting. Moreover, insofar as we regard the sources of power as including weapons, wealth, organization, and technology, we recognize that at least in theory there are no limits to its accumulation. To put it another way, one could suggest that the total amount of

[10]I use *modern European concept* as a convenient shorthand term. The four basic notions about power that I am proposing did not spring into existence all at once; their emergence was a slow, uneven process. Although some of these notions may be evident in Classical philosophy, they were largely submerged in the Middle Ages and only developed fully during later periods. Explicit theorizing about the relationship of power and legitimacy emerged historically from the long conflict between the papacy and the rulers of medieval Europe. The modern concept of power as something abstract goes back at least as far as Machiavelli. The idea of the heterogeneous sources of power came into full philosophic flower with Montesquieu and his successors of the Enlightenment. What one might call the "non-zero-sum" view of power probably did not arise until the Industrial Revolution. (These datings are of course no more than rough marking points.) Thus the "modern European concept" of power outlined here is essentially the culmination of a long process of intellectual evolution.

power in the world today is significantly larger than it was thirty years ago (as the result, for example, of the invention of the hydrogen bomb), and that this sum of power will probably continue to increase in the thirty years to come. In this sense our concept of power is directly conditioned by the accelerating development of modern technology.

4. *Power is morally ambiguous.* It follows logically from the secular conception of political power as a relationship between human beings that such power is not inherently legitimate. This moral ambiguity is, of course, enhanced by our view of power as deriving from heterogeneous sources. This heterogeneity has accentuated the prominence and complexity of a question that continues to preoccupy political theorists: What kinds of power are legitimate? Or, more pointedly, what is the relationship between the positivist concept of power and the ethical concept of right?

Briefly, then, the contemporary Western concept of power is an abstraction deduced from observed patterns of social interaction; it is believed to derive from heterogeneous sources; it is in no way inherently self-limiting; and it is morally ambiguous.

In essence, each of these premises about power runs counter to an equivalent premise in the Javanese tradition, and it is from the interrelations between these contrasting premises that the coherence and consistency of that tradition derive.

1. *Power is concrete.* This is the first and central premise of Javanese political thought. Power exists, independent of its possible users. It is not a theoretical postulate but an existential reality. Power is that intangible, mysterious, and divine energy which animates the universe. It is manifested in every aspect of the natural world, in stones, trees, clouds, and fire, but is expressed quintessentially in the central mystery of life, the process of generation and regeneration. In Javanese traditional thinking there is no sharp division between organic and inorganic matter, for everything is sustained by the same invisible power. This conception of the entire cosmos being suffused by a formless, constantly creative energy provides the basic link between the "animism" of the Javanese villages, and the high metaphysical pantheism of the urban centers.[11]

2. *Power is homogeneous.* It follows from this conception that all power is of the same type and has the same source. Power in the hands

---

[11]Thus, the well-known mystical formula *Tuhan adalah Aku* (God is I) expresses the concreteness of the Javanese idea of power. The divine power is the essence of I.

of one individual or one group is identical with power in the hands of any other individual or group.

3. *The quantum of power in the universe is constant.* In the Javanese view, the cosmos is neither expanding nor contracting. The total amount of power within it also remains fixed. Since power simply exists, and is not the product of organization, wealth, weapons, or anything else—indeed, precedes all of these and makes them what they are—its total quantity does not change, even though the distribution of power in the universe may vary. For political theory, this conception has the important corollary that concentration of power in one place or in one person requires a proportional diminution elsewhere.

4. *Power does not raise the question of legitimacy.*[12] Since all power derives from a single homogeneous source, power itself antecedes questions of good and evil. To the Javanese way of thinking it would be meaningless to claim the right to rule on the basis of differential sources of power—for example, to say that power based on wealth is legitimate, whereas power based on guns is illegitimate. Power is neither legitimate nor illegitimate. Power is.

In summary, then, the Javanese see power as something concrete, homogeneous, constant in total quantity, and without inherent moral implications as such.[13] (Henceforward, when the word *power* is used in the Javanese, rather than European, sense, it will be capitalized.)

The Quest for Power

The central problem raised by the Javanese conception of Power, by contrast with the Western tradition of political theory, is not the exercise of Power but its accumulation. Accordingly, a very considerable portion of the traditional literature deals with the problems of concentrating and preserving Power, rather than with its proper uses. In the orthodox tradition, the quest for Power is pursued through yogaistic practices and extreme ascesis. Although these yogaistic practices in various parts of Java take different forms, including fasting, going without sleep, meditation, sexual abstinence, ritual purification,

---

[12]At least not in the form to which we are accustomed. For a fuller discussion, see the section "Power and Ethics."

[13]This contrast is discussed from a slightly different point of view in Maruyama, *Thought and Behaviour,* chap. 9 ("Some Problems of Political Power"), especially the section on "substantive and functional concepts of power" (pp. 269–75).

and sacrifices of various types, one central idea underlies them: All are designed to focus or concentrate the primordial essence. The best guide for sensing the contours of the conception is perhaps the image of the burning-glass or the laser beam, where an extraordinary concentration of light creates an extraordinary outpouring of heat. The analogy is especially apt since, in the classical imagery of Javanese literature, extreme ascesis has precisely this quality of generating physical heat. The legendary kris-makers[14] of the past were supposed to be able to forge the iron blades with their exquisite inlay solely by the heat concentrated in their thumbs. In the typical *gara-gara* section of the *wayang* plays,[15] where an unknown ascetic is practicing meditation, the most signal expression of his concentration is that, in the words of the *dhalang* (puppeteer), the ocean begins to boil and bubble.[16]

The inward significance of such ascesis is in no sense self-mortification with ethical objectives in mind, but solely and singly the acquisition of Power. In the orthodox tradition, ascesis follows the law of compensation that is fundamental to the Javanese sense of the balance of the cosmos. Thus, self-deprivation is more or less equivalent to self-aggrandizement within the ascetic mode; and, as we shall see, by a typical Javanese paradox, self-aggrandizement (in the sense of personal acquisitiveness or personal indulgence) comes to mean self-deprivation (in the sense of loss of Power or loss of concentration). The conception of *concentration* that underlies the practice of asceticism is also correlated closely with the idea of purity; conversely, the idea of impurity is intimately related to *diffusion* and *disintegration*. The world, the flesh, and the devil are not necessarily conceived as evil or immoral, but rather as distracting and diffusing, and thus as leading to the loss of Power. One finds many examples of this line of thought in

---

[14]The *kris* is the short dagger traditionally a basic possession of every male Javanese. Many are believed to contain deposits of Power and are eagerly sought after even if their workmanship is not of the first quality. For a discussion of the symbolic and social significance of the kris, see Willem Huibert Rassers, *Pañji, the Culture Hero, A Structural Study of Religion in Java* (The Hague: Nijhoff, 1959), pp. 219–97.

[15]*Wayang* is the generic name for a variety of types of Javanese drama, the best known of which is the shadow play. The *gara-gara* is a climactic section of the play, in which the order and tranquillity of the cosmos is disturbed.

[16]Cf., e.g., Ki Siswoharsojo, *Pakem Pedhalangan Lampahan Makutharama* (Yogyakarta: n.p., 1963), pp. 44–45; Jacob Kats, *Het Javaansche Toneel*, 1 (*Wajang Poerwa*) (Weltevreden: Commissie voor de Volkslectuur, 1923), p. 52; and for a historical parallel, in which Panembahan Sénapati's ascetic practices have the same effect, see Soemarsaid Moertono, *State and Statecraft in Old Java*, Cornell Modern Indonesia Project Monograph Series (Ithaca, N.Y.: Cornell University, 1968), p. 19, citing Johannes Jacobus Meinsma, ed., *Babad Tanah Djawi* (The Hague: Nijhoff, 1941), p. 77.

the traditional literature. Not only heroes indulge in ascetic practices—some of the most notable practitioners come from the ranks of
the demons and giants who in the wayang stories are the traditional
enemies of gods and men. Accordingly, their Power is often enormous,
on occasion even exceeding that of the gods. The essential difference
between the heroes and their adversaries, however, is that the latter
eventually permit their Power to be diffused by indulging their passions without restraint, whereas the former maintain that steadfastness, that tense singleness of purpose, which insures the maintenance and continued accumulation of Power.[17]

Besides this orthodox view of the road to Power, another, heterodox
tradition exists in Java, historically best exemplified in the person of
the last ruler of Singhasari, King Kertanagara. In this Bhairavist (Tantric) tradition, Power is sought through a kind of Rimbaudian *dérègle-
ment systématique des sens*—drunkenness, sexual orgies, and ritual
murder.[18] But even this tradition, which still finds more or less clan-
destine adherents in contemporary Indonesia, ultimately aims at the
same objectives as the more orthodox tradition. For in the Bhairavist
belief-system, the systematic indulgence of the sensual passions in
their most extreme form was believed to exhaust these passions, and
therefore to allow a man's Power to be concentrated without further
hindrance. Thus, in both traditions the ultimate aim was concentration for the sake of Power, although the paths chosen to reach this
purpose radically diverged.

While personal ascesis was generally regarded as the fundamental
way to accumulate and absorb Power, traditional Javanese thinking
also recognized that this process of absorption or accumulation could
be furthered both by certain rituals, often containing a core of asceticism, such as fasting, meditation, and the like, and by the possession of certain objects or persons regarded as being "filled" with
Power. Since C. C. Berg has written at length about the ritual mobilization of Power through "verbal magic" in the chronicles of Old Java,
further exploration of the subject here is unnecessary.[19] But it is diffi-

[17]It may be suggested that a kind of moral judgment about Power is implicit in this
difference between heroes and demons. My inclination, however, is to believe that insofar as
a moral judgment is made, it is not about the use of Power but about its retention or
dispersal. Criticism of the demons is leveled at their inability or unwillingness to conserve
the Power they have accumulated.

[18]On this topic, see Willem Frederik Stutterheim, *Het Hinduisme in de Archipel*, 3d ed.
(Jakarta and Groningen: Wolters, 1952), pp. 63, 67, 138; and his *Studies in Indonesian
Archaeology* (The Hague: Nijhoff, 1956), pp. 107–43.

[19]A large part of Berg's writings center on this theme. For a good, brief, and comprehensive formulation, see Cornelis Christiaan Berg, "The Javanese Picture of the Past," in Soe-

cult to understand the great importance attached to ceremonies of state in the contemporary period without bearing this part of the tradition clearly in mind. This obsession with ceremony has commonly been interpreted either as simple love of ideologizing; as manipulative sleight-of-hand, concealing political and economic realities from the population; or as a way of formally integrating conflicting groups and interests in a nation where institutional devices for this purpose have always been exceedingly weak. Such judgments are doubtless partly valid (although opinions may well differ over the extent to which Indonesian political leaders were consciously motivated in this way). But it would be unreasonable to deny that the importance attached to ceremonies may also have a more traditional basis, certainly in the minds of the spectators and probably, if to a lesser degree, in the minds of the leaders themselves. One should not underestimate the dynamic and aggressive aspect of these ceremonies and the degree to which they represent to the participants the conjuring of Power.[20]

Some ceremonies are quite openly of this conjuring character: for example, the presentation at the president's palace of wayang shows, with plots specifically chosen for their relevant political symbolism; the summoning of leaders of various spiritualist or mystical groups to participate in the 1961–62 campaign to reclaim West Irian from the Dutch; and in the National Monument the erection of a modernized *lingga* (sacred phallus). But many other typical aspects of modern Indonesian public political behavior—mass rallies, symbolic marches, hortatory speeches, evocations of the Revolution—while overtly having little connection with tradition, and indeed deriving formally from Western political practice, are in the esoteric sense strongly Power oriented, intended to concentrate and display Power absorbed from various sources—Power-full words (Pancasila, Révolusi, Sapta Marga),[21] Power-full experiences (the Revolution) and Power-full collec-

---

djatmoko et al., ed., *An Introduction to Indonesian Historiography* (Ithaca, N.Y.: Cornell University Press, 1965), pp. 87–117.

[20]For a rather different interpretation of the political function of ceremony, defining it as more or less an end in itself, under the rubric of the Doctrine of the Theater State, see Clifford Geertz, *Islam Observed* (New Haven: Yale University Press, 1968), p. 38.

[21]The Pancasila are the Five Principles—belief in God, nationalism, humanitarianism, democracy, and social justice—first formulated by Sukarno in a historic speech on June 1, 1945, and later accepted as a key element in the national ideology. Révolusi is self-explanatory. The Sapta Marga (Seven Principles) is the code of the Indonesian Armed Forces, formulated by Colonel Bambang Supeno in the early 1950s.

tivities (the People).22 In effect, many of Sukarno's political rallies, ostensibly designed to convey a particular message to the population or to demonstrate the president's popular backing, were no less important as methods of accumulating and demonstrating Power from the willing submission of so many thousands of persons. The greater the extent to which different and even hostile political groups could be brought into these ceremonies, the greater the real and the perceived Power of the master of ceremonies. Sukarno's highly traditional style of incantatory rhetoric naturally added to the political impact of the ceremony as a whole.23

Moreover, it was an old tradition in Java that the ruler should concentrate around him any objects or persons held to have or contain unusual Power. His palace would be filled not only with the traditional array of *pusaka* (heirlooms), such as krisses, spears, sacred musical instruments, carriages, and the like, but also various types of extraordinary human beings, such as albinos, clowns, dwarves, and fortune-tellers. Being in the palace, their Power was absorbed by, and further added to, the ruler's own. Their loss, by whatever means, was seen as an actual diminution of the king's Power and often as a sign of the impending collapse of the dynasty. The extent to which this tradition survives even in elite political circles is no secret to observers of the Indonesian scene, under both Sukarno and his successor. It should perhaps be noted, however, that being *thought* to have such objects or persons at one's disposal is just as politically advantageous as actually having or making serious use of them. A striking illustration of this phenomenon has been the tendency for many prominent non-Javanese politicians to let it be known that they too have some of the regalia of Power.24

22It may be pointed out that marches, rallies, and so forth are used to gain power or demonstrate it in the West as well. My point here is that the power gained and demonstrated is seen very differently in the two cultures.

23Mohammad Roem, in talks with the writer in Ithaca early in 1968, remarked that prior to the rise of the nationalist leader H. O. S. Tjokroaminoto in the 1910s, political speech-makers borrowed their oratorical style from the *bangsawan* stage plays, which in turn derived largely from the European theater. Gesture and imagery tended to be mechanical and formal. The great innovation of Tjokroaminoto, which was picked up and developed by Sukarno, was to base his oratorical style on the dhalang's manner of recitation. This allowed for the skillful use of traditional imagery and traditional sonorities by these two master orators to build up unprecedented rapport with their audiences.

24Some of them, of course, are sufficiently Javanized to make serious efforts actually to acquire Javanese types of regalia.

The Signs of Power

The Javanese tradition of political thought, therefore, typically emphasizes the signs of Power's concentration, not the demonstration of its exercise or use. These signs are looked for both in the person of the Power holder and in the society in which he wields his Power. The two are, of course, intimately related. In the words of one of Indonesia's most prominent contemporary intellectuals, "A central concept in the Javanese traditional view of life is the direct relationship between the state of a person's inner self and his capacity to control the environment."[25]

The most obvious sign of the man of Power is, quite consistently, his ability to concentrate: to focus his own inner Power, to absorb Power from the outside, and to concentrate within himself apparently antagonistic opposites. The first type of concentration we have already dealt with briefly; it suffices to say here that the image of asceticism is the prime expression of concentrated Power. The ability to absorb external concentrations of Power is a frequent theme in both the wayang legends and historical tradition.[26] One typical image, which links this type of absorption with the concentration of opposites, is a battle between a hero and a powerful adversary, in which the defeated adversary in death enters the hero's body, adding to his conqueror's strength. A famous example in the wayang literature is the story of King Parta entering the body of Arjuna after defeat in battle.[27] Other stories, such as those describing the spirit of Begawan Bagaspati descending into Yudhisthira to enable him to kill King Salya, or the fusion of Srikandhi and Ambalika to encompass the destruction of Resi Bisma at the outset of the Bratayuda War, reveal parallel patterns in which Power is absorbed from external sources.[28]

No less striking, and in historical perspective of perhaps more enduring significance, is the ability to concentrate opposites. The classical iconographic symbol of this is the combination of male and female. In ancient Javanese art this combination does not take the

[25]Soedjatmoko, "Indonesia: Problems and Opportunities," *Australian Outlook* 21 (December 1967): 266.

[26]One familiar aspect of Old Javanese historical writing, namely references to historical kings as being incarnate deities, can be interpreted in this light to signify the absorption of external Power into the person of the ruler. See, for example, Berg, "Javanese Picture," pp. 93, 112.

[27]See the plot of the play *Arimba*, summarized in Kats, *Javaansche Toneel*, p. 282.

[28]See the plots of the plays *Pejahipun Suyudana and Pejahipun Bisma lan Séta*, summarized in ibid., pp. 436, 428.

form of the hermaphrodite of the Hellenistic world, an ambiguous transitional being between the sexes, but rather the form of a being in whom masculine and feminine characteristics are sharply juxtaposed. One finds, for example, in the *ardhanari* type of image that the left side of the statues is physiologically female, the right side male.[29] The essential characteristic of this combination of opposites is not their merging but their dynamic simultaneous incorporation within a single entity. Thus the ardhanari image expresses the vitality of the ruler, his oneness, and his center-ness. He is at once masculine and feminine, containing both elements within himself and holding them in a tense, electric balance.[30]

Although in the world of art the masculine-feminine combination remains a vivid representation of Power, in the world of politics, for obvious reasons, the dynamic syncretism of Javanese thinking expresses itself in other ways. The most striking recent expression was the so-called Nasakom-politique of former President Sukarno.[31] When Sukarno proclaimed himself at once nationalist, religious man, and Communist, he was frequently interpreted by observers outside the Javanese political tradition to be talking the language of maneuver and compromise. The Nasakom formula tended to be seen either as

[29]A beautiful example of a *hari-hara ardhanari* image can be found in Claire Holt, *Art in Indonesia: Continuity and Change* (Ithaca, N.Y.: Cornell University Press, 1967), p. 81.

[30]My interpretation here derives in part from Justus Maria van der Kroef's essay on "Transvestitism and the Religious Hermaphrodite," in his *Indonesia in the Modern World* (Bandung: Masa Baru, 1956), pp. 182–95, though my analytic method differs markedly from his. One can perhaps see another version of the male-female conjuncture as an image of Power in an interesting institution of the Central Javanese *kraton* (court). Among the various types of royal regalia, thus part of the ruler's emblems of Power, one finds the *bedhaya*, a special group, usually composed of women, responsible both for guarding the other regalia and for performing the most sacred of the court dances. The interesting thing is that when the king went off to battle, the bedhaya were always brought along; and many of the texts of the songs accompanying bedhaya dances celebrate royal victories. Significantly, it was not the *praméswari* (senior queen) or other official consorts of the ruler who thus performed the function of representing the female component of his Power, but rather the bedhaya. A further involution of this juxtaposition of male and female elements is suggested by the fact that, at least in Yogyakarta, up to the reign of Sultan Hamengku Buwana VII, the bedhaya dances were performed by prepubescent boys dressed in female garments.
The traditional guardians of the regalia of the Buginese and Makassarese rulers of Southwest Sulawesi were the so-called *bissu*, men who dressed in a special combination of male and female garments. For an excellent description of these bissu, with photographs, see Claire Holt, *Dance Quest in Celebes* (Paris: Archives Internationales de la Danse, 1939), pp. 27–36, 87–89; plates 15–18, 94–97.

[31]*Nasakom* is an acronym formed from the words *nasionalisme* (nationalism), *agama* (religion), and *komunisme* (communism). The Nasakom-politique, pursued by Sukarno during the period of Guided Democracy, was designed to encourage mutual trust and cooperation between the groups and parties normally classified under each of these three rubrics.

an irresponsible and intellectually incoherent slogan or as a subtle device for weakening the anti-Communist prejudices of powerful nationalist and religious groups. Such interpretations, however, failed to place the Nasakom-politique within the context of Javanese political thinking. In this world orientation, Sukarno's formula could be interpreted not as a compromise or stratagem, but as a powerful claim to the possession of Power by the ruler. By its terms all other political actors were condemned to subordinate roles as parts of the system: Sukarno alone was whole, *sembada,* absorbing all within himself, making the syncretic conquest.

But it is not only in the overt symbolism of Nasakom that one finds the unity-in-opposites formula of Power.[32] The same relationship can also be found in the powerful appeal made in the prewar period by the PNI (Indonesian National Party) and in the 1960s especially by the PKI (Indonesian Communist Party)—an appeal at once to modernity and to tradition, or perhaps more exactly a mediation of tradition through modernity. Ruth McVey has given a subtle account of the development of Indonesian cultural nationalism in the Taman Siswa school system before World War II.[33] She has shown how the Taman Siswa's founder, Ki Hadjar Dewantara, was able to combine what at the time were ultramodern humanist educational theories with traditional elements in Javanese education, to provide, for that period at least, a particularly effective dynamic combination of new and old, radical and conservative. Whereas Dutch sympathizers attributed Ki Hadjar's ideas to Froebel and Montessori, Javanese adherents saw them as emerging from the formulations drawn up by the traditionalist *kebatinan* (meditation) group, Paguyuban Selasa-Kliwon, led by a group of Ki Hadjar's friends. This typical two-sided quality of radical nationalism has, of course, a clear sociological and historical explanation. But the doubleness can also be seen as reflecting the dynamic Power orientation of Javanese thinking.[34]

[32]Interestingly enough, this formula is most succinctly expressed in the Indonesian national motto, "Bhinneka Tunggal Ika." This motto is usually translated as "Unity in Diversity" and is often regarded as equivalent to the American national motto, "E pluribus unum." There is, however, an important difference of nuance between the two. The American motto implies a process of unification out of divergent elements, while the Indonesian suggests the inseparability of unity and diversity.

[33]Ruth Thomas McVey, "Taman Siswa and the Indonesian National Awakening," *Indonesia* 4 (October 1967): 128–49.

[34]In the 1960s the Indonesian Communist party was particularly successful in reviving, developing, and adapting traditional forms of popular art and theater. By presenting these adaptations of traditional art as ultimately more modern and progressive, as well as more *asli* (indigenous) than the uprooted, derivative, bourgeois culture of the cities, the party played successfully on Javanese sensibilities about the nature of Power.

If the ability to contain opposites and to absorb his adversaries are important elements in a leader's claim to have Power, one key public sign of it has traditionally been what the Javanese call the *wahyu* (divine radiance). Of this emanation Moertono writes: "It was visualized in different shapes and forms—bright luminescence, a 'star,' but most often it was seen as a dazzling blue, green or white ball of light [*andaru, pulung*], streaking through the night sky."35 (This imagery reveals the pervasive identification of Power and light in Javanese thought.) The movement of the wahyu typically marked the fall of one dynasty and the transfer of the light source to another. The everyday presence of Power was more usually marked by the *téja* (radiance) that was thought to emanate softly from the face or person of the man of Power. The psychological grip of this image can be glimpsed in a remarkable speech given by Sukarno in 1963, on the occasion of receiving an honorary doctorate at the University of Indonesia in Jakarta.36 On that occasion he spoke at length about the téja, noting that various European figures had possessed it, among the most notable of whom was Adolf Hitler. Sukarno's discussion of Hitler and his téja evoked dismay among some Western observers present, who judged it within the frame of reference of European history. But seen within the Javanese tradition, Sukarno's references were calmly analytical. Nowhere in his references to Hitler was there any mention of the moral qualities of the Führer's rule. The reason for this omission was not that Sukarno lacked appreciation for moral questions, but rather that within the categories of Javanese political theory, the specific morality of a government is quite secondary (both in historical and in analytical terms) to its Power aspects. The *fact* that Hitler had the téja was central and formed the starting point of any analysis of his regime.37

The glow of the téja was traditionally associated with the public visage of the ruler. Moertono cites the case of Amangkurat III (1703–1708), of whom it was said, when he was about to be deposed, that having "lost his *cahya* [radiance], he looked pale as a Chinese with a stomachache."38 By contrast, it was related of Amangkurat II (1677–1703), at the moment of his resolve to resist the incursion of Trunajaya

---

35Moertono, *State,* p. 56.

36Soekarno, *Ilmu Pengetahuan Sekadar Alat Mentjapai Sesuatu* (Jakarta: Departemen Penerangan Republik Indonesia, Penerbitan Chusus 253, 1963). The speech was delivered on February 2, 1963. (See further in chap. 2, below.)

37As we shall see below, a ruler can lose his téja by indulging in evil actions, but the téja comes first and is not acquired by good actions as such.

38Moertono, *State,* p. 40, citing *Babad Tanah Djawi,* p. 273. My translation differs slightly from Moertono's, both here and in the two notes following.

and to defend the crumbling empire of Mataram, that his followers "did not recognize their lord; formerly his expression was wan and without expression, now his countenance became bright and of a stately gravity."[39]

But since the téja was merely an external manifestation of the inner creative energy of the universe, it could appear not only in the ruler's visage but also in his sexual power. The following remarkable anecdote, which refers to the succession crisis after the death of Amangkurat II in 1703, was intended to indicate why Pangéran Puger, who with Dutch assistance usurped the throne from his nephew Amangkurat III, was the deceased sovereign's legitimate successor. "The story is told that the [dead] king's manhood stood erect and on the top of it was a radiant light (*tjahja*), only the size of a grain of pepper. But nobody observed it. Only Pangéran Puger saw it. Pangéran Puger quickly sipped up the [drop of] light. As soon as the light had been sipped, the manhood ceased to stand erect. It was Allah's will that Pangéran Puger should succeed to the throne."[40] Indeed, the sexual fertility of the ruler is one essential sign of the Power that he holds, for his seed is the microcosmic expression of the Power he has concentrated. The fertility of the ruler was seen as simultaneously invoking and guaranteeing the fertility of the land, the prosperity of the society, and the expansionist vitality of the empire. The Sukarno period once again provides a striking modern parallel to this old idea. Outside observers of Indonesian politics frequently remarked that Sukarno's well-publicized sexual activities appeared to do him no political harm. It was even said that the Javanese indulgently expect their rulers to act in this way. But if the foregoing analysis is correct, the political aspects of Sukarno's personal life are overlooked in such a perspective, for signs of the ruler's virility are political indicators that he still has the Power. Conversely, any marked decline in sexual activity could be taken as a sign of waning Power in other respects. More sophisticated observers of late Guided Democracy were, indeed, inclined to suspect that palace officials deliberately spread exaggerated stories about the president's personal life as part of a continuing effort to maintain his authority.

The social signs of the concentration of power were fertility, prosperity, stability, and glory. At the dhalang of the *wayang bèbèr* puts it in the classical imagery of the ancient Javanese kingdom of Kedhiri:

---

[39]Ibid., p. 57, citing *Babad Tanah Djawi*, p. 174.
[40]Ibid., p. 58, citing *Babad Tanah Djawi*, p. 260.

The land of Kedhiri may be described as stretching far and wide, with long shores, high mountains, rich, fertile, prosperous, tranquil and well-ordered. If fertile, it was the villages which were fertile; if prosperous, it was the Kingdom which was prosperous, food and clothing were very cheap. Even the lowliest widow could keep her own elephant with its mahout. Such was the richness and prosperity of the Kingdom. . . . There were no men who begged from one another; each had possessions of his own. All this was because of the richness and good ordering of the Kingdom.[41]

The two fundamental ideas behind these conventional images are creativity (fertility-prosperity) and harmony (tranquility-order), expressed in the age-old motto so often on the lips of the contemporary elite: *tata tentrem karta raharja* (order, peace, prosperity, good fortune). Both fertility and order are simply expressions of Power. Power is the ability to give life. Power is also the ability to maintain a smooth tautness and to act like a magnet that aligns scattered iron filings in a patterned field of force. Conversely, the signs of a lessening in the tautness of a ruler's Power and of a diffusion of his strength are seen equally in manifestations of disorder in the natural world—floods, eruptions, and plagues—and in inappropriate modes of social behavior—theft, greed, and murder.[42] Again, one should bear in mind that in Javanese thought there is no reciprocal effect between declining power and the appearance of these undesirable phenomena. Antisocial behavior arises from a ruler's declining Power, but does not in itself further diminish that Power. It is a symptom, not a cause, of his decline. Therefore, a ruler who has once permitted natural and social disorders to appear finds it particularly difficult to reconstitute his authority. Javanese would tend to believe that, if he still had the Power, the disorders would never have arisen: They do not stem ultimately from autonomous social or economic conditions, but from a looseness or diffusion of Power within the state.

Power and History

How does the idea of Power affect the traditional Javanese view of the nature or structure of the historical process? Sartono has argued

[41]The citation is drawn from an unpublished transcription and translation of a wayang bèbèr performance recorded in Donorojo, Central Java, in 1963, made by the writer. On the wayang bèbèr see Holt, *Art in Indonesia*, pp. 127–28.

[42]For a good, detailed list of the undesirable natural and social phenomena that appear in a time of decline, see Tjantrik Mataram (pseud.), *Peranan ramalan Djojobojo dalam revolusi kita*, 3d. ed. (Bandung: Masa Baru, 1954), pp. 29–31.

that the essential difference between the traditional Javanese view of history and the modern Western perspective is that, in the modern view, history is seen as a linear movement through time, whereas Javanese traditionally tended to see their history as a series of recurrent cycles. He suggests that while Western historians and political scientists differ on the direction of history's linear movement and the degree to which it is determined by objective factors, all share the sense, essentially derived from the technological revolution of the past two hundred years, that history is noniterative, a series of unique events linked by a complex causality. By contrast, he believes that traditional Javanese historical thinking, influenced in part by Sanskrit cosmological writings, saw history as a cycle of ages (*yuga*) moving from the Golden Age (Krtayuga or Jaman Mas) through successively less happy epochs (Tretayuga and Dyapara Yuga) to the evil Kaliyuga—before the wheel turned again and brought back a renewed Krtayuga.[43] My own interpretation, however, would be that while the Javanese may have utilized elements from Indic cosmology for formal classificatory purposes, their intuitive sense of the historical process was fundamentally a logical corollary of their concept of Power. In popular Javanese thought today, and in the rich eschatological literature of the past, one finds little sense of cycles and of orderly decline and rebirth; instead, one sees a sharp contrast drawn between the Jaman Mas and the Jaman Edan, the Golden Age and the Age of Madness.[44] These two types of historical epoch were seen typically as times of order and of disorder. The critical point is that the Javanese view of history was one of cosmological oscillation between periods of concentration of Power and periods of its diffusion. The typical historical sequence is concentration–diffusion–concentration–diffusion, without any ultimate resting point.[45] In each period of concentration new centers of Power (dynasties, rulers) are constituted and unity is recreated; in each period of diffusion, Power begins to ebb away from

[43]See Sartono Kartodirdjo, *Tjatatan tentang segi-segi messianistis dalam Sedjarah Indonesia* (Yogyakarta: Gajah Mada, 1959). My comments on Sartono's subtle work by no means do it justice. Its main theme is actually to show how the prophetic *Serat Djojobojo* marks a decisive shift from a cyclical to a linear historical perspective under the influence of Islamic eschatology. Cf. also Moertono, *State*, pp. 81–82; and Heinrich Zimmer, *Myths and Symbols in Indian Art and Civilization* (New York: Harper Torchbooks, 1962), pp. 13–19, 35–37.

[44]Even Hindu cosmology points in this direction, since the pattern of change is not strictly circular; the change from the Kaliyuga to the Krtayuga does not pass through gradual stages of reintegration symmetrical to the process of disintegration.

[45]I would like to stress that what I am saying here is meant as an interpretation of the Javanese view of *history* in a quite specific sense. It is not an interpretation of the Javanese concept of *time*, which is probably closely comparable to the Balinese concept based on the combinatorial calendar, so brilliantly elucidated by Clifford Geertz (see Geertz, *Person, Time,*

the center, the reigning dynasty loses its claim to rule, and disorder appears—until the concentrating process begins again. The historical necessity of diffusion is no less compelling than that of concentration, since Power is immensely hard to retain and has perpetually to be struggled for. The slightest slackness or lack of vigilance may begin the process of disintegration, which, once it sets in, is irreversible. (The loosening of cosmological tautness stems from *pamrih*, which essentially means the use of Power for personal indulgence or the wasting of concentrated Power on the satisfaction of personal passions).[46]

This conception of history helps to explain two notable but apparently contradictory features of Javanese political psychology: its underlying pessimism and its susceptibility to messianic appeals. The pessimism derives from the sense of the impermanence of concentrated Power, the difficulty involved in its accumulation and retention, and the inevitability of disorder on the far side of order. The susceptibility to messianism in times of disorder, however, arises from the sense that a new concentration of Power is always preparing itself within that disorder, that one must be alert for portents of its imminent appearance and then approach the germinal center as rapidly as possible, attaching oneself to the new order as it emerges. This messianism clearly has little of the linear quality of many European millenary movements, which saw the world coming to an end with the arrival of the Messiah. Traditional Javanese sense that history does not come to an end, that messiahs are only for their time, and that the primordial oscillations of Power will continue as before.

Unity and the Center

It may be useful to begin discussion of the traditional polity not with its concrete structures but with its ideal symbolic form. Perhaps

---

and Conduct, pp. 45–53). My feeling, essentially intuitive, is that the calendrical, "punctuational" concept of time is in Java the framework within which everyday social life takes place, and applies primarily to familial and local contexts. Perhaps because of the long imperial history of Java, the dramatic rise and fall of dynasties whose names are familiar even to illiterate peasants through the oral wayang tradition, and the long period of colonial subjugation, there is a distinct view of what one would call political history, which is not calendrical at all. This *historical* perspective comes out very clearly in the chronicles (*babad*) of the courts, and the long tradition of messianic and millenarian beliefs among the peasantry. To my limited knowledge, Bali shows a relative lack of both dynastic historiography and peasant millenarianism.

[46]See the section "Power and Ethics" for a fuller discussion of the meaning and significance of pamrih.

the most exact image of the ordered Javanese polity is that of a cone of light cast downward by a reflector lamp. This image conveys, I think more accurately than more conventional terminology, some of the nuances of Javanese political thought. The good society is not strictly hierarchical, since a hierarchy presupposes a certain degree of autonomy at each of its various levels. The movement of traditional Javanese thought implicitly denies this, seeking ideally a single, pervasive source of Power and authority. As we shall see, the gradual, even diminution of the radiance of the lamp with increasing distance from the bulb is an apt metaphor for the Javanese conception not only of the structure of the state but also of center-periphery relationships and of territorial sovereignty. While the undifferentiated quality of the light expresses the idea of the homogeneity of Power, the white color of the light, itself the "syncretic" fusion of all the colors of the spectrum, symbolizes the unifying and concentrating aspects of Power.

The core of the traditional polity has always been the ruler, who personifies the unity of society.[47] This unity is in itself a central symbol of Power, and it is this fact as much as the overt goals of statist ideologies that helps to account for the obsessive concern with oneness that suffuses the political thinking of many contemporary Javanese. The popular hostility expressed toward the Federal Republic of Indonesia (1949–50) reflected, I would argue, not simply the explicit suspicion that its component states were puppets of Dutch creation, but also the sense that oneness is Power and multiplicity is diffusion and weakness.[48]

Sukarno's constant appeals for national unity can in part be attributed to traditional anxiety about a dispersion of Power. Within a traditionalist Javanese framework the multiparty system, the constitutional separation of powers, and federalism were easily interpreted to mean the decline of Indonesia's international Power and that of Sukarno himself as its political focus. The Sumpah Pemuda (Oath of Youth) of 1928—One Country, One Flag, One Language—reiterates the same theme. One can detect it also in the program and strategy of the PKI in the period before its destruction; there the

---

[47]Cf. Geertz, *Islam Observed,* p. 36, on the Doctrine of the Exemplary Center.

[48]Javanese hostility to the concept of federalism has continued long after the departure of the Dutch and the political destruction of their Federalist allies. What I am suggesting here is not meant to devalue the sociological and historical reasons for this hostility. The Javanese imperial tradition and the concrete material interests of Java vis-à-vis the Outer Islands in themselves would lessen Javanese enthusiasm for federalism. What I am pointing out is the mutual reinforcement of interests and perceptions involved in this question.

traditional Marxist formulas of class struggle were transformed into a style of propaganda in which essentially one Rakyat (People), with all its deserving components, was arrayed not so much against an adversary *class* as against small clusters of foreign elements, who by their reactionary or compradore character endangered the wholeness and the unity of the nation.[49] One can find the same style of thought in the defense speech of Sudisman, secretary-general of the PKI, before the Extraordinary Military Tribunal in July 1967, where the deeply emotive Javanese word *manunggal* (to become one) occurs again and again. As he put it, the leadership of the party consisted of five men—Aidit, Lukman, Njoto, Sakirman, and himself—but these five *manunggal jadi satu* (were united as one) in life and in death.[50]

The urge to oneness, so central to Javanese political attitudes, helps to explain the deep psychological power of the idea of nationalism in Java. Far more than a political credo, nationalism expresses a fundamental drive to solidarity and unity in the face of the disintegration of traditional society under colonial capitalism, and other powerful external forces, from the late nineteenth century on. Nationalism of this type is something far stronger than patriotism; it is an attempt to reconquer a primordial oneness.

The same sense of the polity helps, I think, to explain the psychological malaise experienced by the Javanese under the system of multiparty parliamentary democracy in the early 1950s. Herbert Feith has written acutely about this uneasiness as a sense of letdown after the élan of the Revolution, a sense of what both the left-wing politician Sudisman and the right-wing journalist Rosihan Anwar have referred to as *sleur* (a rut).[51] Feith connects this feeling with the impotence of the governments of that period, the inability of weak cabinets to sus-

[49]At the risk of annoying repetition, I should say that I am not trying to suggest that the PKI leaders adopted this strategy because they were Javanese traditionalists. One could, from a Western vantage point, suggest that the crucial influences on the PKI leadership were the history of the Popular Front, their experiences in World War II, the example of Mao, and practical calculations of advantage in political maneuver. I would argue, however, that for much of the PKI's traditionalist constituency, and perhaps for some of its more traditionalist leaders, the national united front line was "culturally comfortable."

[50]Sudisman, *Analysis of Responsibility*, trans. Benedict R. O'G. Anderson (Melbourne: The Works Cooperative, 1975), p. 4. There is little doubt in my mind that Sudisman was also alluding very consciously to the five Pandawa brothers, the heroes of the wayang stories, and identifying the PKI leaders with them.

[51]Herbert Feith, *The Decline of Constitutional Democracy in Indonesia* (Ithaca, N.Y.: Cornell University Press, 1962), pp. 221–24. See also Sudisman, *Analysis*, pp. 8–9; and Rosihan Anwar's column in *Kompas*, August 7, 1968.

tain themselves in power, to carry out their programs, indeed to make their weight felt in the community at large. But I suspect that this argument reverses the intellectual sequence in many Javanese minds; for, seen through a traditional lens, it is less that the various parties *in practice* were unsuccessful in cooperating to carry out a program than that the very structure of parliamentary government, with its formal divisions between opposition and government and between executive, legislature, and judiciary, expressed a looseness at the center. In this perspective, inflation, factionalism, and regionalism would be interpreted as consequences rather than as causes of the diffusion of Power, which was the inner reason for the rapid demise of parliamentary government. Not only were the parties by definition segmental, but nothing in the structure of the state promised to resolve this cluster of partialities into a higher unity. It was surely Sukarno's—and presumably General Suharto's—intuition of this problem that led both men to what some observers have described as a "centrist" politique; an apt enough term, if understood to mean not "in the middle" but "of the center."[52]

Accession and Succession

I have suggested that the logic of the Javanese traditional conception of Power required a center, syncretic and absorptive in character, and that this center was usually realized in the person of a ruler. How was the ruler discovered or recognized? In the historical tradition, the ruler emerged typically in one of two ways. If he represented the first ruler of a new dynasty, he emerged as the man believed to have received the *wahyu*, the divine radiance that passed from the disintegrating Power of one kingdom to the founder of its successor. Very often, the new ruler would be a parvenu of relatively humble origins—such as Kèn Angrok, Panembahan Sénapati, Sukarno, and Suharto—coming to power after a period of turmoil and bloodshed, usually instigated by the new ruler himself. Though Javanese history is replete with stories

[52]For an explication of this point, see, e.g., my "Indonesia: Unity vs. Progress," *Current History* (February 1965): 75–81; Donald Hindley, "President Sukarno and the Communists: The Politics of Domestication," *American Political Science Review* 56 (December 1962): 915–26; Daniel S. Lev, "Political Parties of Indonesia," *Journal of Southeast Asian History* 8 (March 1967): 52–67, esp. 61–64; and Herbert Feith, "Suharto's Search for a Political Format," *Indonesia* 6 (October 1968): 88–105.

of rebellions, their leaders were never said to have the wahyu unless they succeeded in establishing a new dynasty. Failure in itself meant, retrospectively, that the rebel leader did not have the Power; if he had, he would have succeeded. The main claim to legitimacy of the founder of a new dynasty rested on his successful destruction of a previous center of Power and the belief that in so doing he had received the divine wahyu. But it is typical of the Javanese urge toward the center, toward the accumulation of all pools of Power, that the parvenu ruler frequently tried to associate himself through court chronicles with the residues of previous centers of Power and greatness. Schrieke, Berg, and Moertono have amply demonstrated the concerted attempts to link parvenu founders of dynasties with their predecessors through complicated (and often falsified) lines of descent.[53] This characteristic is of course not exclusively Javanese. But the most interesting feature of Javanese "falsification" of history is that it does not primarily involve the establishing of ancestral links with previous dynasties to demonstrate legal, inherited legitimacy—in which case almost any ancestor would do. Typically, ancestral links are made with the most powerful and celebrated representatives of those dynasties.

Thus, in the modern period one finds Javanese claiming descent from the great Sultan Agung of the Mataram dynasty (1613–46), or possession of potent relics (gongs, krisses, and so forth) of the same ruler. A claim to descent from his no less polyphiloprogenitive but considerably less politically adept successors, Amangkurat I, II, III, and IV, is virtually unknown. The point here is not simply the historical glory of Sultan Agung's rule, but also the character of traditional Javanese cosmological thought, which makes no sharp distinction between the living and the dead. The dead may have Power as well as the living. A ruler of such preeminent Power as Sultan Agung retains in death at least some residue of the great concentration of Power that was his in life. Thus, the typical linkages with Sultan Agung are in part for the sake of historical continuity, but more significantly for the sake of coopting and absorbing a recognized pool of Power. In this same tradition one finds Sukarno claiming direct descent from, not just any royal ancestors, but a celebrated king of Singaraja, North Bali; the legendary, prophetic King Jayabaya of Kedhiri; and the great-

---

[53]Bertram Johannes Otto Schrieke, *Indonesian Sociological Studies* (The Hague and Bandung: van Hoeve, 1957), vol. 2, bk. 1, chaps. 1, 2; Moertono, *State*, pp. 52–54, 63–64; Cornelis Christiaan Berg, "Javaansche Geschiedschrijving," in Frederik Willem Stapel, ed., *Geschiedenis van Nederlandsch Indië* (Amsterdam: Joost van den Vondel, 1938).

est of the early Moslem proselytizing saints, Sunan Kalijaga.[54] Contemporary rumors that President Suharto is the son of the late Sultan Hamengku Buwana VIII of Yogyakarta fall into the same conceptual framework. Conversely, the fall of a ruler gives wide currency to underground oppositionist stories that the ruler is not really the son of this or that potentate, but, for example, the offspring of a Dutch planter or a Eurasian.

The fact, however, that ultimately the link sought is a genetic one points again to the linking of sexuality and Power in Javanese thought, and the idea that the human seed, and especially the seed of a man of Power, is itself a concentration of Power and a means of its transmission.[55] Indeed, in normal times, when a dynasty was in assured control, succession to political power ran through the royal descent group. But this conception of succession differed markedly from that of European dynastic inheritance, where the predominant considerations were legal and bureaucratic. In the Javanese tradition each successive generation removed from a particular ruler dropped one degree in rank until, after the seventh generation, the lineal descendants merged back into the wide group of commoners, unless in the meantime they had established newer, fresher descent links with succeeding rulers. In this process one can see clearly the conception of the royal

[54]For the first two claims, see Cindy Adams, *Sukarno: An Autobiography as Told to Cindy Adams* (Indianapolis: Bobbs-Merrill, 1965), p. 19. The last claim is referred to in *Sin Po*, April 13, 1958. Sukarno revealed this part of his ancestry after a visit to Kadilangu, near Demak, where Sunan Kalijaga's grave is reputedly located. We need not concern ourselves with the genealogical truth or falsity of these claims. What is important is *why* they were made.

[55]One should note here that at least one reason for the stress on sexual abstinence for the accumulation of Power is that a man thereby retains his seed within himself, and does not permit its wasteful outflow. It may be asked how the Javanese reconciled this stress on sexual abstinence with their emphasis on the sexuality of the ruler as a sign of the vitality of the kingdom and society. There are various possible answers. One is that they are not fully reconcilable, but derive from the orthodox and heterodox traditions about the acquisition of Power, discussed previously. Another is that the ruler has such an extraordinary superabundance of Power within himself that he can "afford" to dispense some of it in extensive sexual activity. My own inclination is to believe that the apparent contradiction resolves itself if sexuality is linked directly to fertility: The Power of the dynast is revealed by his ability to create successors and transmit his Power to them. The ordinary Javanese has no means of gauging the ruler's virility except by the number of children that he produces. Should the ruler be impotent or sterile, it would be taken as a sign of political weakness. The ruler's intermittent periods of asceticism become that much more credible if his sexual vitality is otherwise so conspicuously evident. Significantly, in the wayang stories there is very little mention of sexual intercourse between heroes and their women that does not produce instant pregnancy. This fertility in sexual intercourse is taken to farcical extremes in some comic plays in which the Gods themselves become pregnant when they bathe in a pool in which the Pandawa hero Arjuna is having submerged relations with a *widadari* (heavenly nymph). Sexuality without pregnancy, then, would have no political value.

seed as a source of Power that progressively diminishes in concentration through increasing historical distance from the original source and through growing admixtures of nonroyal seeds. Thus, the essential link to the ruler is measured in terms of proximity, whether through genetic descent or, as we shall see, along other axes of royal power. The successors to the dynasty's founder derived their original Power from the initial impulse provided by the founder himself. But this Power tended to grow diffuse over generations; unless it was renewed and reintegrated by the personal efforts of a particular descendant, the dynasty would fall of its own enfeebled lack of weight.

Power and Empire

The Javanese idea of Power also has implications for conceptions of sovereignty, territorial integrity, and foreign relations. Moertono and others have pointed out the almost invariable rule both in Javanese wayang stories and in the historical tradition that the names of empires and kingdoms are those of the capital cities. Among the well-known examples are Majapahit, Singhasari, Kedhiri, and Demak.[56] Indeed, the Javanese language makes no clear etymological distinction between the idea of capital city and that of kingdom. In the word *negari* both are included. Thus, the state is typically defined not by its perimeter, but by its center. The territorial extension of the state is always in flux; it varies according to the amount of Power concentrated at the center. Certain frontiers were generally recognized in practice: formidable geographical obstacles like mountains and seas, which, however, tended to be regarded as the abodes of powerful unseen forces. Otherwise the kingdoms were regarded not as having fixed and charted limits, but rather flexible, fluctuating perimeters. In a real sense, there were no political frontiers at all, the Power of one ruler gradually fading into the distance and merging imperceptibly with the ascending Power of a neighboring sovereign.

This perspective brings into relief the fundamental difference between the old idea of a Southeast Asian kingdom and the modern state, which derives from totally contrasting views about the meaning of frontiers. Implicit in the idea of the modern state is the conception that a frontier marks a critical fall in the power voltage of the state's rulers. Ten yards this side of the frontier, their power is sovereign; ten

[56]The same seems to be true of Burma, Siam, and Cambodia.

yards the other side, it does not exist.[57] Moreover, within the perimeter of the state, the power of the center is theoretically of uniform weight. Citizens at the periphery should share status equally with citizens at the center, and legal obligations should apply uniformly throughout the territory. Since the traditional idea of power is totally different in character, and the idea of the uniform lateral application of power is meaningless, the concept of the frontier assumes very limited importance: The traditional state is defined by its center, not by its perimeter.[58]

The highly centripetal character of traditional Javanese thought is strikingly illustrated by the division of the world into two types of states: Java and Sabrang (an undifferentiated word meaning "overseas" but essentially applied to all non-Javanese groups and political entities). Although contemporary politesse and the ideological requirements of Indonesian nationalism make this kind of division no longer publicly acceptable, one finds in private discussion with many Javanese strong and obvious residues of this conception. Indeed, so strongly imbedded was the idea that the Dutch more or less unconsciously adopted it, dividing their own colonial territories into Java and the Outer Regions. Many Javanese still find it extraordinarily difficult to accept fully the idea of Indonesia's being composed of a cluster of equal, interacting islands—Sumatra, Sulawesi, Kalimantan, Java, and the rest. All tend to be seen in their relationship to the center (Java). Similarly, many Javanese find it hard to conceive of the existence of two related *negari*, at least in Java. Thus, although the principalities of Yogyakarta and Surakarta have led separate existences for more than two hundred years and are situated less than forty miles apart, most Javanese will use the word *negari*—for instance in the

[57]The recognition of spheres of influence extending beyond legal-cartographic frontiers is a partial modification of this idea, but it is striking that the word *influence* is used, partly in deference to the idea of the sovereign national state, to mark a qualitative shift from the idea of internally organized power.

[58]Compare the case of Siam, where the problem of "regionalism" in the Northeast, for example, only becomes meaningful in the context of the nation-state. Regionalism implies recognition of the center but political disaffection toward it, rather than an autonomous center in an antagonistic relationship with another center. Prior to the twentieth century, Thai rulers had at different times varying degrees of control over the Northeast, but the problem was never defined as a regional one, since disaffection with, say, Bangkok resulted either in the formation of new centers or the drift of parts of the area into the kingdom of, say, Laos, without any implication of historical permanency either way. This fluidity was significantly enhanced by the rulers' preoccupation with control over populations rather than land. In a sense, then, we can date the inception of the regional problem in Siam to the intellectual shift in the Siamese view of the political entity they lived in from a kingdom to a nation-state.

phrase *kula badhé dhateng negari* (I am going to the negari)—to mean one capital and will refer to the other by its name, as they would any other city in Indonesia.[59]

The centripetality of Javanese political thinking, combined with the conceptions of graduated sovereignty sketched out above, leads logically to a specific perspective on foreign relations. In the first place, it implies a stress on the control of populations rather than of territory. Historically, there were practical reasons for this emphasis. Only the concentration of large populations made possible by intensive rice cultivation could provide the economic surplus and reserve of manpower necessary for building monuments or armies. But the concentration of large populations around a ruler was also the best sign of his having the Power, the magnetic attraction of which revealed the continuing possession of the wahyu. This idea may help to account for one well-known aspect of interdynastic conflict, not merely in Java but also in mainland Southeast Asia—wholesale deportations of populations by victorious rulers. Bringing these conquered populations near to the center augmented royal Power that much more. One can perhaps discern this importance attached to density of population behind Sukarno's consistent opposition to birth control, partly out of personal conviction, but evidently also from political considerations.[60]

In the second place, a certain logic in the *pattern* of foreign relations becomes evident. Moertono describes this pattern well in his discussion of the concept of *mandala,* which derives from Indian political theory, but which finds itself very comfortably at home in Java:

> The *mandala* (circle, namely of influence, interest or ambitions) can be described as a complex of geopolitical relations, relating to boundaries and to contact with foreign countries. The doctrine emphasized the cult of expansion, a necessary spur to the struggle for existence, self-assertion and world domination, and the dynamic factor calculated to disturb the equilibrium of inter-state relations. A state's belligerence is in the first place directed towards its closest neighbor(s), thus making necessary the friendship of the state next to the foe, which, because of its proximity, is also a natural enemy of the foe. But if the mutual foe should be conquered, the two allies would become close neighbors,

[59]Similarly, the Thai refer to their capital as *Krung Thep* (City of the God [Indra]): *Bangkok* is a name used only by and to foreigners.
[60]Cf. Louis Fischer, *The Story of Indonesia* (New York: Harper, 1959), p. 165. One should note the pride with which Sukarno frequently referred to Indonesia's population as the fifth largest in the world.

which would create a new enmity. So this circle of alignment and alienation would steadily expand until a universal peace is reached by the
establishment of a world-state with a sole and supreme ruler (*chakravartin*).[61]

Several important points emerge from this description of the mandala as the basis for international, or rather interkingdom, relations.
The first is that the a priori enemy of the ruler is his closest neighbor.
Moertono does not elaborate on the reasons why this pattern should
exist. But if our general line of argument is correct, the logic is quite
clear. We have seen how in Javanese thinking the Power of the ruler is
by no means equally distributed throughout his realm, but tends to
diminish evenly toward the periphery, so that he is weakest just at the
point where his sphere of Power merges into the perimeter of his
neighbor's. Thus, if his control is not to be diminished and weakened
by the pull of his neighbor's Power, he must first exert his own Power
against the neighbor. We may recall how the idea that the total quantum of Power in the universe is constant implies that any increase of
Power in one place means an equivalent diminution elsewhere. Since
Power is also fluid and unstable, always ready for dispersal and diffusion, interstate aggression necessarily becomes a basic assumption
about interstate relations.

There are three possible methods of dealing with the threat posed
by proximate concentrations of Power—destruction and dispersal,
absorption, or a combination of the two. Destruction of the opponent,
as practiced, for example, by Sultan Agung in his murderous campaigns against the trading city-states or Java's *pasisir* (north coast), has
its disadvantages. On the purely practical level, massive destruction
leads to local depopulation, disorder, and economic decline, and possibly later to rebellions or guerrilla resistance. (Deportation of populations may partly prevent this latter problem, but, insofar as the deportation is not total, it may not do so decisively.)[62] On the more
theoretical level, destruction of others does not in itself automatically
mean any enlargement or renewal of the ruler's Power, but merely the
dispersal of his rival's, which may be picked up or absorbed by other
rivals. Moreover, destruction itself is the most blatant and *kasar*
(crude, rough) means of subduing a rival, and on this account the least
desirable. More satisfactory is the method of absorption, which in
practice involves diplomatic pressure, and other *halus* (smooth, civi-

[61]Moertono, *State*, p. 71, n. 207.
[62]Sultan Agung did in fact deport large numbers of people to Mataram.

lized) methods of inducing recognition of superiority or suzerainty.[63] In theory, absorption is seen as the voluntary submission of neighboring kingdoms to the supreme Power of the ruler. One finds, therefore, in the classical description of the great kings of the past that *raja séwu negara nungkul (sujud)*—the kings of a thousand kingdoms offer submission to them. Significantly, the glorification of the ruler does not mention his prowess in battle, as might be the case with a European medieval monarch. That the ruler has to use the methods of warfare is a theoretical admission of weakness. The idea of "a thousand kings offering their submission" also implies the absorption of their smaller centers of Power into the Great King's, and thus a directly proportional increase in his majesty.[64]

Thirdly, the logical end result of intermandala relationships is the emergence of the chakravartin—in Javanese, *prabu murbèng wisésa anyakrawati* (world ruler). The ideal form of temporal power is a world empire, in which all political entities are combined in a coherent unity, and the ebb and flow of Power implied in a universe of multiple mandala locked in conflict with one another (for a time) no longer exists. One striking illustration of the centrality of this universalism in Javanese political thought is that words meaning universe (*buwana*) or natural world (*alam*) occur in the titles of three of the four rulers in contemporary Java—Paku Buwana (Nail of the Universe), Hamengku Buwana (Sustainer of the Universe), and Paku Alam (Nail of the World).

Finally, it is perhaps more than a coincidence that the typical pattern of political relationships between Java and the Outer Islands has tended to resemble the "leapfrogging" relationship described by Moertono in his discussion of the mandala. In the period of independence alone, one finds striking examples of this pattern in the close connections between the center and the subordinate Karo Batak against the dominate Toba Batak of East Sumatra; between the center and the inland Dayak groups against the Banjarese of South Kalimantan; and between the center and the upland Toraja against the Buginese and Makassarese in South Sulawesi. Although this leapfrogging pattern can perfectly well be understood in the light of Western political theory, it is also quite consistent with a very different intellectual framework.

[63]Cf. Schrieke, *Indonesian Sociological Studies* 2:142.
[64]One can speculate that in a period when administrative control over distant regions was difficult, formal submission combined with practical autonomy was for both parties a convenient form of interstate relations.

Ruler and Ruling Class

If we now turn to the traditional relationship between the ruler and the governmental structure through which he ruled, the concept of Power may help to throw light on the perspective in which this relationship was viewed. Schrieke has drawn a detailed picture of the administrative structure of the precolonial Javanese kingdom, which admirably fits Max Weber's model of the patrimonial state.[65] According to this model, the central government is essentially an extension of the ruler's personal household and staff. Officials are granted their positions, and the perquisites that go with them, as personal favors of the ruler, and they may be dismissed or degraded at his whim. No feudal caste exists as such. Payment of officials is essentially in the form of benefices allotted by the ruler for the period of tenure of each particular office. Within the central government latent or overt tension persists between the royal descent group, or the ruler's extended family, and the *ministeriales,* high-ranking officials of common origin who have risen to power on the basis of their administrative capacities and personal loyalty to the ruler. Since commoners have no hope of succeeding to the throne, barring the complete collapse of the dynasty, they are not regarded as a political threat by the ruler, and insofar as he is a powerful, strong-minded man, the ministeriales tend to be assigned to key positions at the expense of the royal descent group.

While the power of the ruler in the immediate environment of his capital is unquestioned, the poor quality of communications and perennial financial difficulties in a largely nonmonetary economy make it difficult for him, in spite of periodic and impressive military expeditions, to maintain tight administrative control as his empire grows in size. He must inevitably attempt to coopt regional notables and to devolve a great deal of informal power to them.[66] He is not in a position to "hire and fire" them as he can his own ministeriales. Though he will try to replace such local notables as he can with personal aides, these notables will naturally resist his centralizing encroachments. The ruler has also to face the danger that a ministerialis assigned to govern some remote province may develop such strong roots there that he assumes leadership over, or is coopted into,

[65]See Bertram Johannes Otto Schrieke, *Indonesian Sociological Studies* 1 (The Hague and Bandung: van Hoeve, 1955), pp. 169–221; and Bendix, *Max Weber,* chap. 11. Cf. Theodoor Gautier Thomas Pigeaud, *Java in the Fourteenth Century* (The Hague: Nijhoff, 1962), 4:521–36.

[66]This may be done by arranging marriages with prominent regional families, by insisting on periodic residence at the royal court, and by the delivery of hostages to the center.

the group of local notables and in effect joins the latent opposition. The ruler has constantly to shift such men to prevent them losing their ultimate dependency on himself.

The administrative structure, while formally hierarchical, is in effect composed of stratified clusters of patron-client relationships. Both in the regions and in the center, officials gather around them clusters of personal dependents, on the model of the ruler himself. These dependents' destinies are linked with the success or failure of their patrons. They work as administrative and political aides, and have no real autonomous status. They are financed by portions of the benefices allotted to their patron by his patron, or by the ruler himself, if their master is highly enough placed. Just as the power of the ruler is measured by the size of the populations he controls, so the power of the subordinate official (patron) is gauged by the size of the clientele that he heads.

In the case of Java, Schrieke pointed out the constant tug-of-war between provincial notables, who often had lineages older than the ruler's, and the ministeriales of the court; and between the ministeriales and the royal descent group. He stressed the arbitrary and personalistic features of the personnel and public policies of the rulers of Mataram, and the financing of the state administration through both royal monopolies and the appanage system of benefices, whereby officials were assigned the usufruct over specified (and often dispersed) lands, including the labor of the peasants living on them.

It should be readily apparent that the traditional concept of Power in Java provides a coherent perspective within which to view the structure and operations of the patrimonial state. In the first place, the image of the proportional fading of the lamps' radiance with increasing distance does not merely correspond to the decline of a ruler's Power vis-à-vis a neighboring ruler at the periphery of his domains. It can be applied with equal aptness to the center-province struggle, to which Weber and Schrieke attach such importance. Indeed, within the traditional perspective no clear analytical distinction can be made between a powerful provincial notable and a rival sovereign. Each is potentially the other, depending on the Power that the center can accumulate. The cone of light's luminosity expands as the ruler is able to force the submission of rival rulers and demote them to the status of provincial notables; it contracts as provincial notables free themselves from the center and establish their own independent areas of rule. The dreaded "looseness" at the center corresponds, then, to successful pressures for decentralization, and the admired "tautness" to the successful imposition of centralization.

Second, what Weber and Schrieke note as the highly personalistic character of patrimonial rule, in which the corps of officials is regarded as an extension of the person of the ruler, implies that proximity to the ruler, rather than formal rank, is the key to power in such a state. The commoner ministeriales owe their ascendancy over the royal descent group under powerful dynasts precisely to this proximity. Ultimately everything depends on the personal Power of the ruler. The emanation of this Power reveals itself in a quite undifferentiated way along three separate axes: the center-periphery axis, already discussed; the "ascriptive" axis, or the diachronic diffusion of a powerful ruler's seminal Power through seven generations of descendants; and the patron-client or administrative axis, whereby the Power of the highest patron (the ruler) seeps down through descending strata of patron-client clusters until it reaches the peasant base of the society. Thus, although sharp distinctions were made between the ruler's immediate family and high-ranking ministeriales of common origins, these distinctions tended to be less politically significant than might otherwise have been expected; they were subordinate in importance to the crucial factor of proximity to the ruler.[67]

These points may be useful for understanding some aspects of political behavior in contemporary Indonesia. What we have seen, in effect, is the marked consonance of the traditional Javanese concept of Power with the political structures and behavior of the patrimonial state. We can further take note that the indigenization of bureaucratic structures and behavior in Indonesia that was so marked after the middle 1950s can be usefully viewed as a reemergence of the patrimonial model.[68] A full analysis of the reasons for this reemergence of patrimonialism would take us too far afield. Doubtless the major cause was the fact that the rational-legal bureaucracy bequeathed by the Dutch proved economically unsustainable in this period of secular economic decline.[69] But the holding power of patrimonialism was probably also accentuated by the persistence of traditional perspectives so consonant with it.

[67]Compare Maruyama, *Thought and Behaviour*, pp. 12–20. On p. 13 he writes: "The standard of values, then, that determined a person's position in society and in the nation was based less on social function than on relative distance from the Emperor."

[68]This process of "indigenization" is excellently treated in Ann Ruth Willner, *The Neo-Traditional Accommodation to Political Independence: The Case of Indonesia*, Center of International Studies, Research Monograph no. 26 (Princeton, N.J.: Princeton University, 1966).

[69]I am indebted to Daniel Lev for this insight.

The signal unwillingness of the *pusat* (center) to accede to demands for decentralization and regional autonomy in the late parliamentary period (1956–58), while clearly stemming from fears for the national exchequer if the foreign-exchange-producing areas in Sumatra and Sulawesi increased their power, can also be attributed in part to the continuing impact of old conceptions about relationships between center and provinces as indicators of the "health" of the realm. The subsequent triumph over the regional rebellion in 1958 and the consolidation of Guided Democracy were marked by a great increase in the appointment of ministeriales to key military and civilian positions in the regional bureaucracy, and the absorption of the office of *kepala daérah* (elective regional head) into the centrally appointed administrative positions of governor and *bupati*.[70] These ministeriales were, in the old tradition, appointed largely on the basis of their loyalty to Jakarta rather than of any special administrative competence.

A parallel line of argument can be pursued for patterns of administrative behavior at the center, particularly after the restoration of the 1945 Constitution in 1959. This constitution provides explicitly that cabinet ministers are to be the assistants of the president and responsible to him alone. While its models are to be found in Kuomintang China, post-Meiji Japan, and perhaps the United States, one can discern the influence of the old patrimonial style in the sense of comfort with which many Javanese accepted it and abandoned the liberal parliamentary constitution of 1950. The psychological unwillingness of many cabinet ministers to accept any kind of autonomous responsibility, particularly responsibility to parliamentarians and the general public, was quite evident in the liberal period but was out of kilter with the ethical norms implicit in a parliamentary constitution. Under the 1945 Constitution, formal norms and traditional propensities tended to coincide. Insofar as real Power is seen to flow out of the concentrated center and not from the diffuse perimeter, ministerial behavior should reflect the wishes of the former rather than the latter.[71] The same argument helps to explain the ease with which many Javanese accepted the emergence under the authoritarian Sukarno and

---

[70]On the decentralizing and centralizing trends of the period 1955–59, and the creation and virtual abolition of the independent office of *kepala daérah*, see John D. Legge, *Central Authority and Regional Autonomy in Indonesia: A Study in Local Administration, 1950–1960* (Ithaca, N.Y.: Cornell University Press, 1961), chaps. 4, 9.

[71]Ultimately, personal responsibility must be based on autonomous personal power; this is a difficult norm to sustain in combination with the traditional view that the assistants of the ruler have no Power of their own independent of their master.

Suharto regimes of informal power groups outside the "rational-legal" structure of the inherited colonial bureaucracy. The so-called *golongan istana* (palace group) under Guided Democracy and the president's Spri (private staff) under the New Order represented the kitchen cabinet of the ruler, his personal agents and confidants.[72] The enormous power they in fact wielded depended solely on the fact that their proximity to the center was recognized by the entire politico-administrative elite.

Power and Ethics

Although the ruling class of traditional Java could be defined in structural terms as the hierarchy of officials and their extended families, like any other ruling class they were also marked off—indeed, marked themselves off—from the rest of the population by their style of life and self-consciously espoused system of values. Today, the word *priyayi*, which is the most common appellation for this class, primarily connotes ethical values and modes of behavior rather than official position. Yet these values and modes of behavior are linked closely with the traditional functions of this class; and the concept of Power reveals the nexus very clearly.

The quality that the priyayi have traditionally stressed as distinguishing them from the rest of the population is that of being halus. The meaning of this term—which eludes precise definition in English, though some notable efforts have been made by Clifford Geertz[73] and others—is to a certain extent covered by the idea of smoothness, the quality of not being disturbed, spotted, uneven, or discolored. Smoothness of spirit means self-control, smoothness of appearance means beauty and elegance, smoothness of behavior means politeness and sensitivity. The antithetical quality of being kasar means lack of control, irregularity, imbalance, disharmony, ugliness, coarseness, and impurity. Since being kasar is the natural state of man, in which his energies, thoughts, and behavior lack all control and concentration, no effort is required to achieve it. Being halus, on the other hand, requires constant effort and control to reach a reduction of the spec-

---

[72]*Spri* is a standard acronym for *staf pribadi* (private staff). Although it was Suharto who first created this official nomenclature, his example has been widely followed. Today, almost anyone of any importance in the Indonesian government has his own Spri.

[73]See Clifford Geertz, *The Religion of Java* (New York: Free Press, 1964), p. 232.

trum of human feeling and thought to a single smooth "white" radiance of concentrated energy. The connection between halus-ness and Power is readily evident; Power is the essential link between natural man and the halus *satria* (knight) of wayang mythology and Javanese priyayi etiquette. In the minds of traditional Javanese, being halus is in itself a sign of Power, since halus-ness is achieved only by the concentration of energy. In Javanese legends and folk history the slight, halus satria almost invariably overcomes the demonic *raseksa* (giant), *buta* (ogre), or wild man from overseas. In the typical battle scenes of the wayang plays the contrast between the two becomes strikingly apparent in the slow, smooth, impassive, and elegant movements of the satria, who scarcely stirs from his place, and the acrobatic leaps, somersaults, shrieks, taunts, lunges, and rapid sallies of his demonic opponent. The clash is especially well symbolized at the moment when the satria stands perfectly still, eyes downcast, apparently defenseless, while his demonic adversary repeatedly strikes at him with dagger, club, or sword—but to no avail. The concentrated Power of the satria makes him invulnerable.

This smooth invulnerability is the much prized hallmark of the satria, both as military man and as statesman. But it is achieved only by the self-discipline that we have seen as the key to the accumulation of Power. The single most imminent threat to this invulnerability is not the satria's adversary, but pamrih, perhaps best translated as "concealed personal motive." This complex term means doing something not because the act has to be done, but because one's personal interests or desires are thereby satisfied. The traditional motto of the Javanese administrator, *sepi ing pamrih, ramé ing gawé,* still frequently quoted by politicians and officials, means that the correct attitude of the priyayi official should be to refrain from indulging personal motives, while working hard for the good of the state. At the level of everyday morality, pamrih is the socially undesirable quality of selfishness and personal aggrandizement. But on a deeper level, the pamrih of the administrator or the military man is really a threat to his own ultimate interests, since the indulgence of personal, and therefore partial, passions or prejudices means interior imbalance and a diffusion of personal concentration and Power. This idea of pamrih is a constant motif in the "morality" of the wayang plays. It forms the essential contrast between the Pandawa and the Kurawa in the Bratayuda cycle, and between Rama and Dasamuka in the Ramayana cycle. In each case the "evil" party is destined to be defeated not so much because of his evilness as because "evil" means the indulgence of personal passion, which ultimately undermines the concentration of Power.[74]

This theme is strikingly illustrated in two critical episodes of the Bratayuda cycle. The first instance is the final dialogue between Sri Bathara Kresna and Adipati Karna on the eve of the war between the Pandawa and Kurawa, in which Kresna tries to persuade Karna to abandon the cause of the Kurawa and fight on the side of his half-brothers, the Pandawa. At the heart of Karna's eloquent refusal is his rejection of pamrih. He tells Kresna that he knows perfectly well that the Kurawa have done wrong and that the Pandawa will win the war. But everything that he is he owes to Suyudana, the eldest of the Kurawa, and disinterested loyalty is the first quality of the satria. Moreover, should he go over to the side of the Pandawa he would not only be "climbing on the bandwagon" but would also lower the prestige of the Pandawa's ultimate victory. Without Karna on their side, the Kurawa would be no match for their cousins, and the destined Great Bratayuda War would be an inglorious, one-sided military operation. Thus, vis-à-vis both the Kurawa and the Pandawa, he will fulfill his *darma* by siding with King Suyudana, though he knows it will cost him his life.[75]

In an even better-known passage of the epic, Arjuna and Karna face each other on the field of battle. Confronted with his own half-brother, Arjuna "weakens." Turning to Kresna, he says that he cannot bring himself to kill his brother and cannot face the prospect of so much suffering and death. Kresna's famous response is that this humane sentiment is essentially a form of pamrih. Personal ties should not be permitted to sway a satria from the responsibilities laid upon him. The satria goes into battle ready to die, if necessary, but he fights not out of personal hatred or passion, but because of darma. Arjuna should be no less a satria than Karna, who is performing his darma though foreseeing his own death. The purposes of destiny are above those of individual mortals. Recalled to his responsibilities, Arjuna reenters the fray.

Only in the light of the concept of pamrih can the attitude of many

[74]The prototypical example of this is the rape of Rama's wife, Sita, by the demonic Prabu Dasamuka. One could almost say, however, that the act of abduction itself is less evil than Dasamuka's self-indulgence in executing it. In this sense the evil is done to Dasamuka rather than to Sita.
[75]*Darma* is usually translated *duty,* a word that has unfortunate Christian overtones. It is really a caste or status-obligation: Being a satria, one acts as a satria. In a more general sense, it has some of the connotations of *justice*.

Javanese toward the accumulation of wealth be properly understood. Personal acquisitiveness, like sexual indulgence and political ambition, is one of the most obvious types of personal indulgence or pamrih. Accordingly, the overt pursuit of wealth that is characteristic of the merchant or businessman shows a lack of Power, and therefore lack of status. This judgment should not be taken to suggest that the typical high-status Javanese is not a man of wealth or that the Javanese tradition does not conceive of riches as an important attribute of the ruler and his closest associates. But money in itself should never be the object of active pursuit. Wealth should flow to the holder of Power as a consequence of the Power, in the same way that pusaka, large populations, wives, neighboring kingdoms or states flow toward the ruler, as it were, magnetically attracted to the center. The vast wealth that the great rulers of the Javanese past are described as possessing is always an attribute of Power, not the means for acquiring it. Thus, in the Javanese political tradition wealth necessarily follows Power, not Power wealth.

One important reason for widespread anxiety about the regime of late Guided Democracy (and, incidentally, of the New Order) was that some of the highest figures in the state were believed to be bent on the acquisition of personal wealth. The issue of corruption has wider resonances than simply the lack of personal probity among high officials or the waste of national resources, since personal corruption is interpreted as a sign of a regime's decay. A most significant element in the 1966–67 campaign to drive Sukarno from public life was the publicity given to evidence of the president's pamrih in the matter of corruption and other forms of abuse of power for personal advantage. Conversely, one of the most powerful cards in the PKI's hands under both liberal and Guided Democracy was its largely deserved reputation for incorruptibility. This lack of corruption in the PKI appealed not only to the "modern" desire for rationality, probity, and discipline in public life but also to the traditional respect for the man without pamrih, the potential source of new-rising Power. Thus, among the first steps taken by the military propaganda apparatus in the anti-Communist campaign of late 1965 was an attempt to demonstrate that the PKI leaders were secretly sexual libertines (Njoto) and embezzlers (Aidit), because of the powerful images thereby evoked.[76]

[76]One can speculate in passing that the strategy of the PKI in 1963–65 of trying to create a sense of an irresistible tide flowing in their direction, a snowballing accumulation of adherents, was partly conscious harnessing of traditional ideas about the flow of Power from a decaying to a rising center.

The same argument helps to clarify one well-established tradition of Javanese administrative behavior—the so-called *perintah halus*. This phrase is generally understood to mean the giving of orders in polite and indirect language, sometimes even in the form of a request rather than a command; the request is nonetheless understood by both parties to be a command. The nuances of the concept have been sensitively treated from the political and sociological perspective by Ann Willner and Donald Fagg, who see the perintah halus as the result of a highly formalized pattern of interpersonal relations among the Javanese or as a necessary device to conceal the bargaining and bluffing that characterize Javanese power relationships.[77] But within the context of traditional Javanese thinking, the perintah halus is by no means a weak or indirect command designed to cover the uncertainty of the order-giver as to how far his authority will be obeyed. On the contrary, it is a more powerful command than an express order, because it is necessarily given by a halus person, one of higher power and status and closer to the center of Power. We should bear in mind, moreover, the symbolism of the satria in battle. The man of Power should have to exert himself as little as possible in any action. The slightest lifting of his finger should be able to set a chain of actions in motion. The man of real Power does not have to raise his voice nor give overt orders. The halusness of his command is the external expression of his authority. The whole Javanese style of administration is therefore marked by the attempt, wherever possible, to give an impression of minimum effort, as through the perintah halus. The ethics of halus-ness are at bottom the ethics of Power.

Power and Knowledge

If halus-ness is the hallmark of the priyayi, the focus of his ethics, and the expression of his Power, how is it attained? In one sense, the answer has already been given: Since halus-ness is a manifestation of Power, it can be achieved by the traditional road of asceticism and spiritual discipline. Yet this spiritual discipline cannot be achieved by haphazard methods; its attainment is only possible through education

[77]See Donald R. Fagg, "Authority and Social Structure: A Study in Javanese Bureaucracy" (Ph.D. thesis, Harvard University, 1958), p. 362–68, 372–429, and Willner, *Neo-Traditional Accommodation,* especially pp. 44–57. In both Fagg's and Willner's analysis there is a certain lack of historical and cultural perspective. The *perintah halus* in the postindependence period was necessarily in part a bluff. Not only was the belief-system out of which the perintah halus arose being eroded by conflicting norms derived from the secular, skeptical West, but the monolithic power of the Dutch and Japanese colonial governments, which had

in certain specific forms of knowledge. In this perspective, knowledge becomes the key to Power.

Traditional Javanese education can fairly be described as an initiation into a more or less permanent arcane lore. Samudja Asjari has described in detail the process of traditional education in the rural *pesantrèn* under the leadership of the *kyai*.[78] In these pesantrèn the *santri* (pupils) go through a carefully graded series of levels of knowledge, from the simplest, most earthly type through increasingly esoteric studies, till they reach the stage of the *ngèlmu makripat* (the secrets of being, of divinity).[79] The progress of the santri is seen as a long process of moving closer and closer to the ultimate secrets of the cosmos, finally attainable only through illumination.[80] Only a few of the santri ever reach the final stage—one can envisage them spread out like planets in ever narrowing orbits around an inner sun. Education thus provides a key (*kunci*) to the door separating ignorance from knowledge, and that knowledge is access to an ontological reality.[81]

But this pattern of education has not been (and is not) confined to the rural Islamic schools; it underlies the education of the traditional elite as well. In the wayang stories and in the historical chronicles, a critical period in the life of a young satria is a period of isolation and training in a hermitage or mountain grotto. There, under the tutelage of a *resi* (seer), he undergoes initiation into the esoteric sciences. The initiation may include studying the arts of combat (*ngèlmu kadigdayan*) but is mainly devoted to magico-religious introspection. *Déwa Ruci*, perhaps the best known of the wayang plays, is an exact dramatic representation of this process.[82]

---

previously been present to reinforce the perintah halus with indisputable physical coercion, no longer existed. The weakness and multiplicity of authorities in postindependence Indonesia exposed the hollowness of the perintah halus, which had been caused by the colonial experience but concealed by the total domination of the colonial government.

[78]Samudja Asjari, "Kedudukan Kjai Dalam Pondok Pesantrèn" (M.A. thesis, Gajah Mada University, Yogyakarta, 1967), especially pp. 120–36. *Pesantrèn* are rural Islamic schools. *Kyai* is a general Javanese term of high respect, which may refer to human beings or to inanimate objects. In this instance it refers to the venerated Islamic teachers who head the pesantrèn schools.

[79]Cf. Geertz, *Islam Observed*, pp. 36–37, on "graded spirituality" in a slightly different context.

[80]At a cruder level, the santri may also gradually learn the secrets of *ngèlmu kedhotan* (invulnerability).

[81]For an elaboration of this theme and its implications, see chap. 4, below, especially at pp. 127–29.

[82]For a fuller account of this play and a detailed, authoritative analysis of its mystical significance, see K. G. P. A. A. Mangkunagara VII, *On the Wayang Kulit (Purwa) and Its Symbolic and Mystical Elements,* translated from the original Dutch by Claire Holt, Southeast Asia Program Data Paper no. 27 (Ithaca, N.Y.: Cornell University, 1957), especially pp. 16–19, 23–24.

In this play, the young hero Brataséna asks his teacher, Pandhita Durna, how to learn the secret of life, and is told to seek it at the bottom of the sea. In the depths of the ocean he is attacked by a monstrous serpent (*naga*), but finally wins the day. Then there appears before him a tiny divinity, Déwa Ruci, a miniature replica of himself, who tells Brataséna to enter his ear. Brataséna obeys this impossible command and, passing through the ear of Déwa Ruci, reaches the Unattainable. Common folk interpretations of the play stress that the serpent and the sea represent the distracting human passions, and that therefore the struggle with the naga means the struggle to master these base impulses. Déwa Ruci represents the Aku, the divine inner essence, only to be encountered after victory over the serpent. The paradoxical entry of the gigantic Brataséna into the miniature deity's ear symbolizes the idea that inner knowledge is not reached by ordinary study but by a suprarational moment of illumination. Only after going through this test does Brataséna emerge from the sea with altered visage and his full adult name of Wrekudara.[83]

The traditional image of the acquisition of knowledge is that of a search for a key that opens the door between ignorance and knowledge, making possible the qualitative leap from one to the other. Such a learning process contains nothing in the slightest degree heuristic or pragmatic. The residual power of this old conception is not hard to detect in contemporary Indonesian thinking. Bearing it in mind does much to render comprehensible the typical division of the population by the political elite into two radically separate groups, those who are *masih bodoh* (still stupid, still unenlightened) and those who are *insyaf* or *terpelajar* (aware, educated).[84]

Such a viewpoint possibly also helps to explain the immense appeal of explicitly ideological thinking in Indonesia today. The most powerful ideological currents in Indonesia—communism, radical nationalism, and Islam (both reformist and orthodox)—are all seen as keys for explaining the complexities and confusions of the contemporary world. The adepts of each of these *aliran* (currents) feel themselves to have acquired, through a process of politico-religious initiation, an esoteric but comprehensive picture of the universe and its workings.[85]

---

[83]The prestige of learning of this kind is well illustrated by the fact that the highest type of ruler is referred to as the *pandhita ratu* (Sage-King), of whom the classical model is the eldest of the Pandawa brothers, King Yudhisthira of Ngamarta.

[84]See chap. 4, below, pp. 145–46.

[85]For an extended discussion of the aliran see Clifford Geertz, "The Javanese Village," in G. William Skinner, ed., *Local, Ethnic, and National Loyalties in Village Indonesia: A Symposium*, Southeast Asia Studies, Cultural Report Series no. 8 (New Haven: Yale Univer-

While each aliran contains within it powerful expansionist and proselytizing elements, nonetheless each retains a highly introverted character. The hermetic quality of the aliran has been noted by many
observers. The general lack of congruence between them, the rarity of
intimate social contact, the virtually total absence of intellectual exchange, and the sharp dividing line between adherents and non-
adherents, at least in the minds of the adepts, can be seen as similar to
the structures and values of the pesantrèn and other traditional institutions concerned with the acquisition of knowledge.[86]

Here we come full circle to the intimate relationship between
knowledge and Power. It is not simply—as the history of the Republic
shows—that ideologies offer a ready means to local and national
power through the mechanism of political parties, or that within each
aliran those who claim greater knowledge of and deeper initiation
into the aliran's inner lore have obtained positions of high respect and
authority. Ideologies have developed deep roots precisely because they
can be seen as giving Power. The more closely the "initiation" into a
particular ideology approximates traditional educational practices
and conceptions, the more effective the ideology is in developing a
powerful psychological hold on the new adherent. This factor certainly contributed to the striking success of PKI educational work
under the Aidit leadership; for the period of candidacy and the clear-
cut conception of the party as a hierarchical educational pyramid
reveal strong similarities with the structure of pesantrèn education.
One should also not underestimate the powerful appeal that the discipline and secrecy demanded of party members exerted in traditionalist milieux.[87] The radical nature of the party's criticism of the
existing order might be thought to be an obstacle to successful pros-
elytization. But in fact it proved in many instances quite the opposite,

---

sity, 1959), pp. 37–41. Geertz offers two definitions of aliran: "a political party surrounded
by a set of voluntary social organizations formally or informally linked to it," and "a
comprehensive pattern of social integration." My own sense of what an aliran is would be
closer to the second definition: a distinctive, integrated cultural outlook, together with its
organized and unorganized (but potentially organizable) adherents. For a highly sophisticated discussion of the relationships of aliran, class, and political organization, see the
introduction by Ruth McVey to Karel Warouw and Peter Weldon's translation of Sukarno's
Nationalism, Islam, and Marxism, Cornell Modern Indonesia Project Translation Series
(Ithaca, N.Y.: Cornell University, 1969).

[86]For a good description of this "closed" aspect of pesantrèn society, see Samudja Asjari,
"Kedudukan," pp. 130–55, 160–66.

[87]Compare the character of the *tarékat* (Sufi brotherhoods) so excellently described in
Sartono Kartodirdjo, *The Peasants' Revolt of Banten in 1888, Its Conditions, Course, and
Sequel: A Case Study of Social Movements in Indonesia* (The Hague: De Nederlandsche
Boek- en Steendrukkerij v/h Smits, 1966), pp. 157–65.

since the criticism was seen to provide a coherence of vision and an implied renewal of order from within the confusions and antagonisms of everyday life. A more partial, piecemeal critical approach, more ready to accept major elements of the existing situation, would and did find it difficult to match the unity, certainty, and centripetalism of Indonesian Marxism-Leninism.

One should not, in this connection, overlook the peculiar political power of literate men in a largely illiterate traditional society. Where illiteracy is the rule, writing has an enormous power-creating potential, both because of its esoteric character and because it allows mysterious and rapid communication among its adepts. Significantly, in the wayang stories the single most powerful weapon in the hands of the favored Pandawa is not an arrow, club, or spear but a piece of writing, the Serat Kalimasada, the special pusaka of the eldest Pandawa brother, King Yudhisthira. What is actually written in this pusaka is never made clear; indeed, in one sense the power of the pusaka rests in its opaqueness to all but the initiated.[88] Seen in this light, literacy is simply an external sign of the possession of knowledge. Although in practice by no means all priyayi were functionally literate, the priyayi as a status group tended in the traditional world to be identified as the literati. The literacy of the ruling class was a symbol of Power largely because it presupposed the ability to make the qualitative leap out of illiteracy. The literati were not just better educated—they were the educated in a society of uneducated. Their power derived not from their ability to disseminate new concepts through society, but from their ability to penetrate to and conserve old and secret knowledge.

Rulers and Ruled

The centripetal propensities of traditional political thought naturally affected Javanese conceptions of the proper relations between ruler and ruled, between patron and client, and between priyayi and peasant.

Traditional thought clearly did not allow for any form of social contract or conceptualized system of mutual obligations between superior and subordinate. Any such system would have had to admit a

---

[88]Note the prestige and strategic advantage of those in a village who can read the newspaper to the rest. *Koran bilang* (the newspaper says) was, at least until quite recently, a special kind of invocation of authority in the village sphere.

formal reciprocity in political relationships fundamentally alien to Javanese thinking. It would have necessitated the recognition that being halus and powerful imposed obligations toward others less favored *because* they were kasar and unpowerful. As we shall see, the halus and powerful did recognize certain social duties, but the rationale for such obligations had a logic of its own, quite unconnected with the ideas of contract or even, strictly speaking, of noblesse oblige.

If we turn first to relationships within the ruling class itself we find a conspicuous absence of the contractual element implicit in the European feudal institution of vassalage. This absence can be explained empirically by the centralizing tendencies and financial structure of the patrimonial state, which Weber contrasted with classical feudalism. The economic base of the priyayi ruling class was not independent landownership but the system of appanage benefices, previously discussed. And part of the patrimonial ruler's policy was to prevent such appanages from becoming hereditary (and thus ultimately the basis for a more strictly feudal social structure) and to scatter the appanages attached to a particular position in order to prevent local consolidations of economic power that might ultimately give rise to a type of entrenched landlordism.[89]

The appanage system in effect meant that the land of the realm belonged to the ruler and its economic surplus (including the labor of the peasants who tilled it) was in his gift, to be distributed at his discretion to deserving officials. A clear harmony exists between such a system and the concept of Power, since the former naturally encourages ideas that we have already encountered: Wealth (or property) is an *attribute* of power, not its provenance; and socioeconomic status derives from the center and has no meaning except in relation to that center. Such a system also suggests that the wealth of the state is in the gift of the ruler and may be distributed downward through officialdom as the perquisites of office; but that this distribution is to be conceived not as an obligation of the ruler to his officials, but rather as a mark of his favor.

In view of what we have described as the reemergence of patrimonialism in independent Indonesia, the residual influences of the appanage system in contemporary administrative behavior can be clearly seen, particularly in the morphology of corruption. If one leaves

---

[89]For a good account of the gradual evolution of the appanage system in Java from precolonial through colonial times, see Selosoemardjan, *Social Changes in Jogjakarta* (Ithaca, N.Y.: Cornell University Press, 1962), pp. 25–27, 31–33, 216–20, 272–75.

aside the petty corruption-of-necessity arising from critical economic conditions, inflation, and low government salaries and focuses on the large-scale corruption that assumes quasi-official form, it is striking how little evidence there is of the classic European buying and selling of offices. Millionaires, entrepreneurial or landed, usually cannot buy themselves administrative positions of power and prestige. Indeed, this inability is a habitual cause for complaint among certain members of this tiny group. Corruption on a large scale typically takes the form of the allotting of the "surplus" of certain key sectors of the economy to favored officials or cliques of officials, whether civilian or military.[90] Rice collection, tin mining, oil production and distribution, and tax collection are only some examples of the areas in which officially supervised venality occurs. In most cases the corruption is not chiefly for the immediate personal advantage of the official assigned to supervise a particular sector of the economy (though such an official is rarely in straitened circumstances). The corruption is typically used to finance a whole subsector of the administrative apparatus. That is to say, there is a system of parallel financing of favored sectors of the bureaucracy through the invisible flow of corruption running alongside the formal salary structure. The flow, channeled down through an informal pyramid of patron-client clusters on a typical patrimonial model, serves to reinforce the cohesion of such clusters. Cuts and commissions are often standardized enough to be called benefices in the traditional sense. Thus, in many sectors, corruption has become an essential element in the stability of bureaucratic organization.

To the degree that corruption provides a predominant part of an official's earnings and takes the form of quasi-official benefices, his bureaucratic orientation tends to shift increasingly toward immediate patrons or the rulers at the center. A more or less genuine service ethic toward the public, which is sustainable in a system dominated by adequate, fixed salaries and rational-legal norms, is naturally difficult to preserve under reemergent patrimonialism. One could also suggest that this orientation toward patrons and rulers on the part of corrupt officials is even heightened by the dubious legality or open illegality of such corruption today. Under such conditions the protection of one's

[90]This system of organized corruption has of course been enormously extended since the Indonesian state took control of the economic resources of the country in the anti-Dutch campaign of 1957–58.

superiors is especially necessary, and one's dependence on them is enhanced.[91]

While the structures of patrimonialism and the traditional concept of Power work in the same direction, focusing the loyalties of the ruling class inward and upward, this fact alone does not adequately account for the striking lack of *prise* of social contract ideas on modern Indonesian political elites. Insofar as such ideas form a central part of the Western conservative and liberal thought to which these elites were exposed in the colonial educational system, some further explanation seems necessary. In part this phenomenon can be explained by the wide influence of Marxism, in however diluted and distorted a form. The Marxist critique of social contract theory was particularly telling under a colonial regime which, for all its pronouncements of ethical aims, in practice made a mockery of any theory of mutual obligations between ruled and ruler.

We may note, however, that in the postcolonial era, particularly the so-called liberal period (1950–59), social contract ideas acquired very little new influence or prestige. The PKI was naturally impervious to such notions. But the remaining power groups in Indonesian politics tended typically to cling to holistic conceptions of Indonesian society, thus denying theories both of class contradictions and of class obligations.

In general, little thinking was devoted to the sociology of Indonesian politics. Insofar as there was any sociological perspective at all, it centered on an elite-mass dichotomy, symbolized by the words *pemimpin* and *rakyat*. The word *pemimpin* (leader, big shot), like its synonyms *tokoh, orang gedé,* and *pembesar,* is quite undifferentiated in character and is applied without any sense of disjuncture to officials, generals, and politicians alike. At the bottom of the political system are the rakyat (often translated as "the people" or "the common people"), again a term without any precise sociological contours. The rakyat are those who are masih bodoh (nonelite or nonleaders). Obvious parallels can be drawn with the older divisions priyayi and *wong cilik* (little man), and literati and illiterates.

Yet, at the same time, the rakyat has all along been a central symbol of Indonesian nationalism. Ideologically speaking, the national revo-

[91]The extent to which this quasi-official corruption is dependent on the tenure of particular bureaucratic positions is striking. Little evidence exists that control of such benefices gives the particular official an independent basis of power within the political system, which would prevent his relatively easy removal.

lution of 1945 was to secure the liberation of the rakyat; in more radical minds, indeed, the national revolution was the work of the rakyat. We find here an attitude that is ostensibly a complete intellectual reversal of the older viewpoint that the people are quite peripheral to the political system, which is oriented toward the powerful center.

But in many respects this reversal is more apparent than real. The formal contradiction was resolved without difficulty in much of contemporary Indonesian political thinking.[92] One well-known solution was Sukarno's claim that he was the *penyambung lidah rakyat*— literally, the "extension of the people's tongue," perhaps more concisely, vox populi. Although some skeptics have felt that Sukarno and most of his generation in practice kept the people's tongue rather short, the formula represents an interesting mélange of modern populism and traditional ideas. The populism appears in the negation of any liberal theory of representation and thereby of the complex ideas of social contract or obligation implicit in such theories. A traditional theme appears in the close similarity of the concept of an undifferentiated, silent rakyat to the old idea of massed populations as an essential attribute of Power. In such a framework the penyambung lidah rakyat turns out to be less an extension of the people's tongue than the concentrated focus of the Power of the community as a whole. Sukarno's claim thus appears less a statement of ethical commitment than a claim to the possession of Power.

Thus, while the formally populist aspect of Sukarno's title contains an element of obligation—the obligation of the penyambung to express the demands of the people—its informal traditionalist character implies nothing of the kind. The humility implied in the self-bestowed title should not disguise its essential similarity to the many other glory-building titles—Great Leader of the Revolution, Supreme Boy Scout, and the like—which the president assumed. All such titles were claims to having Power, by the association of its symbols with his name.

It would nonetheless be a mistake to infer from what has just been said that there is no inherent sense of obligation and responsibility in the traditional Javanese world view. But this sense of obligation was and is an obligation to Power itself. We have seen that the well-being of the community is regarded as depending on the center's ability to concentrate Power, and the external sign of a decline of that Power is

---

[92]While Sukarno is used here as the prime example, lesser political figures have revealed patterns of thought very similar to his.

the decay or disruption of the community. There is thus no inherent contradiction between the accumulation of central Power and the well-being of the collectivity; indeed, the two are interrelated. The welfare of the collectivity depends not on the activities of its individual components but on the concentrated energy of the center. The center's fundamental obligation is to itself. If this obligation is fulfilled, popular welfare will necessarily be assured. So, while traditional Javanese writers frequently devote long passages to the proper conduct for a king and the art of statecraft, to suppose that the behavior required of the ruler is predicated on the stated or unstated needs of his subjects would be an error. The ruler must behave properly or his Power will ebb and vanish, and with it the good ordering and smoothness of the social system.

The Ruler and His Critics

Although the great majority of what could be defined as the intelligentsia in traditional Java were incorporated into the structure of administration, there remained on the fringes of society one important type of intellectual with a special role to play.[93] This type is represented in pre-Islamic traditional literature by hermits and sages (resi, *begawan, ajar*), usually residing in isolated caves or lonely mountainsides, remote from society. Their physical isolation expressed a fundamental separation from the interdependencies of community life. The ajar (with his *cantrik,* or pupils) was self-sufficient, outside the political order. He withdrew from society to cultivate clairvoyance, study the secrets of the cosmos, and prepare himself for death. The wayang stories and chronicles are filled with descriptions of these revered figures, whose asceticism gives them special insight into the inner state of the world and into the future flow of Power within it. The typical role of the seer is to diagnose decay within the kingdom and warn of the impending downfall of the dynasty. The usual recorded reaction of the ruler is violent: The seer is beaten, tortured, or put to death. But the violence done is itself a sign that the seer's predictions are being fulfilled: The ruler's resort to violence shows that he is dominated by

---

[93]In a general sense, *intelligentsia* can be thought of as referring to the whole of the literate official class. In a narrower sense, it can be confined to the group of *pujangga* (court poets and chroniclers), astrologers, and unofficial policy advisers to the throne. In the wayang literature the preeminent example is Pandhita Durna, brahmin, educator of princes, and *éminence grise* of the Kurawa.

personal passions. On the other hand, precisely because the seer has withdrawn from society, there can be no question of his being infected by pamrih. Indeed, since the seer was held to possess the gift of clairvoyance, his blessing was usually thought essential to the success of a pretender to the throne or the ambitious would-be founder of a new dynasty. No blessing would be forthcoming unless the seer was certain that the recipient would succeed. It was he who detected the first signs of the shifting of the wahyu and located its ultimate destination.

The withdrawal of the ajar from society and politics was an essential element in his prestige, and, in our sense of the word, his power; and his criticism of the ruler depended for its authority on this condition. The seer was not an emanation of the center and not dependent upon it. His political disinterestedness made him a respected (and feared) barometer of the fortunes of the rulers, in the eyes of the rulers themselves and in those of interested third parties (rebels, subjects, and others).

The classic ajar largely vanished from the scene with the penetration of Islam and the later superimposition of bureaucratic colonial authority. But his social and political role, to speak paradoxically, by no means disappeared. Samudja Asjari has explicitly made the linkage between the ajar and the rural Islamic kyai of the late precolonial and colonial periods. In his description of the pesantrèn we find essentially the same features that marked the ajar-cantrik community of an earlier era: physical separation from civil society, asceticism, the search for knowledge, and virtual isolation from the politico-administrative structures of the state.[94] The normal withdrawal of the kyai from political life made their intervention, when it occurred, of great psychological importance. The fact that the kyai were Islamic religious figures made no fundamental change, for the Islam of the kyai was a kind in which traditional elements remained exceedingly powerful: intuitive, personal, and mystical in character, it inherited much of the pre-Islamic religion.

Although the rulers maintained Islamic officials (the *penghulu* and his subordinates) in their entourage as part of the court intelligentsia, with the function of contributing to the glory and Power of the center, these religious figures had little independent prestige. By contrast, the wild" rural kyai, who were never absorbed into the state structure,

---

[94]Samudja Asjari, "Kedudukan," pp. 84, 101–5.

built independent reputations, most often in villages remote from the court centers.

The kyai normally remained aloof from the political life of the state. Only in times of distress and confusion were they likely to emerge from their pesantrèn at the head of their faithful santri, to play brief but at times decisive roles in the collapse of an old order and the emergence of a new before retiring once again to their former isolation. The contemporary sociologist would probably expect such charismatic leaders to emerge in times of social unrest; most writings about Javanese messianic movements stress this point.[95] But from within the traditional intellectual framework, once again causality must be reversed. It is the abrupt emergence of such figures into the political arena that reveals the inner decay or disruption of the social order. Indeed precipitates it. The kyai has thus appeared to have inherited much of the role and status of the ajar before him.

In the colonial period, the rural kyai, not the urban penghulu, were the ones who remained an abiding preoccupation of the alien rulers. Like the traditional kingdoms, the bureaucratic colonial polity found no structural place for the kyai and their pesantrèn. The colonial authorities might repress the insurgence of the kyai when it occurred, but the repression scarcely augmented the prestige and authority of the government. Just as the violence done to the ajar did not disprove his foresight, but rather signaled the pamrih-filled character of the regime, so the repression of the kyai could be taken as a sign of the inner turpitude and decay of the colonial government.

Can the ajar's intellectual lineage be traced to our own time? The kyai have by no means vanished from the rural scene. Their massive intrusion into politics has only occurred twice in the postwar era—in 1945 and 1965.[96] In both cases their intervention presaged and indeed helped bring about a fundamental change of regime—from Japanese to Republican authority in 1945, from Guided Democracy to the New Order in 1965–66. In both instances they acted outside the established political framework and in many important respects outside the control of both declining and ascending ruling groups. (In

[95]Cf. Sartono Kartodirdjo, *The Peasants' Revolt*, especially pp. 154–75; Gerardus Willebrordus Johannes Drewes, *Drie Javaansche Goeroe's. Hun Leven, Onderricht en MessiaspMrediking* (Leiden: Vros, 1925); Justus Maria van der Kroef, "Javanese Messianic Expectations: Their Origin and Cultural Context," *Comparative Studies in Society and History* (1959):299–323.

[96]For some material on the 1945 period, see my *Java in a Time of Revolution* (Ithaca, N.Y.: Cornell University Press, 1972), pp. 4–10, 157, 219–24.

neither case did they remain to take part in the new central authority.) In addition, the roles played by parts of the modern urban intelligentsia,[97] and the attitudes displayed toward them by the rulers and by certain sections of contemporary society, reveal striking morphological similarities to the tradition we have been discussing.[98]

In the later colonial period, one finds clear structural parallels with the older dichotomy between the official literati of the patrimonial center and the isolated ajar and kyai. Whereas the bulk of the indigenous literati formed part of the colonial bureaucracy or became appendages of it, the small nationalist intelligentsia was, partly by choice and partly by necessity, excluded from the colonial power structure. It, too, depended for its prestige on an ostensible absence of pamrih— insofar as it claimed to speak, not for itself, but for the whole oppressed rakyat. It, too, claimed, largely on the basis of the Leninist critique of imperialism which it had absorbed from the West, a special, esoteric insight into the course of historical development and the inner decay of the existing order.

With the ascendance to power of the nationalist intelligentsia after 1945, one might have expected such structural similarities to disappear. Yet, particularly with regard to the behavior and attitudes of the nontechnical intelligentsia, one could argue that the same traditions are still at work: the dominant tradition of service to and glorification of the center, and the secondary tradition of isolation and criticism (as opposed to participatory opposition). During Sukarno's ascendancy, when the attractive power of the center was very great, particular ministers, such as Subandrio, Ruslan Abdulgani, and Prijono, as well as certain well-known Islamic politicians, were perceived by many observers as fulfilling ancient functions in modern guise. It was not entirely in jest that they were sometimes referred to as the pujangga or penghulu of Guided Democracy.[99]

[97]I use the term *intelligentsia* as a translation of *kaum intelèk,* which roughly embraces those who have received a higher Western-style education.

[98]This suggestion can be made without overlooking the fact that in any discussion of the conscious roles played by the urban intellectuals in contemporary Indonesia, Western antecedents and sociological imperatives are of central importance. The Western-educated intelligentsia have inherited that powerful tradition of dissent in modern Western history so eloquently described in Julien Benda's *La Trahison des clercs.* The prestige attached to opposition and skepticism in Western intellectual history has certainly profoundly affected the Indonesian intelligentsia's conception of itself. See Suardi Tasrif, "Situasi Kaum Intelektuil di Indonesia," *Budaja Djaja* (September 1968), for an extended discussion of Benda's book and its implications for the intellectuals under the Sukarno and Suharto regimes. Moreover, the ever-growing disproportion between the numbers of the intellectuals and of available administrative and political positions has necessarily created a large body of educated or semieducated people who cannot be incorporated into the government apparatus.

[99]The New Order has found men to fulfill a similar role. Among those who were opposed

Among the critics of the regime, on the other hand, there were significant numbers who played, or were perceived to play, something of the role of the ajar or kyai. Around certain of these isolated figures there collected devoted cantrik, young men from the provinces, who depended on them for intellectual education and spiritual guidance.[100] Such figures, standing outside the authority structure, depended for their following on their charisma, their moral disinterestedness, and their reputation for insight into the destiny of the center and the identity of its potential successors.[101] The political impotence of such intellectuals may, paradoxically, reveal their real power. This is not to say that the authorities, whether Sukarno or the military, will refrain from suppressing their critics. But repression will tend not to augment the authorities' power, insofar as the role of the critic is felt or perceived in more or less traditional terms. Thus, it may ultimately be at least as dangerous for the authorities to repress these impotent critics, who stand more or less outside the political system, as to suppress a potent opposition within it. For while suppression of the latter may be seen as revealing and augmenting the Power of the center, the crushing of the former may be taken as a sign of the center's impending disintegration. By doing violence to its powerless critics, the regime confirms their criticism and reinforces the authority of their predictions. Once again, in altered form, we find a restatement of an earlier paradox: the grasp for Power may mean its loss and the withdrawal from Power its acquisition.

A Note on Islam

Having carried the argument thus far, we can turn briefly to explore the relationship between this tradition of political thought and that of Javanese Islam. Such an analysis may throw additional light on the

---

to Guided Democracy there were not a few who aspired to play pujangga and penghulu to a different leadership and in a new center.

[100]Such men are often regarded by their young followers as possessing the key (*kunci*) to political and other types of problems, which will eventually be revealed to the most deserving among them. Kunci-ism is also a marked feature of many students' attitudes to aspects of formal university education.

[101]Since the onset of the New Order, a similar dichotomy can be said to have divided the student movement. Some student leaders have associated themselves with the hierarchy of the center—advising the government, speaking for it, and committing themselves to active participation in its structures. Others have insisted on remaining aloof and isolated. This is the group that wishes to see the students and intellectuals remain a moral force, committed not to the regime but to the ideas that the regime claims to practice.

growing antagonism between important Islamic groups and the main bearers of the Javanese tradition, which has become a central theme of contemporary Indonesian politics. Moreover, from the rise of what Geertz has aptly referred to as Islamic "scripturalism"[102] in twentieth-century Java, significant implications can be drawn concerning the general phenomenon of charisma.

It has been suggested that in the early days of its penetration of Java Islam took over certain pre-Islamic traditional roles, such as court adviser, astrologer, brahmin, and hermit-sage. This assimilation would have been unlikely had there not existed a large element of congruence and compatibility between the types of Islam that entered Java in the fifteenth and sixteenth centuries and the cultural tradition that they encountered. The "orthodox" stream in Javanese Islam sufficiently demonstrates this point. In popular folklore, the rivets linking the new religion to the old tradition are still conspicuous—especially in the association of Islam with the Power symbols of the preceding era. One obvious illustration of this is the body of legends that attributes the invention or development of such key elements of the pre-Islamic culture as wayang or the *gamelan* orchestra to the *wali,* the proselytizing saints of old Javanese Islam. Another well-known example is the common interpretation of the name of King Yudhisthira's pusaka, the Serat Kalimasada, as the Kalimah Sahadat, the Koranic confession of faith.[103]

That the penetration of Islam was more assimilative than revolutionary can be attributed to the fact that Islam came to Java "on the heels not of conquest but of trade."[104] It was first brought by traders and has never lost the marks of its provenance, developing its strongest hold in the intermediate, commercial rather than the upper, official or lower, peasant strata. After an initial period of zealotry, the devout Islamic groups were more or less absorbed into the patrimonial state. On the one hand, an Islam that had passed to Java through Persia and India was already patrimonialized and thus generally congruent with

---

[102]Geertz, *Islam Observed,* especially pp. 56–74.

[103]See, for example, Solichin Salam, *Sekitar Wali Sanga* (Kudus: Menara Kudus, 1960), pp. 35–51, for the culturally innovative role of the wali. Solichin Salam actually uses the words *assimilasi kebudayaan* (cultural assimilation) in describing the work of Sunan Kalijaga (p. 48). For the Kalimasada-Kalimah Sahadat fusion, see p. 66 of the same work. For a detailed account of the reputed role of the wali in developing the wayang into its modern forms, see Lindor Serrurier, *De Wajang Poerwa* (Leiden: Brill, 1896), pp. 98–107. Much of Serrurier's information is based on an unpublished manuscript from R. Adipati Sasranegara, the Patih of Surakarta, sent to Amsterdam in 1883.

[104]Geertz, *Islam Observed,* p. 12.

the traditional Javanese world view (particularly with regard to the role and significance of the ruler). On the other hand, after the fifteenth century the rulers assumed Islamic titles, kept Islamic officials in their entourage, and added Islam to the panoply of their attributes. Yet this overt Islamization of the rulers does not seem to have caused major alterations in their way of life or outlook. The penetration of Islam scarcely changed the composition and the recruitment of the Javanese political elite or affected the basic intellectual framework of traditional political thought.[105] To use Gramsci's term, at no point did a "hegemonic" Islamic culture develop in Java. The self-consciousness of pious Moslems remained strictly "corporate."[106] Political and cultural subordination went hand in hand.

In the last quarter of the nineteenth century, both the socioeconomic position and the world view of devout Moslem elements in Java began to change. The opening of the Suez Canal in 1870 vastly increased Javanese contact with the Near East at a time when the so-called Islamic Reform movement was in its heyday. Returning pilgrims transmitted to highly receptive audiences in colonial Java the central idea of this movement: the need to regain the "uncorrupted" and "progressive" Islam of the time of the Prophet, and to discredit the "non-Islamic," heterodox accretions of the intervening centuries.

The reasons for the great receptivity to "scripturalist" ideas must ultimately be traced to the deepening impact of Dutch capitalism and technology on traditional social and economic life and of secularizing rationalism on traditional beliefs. Reform Islam, as it grew and spread

---

[105]Denys Lombard has pointed out to me, however, that in the nineteenth century, at least one important example of Islamic political thought was studied in court circles in Central Java. This was the Tādj-us-Salātīn, allegedly written by Imam Buchārī-ul Djauhārī in 1603, which Hooykaas aptly describes as "Arabic in title, Persian-Moslem in content, Malay in language, and composed in Atjeh" (Christiaan Hooykaas, *Over Maleise Literatuur* [Leiden: Brill, 1947], p. 166). According to Soebardi, "The Book of Tjabolèk" (Ph.D. thesis, Australian National University, Canberra, 1967), pp. 69–70, the Tādj-us-Salātīn was translated and adapted into Javanese verse by the great pujangga of Surakarta, Jasadipura I (1729–1803), most likely in 1759. According to Radèn Mas Ngabèhi Poerbatjaraka, *Kapustakan Djawi* (Jakarta: Djambatan, 1952), pp. 143–44, Jasadipura composed this work in 1726, which seems improbable given his date of birth; the situation is further confused by Theodoor Gautier Thomas Pigeaud, *Literature of Java* (The Hague: Nijhoff, 1967), 1:100, who quotes Poerbatjaraka's view but refers to Jasadipura as an early-nineteenth-century poet! In any event, Jasadipura's version was frequently printed in book form from the end of the nineteenth century, editions appearing in Semarang in 1873 and 1875 and in Surakarta in 1905 and 1922 (Poerbatjaraka, *Kapustakan Djawi*, p. 144). Presumably, then, its major impact came at a time when the influence of Islam in general was increasing rapidly in Java as a result of the Reform movement in the Middle East.

[106]Antonio Gramsci, *The Modern Prince and Other Writings* (New York: International, 1957), pp. 154–56, 168–73.

in twentieth-century Java, represented a rationalist religious response to the challenges created by these developments. Almost every component of traditional Islam, except the fundamental articles of faith, was subjected to this rationalizing tendency. In the process, many traditional elements were discarded, including those which had permitted the long-standing accommodation between Islam and traditional Javanese political thought. The result was ever-increasing self-consciousness and hostility between pious reformist Moslems and their fellow Javanese. In this conflict, the reformists were handicapped not only by their sociologically intermediate and economically weak position but also by the intellectual problems involved in abandoning assimilationist traditionalism. For since the fundamental assumptions of reformist Islam departed drastically from traditional Javanese assumptions, its adherents faced the need to find new answers to political questions that the older tradition had answered more or less satisfactorily for its time.

In the modernist Islamic cosmology, the older Javanese conception of divinity as something formless and intangible suffusing the whole universe is replaced by a divinity sharply separated from the works of His hand. Between God and man there is an immeasurable distance. God is all powerful, all knowing, and all merciful; man is nothing more than His creature. Thus power is, in a sense, removed from the world, since it lies with God, Who is not of this world but above and antecedent to it. Furthermore, since the gulf between God and man is vast and God's power is absolute, all men are seen as equally insignificant before His majesty. But this very equality poses problems for any political theory and any permanent legitimation of political inequality and power. If all men are equally abject in the eyes of God, what is the religious basis for the political rule of one man over another?

Since Javanese cosmology made no sharp division between the terrestrial and the transcendental world, there was no extramundane referent by which to judge men's actions. For the traditionalist Javanese, possessed with the idea of divinity immanent in the world, virtually all aspects of behavior had, as it were, a "political" content insofar as they might affect the distribution and concentration of that Power which alone made the society they lived in well ordered, prosperous, and stable. The edicts of the ruler had no inherent, fixed ethical content; they were judged by the degree to which, in any given situation or period, they enhanced or undermined the concentration of Power. Hence the relativism of traditional Javanese thought, which has been so much commented upon.

By contrast, the newer currents in Islam stressed particularly the idea that Islamic law was based on God's prescriptions to the faithful, transmitted through the person of the Prophet. These prescriptions had a permanent transcendent value and served as a fixed basis for judging any man-made, political law. Such law had no inherent status. Ethics and terrestrial power were thus radically separated.

The logic of this rationalist perspective would appear to point toward a political and legal structure in strict conformity with the tenets of purified Islam. The question arises as to the status, in reformist eyes, of political and legal structures not so constituted. The problem is posed in particularly acute form in a highly pluralistic society like Indonesia and lies at the heart of the controversy over the "Islamic State." Pursuing the logic of Islamic rationalism to its conclusion under such conditions must inevitably arouse antagonism on the part of "statistical" Moslems, Christians, secularists, and others. Failure to pursue it is bound to create frustration among the Islamic devout.

We have already noted the close connection between Power and status in the Javanese world view. It is therefore not surprising that traditional Javanese usually regard the politician as a man of high prestige—unless he abuses his Power through pamrih, in which case his Power will decline. In the modernist Islamic world view, however, we have seen that little status is attached to terrestrial power precisely because all real power is in God's hands. Accordingly, the Islamic politician has no inherent claim to power, except, perhaps, insofar as he speaks for God. Yet any politician who sets himself up as God's spokesman is in a highly vulnerable position. In the Islamic community (*ummat*) the highest status is accorded to the religious scholar, the man with a deep knowledge of religious law and the teachings of the Prophet. This status derives exclusively from within the community. The politician, on the other hand, particularly in a heterogeneous society like contemporary Indonesia, is constantly faced with the need to deal with non-Moslem and nominally Moslem groups. Where these dealings are not purely coercive in character, they tend to be seen both as blurring the boundaries between "we" and "they" and as contaminating the purity of Islamic teaching.[107] With a few rare excep-

[107]The centripetality of Javanese thought connotes a lack of strong concern for external boundaries and the outer perimeters of society. By contrast, Islam, as one of the great proselytizing religions of the world, has always, I think, been conscious of its perimeters and the line between the "we" of the ummat and the "they" of the *kafir* (unbelievers). In twentieth-century Indonesia, this sense of "we-ness" has, of course, been powerfully heightened by Dutch colonial policies of manipulation and repression, competition with aggressive and wealthy Christian missions, and the spread of secular ideas. One could almost suggest that precisely because of a growing lack of a sense of the center, the modernist Islamic community has increasingly tended to define itself by its frontiers.

tions, the modernist Islamic politician is caught in a critical dilemma. To the extent that he authentically represents the claims of Islam, he will have high prestige within his own community but little purchase on the nation as a whole; to the extent that he succeeds in working out relationships with non-ummat groups and spreading his effective influence in the society at large, his prestige within his own community may be weakened. The dilemma arises from the absence in modernist rationalist Islam of any acceptable justification for the kind of dynamic syncretism typical of traditional Javanese thought. A Sukarno's prestige with traditional Javanese might be all the greater to the extent that he could successfully absorb the symbols of Islam into his regalia. A Natsir could not afford to absorb the symbols of non-Islam, for fear of destroying his influence and authority within his own community.[108]

Conclusions

If the overall argument of this essay has any validity, two very general considerations emerge. The first involves the relationship between the intellectual structure of traditional culture and the acceptance, transformation, or rejection of various institutional and ideational aspects of so-called modernization. The second concerns the extent to which the analysis of the Javanese conception of power may be of help in thinking about forms of domination outside the Javanese world, both in other preindustrial societies and in the industrial nations of the West.

I have tried to demonstrate the intellectual coherence of the traditional Javanese perspective on Power and politics and to show how various political institutions and processes look when seen through this lens. In spite of Dutch colonialism, the Japanese occupation, the nationalist revolution, and the socioeconomic changes they brought about, the cultural grip of this traditional perspective remains very strong. Such apparently discrete aspects of Javanese political thought and behavior in the contemporary period as the rejection of parliamentary democracy, the characteristic traits of Jakarta's interethnic and international politics, the patterns of administrative organization and internal bureaucratic relationships, the styles of postindependence leadership, the forms of corruption, and the ambiguous political posi-

---

[108]Natsir, former prime minister and leader of the reformist Islamic political party Masyumi, was probably the most prestigious Moslem politician of the postindependence period.

tion of the urban intelligentsia can and indeed should be seen as inextricably related to one another; the link between them is precisely the continuing cultural hold of traditional conceptions, including conceptions about Power.

If, then, a radical transformation of Javanese politics and society is to take place, in what perspective should traditional political ideas be regarded? From one perspective one could argue the need for a frontal attack on these ideas, insofar as they were the linchpin of the traditional order and continue to reinforce powerful conservative tendencies in Indonesian society. In this view, if the linchpin can be displaced, overcoming resistance to a whole spectrum of social changes may be greatly facilitated. The thrust of modernist Islam and the political propaganda of the New Order intellectuals is largely in this direction. But the success of this "strategy" will depend in the first instance on a clear conception of the nature of the "adversary" and the strength of its defenses. In the second instance, success will depend on the ability to provide a coherent and persuasive alternative to a deep-seated traditional orientation. As of now, my impression is that the self-styled modernizers are paying little attention to either problem. In spite of a large volume of abuse leveled at what is frequently called *méntal lama* (the old mentality), scarcely any attempt is being made to understand this mentality and assess its strengths and weaknesses.

From another perspective, one could argue that the mode of social transformation must be adapted to traditional ideas. But such a strategy presupposes a leadership sophisticated enough to be deeply familiar with these ideas, yet not bound by them, and disciplined enough to use them without succumbing to them. The career of Sukarno is instructive in this respect. No one in modern Indonesian history used traditional ideas with greater success for mobilizing populations and enhancing his own personal authority. Yet Sukarno's ultimate failure, the growing conservatism of his regime and the internal impasse to which his policies led, can in part be attributed to his inability to liberate himself sufficiently from the hold of the ideas he manipulated. Too often the concepts of the center, of dynamic syncretism, of power as an end rather than a means, dominated his own innermost thinking as well as his public posture and private maneuverings. Guided Democracy was a very Power-full state in the traditional meaning of the word but not at all a powerful state in the sense of an organization capable of carrying out sustained and planned change. Yet it is doubtful to what extent the former president in his own mind clearly distinguished between the two.

I suggested at the start of this essay that a careful analysis of the

Javanese conception of Power and politics might be of some value for political analysis outside the restricted geographical limits of Java or Indonesia. This value, I think, may lie in helping to elucidate the much-vexed problem of "charisma." The enormously wide range of personality types among the "charismatic leaders" of our time, their contradictory ideologies, the vastly differing socioeconomic, religious, and ethnic character of their clienteles, the great variety of the types and levels of political organization in which they have appeared, pose in themselves difficult questions of analysis and conceptualization.[109] Continuing difficulties have been encountered in classifying "charisma" with more conventional sources of power, such as wealth, arms, population, and so forth. The apparent instability and fluidity of "charisma" as reflected in the meteoric rise and fall of such men as Nkrumah, Ben Bella, and Sukarno suggests that this type of power is in some way sui generis. But what the genus may be is by no means clear.[110]

Today the prevailing view is that "charisma" lies in the eye of the beholder: It is less a real quality of the leader than a quality attributed to him by his followers, who see him as someone extraordinary, sometimes with a historic mission, sometimes with the grace of God, in any case with preternatural capabilities. What is the explanation of this perception? I would argue that the perception derives from ideas analogous to the Javanese conception of Power, and that the charismatic leader has Power in much the same sense that the traditional rulers of Java had it. He is regarded as the center from which Power radiates, and the believer attaches himself to this Power, rather than submitting to it, as he might to rational-legal authority. The charismatic leader's Power is revealed rather than demonstrated. The difficulty facing such a leader trying to make a political comeback is exactly that of the weakened center, as the Javanese think of it. If he really still had the Power he would never have lost it; if he had the answer to disorder, the problem would never have come up. (We can also note that modern charismatic leaders, precisely like the figures of Power in Javanese legend and history, are often associated with asceticism, syncretic dynamism, and conjuring ceremonial.)[111]

[109]For an interesting recent discussion of these difficulties and some suggestions for their resolution see Ann Ruth Willner, *Charismatic Political Leadership: A Theory*, Center of International Studies, Research Monograph no. 32 (Princeton, N.J.: Princeton University, 1968).

[110]These uncertainties help to account for the constant, almost unconscious tendency toward reification of the concept of charisma, both in popular literature and scholarly writing. To avoid the dangers of reification, I have resorted to the irritating typographical device of putting the word *charisma* in quotation marks.

I would therefore propose, very tentatively, that we have the basis for a useful simplification of Max Weber's description of "charisma."112 In the first place, I believe that the difficulties and imprecisions of Weber's concept of "charisma" stem from the fact that he tended to view it primarily from the sociological and psychological, rather than the cultural anthropological, perspective. That is to say, he focused his attention on the social, economic, and political conditions in which charismatic leaders emerged and on the personalities of such leaders rather than on the culture of their followers. He was inclined to show the extraordinary *qualities* attributed to these leaders, without being able to define what these qualities were or had in common.

I would suggest that these discrete qualities can be reduced to a common denominator: the belief on the part of followers that their leader has Power. The *signs* of this Power—its particular qualities—will be determined by the contingent idiosyncratic character of particular cultures.113 One might suggest asceticism in Southeast Asia, and virility (*machismo*) in Latin America, as examples. Asceticism in the one cultural area, machismo in the other, signify the same thing—Power.

In general, Weber was inclined to view "charisma" as something short-lived, spontaneous, unpredictable, and revolutionary, although under certain conditions it could become depersonalized and institionalized.114 Political "charisma" typically emerged when a given patrimonial, feudal, or rational-legal bureaucratic system entered a period of stress. Later, "charisma" tended to undergo a process of routinization and bureaucratization—until crisis produced a new charismatic leader. The implication of this view is that there is an endless historical oscillation between charismatic and traditional or bureaucratic rule; like the chicken and the egg, neither can be said definitely to precede the other.

111Compare the description of charismatic leadership given by Weber in Hans Heinrich Gerth and C. Wright Mills, trans. and ed., *From Max Weber: Essays in Sociology* (New York: Oxford University Press, 1958), pp. 245–52; cf. also Bendix, *Max Weber,* pp. 298–328.

112In the discussion that follows, I give a somewhat one-sided view of Weber's thinking. Weber's discussion of charisma is often rather confusing, not least because of repeated reification of his concept. Weber's ideas are here deliberately simplified for the purpose of clarifying the essential point that I want to make.

113Cf. Willner, *Charismatic Political Leadership,* pp. 81–87, for an informative discussion of the way various contemporary charismatic leaders evoke the folk heroes of their respective cultures.

114Cf. Bendix, *Max Weber,* pp. 309–14.

If, however, we can accept that "charisma" involves belief in Power, it should be clear that in both the historical and analytical sense, "charisma" precedes rational-legal domination.[115] Study of the Javanese political tradition demonstrates that in Old Java, all rule was charismatic insofar as it was based on belief in Power. Bureaucracy there was, but it drew its legitimacy and authority from the radiant center, which was seen to suffuse the whole structure with its energy. In such a society, "charisma" was not a temporary phenomenon of crisis, but the permanent, routine, organizing principle of the state. This suggests that the short-lived, unpredictable, revolutionary character that Weber attributed to "charisma" may be purely contingent and time bound and, with an important qualification shortly to be discussed, all presecular societies may be said to be under charismatic domination. The question arises as to why Weber limited his use of the idea of " charisma" largely to situations of stress and crisis. It seems to me that the answer lies in a rather untypical absence of historical perspective. While Weber drew his general theory of the rise of rational-legal bureaucracy from what he saw as the *historical* spread of rationalism and secularism, in his discussion of "charisma" the historical element is largely absent.

If the historical component is restored, the argument shifts in the following direction. In the later historical evolution of the West the rapid pace of economic, technological, and social change has been paralleled by a cultural transformation of unprecedented extent. This development can be seen, from the contemporary social science perspective, as the movement from magical religion through religious rationalism to secular rationalism, as traditional ontologies have been challenged by scientific discoveries, technological innovations, and the immensely increased complexity of social and economic life. This movement has, of course, by no means been confined to the West, although it has gone further there than elsewhere. In Geertz's description of Islamic evolution in Morocco, for example, the rise of the scripturalists at the expense of the marabouts can be seen as the ascendancy of religious rationalism vis-à-vis magical religion. One could perhaps argue a comparable evolution in China from the magical religion of the Shang era to the marginally religious rationalism of Confucian thought. In Indonesia, the spread of reformist Islam in the twentieth century is probably a comparable phenomenon.

As the West moved toward secular rationalism, a new conception of

[115]One could probably also say, depending on one's precise interpretation of "traditional domination," that it is subsumed under charismatic domination.

power was crystallized bit by bit, at first by political philosophers like Machiavelli and Hobbes and later by the proliferating apparatus of scientific-industrial education and research.[116] In its final form this concept of power is at radical variance with its ancestor, as I tried to indicate in the introduction. Nonetheless, as Marx pointed out, the culture of a society, while following the general trajectory of technological and social development, always tends to change more slowly and in a more piecemeal, fragmentary fashion. In all societies whose cultures are dominated by religious or secular rationalism, one can expect to find residues of previous cultural modes. Older and newer cultural elements will exist in contradictory juxtaposition.

I would suggest that this is the case with so central a component of any culture as its ideas about power. In most contemporary cultures, including our own, the two polar conceptions of power that I have outlined exist side by side, with one or the other more or less predominant.[117] In our society the older conception of Power appears residually in the interstices of legal-scientific culture—in faith healing, psychiatry, prayer, and what is referred to as "charisma." Although the older idea of Power may be residual in societies dominated by religious or secular rationalism, it is likely to emerge into prominence under conditions of severe stress and disturbance of routine assumptions—when institutions explained and legitimized in terms of the hegemonic cultural mode appear to be breaking down or to be in decay.[118] Such circumstances evoke not so much new types of leaders or new forms of domination as ancient conceptions and ancient sources of authority.

[116]The decline of traditional European ideas of power in late medieval and early modern times under the impact first of religious and later of secular rationalism is beautifully described in Marc Bloch, *Les Rois Thaumaturges* (Strasbourg: Librairie Istra, 1924). Bloch focuses particularly on the healing power attributed to the monarchs of France and England (in the former case up till the French Revolution, in the latter up to the reign of Queen Anne), but, especially on pp. 51–79, he discusses in more general terms the cultural roots of the European monarchical idea. Curiously enough, on pp. 52–53 he makes explicit comparisons with cultural conceptions prevalent in Polynesia, drawing his data from Frazer's *Golden Bough*. For this reference, I am indebted to Denys Lombard.

[117]By stressing the crystallization process in the development of the modern Western concept of power, I mean to indicate that between the two polar ideal types, various intermediate types can be envisaged.

[118]It should come as no surprise in this perspective that the religious rationalism of the scripturalists in Morocco was superseded, during the crisis of decolonization, by the more ancient "maraboutic" tradition in the person of Sultan Muhammed V (cf. Geertz, *Islam Observed*, p. 81, where the author observes that "French rule had produced what, left to itself, the dynasty was almost certainly no longer capable of creating—a maraboutic king")—nor that the secular rationalism of the West was for a time successfully challenged, in the aftermath of the Great War and during the World Depression, by charismatic leaders like Adolf Hitler and Benito Mussolini.

CHAPTER 2

Further Adventures of Charisma

When I wrote "The Idea of Power in Javanese Culture," I felt rather confident that I had resolved certain problems in Max Weber's concept of "charisma," and certain oddities in the way that he had characteristically employed it. For example, he had at times given the impression that "charisma" was a *real* attribute of certain religious or political leaders, rather than simply something projected onto them by followers; and that he insisted on associating "charisma" with irrationality, unpredictability, and creativity. Indeed, it was these features that for him sharply distinguished charismatic from traditional and rational-legal forms of domination. Yet, in thinking about those modern Third World leaders often described as "charismatic"— Sukarno, U Nu, Nasser, Nehru, Ho Chi Minh, Castro, and so on— two things had struck me in particular. First, one could easily draw portraits of them that would with some plausibility emphasize traditionalism, rationality, and predictability as essential elements of their public personae. Second, their "charisma" had very narrow territorial/cultural limits. Castro in Indiana, Sukarno in Riga, Nehru in Mexico City, seemed very unlikely to command much beyond a certain "show-biz" interest.

Under these circumstances, it appeared to me necessary to locate charisma firmly in the perceptions of particular, historically and geographically bounded followings. At the same time, given the worldwide, if random, distribution of "charisma," one had to look for some

Based on a paper delivered in 1985 to the American Anthropological Association as "The Discourse of Charisma."

common cross-cultural assumptions linking these culturally specific perceptions together. I thought I had found the answer in identifying, not a typology of charismatic persons, but some fundamental assumptions about power, which, in any culture, is fundamentally a metaphor for causality—why things happen the way they do. From the Javanese data it seemed plausible to argue that all human societies at one time or another had had a *substantive* view of power as an emanation of the cosmic or divine; but that each culture had probably developed its own idiosyncratic diagnostic of this power: how it could be accumulated and deployed, and how one tracked its operations. One could then argue that when Weber contrasted charismatic with traditional or rational-legal domination, he was the victim of a sort of optical illusion. In reality, there were only *two* general forms of domination, one linked to substantive and the other to instrumental/relational concepts of power. When Weber posited charismatic domination as quite different from traditional domination, he had failed to see that they were at bottom the same; thus, the appearance of "charisma" in modern, rational-legal systems of domination simply represented the spectacular reemergence, under conditions of severe social and economic crisis, of older imaginings. Far from being novel and innovative, it represented a temporary archaism born of crisis. If this were so, then, properly understood, all traditional authority was charismatic, and all charismatic authority traditional.

I was able, in 1972, to convince myself that Weber had made a serious "category error," because I was unselfconscious about the status of the sociological discourse that we shared. Thus, I had no trouble in adopting the historicist perspective that dominated Weber's thought: history as a progressive disenchantment of the world through the processes of secularization and rationalization, in which capitalism and bureaucratization were two sides of the same ominous coin. It never occurred to me to think that Weber's "types" were really "tropes," i.e., that they were the necessary metaphorical elements for a rhetoric he hoped would be adequate to his vision of the *longue durée*. Today, I am inclined to read Weber in a less strictly sociological way, not least because of the general exclusion of his categories from Marxist discourse, and their lack of easy prise on the vocabularies of the Southeast Asian political systems with which I am most familiar.

It is characteristic that the most famous passage describing charisma appears in the introduction to Weber's *Economic Ethics of the World-Religions*. We should note right away the significance of the word *world* in this title: that Weber was actually less concerned with religion, or religions in general, than with those religions, or sacred systems of belief, whose metaphysical elaboration, speculative grandeur, and ethical amplitude allowed them to become the bases of vast and, in his view, astonishingly stable civilizations. These religions are, or were, "first class," World Religions, because, so it seemed to him, they were conceived in terms which, *in principle,* made them open to all human beings. The advent of these religions—Buddhism, Hinduism, Judaism, Christianity, Islam, and Confucianism—struck him as absolutely astonishing and revolutionary, and as (quite often) the product of "extraordinary" individuals—Gautama, Jesus Christ, Muhammad—who by their visions brought about radical breaks in the civilizations into which they had been born. He was, however, no less profoundly impressed by the way that these revolutionary religious visions were later successfully institutionalized, or "routinized," by followers and successors, and above all, perhaps, by the systematic transmission of written texts.

In this way, the original models of charisma, charismatic leadership, and the routinization of charisma were derived from the old "world religions"; in other words, from a historical epoch in which the disenchantment of the world had yet seriously to begin. At the same time, since Weber did not himself believe in any of these "world religions," and regarded himself as a comparative historical sociologist, he was led to a generalized suprahistorical and supracultural schema for these phenomena, which could not logically be limited to the religious sphere. Hence the curious tone of this famous passage:

> "Charisma" shall be understood to refer to an *extraordinary* quality of a person, regardless of whether this quality is actual, alleged or presumed [notice that it may be "actual"]. "Charismatic authority," hence shall refer to rule over men . . . to which the governed submit because of their belief in the extraordinary quality of the specific *person.* The magical sorcerer, the prophet, the leader of hunting and booty expeditions, the warrior chieftain, the . . . "Caesarist" ruler . . . are such types . . . . The legitimacy of charismatic rule thus rests upon the belief in magical powers, revelations, and hero worship . . . . Charismatic rule is not managed according to general norms, either traditional or rational . . . and in this sense is "irrational." It is "revolutionary" in the sense of not being bound to the existing order.[1]

---

[1]The translation is taken from H. Stuart Hughes, *Consciousness and Society: The Reorientation of European Social Thought, 1890–1930* (New York: Vintage Books, 1958), pp. 289–90. Italics added.

In this formulation we will notice some characteristic elisions, and at the same time a certain absence of sociological rigor. Weber assumes that leaders of hunting and booty expeditions, sorcerers, warrior chieftains, and Caesarist rulers all derive their authority from something that is *acultural:* a quality of personhood independent of even traditional, general norms and radically distinct from the society or community's existing ideas about: sorcerers, chieftains, and Caesarist rulers. This assumption is very difficult to fit with the overwhelming bulk of the historical and ethnographical record—and Weber was not in the least ignorant of much of this record. Furthermore, Weber's formulation concedes that the extraordinariness of all these charismatic figures may be "alleged" or "presumed," i.e., by *other, presumably non-charismatic* people, which indicates that these people must have some "ordinary" criteria of their own by which they can distinguish who the "extraordinary" charismatic person is. Yet it is precisely the configurations of these criteria or expectations that he is reluctant to investigate. Above all, the idea that many cultures may think in terms of the normality of the extraordinary, or at least a certain definition of the extraordinary, lies outside his frame of reference.

On the other hand, these elisions turn out to be necessary if "charisma" is to be allowed to appear in a disenchanted world, where magic, sorcerers, warrior chieftains, and so on have been effectively marginalized. In their place appear revivalist preachers—*of old religions;* mesmerizing politicians—*in institutionalized offices;* flamboyant generals—*in regular military hierarchies;* guerrilla leaders—*following internationally regularized manuals for guerrilla warfare;* boxers—*who become world champions in carefully regulated and monitored competitions;* media celebrities—*products of gigantic communications conglomerates;* and so on. In other words, these epigones of sorcerers, priests, and leaders of hunting and booty expeditions exist in a world that is overwhelmingly institutionalized, and in which the possibility of a "charismatic" personality who is "revolutionary" in the sense of not bound to the existing order—which order, after all?—is harder and harder to imagine. A figure like Mao Tse-tung, for example, in some phases of his life might certainly be thought of as charismatic, and even "revolutionary" in Weber's terms, *within the confined Chinese context.* But the same Mao created and chaired a party constructed according to the traditional norms of international Bolshevism, and he proclaimed himself guided by the Marxist-Leninist canon—such that within the larger "world revolutionary" context he appeared "normal" rather than extraordinary.

What, then, induced Weber to develop his suprahistorical concept of charismatic leadership, when his other modes of domination, traditional and rational-legal, appear to be thoroughly, and sequentially, historical? It is tempting to argue that the trope of charisma was a necessary adjunct of the concept of rational-legal authority itself. A European man of his time, the eve of World War I, when Europe's global hegemony was at its zenith, Weber was profoundly convinced that Western civilization represented a more advanced civilization than anything that had occurred before or elsewhere; that what underlay this civilization was an astonishing, sustained application of reason/rationality to the natural world and human society; and that the rest of the world was probably bound to follow in Europe's footsteps. The two most spectacular manifestations of this rationality were capitalism and modern administrative organization. Yet Weber was also aware that this rationality was fundamentally instrumental in character, and that it had no satisfactory ethical basis. If man's rational faculties were what made him the only "free" species in the animal world, they had produced hierachies and institutions of such powerful instrumental rationality that they gravely endangered that freedom. And since nothing in the nature of rationality itself appeared to him capable of transcending or transforming it, he felt compelled to look for a deus ex machina—something both "irrational" and "revolutionary" vis-à-vis the calculus of the market and the bureau. It is in this sense that "charisma," extrapolated from the legendary origins of the world religions, seemed to him a necessary, redemptionist counterpoint to rational-legal domination. In other words, it was "imaginable," or needed to be conjured up, only if the modern world itself was understood according to the trope of bureaucratization.

Here the contrast with Marx is illuminating. For Marx's dialectical vision of the historical process led him to make a sharp distinction between the instrumental rationality of capitalism and its substantive irrationality. Capitalism, in his view, had created a worldwide system of domination of extraordinary dynamism, but at the same time of enormous instability. With every instrumentally rational step it forward took, it compounded its own inner irrationalities and contradictions, thereby summoning into being the forces that would ensure its dissolution and transcendence. In Marx's vision redemption was located in the revolution. At the same time, the revolution itself was a necessary outcome of capitalism's own development. It was absolutely predictable, unquestionably "rational"—in the substantive sense— resolutely social and collective, and revolutionary precisely by being bound to the existing order of late capitalism. Thus the trope "revolution" stands in every way radically counterposed to that of "charisma." But, at the same time, it serves, if more radically and forcefully, the same function: the hope of freedom in a disenchanted world. This is the main reason why "charisma" has no place within Marxist discourse.

What I am suggesting is that the trope "charisma" was created because it was a needed node in the characteristic Weberian discourse that links together "disenchantment of the world," "rationality," "capitalism," "bureaucratization," "freedom," and "person." Theologically, this has the bittersweet taste of agnosticism. Politically, it manifests the contrieties of sociological pessimism and liberal will to human freedom that formed the basis of Weber's personal political stance and that led him to make his celebrated separation between the vocations of science and of politics.

Before turning to the question of how Weber's turn-of-the-century coinage came to live on, even if with strikingly different connotations, when so many other academic coinages melt on the doorstep of the mint, it may be useful to look briefly at what appear to be the reasons why "charisma" does not appear in the discourse of Indonesian politics, or indeed most of the Indonesian historical writing about politics. I take Indonesia here as probably characteristic of most Third World countries (it is certainly very similar, in this respect, to what I know of other Southeast Asian countries). Let me begin by offering an extended quotation from a remarkable speech by the late President Sukarno, the modern Indonesian leader most generally regarded in the West as a prototypical charismatic Third World luminary. The speech is unusually interesting in that, although Sukarno never mentions the word, he nonetheless appears to be talking about something *like* "charisma," and at the same time links this discussion to the historical figure we are most likely to think of as the prototypical First World charismatic leader: Adolf Hitler. Here is what Sukarno, addressing the students and faculty of Indonesia's leading university, on the occasion of accepting an honorary degree on February 2, 1963, had to say:[2]

> Brothers and sisters, if today I accept the conferral of [an honorary degree] from the University of Indonesia, then I would like to express at

[2]Soekarno, *Ilmu Pengetahuan Sekadar Alat Mentjapai Sesuatu* (Jakarta: Departemen Penerangan Republik Indonesia, Penerbitan Chusus No. 253, 1963), pp. 25–27, 36. I have altered the spelling to conform to current official usage.

the start a hope that this honorary doctorate is not being conferred in order to provide me with an *aureool* [aureola]—by *aureool* I mean *téja*—is not being conferred on me with the aim of providing me with the *aureool* of the Great Leader of the Revolution, an appellation also given me not at my own request, but by a decision of the MPRS,[3] whose chairman, beloved brother Chaerul Saleh, is here with us today.

Brothers and sisters, if some time ago I affirmed to Indonesian society the need for leadership in the Revolution, in the State, I did so simply as an enunciation of a principle of history—in fact more than a principle of history—actually a fact of history. This principle of history, this *historis principe,* or rather something more than a principle of history, actually a fact of history, is that throughout the course of historical eventualities no great revolution has proceeded properly without leadership. And since I deeply wish—as you, brothers and sisters, also wish—that the Indonesian Revolution proceed as mightily as possible until the aims of this our Revolution are achieved and accomplished, that was why in that speech I stressed the need for Leadership, and why I linked it with other principles, or other aims, and why I finally ended up with proclaiming the slogan: *Re-So-Pim:* Revolution, Socialism, Leadership.[4]

These three things . . . form an indivisible Trinity. But I ask you, brothers and sisters, to understand that if I give the content to the Leadership element in Resopim, I do not do so for my own sake—not at all!—but simply as a fact of history. . . . As I just stated, the fact is that in the centuries-old course of history no great revolution has been able to proceed without Leadership. This is why our Revolution too must have leadership. As for who should hold the Leadership, well, that's another question. . . . Thus on this day let it not be that I am honored by the University of Indonesia by being granted an Honorary Doctorate simply to provide me with an *aureool,* a *téja,* because in the course of history there have been cases of the conferral of an *aureool* on a leader, not on account of a principle of history, but because of the principle of personhood.

In the history of fascism, for example, during the Hitler period, two principles were enunciated: the *Vater Prinzip,* the *Vader Principe,* the Father Principle; and the *Führer Prinzip,* the *Leiders Principe,* the Leadership Principle. Of Hitler it was said: *Er ist der Führer,* He is the Leader, he *hat immer recht,* he is always right, he will never make a mistake, we must follow him in everything he does, because *er ist der Führer.* Hitler was exalted as *Führer,* in fact all kinds of fantastic characteristics were ascribed to him, in order that the Personal Principle be implemented as

[3]Majelis Permusyarawatan Rakyat Sementara—Provisional People's Consultative Assembly: formally, the highest constitutional body in the Republic of Indonesia in those days.
[4]Resopim is an acronym for *ré(volusi), so(sialisme),* and *pim(pinan),* or leadership.

thoroughly as possible. Thus to Hitler were attributed all kinds of non-sensical titles, appellations, traits and characteristics. This conferring of an *aureool* on Hitler, this conferring of a *téja,* was done as though he was not an ordinary human being, but one created in what the *dhalang* calls "Téjamaya," or "Tinjumoyo," i.e., *babaran Téjamaya,* or truly a product or Téjamaya.

No, brothers and sisters, though you have elevated me to be the Great Leader of the Revolution, I ask you not to make me a product of Té-jamaya. . . . To you students I say, *téja* means light, *aureool,* while *maya* means illusion. In the Mahabharata, the idea behind Téjamaya is that *kahyangan* or heaven is not something material, its domain should not be thought of as like ours, its trees should not be imagined as like ours, and its beauties not like our earthly beauties either, for heaven is made from *téja,* or *light,* of an ethereal radiance. . . .

Now there are people, like the German nation during the fascist era, who think like this: *Der Führer hat immer recht,* the leader is always right, he is never mistaken, the leader is a super scholar. You here, of course, are all super scholars, but Hitler was called a super-super-super great scholar, *er hat immer recht.* Hitler was called a Super General, far above ordinary generals, a super general, with no equals in the military sphere. Thus every single one of his orders had to be carried out. They said Hitler was also a Super Economist, a Super Politician, a Super Strategist, plus all kinds of other titles, everything of course also Super.

And the need of ideals for a successful Revolution:

Take Hitler, for example—wah, Hitler was extraordinarily clever, really—perhaps he wanted to say that happiness isn't possible on a material basis alone, and thus he pronounced another ideal, the ideal he called the Dritte Reich, the Third Kingdom. This Third Reich would really and truly bring happiness to the people of Germany. The First Kingdom was that of *der alte Fritz,* a kingdom led by Old Fritz; the Second Kingdom was what existed just before the World War, and now this kingdom had been destroyed in the World War. "Come, let us build a Third Kingdom, a Dritte Reich, and in this Third Reich, hey, sisters, you will live happily; hey, brothers, you will live happily; hey, kids, you'll live happily; hey, you German patriots, you will see Germany sitting enthroned above all peoples in this world." How clever Hitler was, brothers and sisters, in depicting these ideals.

And how about me? Aside from depicting for you, brothers and sisters, what socialism will be like, I also state, yes, I state that we are not children of a beancurd nation. I say rather we are children of a nation that in the old days too experienced a golden age.

There are at least three instructive features to these remarks, especially if we bear in mind that Sukarno is speaking to the young educated elite of his country.

In the first place, he reminds his audience of the traditional-popular and court-classical Javanese discourse about Power. In this discourse, which partly originates from the Mahabharata, heaven and earth are on rather intimate terms with one another, the deities make regular trips back and forth between the two spheres, and members of the ruling class may visit heaven and even cohabit sexually with a section of its population. The Power of human beings is fundamentally of the same type and origins as that of the divinities; some of the human beings are described and understood as incarnations of particular gods. It is this view of the world that makes the puppeteer's phrase *babaran Téjamaya,* "product of heaven," intelligible, and also suggests how normally extraordinary such personalities were. Similarly, in many of the traditional Javanese court chronicles (*babad*), Javanese royalty are described matter-of-factly as lineal descendants of the heroes of the Mahabharata (in its Javanized *wayang* form). Hence these chronicles very frequently relate that men destined for rulership were the recipients of the *téja,* an ineffable radiance emanating ultimately from Téjamaya. Again, one might say that this sign of singularity was completely unsingular: It went with kingship and had little to do with "personality" in our sense, let alone with an *intrahistorical* mission or message. In fact I cannot think of an instance where a ruler "never had" the téja, though there are plenty of instances where rulers are said—for various reasons—to have lost it.

But having reminded his listeners of this traditional discourse, Sukarno distances himself from it. He jokes that neither Hitler nor he himself is *babaran Téjamaya*—nor, by implication, is anyone else. He uses the Dutch word *aureool* as a synonym for *téja,* as if the two words were as routinely interchangeable as president and *presidèn,* in a sort of general "comparative politics" vocabulary: *Aureool* is, so to speak, what the white, European, Christian, Dutch call *téja.* Nothing special there. He speaks amusedly of his audience, or the German people, "conferring" this international téja—nothing very mysterious here either.

In the second place, Sukarno sharply segregates this *téja-aureool* from leadership. While jokingly rejecting any *aureool* for himself, he also insists on the central importance of *leadership* to any revolution, and of his own *leadership* to the Indonesian Revolution. What is instructive is the way in which this leadership and the Indonesian

Revolution are characterized. His language makes it clear that the Indonesian Revolution is one of many revolutions in human history, and that its uniqueness if of the limited, territorially restricted type generally characteristic of nationalisms. "We have ours like any other great people." In fact it is this historic *plurality* of revolutions around the world that permits him to draw the conclusion that, *like* the others, the Indonesian Revolution needs leadership. It is also clear that it is not this leadership that"produces" the revolution—which arises from quite other sources—but rather that it is a necessary add-on to ensure that each revolution will proceed as "mightily" as it can. (Even a Mercedes-Benz will end up in a ditch without a competent chauffeur.) This is why he can say that his own leadership is properly based on a principle of history, a "real," ontologically rooted process; whereas Hitler's claims to leadership were based on the "false" transhistorical principles of Vater-dom and Führer-ship. In expressing these views, the president showed himself a faithful heir of Marx and Lenin.

Thirdly, he speaks of Hitler's style of leadership in a decidedly curious manner. The Führer is described initially as *bukan main pandainya,* and this adjective *pandai* is later repeated. Now pandai is a very ordinary modern Indonesian word, which can either mean "intelligent" (one speaks of a pandai schoolboy or student) or "good at something" in a technical or professional sense (one refers to someone being pandai at tennis, or acting, or fixing cars, or playing the piano). The context shows that Sukarno is using the word in the second sense, and that he means that Hitler was "good at" conjuring up a happy future for the German people. What this skill consisted of is suggested by the odd way in which the president has Hitler speak, i.e., in exactly the rhetorical style of "hey, sisters, you will live happily" that Sukarno *himself* patented. Hitler talks like Sukarno. And his skill is public speaking.

In all of this, Sukarno's tone is that of a fellow professional: "I can't stand his mania for playing Liszt and Rachmaninov, but you have to give it to him—his finger control and pedaling are really first class." Thus, from a limited, "technical" point of view, Sukarno is quite prepared to grade Hitler highly—for his audience. What is so valuable about this technical recommendation, from a politician who certainly regarded himself as a man of the left (and was soon to be overthrown precisely for that reason) is that it shows still another reason, beyond the heritage of Lenin and Marx, that Sukarno's political discourse had no room for "charisma." It is exactly the same reason that an expert conjuror, speaking about another conjuror, may well talk about technique, new tricks, style of patter, manual dexterity, stage presence, and so on, but will never talk about . . . magic! Of course, this does not at all mean that there is no element of conjuring in Sukarno's offhand remarks: A certain awe always attaches to the conjuror who says disarmingly that what he does is just a bag of tricks.[5]

It might, of course, be objected that Sukarno was a man of immense vanity, a superficial, derivative thinker and a second-rate Third World nationalist demagogue. Hence the "fellow-illusionist" style of his remarks about other political leaders. But one can find interesting similarities in the writings of first-rate, First World charismatic leaders. Take, for example, these reflections by Charles de Gaulle on Adolf Hitler:

> As for Hitler, it was suicide, not treason, that brought his enterprise to its end. He himself had incarnated it, and himself terminated it. So as not to be bound, Prometheus [*sic*] cast himself into the abyss. . . . Moreover, if Hitler was strong, he was no less cunning. He knew how to entice, and how to caress. Germany, profoundly seduced, followed her Fuehrer ecstatically. Until the very end, she was to serve him slavishly, with greater exertions than any people has ever furnished any leader. . . . Hitler's attempt was superhuman and inhuman. He maintained it without stint, without respite. Until the final hours of agony in the depths of a Berlin bunker, he remained unquestioned, inflexible, pitiless, as he had been during his days of supreme glory. For the terrible greatness of his conflict and his memory, he had chosen never to hesitate, compromise, or retreat. The Titan who tries to lift the world can neither bow nor bend.[6]

---

[5]It ought also to be noted that in almost every speech he made Sukarno did not fail to express a rather comparable "technical" admiration for such varied leaders as Gandhi, Ataturk, Kennedy, Sun Yat-sen, Lassalle, Tito, Lincoln, etc. All were for him *orang besar* (big men) who showed, in their own countries and in their own epochs, that they were politically *pandai*.

[6]Charles de Gaulle, *The Complete War Memoirs* (New York: Simon and Schuster, 1960), pp. 866–67. Compare this passage (pp. 736–37) on Stalin:

Stalin was possessed by the will to power. Accustomed by a life of machination to disguise his features as well as his inmost soul, to dispense with illusions, pity, sincerity, to see in each man an obstacle or a threat, he was all strategy, suspicion and stubbornness. The revolution, the party, the state and the war had offered him the occasions and the means of domination. He had seized them, using a thorough knowledge of the complexities of Marxist dialectic and totalitarian rigor, bringing to bear superhuman boldness and guile, subjugating or liquidating all others. Thenceforth, with all Russia in his hands alone, Stalin regarded his country as more mysterious, mightier and more durable than any theory, any regime. He loved it, in his way. Russia herself accepted him as a czar during a terrible epoch, and tolerated Bolshevism to turn it to her own advantage, as a weapon. To unite the Slavs, to overcome the Germans, to expand in Asia, to gain access to open seas—these were the dreams of Mother Russia, these were the despot's goals.

It remains now to turn quite briefly and schematically to the milieux in which *"charisma"* remains a central trope—what in a rough-and-ready sense could be called Anglo-Saxon liberal social science. One might think, given Weber's enormous prestige in this milieu, that his famous coinage would come down to us essentially intact, its meaning stably positioned within the discourse for which he invented it. Yet I think it can be shown that for the most part it has been borrowed for a different discourse, one, moreover, with which Weber himself would surely have had little sympathy.

It is striking, for example, that in the contemporary social science literature virtually all traces of Weber's hope, his sense of "charisma" as a source of redemption, have disappeared. On the contrary, "charisma" characteristically manifests itself as something demagogic, irrational, regressive, shady, and usually dangerous. The disappearance from the international stage, by death or political eclipse, of Nasser, Nehru, Nkrumah, Toure, Nu, Sukarno, and Khomeini has, on the whole, been greeted with relief. The other side of this coin is a comparable satisfaction that charisma does not much manifest itself in First World political systems. If this or that commentator may on occasion refer to Thatcher's or Reagan's charisma, the word is usually used only half-seriously, as if in shoulder-shrugging quotation marks.

Why has this displacement has taken place, and why has "charisma" itself been retained in the social science lexicon? I suspect that there are two kinds of answer to these questions, but that these answers are indirectly interrelated.

The first is that nowadays most social scientists do not deeply share Weber's eschatological anxiety about rationalization, secularization, and bureaucratization. The central social sciences—economics, sociology, and political science—typically see themselves as exemplars of instrumental rationality and secularization; they are glad to be useful to, and eager for the support of, modern capitalist states. There is no great difficulty in aligning the sensible, in principle quantifiable, objectivities of these fields of enquiry with the rationalist, bureaucratic discourse of public policy. The central goal of these disciplines is, after all, reliable prediction, within definite limits, about collective human behavior. Moreover, academic social science is itself characterized by a high degree of internal division of labor, segmented distribution of knowledges, administrative and technical hierarchy, and professional specialization. In other words, to the extent that the disciplines have become large institutional complexes, they have tended to become incorporated within the existing order, rather than sites for anxious interrogation of that order.

These circumstances explain the disciplines' tacit occlusion of Weber's redemptionism, the desperate hope that permitted him to credit the possibility—among others—that "charisma" could be a "real," transhistorical, transcultural attribute of certain human beings, that there really were "extraordinary people." This occlusion, leaving open only the alternatives of "alleged" and "presumed" charismatic leaders, focused scholarly attention on such leaders' followings: their cultural presuppositions, their social, political, and economic circumstances, and, especially, the profound crises that drew them into the leaders' orbits.[7] Charisma appeared, within this optic, as merely a telltale *symptom* of a newly discovered social disorder called *millenarianism*.[8]

In the post–World War II scholarly tradition inspired by historians Eric Hobsbawm and Vittorio Lanternari and anthropologists Peter Worsley and Kenelm Burridge, millenarianism appeared as the religion of the oppressed, above all members of traditional communities in the Third World and the backward peripheries of Europe, as they experienced the onslaught of capitalism, imperialism, colonialism, Christianity, and commodification.[9] Sympathetic as these mostly left-leaning scholars were to what Hobsbawm termed "primitive rebels," they found it difficult to avoid viewing them from on top of the juggernaut itself. From this elevated perch, the huge variety of the juggernaut's victims perhaps inevitably tended to blur into a single victimized mass of actual or potential "millenarians."[10]

In the hands of less sympathetic, less progressive social scientists, *millenarianism* proved sufficiently flexible to be stretched to cover a good deal of Third World anticolonial political nationalism, especially where this nationalism was articulated by putatively "charismatic" leaders. In this fashion nationalism could be given a socially patholog-

---

[7]This occlusionary spirit has an ancestry at least as old as Gibbon, who with Enlightened glee accused St. Simeon Stylites of "committing" miracles. Weber himself still hoped for miracles.

[8]See the elaborate "theoretical and methodological introduction" to the second, augmented edition of Peter Worsley, *The Trumpet Shall Sound: A Study of "Cargo" Cults in Melanesia* (New York: Schocken, 1968), pp. ix–lxix.

[9]See particularly Eric J. Hobsbawm, *Primitive Rebels: Studies in Archaic Forms of Social Movement in the 19th and 20th Centuries* (New York: The Norton Library, 1965; original publication date 1959); Vittorio Lanternari, *The Religions of the Oppressed: A Study of Modern Messianic Cults* (London: MacGibbon and Kee, 1963); and Kenelm O. Burridge, *New Heaven, New Earth: A Study of Millenarian Activities* (Oxford: Basil Blackwell, 1969).

[10]This may be the reason why Hobsbawm segregates the documentary evidence of his rebels' thinking to a 19-page appendix, significantly titled "In Their Own Voices." *Primitive Rebels*, pp. 174–93.

ical taint, and its vocal representatives figured as cynical or self-deluding charlatans.

The second explanation for charisma's survival and repositioning is suggested by the conclusion to Norman Cohn's pioneering text on certain "millenarian" movements of medieval Europe. For in this valediction he explicitly linked these movements to the enemies of modern liberalism and social democracy—Nazism, Communism, and Libertarian Anarchism.

The story told in this book ended some four centuries ago, but it is not without relevance to our own times. The present writer has shown in another work how closely the Nazi phantasy of a world-wide Jewish conspiracy of destruction is related to the phantasies that inspired Emico of Leiningen and the Master of Hungary; and how mass disorientation and insecurity have fostered the demonization of the Jew in this as in much earlier centuries. The parallels and indeed the continuity are incontestable.

But one may also reflect on the left-wing revolutions and revolutionary movements of this century. For, just like medieval artisans integrated in their guilds, industrial workers in technologically advanced societies have shown themselves very eager to improve their own conditions, their aim has been the eminently practical one of securing a larger share of economic prosperity or social privilege or political power, or any combination of these. But emotionally charged phantasies of a final, apocalyptic struggle or an egalitarian Millenium have had much less attraction for them. Those who are fascinated by such ideas are, on the one hand, the populations of certain technologically backward societies which are not only overpopulated and desperately poor but also involved in a problematic transition to the modern world, and are correspondingly dislocated and disoriented; and, on the other, certain politically marginal elements in technologically advanced societies—chiefly young or unemployed workers and a small minority of intellectuals and students.

One can indeed discern two quite distinct and contrasting tendencies. On the one hand working people have in certain parts of the world been able to improve their lot out of all recognition, through the agency of trade unions, co-operatives and parliamentary parties. On the other hand during the half-century since 1917 there has been a constant repetition, and on an ever-increasing scale, of the socio-psychological process which once joined the Taborite priests or Thomas Müntzer with the most disoriented and desperate of the poor, in phantasies of a final, exterminatory struggle against "the great ones"; and of a perfect world from which self-seeking would be for ever banished.

And if one looks in a somewhat different direction, one can even find an up-to-date version of that alternative route to the Millenium, the cult of the Free Spirit. For the ideal of a total emancipation of the individual from society, even from external reality itself—the ideal, if one will, of self-divinization—which some nowadays try to realize with the help of psychedelic drugs, can be recognized already in that deviant form of medieval mysticism.

The old religious idiom has been replaced by a secular one, and this tends to obscure what otherwise would be obvious. For it is the simple truth that, stripped of their original supernatural sanction, revolutionary millenarianism and mystical anarchism are with us still."[11]

Cohn's words bring us back, first and foremost, to Sukarno's fellow conjuror. For the Führer is, in the modern social science imagination, the ultimate "charismatic leader." Yet he is fixable as such only with a particular stage lighting, one that keeps the following in deep shadow: (1) that Hitler never won an absolute majority of German votes in free elections; (2) that he came to the chancellorship by constitutional Weimarian means; (3) that he proclaimed the *Third* Reich, in continuity with two earlier Reichs, not a *novus ordo saeculorum;* (4) that he inherited from the previous Reich the Wilhelmine adminstrative state and the Prussian-officered, professional standing army; (5)that his regime was unimaginable without the world Depression; (6) that his mass murders were made possible by a highly rationalized bureaucracy; (7) that specific clusters of classes and social strata supported him; (8) and that quite uncharismatic figures can be held responsible for mass political murder (e.g., Maximiliano Martinez and his *matanza* in El Salvador, Suharto in Indonesia and East Timor, Yahya Khan in Bangla Desh). Most important, it is necessary to deep-shadow the fact that the great atrocities of our time are made possible only by the advances of exactly the technological and administrative rationalities (professional armed forces, scientific establishments, police machineries, bureaucratic psychiatry, systematic archives, computers, and so on) about which Weber had his nightmares.

Deep shadow is only intelligible juxtaposed to klieg lighting. Thus, the obscuring of administrative rationality, technology, political organization, financial logic, state planning, and class conflicts serves to highlight Hitler's "uniqueness," his demonic persona, his téja, his psychological abnormalities, and his "revolutionary" message (as opposed to his political skills, diplomatic dexterity, and intelligent support for the innovative economic policies of Hjalmar Schacht); and, at the same time, the pathologically authoritarian, millenarian character of German culture. The complex history of modern Germany is in this way diabolized.

Hence, the trope "charisma" appears as a figure for the satanic, a premonition of hell rather than of redemption. Hitler's black halo illumines the faces of Stalin and Mao (and, more faintly, those of many Third World charismatic political leaders). What all these social science "charismas" do is to deep-shadow the great bureaucracies of the modern world, and the classes from which these instrumentalities are every day recruited. This may be why "charisma," diabolized rather than sanctified, has so vigorously survived. Its formal contraposition to everything administratively rational shows sharply why we still need it. It has become a trope for showing that the disenchanted world is just what Dr. Pangloss ordered.

CHAPTER 3

Old State, New Society: Indonesia's New Order in Comparative Historical Perspective

It is perhaps too easy, in the age of the United Nations, to read *nation* as merely a convenient shorthand expression for *nation-state,* and thereby to overlook the fact that a tiny hyphen links two very different entities with distinct histories, constituents, and "interests." Yet the briefest backward glance reveals that their current marriage is a recent and often uneasy mating. As late as 1914, the dynastic realm was still the "norm"—a realm defined not by common language, customs, memories, or permanently demarcated borders, but rather by high monarchical centers—hence figures like the Tsar of All the Russias, the Son of Heaven, and the Queen of England cum Empress of India. The great majority of today's nation-states were "born" in the period from 1800 to, say, 1975 from titanic conflicts *between* "nations" as extrastate solidarity movements and dynastic or colonial "states." Thus, the youth of most nations was, shall we say, a stateless youth.

Similarly, most states have genealogies older than those of the nations over which they are now perched. The truth of this proposition is exemplified by some entertaining contemporary anomalies. For example, the revolutionary and socialist rulers of the Soviet Union and the People's Republic of China find nothing bizarre in pursuing their territorial quarrels by brandishing maps and treaties produced by absolutist Romanovs and the "feudal" Manchu Ch'ing dynasty. In the same way, there are dozens of cases of ex-colonial states pursuing

First published in 1983. *Journal of Asian Studies* 42 (May 1983): 477–96. Reprinted with permission.

foreign policies that are remarkably similar to those pursued by their predecessors—even though diametrically opposed "national interests" are formally represented by these states. (See, e.g., Neville Maxwell's learned and witty account of independent India's Curzonesque policy along its northern frontiers.)[1] Finally, we are also familiar with the fact that in most of the national states of the Third World (and elsewhere, though less obviously) the narrower lineaments of older states are still quite evident: organizational structures, distributions of functions, personnel, institutional memories in the form of files and dossiers, and so on.

The contemporary conflation of nation and state undoubtedly derives from the following convergence. On the one hand, the imagined (but by no means imaginary) community of the nation, whose legitimacy and right to self-determination have become accepted norms in modern life, finds the gage of that autonomy in a state "of its own." On the other hand, the state, which can never justify its demands on a community's labor, time, and wealth simply by its existence, finds in the nation its modern legitimation. The nation-state is thus a curious amalgam of legitimate fictions and concrete illegitimacies.[2] The conflation is all the easier because *the state* is a notoriously slippery entity for political theory and political sociology. It is only too easy to collapse it into either a legal fiction or a collectivity of persons (the bureaucracy). The fact is that the state has to be understood as an *institution,* of the same species as the church, the university, and the modern corporation. Like them, it ingests and excretes personnel in a continuous, steady process, often over long periods of time. It is characteristic of such institutions that "they" have precise rules for entry—at least age, often sex, education, and so forth—and, no less important, for exit—most notably, mandatory retirement. No more impressive sign exists of these institutions' inner workings than the steady rotation *out* of their top leaders (corporate presidents, senior prelates, distinguished academicians, high civil servants, and so on). And, like its sister institutions, the state not only has its own memory but harbors self-preserving and self-aggrandizing impulses, which at any given moment are "expressed" through its living members but which cannot be reduced to their passing personal ambitions.

Under these circumstances, one would expect to find in the policies

[1]Neville Maxwell, *India's China War* (New York: Pantheon, 1970).
[2]See my *Imagined Communities: Reflections on the Origin and Spread of Nationalism* (London: Verso, 1983).

pursued by nation-states a variable mix of two types of general interests—those we can think of as the state's and those of the nation's,
perhaps best conceived of as "representational" or "participatory"
interests. One can thus imagine a sort of spectrum between the following polar situations. (The ensuing distinctions are a variation on those
drawn with great brio by Alers.)[3] One situation would be a condition
of foreign occupation or colonialism, for example, France under German, or Japan under American occupation; "Indonesia" under Dutch
colonialism or "Vietnam" under French. In all these instances, the
state continues to carry out its modern functions—collecting taxes,
administering services, printing money, organizing judicial proceedings, and so on, and the personnel in the state's employ are to an
overwhelming extent natives. Notice that nothing under these conditions predetermines the level of welfare of the subjected populations.
Under American occupation, Japanese society made a remarkable
recovery from the disaster of war, and no one could deny that, in some
ways, the colonial regimes in Vietnam and Indonesia made signal
contributions to the progress of the colonized. What nonetheless is
clear is that national participatory interests were almost completely
ignored or suppressed. The other situation, one of incipient revolution, is where the state is disintegrating, and power shifts decisively
into the hands of extrastate organizations typically recruited on a
voluntary and mass basis.

If these are the polar cases, under unexceptional circumstances the
policy outcomes in nation-states will typically represent a shifting
balance between the two "interests" sketched above. I propose that
this framework is a useful optic for interpreting modern politics in
Indonesia. In particular, I would argue that the policy outcomes of the
New Order (ca. 1966 to the present) are best understood as maximal
expressions of state interests; and that the validity of this argument
can usefully be gauged by reflecting on the history of the state in
Indonesia. My aim here is *not* primarily to weigh the benefits to the
population of successive regimes, but rather to develop an appropriate
framework for comparative historical analysis.

Ancestry: The Colonial State

The birthdate of the Indonesian state remains a matter of controversy among scholars, but its birthplace is quite clear: the swampy coast-

---

[3]Henri Alers, *Om een rode of groene Merdeka: tien jaren binnenlandse politiek: Indonesië, 1943–1953* (Eindhoven: Vulkaan, 1956).

al township of Batavia, which the Vereenigde Oostindische Compagnie (VOC) made the center of its island empire at the beginning of the seventeenth century. If, from the perspective of Amsterdam, the VOC appeared as a *business* (of varying profitability), in the archipelago it manifested itself almost from the start as a *state*—raising armies, concluding treaties, imposing taxes, punishing lawbreakers, and so forth. Moreover, even in embryo, this state exhibited a concern for its own political-territorial aggrandizement quite aside from considerations of commercial advantage.[4] When it was formally replaced, early in the nineteenth century, by the Dutch Crown, the same impulse continued to be evident. Indeed, the Indonesia we know today is the exact product of the extraordinary extension of Batavia's politico-military power between 1850 and 1910.[5] Many of these conquests made little sense in terms of economic profitability or even of military security.[6] Some were financially disastrous. Frequently, the crucial decisions were made in Batavia rather than in The Hague, and for local *raison d'état*. The Acèh War (1873–1903) is a fine case in point.[7]

By 1910 the colonial state, acting through its own military force, the Royal Netherlands Indies' Army (Koninklijk Nederlandsch-Indische Leger, hereafter cited as KNIL), had successfully imposed *rust en orde* (tranquility and order) throughout its vast possessions, a system of control not seriously disturbed until it was demolished in a few weeks in 1942 by Japanese invaders. If the state's horizontal expansion had come to a halt early in this century, the opposite was true of its vertical penetration. Under the so-called Ethical Policy, inaugurated in 1901, there was a huge extension of the state apparatus deep into native society and a proliferation of its functions.[8] Education, religion, irrigation, agricultural improvements, hygiene, mineral exploitation, political surveillance—all increasingly became the business of

[4]See, e.g., Charles Ralph Boxer, *The Dutch Seaborne Empire, 1600–1800* (London: Hutchison, 1965), pp. 84–97.

[5]Bernard Hubertus Maria Vlekke, *Nusantara: A History of Indonesia* (Brussels: Editions A. Manteau, 1959), chap. 14 ("The Unification of Indonesia").

[6]In this sense, the conquests are the exact lineal forebears of the attempted annexation of East Timor after December 7, 1975.

[7]Vlekke, *Nusantara*, pp. 320–21.

[8]The classic work on this process is John S. Furnivall, *Netherlands India: A Study of Plural Economy* (New York: Macmillan, 1944). The end product is aptly epitomized by *Rumah Kaca* [The Glasshouse] (Jakarta: Hasta Mitra, 1988), the Foucaultian title of vol. 4 of novelist Pramoedya Ananta Toer's great tetralogy on the rise of Indonesian nationalism. A sardonic glimpse of the Glasshouse under construction is in Onghokham, "The Inscrutable and the Paranoid: An Investigation into the Sources of the Brotodiningrat Affair," in Ruth Thomas McVey, ed., *Southeast Asian Transitions: Approaches through Social History* (New Haven: Yale University Press, 1978).

a rapidly expanding officialdom, which unfolded more according to its inner impulses than in response to any organized extrastate demands.

What were the bases for this aggrandizement? The answers become clear when we look at the taxation and personnel policies of the mature colonial state. In 1928, the last good year before the Depression, the state derived roughly 10 percent of its income from *state* monopolies in salt, pawnbroking, and opium (which it sold to its customers at ten times the open-market Singapore rate);[9] 20 percent from the profits of *state*-owned mines, plantations, and industries; 16 percent from import duties; 10 percent from corporation taxes; 6 percent from land rent; and 9 percent from income taxes. Various excise and other regressive indirect taxes made up the remainder.[10] If we remind ourselves that this was an economy that at the time produced 90 percent of the world's quinine, 80 percent of its pepper, 37 percent of its rubber, and 18 percent of its tin—to say nothing of petroleum—it is clear that, like the old VOC state, the late colonial state derived its financial strength largely from its *own* monopolistic operations and an efficient exploitation of local human and natural resources.

For the other side of the picture, we must turn to the pattern of government spending. In 1931, *no less than 50 percent* of the state's expenditures were devoted to its own upkeep.[11] One reason for this pattern was that the Netherlands East Indies (NEI) state imported from Europe nine times as many officials proportional to native population as did British India (excluding the "native" states).[12] (This was a relatively recent development, because in 1865 there were only 165 European officials in the territorial administration of the 12 to 13 million population of Java.)[13] Yet the Europeans still numbered only slightly over 10 percent of the entire state apparatus. In 1928, there were almost a *quarter of a million* native officials on the state payroll.[14] To put it another way, 90 percent of the colonial civil service was composed of "Indonesians," and the state's functioning would have been impossible without them. As Benda has written, this situa-

[9]James R. Rush, *Opium to Java: Revenue Farming and Chinese Enterprise in Colonial Indonesia, 1860–1910* (Ithaca, N.Y.: Cornell University Press, 1990), p. 226.

[10]The above data are calculated from Amry Vandenbosch, *The Dutch East Indies: Its Government, Problems, and Politics* (Berkeley: University of California Press, 1944), pp. 298–305.

[11]Ibid., p. 172.

[12]Ibid., p. 173.

[13]Cornelis Fasseur, *Cultuurstelsel en Koloniale Baten: De Nederlandse Exploitatie van Java, 1840–1860* (Leiden: Universitaire Pers, 1975), p. 9.

[14]Vandenbosch, *The Dutch East Indies*, p. 171.

tion represented the last stage in the long process by which various strata of (largely Javanese) native ruling classes had, since the mid-nineteenth century, been absorbed and encapsulated into an ever more centralized and streamlined colonial *beamtenstaat*.[15] (Sutherland has done an excellent study of the Javanese territorial bureaucracy in later colonial times.)[16]

Three and a half years of Japanese military rule (March 1942 to August 1945) came close to destroying this iron cage. In the first place, the territorial unity of the colonial state was broken up. Java, Sumatra, and eastern Indonesia were ruled separately by the Japanese Sixteenth and Twenty-fifth armies, and an arm of the Japanese navy. In each zone divergent policies were pursued, and there was little administrative contact, let alone rotation of personnel, among them. Second, as a result of this division and of the wartime collapse of the colonial export economy, the resource base of the state(s) disintegrated, along with its (their) inner financial discipline. On Java, the military authorities coped with this crisis by imposing harsh levies in labor and kind, and by reckless printing of money. Hyperinflation rendered official salaries meaningless, and a profoundly demoralizing corruption spread rapidly through the apparatus. Third, the abrupt removal of experienced Dutch officials, their replacement by relatively inexperienced Japanese and suddenly promoted Indonesians, and wartime dislocations and shortages drastically undermined the efficacy of the state machine. Finally, the brutal exploitativeness of occupation policy in its later stages aroused deep popular hatred, a hatred substantially directed at a native officialdom increasingly regarded as quisling. Thus, in the aftermath of the Japanese surrender in August 1945, in many parts of Java and Sumatra the state almost disappeared in the face of popular insurgence.[17] In other parts of Indonesia, fragments of the old beamtenstaat went their own merry way.

State and Society, 1945–65

On August 17, 1945, the well-known nationalist politicians Sukarno and Hatta proclaimed Indonesia's independence in a brief cere-

[15]Harry J. Benda, "The Pattern of Reforms in the Closing Years of Dutch Rule in Indonesia," *Journal of Asian Studies* 25 (1966): 589–605.

[16]Heather Sutherland, *The Making of a Bureaucratic Elite: The Colonial Transformation of the Javanese Priyayi* (Singapore: Heinemann, 1979).

[17]See my *Java in a Time of Revolution* (Ithaca, N.Y.: Cornell University Press, 1972), chaps. 6, 7, 15.

mony in the front yard of Sukarno's private home in Jakarta. Insofar as the two had any official position at all, it was as chairman and vice-chairman of the Committee for the Preparation of Indonesian Independence, a body hastily created by the Japanese less than a week earlier. The following day, the twenty-odd members of this committee "elected" Sukarno to the novel office of president, thus formally combining leadership of the new nation with that of the old state.[18] Even though Sukarno never thereafter submitted himself to any larger electorate, this does not alter the significance of the state-leadership office being defined for the first time in *representative* terms.

The symbolism of these acts, which took place physically and politically *outside the state,* reminds us that Sukarno's previous career was built entirely on the mobilization of popular forces (the nationalist movement) and in long-standing opposition to the colonial state. Not only had Sukarno never been an official of that state, but he had been spied on by its informers, arrested by its police, tried by its judges, and imprisoned and internally exiled for almost eleven years by its top bureaucratic directorate.[19] And many of those who spied on, arrested, and sequestered him—not to speak of those who steadfastly obstructed his political work in the periods when he was free—were Indonesian members of the state apparatus.

During the four years of the Revolution (1945–49) that followed, there were really two states functioning in the archipelago—that of the infant republic and that of the returning Netherlands Indies. Gravely weakened by wartime Nazi occupation and economic devastation, Holland still disposed of far greater military and financial resources than the Indonesian nationalists. By the end of 1946 it had resumed control of the entire eastern half of the archipelago, and a year later it had occupied virtually all the major export-commodity-producing zones in Java and Sumatra. As its power grew, it was able to reassemble many segments of the old beamtenstaat. In the wake of the second "police action," launched on December 19, 1948, the colonial state seized every significant urban center and captured Sukarno, Hatta, and other top Republican leaders.[20]

The rival Republican state was weak from the start and got weaker

[18]Ibid., chap. 4.

[19]John D. Legge, *Sukarno: A Political Biography* (New York: Praeger, 1972), especially chaps. 5, 6.

[20]See George McTurnan Kahin, *Nationalism and Revolution in Indonesia* (Ithaca, N.Y.: Cornell University Press, 1952); Alers, *Om een rode;* Anthony Reid, *The Indonesian National Revolution* (Hawthorn, Victoria: Longmans, 1974).

as the years passed. The political reliability of much of its inherited personnel was suspect; many of its new members entered it laterally, and as revolutionaries with utterly un-beamtenstaat visions, experiences, and skills. Not a few assumed offices within the state without long-term official careers in mind. The state's low inner coherence was accentuated by its poverty. What authority it had it largely borrowed from its old adversaries, the nationalist leaders.[21] These leaders, in turn, now found it in their interest to protect the apparatus, for three tactical reasons: They were anxious to deny the Dutch as much of the old beamtenstaat as possible, recognizing that in many ways it was more important to their adversaries than to themselves; they found it on occasion useful in their internal struggles for power; and they hoped to win international recognition for a sovereign nation, a recognition given only to nations-with-states.

If the Dutch were finally forced to concede defeat, the reasons had little to do with the Republican state. The prime factor was a highly localized popular resistance, above all in Java and Sumatra, expressed through a myriad extrastate politico-military organizations, locally recruited, financed, and led.[22] What linked these myriad resistances together was not the state, but a common vision of a free nation.[23] War weariness among the Dutch and powerful American diplomatic and financial pressures also contributed to the dramatic turnabout by which, at the end of 1949, sovereignty was formally transferred from Holland to the United *States* of Indonesia.

This new, internationally recognized entity represented internally a fragile amalgam of the two adversary states of the preceding four years—militaries, civil bureaucracies, incipient legislatures, financial resources and liabilities, including a $1,130 million debt inherited from the NEI state,[24] as well as complexes of institutional memories. Furthermore, each "half" of the amalgam was, for different reasons,

[21]See Anderson, *Java*, pp. 113–14, for an account of the one-sided negotiations between the nationalist leaders and top representatives of the state on August 30, 1945, and chap. 15 for an analysis of why Sukarno and his associates lent their prestige to reviving the authority of ex-colonial officialdom.
[22]This popular resistance is splendidly described and discussed in Audrey Kahin, "Struggle for Independence: West Sumatra in the Indonesian National Revolution" (Ph.D. thesis, Cornell University, 1979).
[23]The emblem for this condition is Acèh. The first major region to go into rebellion after independence (1953) in protest against meddling from Jakarta, during the Revolution it was the center's most selfless supporter, *freely* contributing large sums of money to the financially hard-pressed Republican authorities in Java (who were in no position to exact taxes through a state).
[24]Kahin, *Nationalism*, pp. 433–53.

weak: The NEI half was politically tainted with collaboration and deprived of its inner Dutch spine; the Republican half had not recovered from its pulverization in 1948–49. And when, in 1950, as a result of popular, extrastate agitation, the United States of Indonesia was turned into the unitary state of the Republic of Indonesia, the fragility of the amalgam was not significantly reduced. It could easily be argued that parliamentary democracy survived in Indonesia until about 1957 simply because *no other form of regime was possible.* There was no coherent civil bureaucracy. No dominant nationwide political party had emerged. No centralized, professionalized armed forces (including an industrial navy and air force for archipelagic control) existed, capable of seizing power. Parliamentary democracy, with its emphasis on popular representation and on extrastate political organization and activity, "fitted," one might say, the existing realities and expressed the current preponderance of nation and society over state.

The weakness of the state, which became ever more conspicuous as the élan of the independence struggle faded into memory, can be seen along three dimensions: military, economic, and administrative.

As early as 1950, hostility between ex-Republicans and ex-KNIL components of the amalgamated armed forces erupted into violence in Java and Sulawesi, and led to the attempted secession of the "Republic of the South Moluccas."[25] Soon afterward, so-called regional revolts occurred in many parts of the archipelago, most notably in formerly strongly Republican areas. Finally, a full-scale civil war broke out in 1958 between the Republic of Indonesia and the self-styled Revolutionary Republic of Indonesia (PRRI), which counted among its leaders some of the best-known political and military figures of the Revolution. These conflicts were made possible because the Revolution had been fought by local guerrilla forces, over which a small and inexperienced central staff had little more than a certain moral authority. The upshot was that, like postwar Burma, the independent state of Indonesia was for years unable to exert military control over sizable parts of its cartographic domain.

In economic terms, the state not only presided over a war- and revolution-shattered economy, but was burdened with heavy inherited debts and had few effective means of levying taxes. Moreover, until 1957, the "Big Five" giant Dutch conglomerates continued to domi-

[25]See the good accounts of the "Westerling Affair" in West Java and the "Andi Aziz Affair" in South Sulawesi contained in Herbert Feith, *The Decline of Constitutional Democracy in Indonesia* (Ithaca, N.Y.: Cornell University Press, 1962), pp. 62, 66–68.

nate much of the advanced revenue-producing sectors, as well as inter-island shipping. The country's oil industry was overwhelmingly in Dutch, American, and British hands. Small wonder that the postcolonial state glowed with the dim, fitful radiance of a klieg lamp powered by flashlight batteries.

During the 1950s, the administrative coherence and discipline of the civil service apparatus continued to crumble. In part, this was the result of the rancor between the two halves of the amalgamated post-1950 *apparat*. In part, memories of how officials had been deposed, kidnapped, and even killed during the Revolution lowered morale and encouraged self-protective passivity. But most important was the penetration of the state by society. Already during the Revolution, some offices and functions of the beamtenstaat had been taken over by persons who would have been walled off from it in the colonial era: elderly Islamic *kyai* (religious scholars) became district officers, teenagers organized medical and alimentary public services, and functional illiterates assumed important local military commands. Such people joined the state, but their fundamental loyalties were typically to nation, ideological grouping, paramilitary organization, local community, and so forth. After 1950 the penetration continued, in the first instance via the political parties. Building nationwide parties in a nation of roughly 100 million people was naturally an expensive proposition. The leaders found that a cheap way to develop their organizations was to enroll supporters inside the state apparatus. Thus, the civil bureaucracy swelled from a 1940 figure of about 250,000 to a 1968 figure of about 2.5 million—a tenfold increase in one generation.[26] An economically weak state was in no position to pay this vast body adequately (and so maintain some inner institutional discipline). The inevitable consequences were spreading corruption (some personal, some for party coffers) and declining efficacy. And insofar as all governments of the 1950–57 period were coalitions of parties, departmental segmentation under patronage politics became ever more serious. By 1957 there was no better indication of the porousness of the state than the passage of Law No. 1/1957, which made regional executives (*kepala daérah*) elective (party supported) rather than centrally appointed.[27]

[26]Donald K. Emmerson, "The Bureaucracy in Context: Weakness in Strength," in Karl D. Jackson and Lucian W. Pye, ed., *Political Power and Communications in Indonesia* (Berkeley: University of California Press, 1978), pp. 82–136, at p. 87.

[27]John D. Legge, *Central Authority and Regional Autonomy in Indonesia: A Study in Local Administration, 1950–1960* (Ithaca, N.Y.: Cornell University Press, 1961), chap. 9.

But it was not only the parties that penetrated the *apparat*. During the Revolution and its immediate aftermath, many of the traditional collaborationist upper classes in the more backward parts of the Outer Islands lost, or feared losing, much of their old power and wealth. Feeling vulnerable in the electoral arena, they were eager to protect their lineages' futures by sending their children into the burgeoning civil service academies. These young minority-aristocrat officials added an often energetically conservative and particularistic ethnic dimension to the kaleidoscopic inner life of the state.[28]

However, at the same time two powerful forces came, toward the end of the parliamentary period, to the state's rescue. The most important of these was the army. Throughout the decade, the army was convulsed by inner conflicts, but gradually the high command in Jakarta succeeded in strengthening its authority.[29] It pursued a policy of promoting professionalism and corporate cohesion through training overseas—mainly in the United States—and, in Indonesia itself, the development of increasingly complex, centrally controlled educational institutions. In addition, it managed to build with heavy external assistance its own elite strike force, which reached maturity in the 1960s as the Army Strategic Reserve (Kostrad). Thanks largely to Soviet aid, the center acquired a sizable navy and air force (organizations that, given their high capitalization, are unlikely to emerge from decentralized guerrilla forces). As a result, by 1962 the army leadership had largely managed to suppress regional military dissidence and to bring the old NEI's territory under unified control for the first time since 1942. Each military success meant the elimination of competitors for intramilitary ascendancy. The grip of Java-based officers on the high command increased, while Javanese troops became de facto occupiers and controllers of much of the Outer Islands.

Finally, the army leadership found the means to resist the forces that had so fractionalized the civilian arms of the state apparatus. The year 1957 marked the turning point. On March 14, President Sukarno declared martial law for the whole country in response to the regional crisis, thereby giving the military vast emergency powers. These powers were used initially to curb the activities of the parties, above all the Communist party (PKI), to suppress party-controlled veterans'

[28]This process is excellently discussed in Burhan Djabier Magenda, "The Surviving Aristocracy in Indonesia: Politics in Three Provinces of the Outer Islands" (Ph.D. dissertation, Cornell University, 1989).
[29]Ruth Thomas McVey, "The Post-Revolutionary Transformation of the Indonesian Army," pts. 1 and 2, *Indonesia* 11 (April 1971): 131–76; 13 (April 1972): 147–82.

organizations and to seal the military off from party linkages. Then, in December, when militant trade unions seized much of the vast Dutch corporate empire in retaliation for The Hague's intransigence on the West New Guinea issue, the high command stepped in to supplant the unions.[30] Quite suddenly, it took control of the bulk of the advanced sectors of the economy. Thus, for the first time it obtained the financial means to attach the officer corps firmly to itself and to give the military as a whole a *corporate economic interest* quite distinct from that of every other sector of Indonesian society. For the first time since 1942, the major *economic* resources of the nation were now under unified local control.

Allied with the army leaders was the charismatic figure of Sukarno. In the development of regional unrest, culminating in the outbreak of civil war in February 1958, he perceived a growing threat of national dismemberment, a threat all the greater in that the United States (at least its left hand, the CIA) was financing and arming the dissidents. He was increasingly convinced by experience that the coalition party cabinets were incapable of overcoming the threat, indeed, that even his own personal prestige was, by itself, insufficient for that task. Only the army had the power and the means. It was necessary, therefore, to give the army leaders what they insisted they needed: martial law, curbing of the political parties, control over the Dutch enterprises, and the cancellation of Law No. 1/1957. It is probable also that he had come to believe that the final retrocession of West New Guinea to the Republic could only be achieved by building up a military force that the Dutch (and the Americans) would have to take seriously.

However, Sukarno was fully aware that the consolidation of the army offered for the first time the possibility of a successful coup and the installation of a military-dominated regime. Accordingly, he was quick to use his political prestige and his legal authority under the 1945 Constitution (reinstated in 1959 by his personal decree) to prevent the suppression of the parties and their affiliated mass organizations.[31] The coalition between the army high command and Sukarno

[30]Daniel S. Lev, *The Transition to Guided Democracy: Indonesian Politics, 1957–1959,* Cornell Modern Indonesia Project Monograph Series (Ithaca, N.Y.: Cornell University, 1966), pp. 34, 69–70.

[31]This is not to deny that Sukarno had chafed under the limits imposed on him by the constitution of 1950 or that he enjoyed the vastly increased powers assigned the presidency under that of 1945. Moreover, in protecting the parties and popular organizations (except for the Socialist party and the Islamic Masyumi, which he banned for participation in the PRRI), he was motivated by a need for organized political support as a counterweight to the army. Indeed, so concerned was he about the army's intentions that he went out of his way to show favor to the navy, air force, and police.

made relatively smooth the transition from "parliamentary" to "Guided Democracy." But it was a coalition of expediency that began to break down as soon as the immediate interests of the partners no longer coincided. The consequences of the conflict between them, and between the forces they increasingly came to champion, were first a period of great instability and ultimately the cataclysmic events of 1965–66.

From Sukarno's point of view, the prime purposes of the coalition— the absorption of the entire former Netherlands East Indies into the Republic and the restoration of unitary authority in the archipelago— had been achieved by early 1963, when a shrewd mixture of diplomacy and military bluff finally succeeded in stirring the Americans to arrange the retrocession of West New Guinea (via an interim United Nations administration). The price for all this, however, had been high. It was not merely that the army had greatly increased its power and inner cohesion. In addition, the long-maturing, intimate ties between the army and the United States had clearly given the regionally dominant foreign military power a dangerous *point d'appui* deep within the Indonesian state.[32] As Sukarno perceived it, this penetration imposed significant limits on the sovereignty of the Indonesian nation and on its ability to manage its internal affairs with the maximum autonomy. Furthermore, the army's control of the former Dutch enterprises had now put it into a directly antagonistic relationship with the popular sector—the workers and peasants employed in the mines, plantations, and other major commercial enterprises. Sukarno thus increasingly came to feel not only that his personal position was threatened, but that the original goals of the nationalist movement were endangered.[33]

One can think of his solution to this problem as having two distinct, if interrelated, components. The first was to encourage a remobilization of extrastate popular organizations ("returning to the rails of our Revolution") under his personal ideological leadership. (On May 1, 1963, immediately after Jakarta assumed sovereignty over what it called Irian Barat [West New Guinea], Sukarno lifted martial law,

---

[32]This point is nicely illustrated by Howard P. Jones, longtime (1958–65) American ambassador to Indonesia, in his inimitable memoir: "In terms of power politics it would mean placing our best bets squarely on the Indonesian army . . . to preserve the pro-American, anti-Communist loyalties of the top officer group in the army." *Indonesia: The Possible Dream* (New York: Harcourt Brace Jovanovich, 1971), pp. 126–27.

[33]Legge, *Sukarno*, chaps 12–13; Peter Christian Hauswedell, "Sukarno: Radical or Conservative? Indonesian Politics, 1964–65," *Indonesia* 15 (April 1973): 63–82.

giving the parties renewed freedom of activity.) Paradoxically enough, this effort was greatly facilitated by the absence of elections under Guided Democracy. The punctuational rhythms and legislative focus of parliamentary constitutionalism were replaced by an accelerando of mass politics penetrating ever more widely down and across Indonesian society. The major political parties of the period—the PKI, the PNI, and the conservative Muslim NU—threw themselves into expanding not merely their own memberships but those of affiliated associations of youth, women, students, farmers, workers, intellectuals, and others. The result was that by the end of Guided Democracy each of these parties claimed, with some justification, to be the core of a huge, organized, ideological "family," each about 20 million strong, which competed fiercely for influence in every sphere of life and on a round-the-clock basis. Hence the popular penetration of the state, which had been stemmed, and even reversed, after the declaration of martial law in 1957, resumed. Even the armed forces were put under penetrative pressure by Sukarno's campaigns for the "Nasakom-ization" of all state institutions and, in 1965, for the formation of a Fifth (*Armed*) Force composed of popular volunteers. (Nasakom was an acronym for *Nasionalis-Agama-Komunis*, i.e., Nationalist-Religious-Communist. The other four forces were, of course, the army, navy, air force, and police.)

Second was an increasing emphasis on economic autarchy and an actively anti-imperialist foreign policy. A full exploration of the reasons for this strongly nationalist policy lies beyond the scope of this essay. For our immediate purposes, it is enough to note that the policy was intended to encourage popular mobilization under Sukarno's direct, personal aegis, while minimizing its disintegrative potential.[34] It was also aimed at decreasing the leverage of the United States in Indonesian domestic politics. Both the president and his political supporters were well aware of the enormous importance to the army leaders of the "American connection" (training, funds, weapons, intelligence, etc.) and saw in a sustained campaign for national political and economic autonomy a subtle but effective way of maneuvering toward the breaking of that connection.[35]

[34]See Donald Hindley, "President Sukarno and the Communists: The Politics of Domestication," *American Political Science Review* 56 (1962): 915–26. Borrowing from Hindley, one could argue that Sukarno in fact aimed at the domestication of *all* Indonesian political groups. Cf. my "Indonesia: Unity vs. Progress," *Current History* 48 (1965): 75–81.

[35]Unsurprisingly, no such campaign was launched against the "Soviet connection"—not because the PKI was on good terms with the CPSU, which it was not, but because Soviet military supplies went to the army's service rivals, the navy and the air force.

Events soon proved, however, that Sukarno's politique was unsustainable—at least under the circumstances of the time. The fundamental reason was economic. Indonesia was simply too poor to afford, simultaneously, a huge military buildup to make a militant foreign policy credible;[36] an autarchic economic policy that worked to extrude much foreign capital and also left the existing advanced productive sectors under inexperienced and venal military management; and a huge mobilization of competing popular movements. The only method available to cope with the resulting financial pressures was the printing of money in ever vaster quantities. In a sort of replay of the Japanese period (and for comparable structural reasons), the value of the *rupiah* fell ever more rapidly; between early 1962 and late 1965 its black-market exchange value with the United States dollar changed from Rp. 470 to Rp. 50,000, in a steeply ascending curve after the middle of 1964.[37] This hyperinflation affected every aspect of Indonesian life and sounded Guided Democracy's death knell.

For present purposes, the most important consequences were two. On the one hand, as in the later Japanese period, the efficacy of the civilian side of the state apparatus disintegrated as corruption and absenteeism proliferated, and communications, transportation, and revenue collection broke down. (This did not stop the bureaucracy from continuing to grow—one might almost say metastasize.) The one apparatus capable of sustaining itself was the army, partly because it was "legally" closed to party penetration, partly because it controlled the bulk of the country's real, as opposed to paper, assets. Thus, the last years of Guided Democracy marked an accelerating ascendancy of the army vis-à-vis all other arms of the state administration. On the other hand, the hyperinflation exacerbated domestic antagonisms to the point of explosion. As the living standards of the poor rapidly declined, the PKI was put under heavy pressure by its constituents to struggle more militantly for their material interests. The legal ban on strikes in so-called vital (i.e., state-controlled) enterprises made trade union militancy difficult and risky. Prospects seemed better in the countryside, and in 1964 the PKI began its *aksi sepihak* (unilateral mass actions) to force implementation of the rather

[36]In particular, the policy of "Confrontation," launched in September 1963, against the newly formed Federation of Malaysia.

[37]James Austin Copland Mackie, *Problems of the Indonesian Inflation*, Cornell Modern Indonesia Project Monograph Series (Ithaca, N.Y.: Cornell University, 1967), pp. 98–99, tab. 3.

mild Share-Cropping and Land Reform laws of 1959 and 1960.[38] The timing could not have been worse, for one consequence of the hyperinflation was a rush out of cash into land (on the part of those who had the cash), and a heightened determination on the part of those who already owned land to hang on to it. In the first group were many officials, civilian and military; in the second, those local notables so strongly represented in the regional leaderships of the NU and the PNI.[39] Anti-PKI rural violence had already begun months before the eruption of Lieutenant-Colonel Untung's September 30th Movement,[40] presaging the massacres of 1965–66 under the direction of the army leadership, which swept Guided Democracy—and soon thereafter Sukarno—into history.

Suharto, the State, and the New Order

The argument of the final section of this essay is that the New Order is best understood as the resurrection of the state and its triumph vis-à-vis society and nation. The basis for this triumph was laid in the physical annihilation of the PKI and its allies, the suppression of popular movements, sweeping purges of the state apparatus, and the removal of President Sukarno as an effective political force—all achieved between October 1965 and April 1966. But the *character* of the triumph cannot be understood without a look at the earlier career of General Suharto, before turning to consider a few of the more arresting components of the policies consistently pursued since 1966; for the two are intimately related.[41]

Born in 1921 as the son of a village official in the central Java

[38]On the aksi sepihak in context, see Rex Alfred Mortimer, *The Indonesian Communist Party and Land Reform, 1959–1965,* Monash Papers on Southeast Asia no. 1 (Clayton, Victoria: Monash University, 1972).

[39]See ibid.; also Margo Lyon, *Bases of Conflict in Rural Java,* Center for South and Southeast Asia Studies, Research Monograph no. 3 (Berkeley: University of California at Berkeley, 1971), and José Eliseo Rocamora, *Nationalism in Search of Ideology: The Indonesian Nationalist Party, 1946–1965* (Quezon City: University of the Philippines, Center for Advanced Studies, 1975).

[40]Mortimer, *The Indonesian Communist Party,* pp. 48–50; and Jacob Walkin, "The Moslem-Communist Confrontation in East Java," *Orbis* 13 (Fall, 1969): 822–32.

[41]The following biographical sketch is drawn from various published and unpublished sources, including Otto Gustav Roeder, *The Smiling General* (Jakarta: Gunung Agung, 1969), and Hamish McDonald, *Suharto's Indonesia* (Blackburn, Victoria: Fontana, 1980), chaps 1, 2.

principality of Yogyakarta, Suharto grew up during the Depression. The economic crisis, his father's inconspicuous social position, and the limited educational opportunities afforded by the NEI regime meant that his formal schooling ended when he graduated in 1939 from a private Muslim secondary school in Solo. In the summer of 1940 he applied for and was admitted to a basic training course offered by the colonial army, and in December he proceeded on for further training. By the time the Japanese invaded Java in March 1942, Suharto had risen to the rank of sergeant. Like his near-contemporaries Ironsi, Amin, Bokassa, Eyadema, and Lamizana, he thus began his ascent to state leadership from the noncommissioned stratum of the colonial state's military apparatus—one quite separate from the Royal Netherlands Army, and one whose small size (about 33,000 in 1942) shows that its essential mission was less external defense than internal security. If the Japanese had not invaded, Suharto would probably have ended his active days as a master-sergeant—officership in the KNIL was essentially a white prerogative. With the crushing and dissolution of the KNIL, Suharto joined the police. Again, had Japan won the Pacific war, Suharto would probably have worked his way up the Japanese colonial security apparatus. But in the autumn of 1943, in the face of steady Allied advances, the Japanese military authorities in Java decided to set up a native auxiliary force named Peta (consisting of sixty-six battalions, locally recruited and deployed, with no central staff, and battalion commander as its highest rank) to assist in the defense of the island. Suharto joined this decentralized force and eventually became a company (about one hundred men) commander in it. This force was in turn dissolved when the Japanese surrendered in August 1945; had the Dutch been in a position to resume control immediately, like the British in Malaya or the Americans in the Philippines, it is quite possible that Suharto would have rejoined a resuscitated KNIL or the colonial police. There is *no* evidence of any nationalist activity on his part until after the proclamation of Indonesia's independence.

But he was quickly swept up by the Revolution. In the largely spontaneously formed, ill-trained, and poorly armed Republican armed forces, his experience in two colonial militaries and his native abilities led to a rapid rise in rank. The twenty-one year-old sergeant of 1942 was in 1950 a twenty-nine-year-old lieutenant-colonel with a good military reputation and excellent prospects. Thereafter, his main field activities were participation in the suppression of regional and Muslim dissidence and leadership of the militarily unsuccessful operations against the Dutch in West New Guinea. Possibly because he was among the minority of senior officers who did not undergo training in the United States, he was appointed by Sukarno as the first commander of the army's elite strike force, Kostrad. It was from this office that Suharto destroyed the September 30th Movement and the PKI in 1965–66. (He held de facto presidential power only after the *coup de force* of March 11, 1966, and formally supplanted Sukarno as president only in 1968.)

These details on Suharto's career have been organized to underline one central point: that it has been made *entirely* within the state, more particularly within the internal security apparatus. (Sukarno was never an official of any kind.) The other side of the coin, however, is that this official lived through and experienced in the most intimate way the collapse of the Dutch and Japanese colonial regimes and the extraordinary vicissitudes of the state in independent Indonesia. Nothing was better calculated to encourage an abiding anxiety about the stability and security of the state (yet, as we have seen, Suharto's present eminence was only made possible *by* that state's fragility).42 It is understandable then that the consistent leitmotiv of New Order governance has been the strengthening of the state qua state. The best evidence for this proposition is the thrust of certain characteristic New Order policies in the economic, sociopolitical, and military areas.

Economic Policy

I have no intention of denying that many of Indonesia's technocratic planners have sincerely aimed at raising the living standards of the population, improving social welfare, and modernizing the structure of the economy—any more than one would deny such intentions to many officials of the colonial beamtenstaat, particularly those of an "Ethical" bent. The interesting question, however, is why Suharto and his closest military associates so quickly adopted the "development strategy" propounded by archtechnocrat Professor Widjojo Nitisastro and his entourage. I am inclined to argue that the basic initial decisions were made in order to overcome the enormous problems created

---

42This said, we should not ignore the fact that much of Suharto's career coincided with periods in Indonesian history in which popular political forces were quite strong relative to the state; and that, accordingly, many officials' survival depended on learning some basic political skills. It would be an error to think of Suharto simply as a bureaucrat, even a wily and intelligent one.

by hyperinflation—which, more than anything else, had destroyed Guided Democracy. Price stabilization was an absolute prerequisite for any new regime (we can be sure that a triumphant PKI would have pursued the same objective, if by different methods). But bringing inflation under control was not merely necessary for the broad purpose of stabilizing the economy and restoring some sense of normalcy to the life of society, it was also essential for reconstituting the discipline, cohesion, efficacy, and power of officialdom. The apparatus had to be provided with a *stable* hierarchy of emoluments, and at a sufficient level to command a unified subordination and loyalty. (Compare the outlays on officialdom in the calm, autocratic days of the colonial beamtenstaat, cited above.) Because the state itself was then still too weak and chaotic to undertake measures to raise the necessary resources domestically, Widjojo had little difficulty in showing Suharto that massive external support was essential and that gaining this support required policies designed to win the sympathy of the Western capitalist powers and Japan. Hence, in rapid succession: the liquidation of "confrontation" with Malaysia and the end of formal (and, of course, ineffective) price controls in 1966; the return of many nationalized enterprises to their former owners[43] and the promulgation of an easygoing Foreign Investment Law in 1967; the rationalization of banking and interest rates in 1968; the end of multiple exchange rates between 1968 and 1971; and so on.

The results were quick in coming: over half a billion dollars in aid in 1968 and an "annual IGGI fix" on a colossal scale ever since. Cumulative aid up to the eve of the great OPEC windfall late in 1973 amounted to over $3 billion. We may gauge the significance of these sums by comparing the *lowest* IGGI commitment of the pre-1974 era—$534 million in 1969—with *total* net government expenditures and receipts in 1957 (the last year of constitutional democracy) and 1960 (a good year for Guided Democracy): These amounted to $660 million and $500 million (1957) and $200 million and $180 million (1960).[44]

---

[43]It might be argued that, because these enterprises passed out of the state's hands into those of foreigners, a significant loss of state power was involved. In fact, these enterprises were so run down by years of military bleeding and economic chaos that the real cost in 1967 was quite small. In return for these retrocessions, the military-dominated state shortly received rewards many times larger, as I note below.

[44]These amounts, converted at prevailing black-market exchange rates, are calculated from Mackie, *Problems,* pp. 96–98, and Franklin B. Weinstein, *Indonesian Foreign Policy and the Dilemma of Dependence: From Sukarno to Suharto* (Ithaca, N.Y.: Cornell University Press, 1976), pp. 369–70, app. B.

It was above all these massive inflows, in some years covering 50 percent of the cost of all imports, that allowed Suharto to build, over the course of the 1970s, the most powerful state in Indonesia since Dutch colonial times. (The OPEC windfall and the revival of raw-material exports simply accelerated the process.) They also permitted him to dissolve with few serious short-term costs the extrastate anti-Communist coalition that had helped to bring him to power in the first place.[45]

We should not forget one other important advantage of the "annual IGGI fix," namely that the money came directly and exclusively to the *center* and without any significant state outlays in the form of a tax-gathering apparatus. In other words, not only was the power of the state vis-à-vis society vastly enhanced, but within the state the center came decisively to dominate the periphery.

Much the same could be said of the New Order's generally amiable attitude toward mono- and multinational foreign investment, despite what might seem substantial political disadvantages—not merely the material alienation of a significant component of the independent indigenous entrepreneurial class, but a much broader dissatisfaction among the population, deriving from the heritage of the nationalist movement and from fear of foreign economic domination. The key to understanding this long-standing complaisance[46] lies in recognizing the advantages that multinationals offer the state qua state. Thanks to their hierarchical structures, they provide the center with sizable, easily accessible revenues (taxes, commissions, etc.). They are ready, up to a point, to be model taxpayers, thereby obviating the need to extract income from domestic property owners. They are what one might call "Grade A pariah entrepreneurs," meaning that their executives have neither the interest nor the capacity to pursue political ambitions inside Indonesia. These corporations present no direct political threat to the state, as a powerful indigenous business class might do. And we should remember that the state does not keep all this wealth to itself: much of it is funneled out into society in the form of contracts, grants-

---

[45]For a brief overview of the components of the coalition and its progressive dismemberment, see my "The Last Days of Indonesia's Suharto?" *Southeast Asia Chronicle* 63 (1978): 2–17. The weakness of this analysis lies in a gross underestimation of the staying power of the beamtenstaat as of 1978.

[46]This stance is by no means without its nuances, and it would be a mistake to regard New Order policy as unqualifiedly "open door." It is useful in this context to bear in mind the twenty-year struggle of the Cultuurstelsel's beamtenstaat against *private* colonial capital (1848–68) and of the twentieth-century colonial state's monopolies and often ambiguous relations with non-Dutch conglomerates.

in-aid, loans, and so on. Thus, indigenous entrepreneurial elements ravaged from one side by the multinationals may profit handsomely from another side—but only by the grace of the state. They may prosper, but their prosperity cannot form the basis of any challenge to officialdom.

Sociopolitical Policy

Under this rubric, three policy lines are of special interest: the state's formula for Indonesia's political future; its handling of "the Chinese," both citizens and aliens; and its relationship with its prime "class base."

It is striking that the New Order has never publicly proclaimed itself an emergency, provisional, or even tutelary regime. It holds out no prospects for a return to civilian rule or a restoration of representative government. In this sense, it belongs in what Nordlinger calls the "ruler-type praetorianism" category, a distinct minority (he estimates no more than 10 percent) among military-dominated regimes.[47] The state leadership has attempted to persuade its audiences that this "no-change" future is legitimate by insisting that a peculiarly Indonesian form of democracy is actually already in place: Pancasila Democracy. It points to the facts that elections are regularly held, that opposition parties are represented in national and provincial legislatures, and that Suharto himself holds office through an (indirect) electoral mechanism.

In reality, elections are carefully manipulated, and with some thermostatic sophistication: Golkar (the state party) won 62.8 percent of the vote in 1971, 62.1 percent in 1977, and about 64 percent in 1982.[48] Opposition parties not only have had their leaderships emasculated by General Ali Murtopo's Special Operations organization, but sit in legislatures with what in practice are permanent state-appointed majorities.[49] No one has ever stood against Suharto in a presidential election.

[47]Eric Nordlinger, *Soldiers in Mufti: Military Coups and Governments* (Englewood Cliffs, N.J.: Prentice-Hall, 1977), p. 26.

[48]For details, see Masashi Nishihara, *Golkar and the Indonesian Elections of 1971,* Cornell Modern Indonesia Project Monograph Series (Ithaca, N.Y.: Cornell University, 1972); Ken Ward, *The 1971 Elections in Indonesia: An East Java Case Study,* Monash Papers on Southeast Asia no. 2 (Clayton, Victoria: Monash University, 1974); R. William Liddle, "Indonesia 1977: The New Order's Second Parliamentary Election," *Asian Survey* 18 (1978): 175–85; and *Far Eastern Economic Review,* May 14–20, 1982, p. 15.

[49]Harold Crouch, *The Army and Politics in Indonesia* (Ithaca, N.Y.: Cornell University Press, 1978), chap. 10; Heri Akhmadi, *Breaking the Chains of Oppression of the Indonesian People,* Cornell Modern Indonesia Project Translation Series (Ithaca, N.Y.: Cornell University, 1981), pp. 58–76.

Furthermore, there is the doctrine of *dwifungsi* (dual function), now enshrined as a fundamental aspect of Pancasila Democracy, which states that the Indonesian Armed Forces have permanent responsibilities in the fields both of national security and of social-political-economic development. Under this banner, the military have massively penetrated all hierarchies of the state apparatus and most aspects of society's life.[50] Finally, the semiofficial doctrine of the "floating mass" (originally coined in 1971) in effect says that Indonesia's unsophisticated rural masses are not to be distracted from the tasks of development by political parties, except in brief state-defined pre-election campaign periods. Under a law established in 1975, political parties are formally banned from establishing branches below the regency level, "virtually confining their activities to big towns and cities."[51] All these ideological formulas serve primarily the power interests of the state qua state.

It is widely, and largely correctly, believed in Indonesia today that "the Chinese" (no distinction between citizens and aliens) dominate the domestic economy under the protection of the state and with the backing of Chinese capital in Taiwan, Hong Kong, and Singapore, as well as the capitalist world's economic giants. Yet the Suharto leadership has also suppressed Chinese culture, closed down Chinese schools, barred Chinese-language publications, and, most significantly, officially installed the derogatory racist word *Cina* in the place of the customary, neutral *Tionghoa*. Moreover, citizens of Chinese extraction have been more drastically excluded from official politics than at any time since 1945. In the entire fourteen years that Suharto has been president, there has never been a "Chinese" cabinet minister, though such ministers were a regular feature of the revolutionary, parliamentary, and Guided Democracy periods.[52] Nor will one find any generals or senior civil servants of obvious Chinese ancestry. This ghettoization of citizen-Chinese—political exclusion and economic privilege—reminds one not only of the colonial era and John Furnivall's "plural society," but of the position of the Jews in Eastern

[50]The data in Emmerson's "Bureaucracy" (pp. 101–5) are strikingly confirmed by the quantitative analysis in John A. MacDougall, "Patterns of Military Control in the Indonesian Higher Central Bureaucracy," *Indonesia* 33 (April 1982): 89–121.
[51]McDonald, *Suharto's Indonesia,* p. 109; cf. James Austin Copland Mackie, "Anti-Chinese Outbreaks in Indonesia, 1959–1968," in J. A. C. Mackie, ed., *The Chinese in Indonesia: Five Essays* (Melbourne: Nelson, 1976), p. 119.
[52]Informally, a number of citizens of Chinese descent, such as Liem Bian-kie, Harry Tjan Silalahi, and Panglaykim, have exercised a good deal of political influence from within Ali Murtopo's Special Operations apparatus. In another sort of regime, men of their abilities would probably long since have achieved cabinet rank.

Europe under the nineteenth-century autocracies. The policy has been consistently maintained throughout the New Order period, in spite of widespread popular dissatisfaction (provincewide racial riots in Central Java in 1980), and we must regard it as a central element in the leadership's strategy. Insofar as the policy of economic favoritism in practice applies to *all* Chinese, aliens as well as citizens, it is difficult to locate it within any obvious "national" interest. From the point of view of the state, however, it makes excellent sense, for it increases the economic resources available to the state without the need for any cession of political power. The more pariah "the Chinese" become, the more they are dependent on the apparatus. (In addition, popular antiforeign feeling can be deflected from Western and Japanese multinationals.)

The class base of the New Order has not yet been the subject of systematic research.[53] But there is no good reason to believe that there was any dramatic change in the class structure between, say, 1955 and 1975. It is generally agreed that in Java the dominant class has all along been the so-called *priyayi*, deriving genealogically from the court, provincial, and village elites of precolonial times and overwhelmingly identified in this century with white-collar occupations. As mentioned earlier, in many parts of the Outer Islands petty feudalities survived intact until after independence. During the 1950s these classes continued (Java) or began (Outer Islands) to send some of their children into the state apparatus. But the weakness of the state vis-à-vis popular organizations, especially the political parties, also encouraged entry into and claims to local leadership of these organizations (where this seemed feasible). Quintessential in this respect was the PNI, the leadership of which was heavily priyayi and which gradually drew into itself segments of Outer Island upper classes.[54] The prewar nationalist credentials of many of its national-level leaders, the apparent favor of President Sukarno, and astute exploitation of the residual social prestige and patronage networks of the classes that dominated it made the PNI the most successful party in Indonesia's only free nationwide parliamentary election, which took place in 1955.[55] From 22.3 percent of the vote in that year, however, its share shrank to 6.9

[53] A partial exception is Richard Robison, "Capitalism and the Bureaucratic State in Indonesia, 1965–1975" (Ph.D. thesis, University of Sydney, 1978).

[54] Rocamora, *Nationalism,* chaps. 4–5; and Magenda, "The Surviving Aristocracy."

[55] Herbert Feith, *The Indonesian Elections of 1955,* Cornell Modern Indonesia Project Interim Report Series (Ithaca, N.Y.: Cornell University, 1957); for the PNI's role, see Rocamora, *Nationalism,* chaps. 4, 5.

percent in 1971. In 1977, after Suharto had coerced it into a merger with two Christian parties and a few other minor non-Muslim parties, the resulting "party" won only 8.6 percent of the vote.[56] In 1982 it won about 8 percent.

The obvious beneficiary of the PNI's eclipse was the *state* party Golkar, summoned into existence for the elections of 1971. Golkar's electoral successes in 1971, 1977, and 1982 have always been principally due to the activities of the two most powerful arms of the state: the Ministry of Defense (using the territorial chain of military command) and the Ministry of the Interior.[57] If I am correct in arguing that the social bases of Golkar and the PNI are similar, then it is difficult to account for the pulverization of the PNI at Golkar's expense in terms of *class*. (In addition to the constituencies of the old PNI, Golkar exploited the cowed residuum of the PKI's former supporters, who sought safety in obedience to officialdom.) It seems clear that the key difference between the two organizations, and the basis for the triumph of the one over the other, is that Golkar articulates the interests of the state qua state, and the PNI merely the interests of the class from which many functionaries of that state have been drawn. In effect, that class has been told that its interests will be served only through the mediation of the *apparat*.

Security Policy

One of the most curious aspects of New Order policy—given the regime's domination by the military—has been its neglect of the armed forces as armed forces, both in terms of basic amenities for the lower ranks and in terms of equipment and training.[58] Military budgets were quite modest during the 1970s, typically less than 20 percent of total official outlays. But sizable additional sums came in from unofficial sources: military-controlled monopolies, institutional corruption, and,

[56]McDonald, *Suharto's Indonesia*, pp. 107, 239.

[57]Thus, interior minister General Amir Machmud arranged for the issuance of Presidential Regulation no. 6/1970, whereby civil servants were "denied the right to engage in political activity (read: party activity) and were required to show 'monoloyalty' to the government (read: GOLKAR)" (Emmerson, "Bureaucracy," pp. 106–7). After the 1971 elections, Korpri, a union for *all* civil servants, was established to enforce "monoloyalty" organizationally.

[58]When the Buginese aristocrat General Andi Muhammad Yusuf replaced General Panggabean as Minister of Defense in the spring of 1978, he won sudden popularity by making unannounced visits to inspect the housing and equipment of the rank-and-file troops and then expressing publicly his concern at the sad conditions he found prevailing.

up to its collapse in 1975, the state oil corporation, Pertamina. Crouch cites a March 4, 1970 editorial in the official armed forces newspaper *Angkatan Bersenjata* to the effect that the forces' budget covered only half of their operational requirements.[59] Sizable new armaments were not acquired until 1976. Nothing better measures the consequences for the professional fighting capacities of the military than the shambles made of the initial December 7, 1975 invasion of East Timor and the fact that, in spite of horrific antipopulation measures taken in 1977–78, the resistance of Fretilin nationalists still had not been crushed seven years later, as 1981's intensified fighting attested. Until recently, the main arms purchases have been such things as OV-10 Broncos, valuable for counterinsurgency operations but useless for external defense. This neglect cannot easily be explained by any sparseness of the state's financial resources, particularly after the OPEC windfall of 1973. The fact is that for a nation of Indonesia's size, population, and strategic location, her military, 250,000 or so strong, remains remarkably small, underarmed, and undertrained.

Many observers have welcomed this modesty as a sign of Suharto's determination to commit the bulk of the nation's resources to the economic development of the country and the welfare of the population. I myself am inclined to emphasize the interesting parallels between the contemporary Indonesian armed forces and the old Dutch-Colonial KNIL. The KNIL was small in size, and poorly trained and equipped by the standards of the day. The colonial state could afford to keep things this way because it relied for external protection on close ties with the hegemonic naval power of the era—Great Britain—which had its own geopolitical reasons for proffering this protection. (Great Britain deliberately cultivated friendly ties with the small powers situated across the Channel [Holland and Belgium] and at the mouth of the Mediterranean [Portugal].) The KNIL nonetheless was quite capable of maintaining order within the huge colony, aided by a complex of police forces and a vast network of informers.

In the same way, the real external security of the contemporary beamtenstaat is provided by the huge naval and air forces of the United States, with which, as we have seen, the Indonesian army has long had the most intimate ties. The state's security has been further enhanced by the development in stages since 1971 of the Washington-Peking-Tokyo entente. Under these circumstances, Indonesia faces no credible external military threat, a situation unlikely to change until Japan becomes a naval, as well as an economic, competitor of the

[59]Crouch, *The Army,* p. 274.

United States in Southeast Asia. From the state's point of view, then, there is no point in a large conventional arms buildup, which, in addition, might cause negative reactions among some of IGGI's European donors, who have few strategic interests in Southeast Asia.

As with the KNIL, a great deal of the Indonesian military's time, resources, and energy have been devoted to the internal defense of the state. The obvious symbol of this is the central locus of power within the armed forces: Kopkamtib, an acronym for Komando Pemulihan Keamanan dan Ketertiban (Command for the Restoration of Security and Order or, in the words of an earlier era, *rust en orde*), which was set up by Suharto in October 1965 to direct the obliteration of the PKI. Seventeen years later, Kopkamtib still exists (its restorative task forever to be unachieved?) and is possibly even more powerful than in its salad days. Supplementing Kopkamtib are the huge official state intelligence apparatus Bakin, Ali Murtopo's Special Operations net, and a plethora of other intelligence cum internal security hierarchies.

As with the KNIL, the activities of the military under Suharto's leadership have involved local aggrandizement. The invasion of East Timor is a case in point. Objectively considered, even a leftist-controlled independent East Timor presented no more substantial a threat than did "fanatically Muslim" Acèh to the Netherlands East Indies a century ago. Nor does East Timor offer more promising economic rewards than did that northern tip of Sumatra. Like Acèh to Batavia, East Timor appeared to Jakarta as a presumptuous nuisance to be disposed of by the methods used for the maintenance of internal security: political manipulations, popular controls, counterinsurgency sweeps, and calculated terror.[60] (In both cases the "enemy" turned out to be much tougher than was initially anticipated.)

Conclusion

I argued at the outset that the amalgam *nation-state* is rather recent and that it often conjoins a popular, participatory nation with an older adversarial state. If this argument makes sense, one should expect the

[60]The secret manipulations carried out by Ali Murtopo's Special Operations apparatus are excellently described by McDonald (*Suharto's Indonesia,* chap. 9). The grim toll taken by the counterinsurgency campaigns has been extensively detailed in a succession of hearings, beginning in 1977, held by the subcommittees on International Organizations and on Asian and Pacific Affairs of the U.S. Congress, House of Representatives (March 23, 1977; June 28, July 19, 1977; February 15, 16, 28, 1978; March 7, 8, 1978; February 4, 6, 7, 1980).

policy behavior of the amalgam to vary in character according to the predominance of one or other of its components. I have attempted to illustrate this argument by a schematic account of the vicissitudes of the state in Indonesia from late colonial times to the present. Finally, I have endeavored to demonstrate the validity of the basic distinction by analyzing key aspects of the policy behavior of the New Order, which may seem unintelligible from the point of view of the new nation's interest but are quite rational from that of the old state. I make this argument in full awareness of the attractions of a more strictly class-based analysis, but the intense and inconclusive debate over "the state" among neo-Marxist theorists in recent years suggests that there is something there that does not straightforwardly fit with such analysis. I hope that this essay may contribute toward some useful rearrangement of the pieces.

PART **II**

LANGUAGE

CHAPTER 4

The Languages of
Indonesian Politics

The languages of contemporary Indonesian politics have recently been the object of a certain cantankerous attention. The eminent Swiss historian and publicist Herbert Luethy describes Indonesian (*bahasa Indonesia*) as a "synthetic" language that has borrowed "copiously and indiscriminately from all the technical terminologies and ideological abstractions of the modern world," and that is "scarcely intelligible, in its newer parts, to the average Indonesian, who listens to the official speeches all the more admiringly for being able to make nothing of them."[1] Luethy proceeds to argue that the public language of contemporary politics is a "hodge-podge of irrational gobbledygook," leading to "ideological intoxication" and "magical syncretism"—all this expressing the "obsession" of "a Javanese élite which is losing its own personality in identifying itself with an artificial nation. . . . The whole of Indonesian politics consists of magical processes derived from Javanese cosmogony." In reply to Luethy, Clifford Geertz concedes that "unreason" has erupted in Indonesia, and that President Sukarno's major recent speeches have been "desperate inanities," but argues that the "retreat to cultural revivalism, racial scapegoating, and the manufacture of external enemies" have been not the result of "any archaic memories of the world of the Mahabharata," but of the state leadership's "panic" at its failure

First published in 1966. *Indonesia* 1 (April 1966): 89–116. Reprinted with permission.
[1]See Herbert Luethy, "Indonesia Confronted," pts. 1 and 2, in *Encounter* 25 (December 1965): 80–89, and 26 (January 1966): 75–83; and Geertz, "Are the Javanese Mad?" in *Encounter* 26 (January 1966): 86–88.

123

to cope with the country's immense demographic, economic, social, and political problems.

Both scholars, despite their vehement disagreements on other matters, seem to see the language of Indonesian politics as a sign, or reflection, of a profound pathology. In this regard, at least, they are joined by most experienced observers of modern Indonesia. No one has yet attempted to look at the language of contemporary Indonesia as an *enterprise* for the mastery of a gigantic cultural crisis, and a partly subconscious project for the assumption of "modernity" within the modalities of an autonomous and autochthonous social-political tradition. Yet this enterprise is of decisive importance for the generations that lie ahead, since with every decade that passes, Indonesian is becoming more and more the one language through which Indonesians of all kinds are coming to grips with modern and ancient realities. The East-West polyglots of the colonial and early postrevolutionary period are slowly beginning to disappear from the scene. The "new Indonesian" language is therefore of paramount importance for the shaping of younger Indonesians' national consciousness.

The extraordinary character of modern "political" Indonesian (with which we are especially concerned) derives from the fact that it is inevitably the heir of three separate languages and two separate linguistic-cultural traditions. The languages are Dutch, Javanese, and "revolutionary-Malay"—the traditions are Dutch-Western and Javanese. The enterprise of modern Indonesian is therefore the synthesis of a new political-cultural intelligence and perspective out of the fragmentation of the colonial and early postcolonial period, and the restoration of a unity of consciousness such as has not existed since the initial confrontation with Dutch colonialism. The new Indonesian language has had to develop into a means of communication that can express not only Indonesian nationalism but also Indonesian aspirations, Indonesian traditions and international realities—within the limits of a single vocabulary. The colossal cultural effort involved, and the remarkable success achieved, seem to me to have been inadequately appreciated, and the morphology of the transformations involved insufficiently studied.

Colonial Indonesia was a bureaucratic Wonderland: a cluster of interacting but basically separate linguistic and cultural universes, linked by the miracle of modern bureaucratic and technical organization. Each language, be it Batak, Sundanese, Javanese, or Dutch, was the product of separate historical experiences, community organizations, literary and cultural specializations, and metaphysical outlooks. The discontinuities among these linguistic-cultural universes were fundamental to the structure of colonialism. The responses to these discontinuities on the part of "Indonesian" literati was inevitably expressed primarily in bilingualism, since only through the mastery of the language of the Other could the chasm between the universes be bridged and the colonial system challenged on something like even ground.

But the leap out of, say, Batak into Dutch meant far more than the acquisition of a new technical vocabulary and the ability to peer into the arcana of Dutch domination. It also involved the development of two interacting or conflicting modes of consciousness. The new generation of bilingual literati (which arose around the end of the nineteenth century) thus became cultural middlemen, but inevitably middlemen who were involved as much in the effort to control two mental universes as in facilitating communication between them. In the colonial situation, bilingualism was not merely a technical but also a grave psychological, and ultimately religious, problem.

For the acquisition of the colonial language implied a change in modalities of consciousness. It was far more than just the discovery of a radically different set of phonetic equivalents for the inventory of one's own language. The structure of Dutch (and through it of European) thought and consciousness was fundamentally different from those of the traditional languages of Indonesia, and the advance to bilingualism therefore *in itself* created a profound mental and spiritual displacement—what our modern economic-cultural missionaries like to call "cultural shock," but at a much deeper level. The profounder the knowledge of the acquired language, and the more this language substituted itself for the aboriginal language as the medium of thought and discourse, the more destructive and/or creative (according to individual talents and situations) became the two-mindedness of the literati.

It is one of the ironies of colonial history that, since the psychological effort to maintain equilibrium between two universes is so immense that few could sustain it, the early radicals who leapt out into Dutch and "conquered" the organization and methodology of colonial society became increasingly isolated from the aboriginal Indonesian world; having acted as pioneers, they later found themselves to a large extent culturally marooned on a farther Western shore. A newer generation then grew up for whom the "conquest" was a thing of the past, and whose basic task was the development of a counterlanguage to Dutch, a modern, nationalist language, which would *in itself* reestablish the connection with Indonesian traditions, without compelling each individual to master the crisis internally through a bilingual conquest. While one generation struggled to work its way out of the traditional modes of thinking, the next has been trying to reestablish contact with and build on them. In this attempt, an immense act of social and national creativity is involved.

The implications of this quest for a fundamental national unity (*not* basically a question of interregional homogenization, but one of spiritual coherence) have too often been ignored, or reduced to superficial maintenance of "folk culture" in a quite synthetic way. There has been too much focus on bureaucratic marination of the external emblems of Tradition (costumes, *adat* [customary law], etc.), and too little on the deeper communal quest for a sense of rooted identity, expressed at all levels of the population, through the adventures and transformations of the national language.

The main thrust of what follows is, therefore, the search for the overall line of this act of creativity. The main focus will be on the Javanese, since a combination of political power, numbers, and strength of cultural identity has made them the single most creative force in developing the new Indonesian. How has "revolutionary Malay" set about the task of disciplining and uniting the bureaucratic colonial vocabulary, the Western democratic-socialist vocabulary, the nationalist-revolutionary vocabulary, and that of Javanese tradition? How has this synthesis been stretched or transformed to adjust to the realities of urban Indonesia today? I believe that the most satisfactory perspective for understanding this development is a growing imposition of Javanese flesh on the skeleton of "revolutionary Malay."

It may be helpful to start with some consideration of an earlier confrontation between the Javanese and an alien civilization—that of Middle Eastern Islam—since the pattern of resolution in that now distant clash is now quite clearly visible.

While political power in Old Java was largely held by bureaucratic functionaries of the rulers, religious and intellectual power was wielded, particularly in those areas where royal authority was weakest, by the *kyai* (Islamic teachers). One found them mainly in the *pasisir* (Java's northern littoral), and in traditional rebel areas (remote valley fortresses such as Ponorogo). The kyai was essentially a man of greater religious wisdom than his fellows, and accordingly the typical institution he headed was the *pesantrèn* or rural Islamic school. Pesantrèn education was explicitly an initiation into the higher wisdom. The social structure of the pesantrèn, in which the kyai was assisted by his more advanced pupils, reflected the conception of education as a path to wisdom (rather than knowledge). The prestige of the kyai rested on many factors, on his reputed ancestry, his powers, his experience, and his personal character—but above all on his mastery of an esoteric vocabulary. The most important element in this vocabulary was, generally speaking, Arabic.

The normal method of instruction of boys and youths in the pesantrèn was the inculcation, by rote, of extensive passages of the Koran, and their subsequent elucidation by the master. It has sometimes been claimed that this rote learning of the Koran represents the decadence or fossilization of Islam in Java. Yet it seems more sensible to see it as a sign of Java's defense against Arabic culture and its final conquest of this alien infiltration. The domestication of Islam and Arabic by the Javanese cultural impulse was done through the transformation of the Koran into a hermetic textbook of riddles and paradoxes. Arabic was maintained as the language of "initiation" precisely because Arabic was *not* understood; the whole point of a spiritual ritual in an uncomprehended language is that it manifests power, and implies a deliberately nonrationalist mode of cognition. Islam had forbidden the continued use of Shivaitic and Tantric *mantra;* Java answered by turning the Koran into a book of mantra. (The fact that until quite recently it was forbidden to translate the Koran *under Islamic law itself* simply served to justify a principle which derived from the local culture.)

The pupils in the pesantrèn thus acquired their Koranic texts by rote, and the excelling pupil was the boy who could recite without mistakes. Since the youth clearly understood little of what he was saying, the importance attached to recital errors has clear "magical" overtones; mistakes are not just mistakes, but errors that forebode trouble for the community if they are not efficaciously corrected.

A second aspect of pesantrèn education was the "decoding" of the Koranic texts and of Javanese-language riddles and paradoxes. This part of the educational system is marvelously depicted in the pages of the great early nineteenth-century Javanese "encyclopedia," the *Serat Centhini,* much of which concerns wandering Islamic devotees, the *santri* (the original meaning is "pupil"), who travel from one pesantrèn to another, testing each other's skill in unraveling puzzles and religious conundrums.

The function of the religious pun or conundrum is to bridge two levels of cognition. Taking a specifically Javanese example, one of the best-known religious puns turns on the name of the magical weapon of King Yudhisthira (hero of the *wayang* shadow-puppet theater)—the Kalimasada. This Kalimasada is not an arrow, club, or spear but a piece of esoteric writing, an incomprehensible document of great power. (It is not what is "said" in the Kalimasada that is important, but that certain syllables are inscribed on it in a certain powerful order by a certain person at a certain time.) Yet while the Kalimasada is an authentic symbol of a pre-Islamic cultural tradition, it is also common to find it referred to in pious Islamic circles: but now under the guise of the Kalimah Sahadat, the five elements of the Koranic confession of faith. (There is even a legend describing how Yudhisthira gave his weapon to Sunan Kalijaga, one of the nine pioneering Islamic "apostles" in Java). The riddle is thus: "When is the Kalimasada not the Kalimasada?" Answer: "When it is the Kalimah Sahadat."

The riddling pun is of great importance to the Javanese Islamic tradition, since it represents a sort of "capsulated" intuition. Neither historical nor linguistic analysis has any real purchase on this intuition, because it is built into the miraculous quality of the pun itself (How can it be coincidental? Is the idea of coincidence meaningful only in certain cultures?), revealing another level of Being flowing in and out of the phenomena. (From an outsider point of view, the pun seems to express the will to unity of the Javanese cultural tradition, the urge to unite or absorb conflicting cultural streams through linguistic symbolism.)

Thus, the inner wisdom taught in the pesantrèn (and this is even truer of the more Hindu-Buddhist *abangan* religious thought of South Central Java) is gained almost entirely by ascetic practices, rituals, and the study of conundrums and paradoxes (*prenèsan*). The common denominator is a sense that the phenomena are not always what they seem to be; what really is, may not appear to be so. One finds, for example, simple paradoxes such as the old tag: "Sing ana, ora ana; sing ora ana, ana" (What is, is not; what is not, is). This is often imaged by the word *longan,* which means the space under a chair, table, or bed. The riddle of being and nonbeing is nicely expressed in the conundrum that longan exists, yet does not exist. No chair can exist without it, yet it cannot exist without a chair.

A third important aspect of the pesantrèn education is that it always had a metaphysical dimension; it was seen as part of a long process of spiritual training, an initiation into something profoundly esoteric, a key to an otherwise locked door. Hence the special character of the well-known "relativism" of the traditional Javanese *weltanschauung.*

Paradoxes are always an expression of an esoteric truth. (By contrast, in Atlantic societies, where any sense of "certainty" in this ultimate sense is getting rarer, paradox, where not merely play, arouses the sense of skating out to sea on melting ice.) Because ontological certitude underlies the quotidian relativism of traditional Javanese philosophy, the phenomena do not have to be "saved," since they are never the sum of what Is. The real and the really real are closely connected, but they are not identical.

It should be clear that the mode of old Javanese Islam is in sharp contrast to that of the modern Middle East. Since the rise of the Cairo-influenced reformist Islamic organization Muhammadiyah in the early years of this century an increasingly self-conscious schism has emerged in the Islamic community (*ummat*) on Java. "Reformists" ("modernists") have made so bold as to say that the Koran means what is says, just that and only that. The Koran is less a key to mystery than a sort of religious Highway Code.

For the true Islamic modernist Arabic is the language of truth and rationality, and therefore it must be *directly understood.* For pesantrèn traditionalists it is still Javanese, partly because Javanese is the mother language, with all its own secret inflections and resonances, partly because the language is so strongly felt to be the major expression of Javanese identity. Its allusive alliterativeness, its highly developed onomatopoeia, and its rich sensory vocabulary provide a treasury of esoteric causalities and an enduring sense of a hidden continuity flowing through the phenomena, down to the most intimate sphere of people's lives. When the *pesindhèn* (female singer) at a wayang performance wishes to rest and to warn the puppeteer (*dhalang*) to take over, she weaves the words *ron ing mlinjo* (leaves of the mlinjo tree) into her song. Since these leaves are also known as *so* and the Javanese verb for rest is *ngaso,* the connection is at once felt, and to the mystification of the uninitiated, the dhalang immediately takes over the burden of the singing.

The Javanese sense of the interrelatedness of the phenomena and yet skepticism about their ultimate reality is fundamental to any understanding of the Javanese political style. In Javanese social intercourse, great stress was traditionally laid on a wide space between facial expression and mental attitude. Regardless of one's emotions, one's face should express "appropriate" feelings of complete impassivity. This sense of the face as a kind of built-in mask has been much commented on by travelers and by students of Javanese life. But it is generally misunderstood as: the *real* is the emotion, the *false* is the face/mask. In fact, it is not nearly as simple as that. In the mask dance, for example, the relationship of the dancer to his mask is highly ambiguous: The mask may formally express an emotion that the dancer feels but dares not express (the mask provides an alibi); it may simply be a disguise; or it may be magnetic (there is a common belief that women will fall madly in love with a masked dancer but not with the same man unmasked); or again it may take possession of him, so that the man becomes the mask. The relationship between the real and really real is thus obscure and intricate. And when the dhalang sits behind the screen, manipulating the puppets he chooses, imitating their various voices, conveying their passions and personalities, he becomes at once all of them and none of them.

The Pamongpraja

Whereas the most autochthonous type of Javanese authority (such as we have just considered) was monolingual, or at least bilingual only in a very special sense—that he had acquired a store of esoteric Arabic—the elaboration of a secular colonial bureaucracy required the cultivation of bi- or even, trilingualism. Well before the rise of the modern nationalist intelligentsia, those Javanese functioning as subordinate administrators for the colonial government started to face the challenge of Dutch rule by the slow acquisition of Dutch and Dutch-Western modes of thinking. Of special interest were the highest-ranking functionaries, the *bupati,* particularly those serving in areas remote from the old royal capitals of Surakarta and Yogyakarta (Jepara, Rembang, Tuban, Banyumas, and Banten are all good examples). Since the bupati was the main nexus between the rural Javanese populace and the colonial government, and thus the middleman between two mutually uncomprehending worlds, he was early on forced to cultivate two-mindedness. Whereas vis-à-vis the Dutch his position was weak and clearly subordinate, vis-à-vis the Javanese population he remained the apex of the social order in a society intensely conscious of status hierarchies. While the Dutch did what they could (within the logic of the colonial system) to maintain the outward grandeur and pomp of the bupati's position, it was clear to those most closely concerned that this was pretty much a show; that the "formal" apparatus of power was quite different from the "real"; that, for example, the Dutch *contrôleur,* though below the Bupati in rank and dignity, nevertheless effectively ran the local government. A similar development had long been in evidence in the twin royal capitals, where, in spite of the formal majesty of the sunan and sultan, it was well understood that effective power was in the hands of the Dutch-appointed *patih* (a sort of grand vizier). The relationship contrôleur-bupati and patih-sunan were in many respects dissimilar, but in one critical respect they were alike—in their disassociation of legitimating and administrative functions. In each case the magico-religious figure was powerless on a day-to-day level, yet his authority was essential for the smooth working of the system controlled by his opposite number: an ambiguous, symbiotic relationship, recalling the mask and its wearer, the dhalang and his wayang.

Although from the colonial point of view the bupati was basically an administrator, from the Javanese point of view he was the most eminent *priyayi* in his district—and *priyayi* is perhaps best defined as literate man of quality. The prestige of literacy in a land where perhaps 90 percent of the population was illiterate is easy to comprehend. Writing assumes a totally different character to the literate and the illiterate man. For the one it is a means of communication; for the other, a sign of inaccessible power. This is why the dominion of the bupati was, at bottom, the dominion of literacy over illiteracy. In the language of the Javanese, the reflection of this stratification appeared, probably not earlier than the late seventeenth century, in a structural differentiation between two major levels of discourse, *krama* and *ngoko*. Krama, par excellence the language of the priyayi, is a consciously archaizing Sanskritic sublanguage, developed largely to emphasize and "build into" the larger Javanese language the increasing hierarchicalization of Javanese society under the influence of Dutch pressure and later control. While krama is essentially an honorific language, and thus largely spoken *up* the social hierarchy, full mastery of the vocabulary requires a high degree of education. To this day social prestige among the Javanese is indicated most clearly by an individual's mastery of the finer forms of this *langage de politesse*. The rolling, melodious, polysyllabic krama words emphasize in themselves the sense of distance and space between the ranks of Javanese society. Ngoko, on the other hand, is terse, acerbic, humorous, and sensuous. It is spoken down the social hierarchy and among very close equals, friends or family. The duality of these two sublanguages reflects not only the stratification of Javanese social structure but a dualism in the Javanese mind. Krama is official, aspirative—a little like a mask.

Ngoko is private, cynical, passionate—a little like the heart. But neither can be fully appreciated without the other, and both "live" in their complementarity.

In his relationships with the Javanese world, the bupati was bounded and conditioned by the structures of Javanese as a language. The values and orientations of that language persisted in his life, since they had real application to what was still largely a traditional community. But in his relationship with his Dutch superiors and with his priyayi colleagues and equals in the outside the *pamongpraja* (territorial civil service), who shared a Dutch education with him, he (especially the younger bupati of the late nineteenth and early twentieth centuries) was compelled to leave Javanese behind him. The acquisition of some Dutch (and also Malay, though Malay had a special role of its own) was necessary to an adequate performance of the increasingly technical-managerial aspect of his role, particularly with the introduction, around the turn of the century, of the Ethical Policy, which called for a great expansion of governmental activity in both the economic and social fields.

In the Indies world—as opposed to the purely Javanese—Dutch came thus to assume some of the functions of krama, a high-status language that denoted the degree of the individual's "literacy" and in which the operations, particularly of the government, were most honorifically expressed.[2] Whereas for the Dutch in Java the Dutch language remained, among themselves, a language without any special prestige, it assumed a quite different place in the *weltanschauung* of the younger Javanese pamongpraja. Precisely because Dutch educational policy (in contrast to British policy in India, for example) was to limit the number of Dutch-speakers to those needed for the purposes of the colonial regime, Dutch acquired the "esoteric" aura of being the language of the inner elite—which it has not lost to the present day. Moreover, since Dutch education tended to be given to people of known lineage—people of "good family"—by a reverse process, knowledge of Dutch was generally taken to indicate breeding and literati ancestry.

It rapidly became fashionable for younger pamongpraja families to speak Dutch in their homes, often with a heavy Javanese accent and including many Javanese words. Particularly in the larger cities, among professional people, Dutch tended to be used also for situa-

---

[2]One still often hears Dutch referred to jokingly as *krama inggilnya Jakarta*—the krama inggil of Jakarta. Krama inggil is a specifically high-status form of krama generally confined to the old royal court capitals.

tions for which the older regional language seemed ill adapted: writing love letters, for example, and discussing women's fashions and the Western amusements and appliances becoming ever more available.

But it was in the offices of the colonial bureaucracy that the political effects of the new bilingualism were most immediately felt. From their Dutch superiors younger Javanese officials divined a new vocabulary of politics, which they rapidly absorbed. For the conventional colonial official, the world divided normally into two: *praters* and *werkers.* Praters (talkers) were the parliamentarians, editors, idealists, "reds" and ideologues. Werkers (doers) were busy and practical men of affairs, who kept their mouths shut, "ran a tight ship," had a strong sense of hierarchy and knew their place down to the last E. The division was in many ways a conventional pejorative distinction between administrators and politicians. Furthermore, Dutch officialdom defined their Great Society as based on *rust en orde* (tranquility and order), which were constantly being threatened by *relletjes* (disturbances), *opstanden* (rebellions), and *revolutionnaire uitbarstingen* (revolutionary outbursts)—in ascending order of seriousness. Any reading of Dutch colonial literature astounds one with its obsessive concern with menaces to order.[3] Society, in all serious matters, was divided between law givers and law receivers, regulators and regulated. The politician was an intruder and an outsider. The danger was always that hierarchy would be disturbed by "lower" elements making claims to power in the name of communal, revolutionary and/or democratic forces.[4]

A curious mutual acculturation took place between the Dutch and Javanese bureaucratic hierarchies, based on a growing communion of interests and outlooks. In the early nineteenth century the osmosis had often taken the form of Javanization of the Dutch, most frequently in the kitchen or in bed through the Dutch official's *huishoudster* or native live-in mistress. Javanese regalia and paraphernalia, such as golden umbrellas, were happily adopted by Dutch administrators. Later on, however, especially after the opening of the Suez Canal had

[3]In those palmy days it was still *orde,* not yet *tata-tertib* (law-'n'-order) and *keamanan* (security).

[4]This tension provides the basis of Henri Alers's fascinating and much neglected study of modern Indonesian politics, where the basic conflict is drawn between "green" and "red" forces. See Henri Alers, *Om een rode of groene Merdeka: tien jaren binnenlandse politiek: Indonesië, 1943–1953* (Eindhoven: Vulkaan, 1956). These colors do not represent Islam and communism, but rather the forces of rule-order-hierarchy and those of revolution-spontaneity-community. Alers's sneaking sympathy for the "reds" scarcely disguises the fact that his analytic framework is essentially the colonial administrators' perspective stood on its head.

permitted a sizable immigration of Dutch women, this Javanization came to an end, signalized by Governor-General van Heutsz's *Hormat* circular, which banned the use of Javanese ceremony and regalia by Dutch officials, and the rapid decline of the older type of interracial concubinage. The osmosis then began to work the other way, with (some) educated Javanese acquiring (mainly in Holland) Dutch wives and the characteristic regalia of Dutch authority.[5]

Acculturation between Dutch and Javanese administrators was all the easier in that certain aspects of Dutch and Javanese bureaucratic culture ran along surprisingly similar lines. The hostility of many of the older Dutch *ambtenaren* (civil servants) to the rising, thrusting capitalist class in the Indies (which often had the ear of The Hague, and which increasingly threatened the power monopoly of officialdom) was not far (especially as these ambtenaren often liked to assume aristocratic airs) from the Javanese priyayi's disdain for *dagang* (trade). The Dutch obsession with detail, rule and rank, categorization and classification, accorded well with the Javanese priyayi love of fussy protocol and elaborate hierarchies. Especially with the rise of the Ethical generation of Dutch administrators, steeped in romantic ideas of adat and the need to protect the *inlander* (native) from the ravages of Westernization, the mutuality became quite close. The pamongpraja, whose whole position was supposed to rest on adat, naturally tended to find this outlook agreeable; and the "moral" emphasis of Ethical rule, concern for what was conceived to be the good of the ruled, echoed older Javanese ideas about the duties of the ruling class. To the classical motto of the priyayi administrator—*sepi ing pamrih, ramé ing gawé, mangayuayuning buwana* (be disinterested, work hard, to perfect the world)—the ambtenaar of the Ethical school could gladly say Amen. Here Leiden and Yogyakarta met and fully understood one another. The ideal priyayi admin-

[5]Alers has an intriguing analysis of what he calls the *mokolo* of colonial society. The mokolo are the apparently alien, aristocratic rule givers of some communities of South Sulawesi whom Alers takes as the model for certain types of "green" rule. These mokolo are typically a closed caste, filled with a "Nietzschean" consciousness of superiority and disdain for the rest of society, whom they regulate, patronize, and exploit. They do not mingle with the rest of society, and live by their own quite separate code, which is not imposed on the rest of the community. Alers describes the Dutch bureaucracy as typically mokolo (the ultimate of "green-ness"), with race coloration substituting for an aristocratic *esprit de corps*. The "inner" bourgeois character of Dutch colonial rule thus assumed an "external" aristocratic mokolo character vis-à-vis the brown-skinned populations. Foreign observers of post revolutionary Javanese administrators in the non-Javanese islands have noted a clear trend towards mokolo-ism in their behavior.

istrator, the polite, honorable man who carries out his duty to the state with a minimum of (overt) ambition, had more than superficial resemblances to the old-fashioned ambtenaar, the man of *eer* (honor) and *hoffelijkheid* (politesse).

For the priyayi, then, the type of Dutch that was acquired often tended to reinforce traditional attitudes. The inner language of the Dutch civil service classified political phenomena (on the grand scale) in terms not too far from those already familiar to the Javanese bureaucrats; the fact that the two organizations were functionally complementary also helped to ease the process of mutual assimilation, or rather, in the twentieth century, the slow assimilation of Javanese to Dutch modes of rule. The inner vocabulary of Dutch bureaucratic intrigue and office gossip percolated rapidly through to the Javanese. The pamongpraja official might also (rarely) have *ruzie met zijn baas* (a row with his boss), complain that some colleague was *erg koppig* (very obstinate), shake his head that some too outspoken friend had been *strafovergeplaatst* (punitively transferred to a remote station), and worry about the *herrie* (trouble) caused by, say, the unaccountable spread of Sarekat Islam. He might worry about *het volk* after a bad harvest, and would certainly fret that his office must be kept *netjes* (tidy), with everything *in orde*.

The most crucial aspect, however, of the bilingualism of the pamongpraja was that in most cases it provided a means to cope with the real social-political position of this class, both vis-à-vis Dutch superiors and Javanese subordinates. The conservatism of the pamongpraja as a group, the fact that their interests lay in defending an established order, also meant that it was easy to absorb out of the Dutch universe only what was essential as sandbags to block the growing breaches in the old Javanese *weltanschauung*. With no mission to fulfil except the maintenance of the existing order, the pamongpraja class was able to make a much more "stable" adjustment to its own bilingualism, and undergo far less stress in the process, than the nationalist intellectual class. Nonetheless, since a great many of the younger nationalist intelligentsia were related to the pamongpraja, and indeed in some ways formed merely a new part of the larger priyayi stratum, the experience of the older generation pamongpraja formed a bridge between the traditional Javanese experience and that of the future nationalist revolution. Rather than simply absorb and adapt Dutch partially, to reinforce Javanese traditions, the younger intelligentsia, drawn mainly into the professions, was to build on the older generation's experience and advance to the radical absorption of Dutch as a "whole"—including the metropolitan spectrum of Dutch culture—and consequently, in the long run, to destroy Dutch colonial power from within.

The Nationalist Intelligentsia

Whereas the pamongpraja was to the end well adapted to the maintenance and continuation of Dutch rule, colonial conservatives very early recognized that even the limited Dutch-language education provided by the colonial authorities was creating a new class of people whose very existence could presage the end of Dutch rule. This group of newcomers, contemptuously referred to a *half-intellectuelen* (semi-intellectuals), *gladakkers* (rascals), *ruziemakers* (troublemakers), even *sloebers* (skunks), was contrasted in the Dutch colonial mind with a sentimentalized *adel* (nobility) and the *eenvoudige tani* (uncorrupted peasant).

For these intellectuals, without a stable function within the structures of the colonial system but potential leaders of a postcolonial society, bilingualism was not the key to a modernization of regional tradition. Rather, it opened the way to a critical conception of colonial society as a whole and a vision of a future society after the disappearance of the colonial regime itself, be it in the simplest and most abstract terms. Here the role of Dutch was of crucial importance, since it provided the necessary means for communicating West European and Russian Marxist theories on colonialism and imperialism to a potential revolutionary elite in Indonesia. This process of transmission is, of course, a commonplace of studies of anticolonial nationalism. What is often insufficiently stressed, however, is the *clarity* of this revolutionary mode of thinking within the mystified colonial world: its coherence, simplicity, and comprehensiveness vis-à-vis the factitious (and real) complications of racial division, adat particularity, and religious schism, which made attempting to think systematically about Dutch power so difficult within the framework of the indigenous languages (even one as highly developed as Javanese). Just because Dutch power stretched wider than any ethnic-linguistic group, and as deep as the full stratification of traditional society, it could only be responded to within terms that it laid down itself. The vehicle of comprehension was therefore necessarily Dutch; the vehicle of attack was subsequently to be Indonesian (revolutionary Malay). Paradoxically enough, the spread of Indonesian as a national language was only possible once Dutch had become the inner language of the intelligensia: Only then could Indonesian be developed to receive the new thinking, and then to diffuse it more widely within colonial society.

It can safely be said that whereas openly conservative Dutch thinking had virtually no impact on Indonesians (the disguised conservatism of the "Ethical" civil servants did, of course, influence pamongpraja circles), Dutch socialist and Communist writing affected virtually the whole of the nationalist intelligentsia of the twenties and thirties. For this reason a *marxisant* vocabulary became the common property of the entire nationalist intelligentsia of those years. The importance of this vocabulary was dual in that it offered a critique of the existing order and suggested a program for its replacement. Because the analysis offered by Marxism was apt and clear, it was taken over wholeheartedly by all important segments of the rising educated elite.

All Indonesian intellectuals of the twenties and thirties were posed the problems of cultural and spiritual dualism in their harshest forms. Rare was the person who could hold the two universes either completely separate or in balance. There was a general tendency for the weight of an individual's perspective to be laid on either the Dutch or the regional-traditional "leg." Those who leaned on the Dutch "leg" came to find that dialogue and intercourse with the Dutch enemy was sometimes easier than with the provincial and rural Indonesian masses. Many of them had lived for at least some years in Holland or in other parts of Europe. Many became active members of the Dutch Left, whether as socialists or Communists. On their return, it was natural for them to adopt a political strategy of "cadre-forming" among Dutch-educated younger intellectuals to whom they could talk in the same general language that they had used with their Dutch socialist or Communist counterparts. It was no coincidence that the strategy of the Hatta-Sjahrir group in the early thirties was thus devoted primarily to building up an elite circle of Dutch-speaking radical intellectuals. On the other side, there were intellectuals whose assimilation of Dutch was more superficial, who had few close relationships with Dutchmen, and who felt more comfortable within traditional milieux than in the "international" socialist-communist intellectual world. For such men and women political action became meaningful not through critical dialogue with the Dutch, but in relation to their communities of origin. Whereas intellectuals in the first group were closer to like-minded Dutchmen than unlikeminded Javanese or Sundanese, the reverse was the case with the second group. To a large extent, though acting as translators of "outside" ideas into the traditional world, they rarely moved effectively or comfortably outside it. For this reason the natural political strategy for them was the mobilization of the masses, within a cultural universe largely incomprehensible to the Dutch. Precisely because this was their strength, their grip on programmatic Marxism remained weak—indeed, the conscious dilemmas of postrevolutionary Indonesia result largely from this fact.[6]

Nonetheless, the two groups abstracted in this analysis (actually there were no such groups, but a whole range of personalities between the two polar "types") were united by the language of the colonial ruler. Since it was the school language of the whole generation of intellectuals which grew up before the Japanese occupation, Dutch remained the inner language of elite discourse, especially among nationalists of different ethnic groups. It was the medium for absorbing those ideas and instructions from the West (including Russia) which promised to liberate the peoples of Indonesia from the grip of their white masters. It also built up elite cohesion vis-à-vis both the Dutch and the indigenous masses. Furthermore, because Dutch education was given mainly to the children of priyayi families, it was subsequently to appear as a sort of sign of high status even *within traditional society*. To this day the vague line dividing those who are *binnen* (in) and those who are *buiten* (out) in Jakarta politics remains fluency in the colonial language.

In spite of the elite's full or partial mastery of Dutch, the colonial government's educational policies made it clear that there would be no possibility of using Dutch (as English was used in India) to unite regional nationalisms into a solid anti-Dutch front. A language had to be found that could be used across ethnic and status lines to fulfill the unifying function at the mass level that Dutch performed for the elite. The language would thus, since it was called into being by the nationalist struggle, represent in itself the pure spirit of resistance to the domineering monopoly of Dutch as the bridge to "modernity." It would in itself declare the impending cultural defeat of Dutch dominion.

[6]One could say that the difference lay between those who basically thought in Dutch and those who, however fluent their Dutch, subconsciously translated as they went along into the structures of their own languages. Later, as we shall see, both translated into Indonesian, some from Dutch and others from Javanese. Compare Sutan Sjahrir's manifesto *Perdjoeangan Kita* (November 1945) and Sukarno's famous statement of basic Indonesian political principles, the Pancasila (June 1945), neither of which is fully comprehensible without the reader knowing something of the mother tongues involved.

What was commonly known as *pasar* (bazaar) Malay, long the lingua franca of the archipelago, became the basis of a new, *essentially political language,* Indonesian (revolutionary Malay). It was a language simple and flexible enough to be rapidly developed into a modern political language, analogous to but also juxtaposable to Dutch, without strong traditional traits (mainly syntax and honorifics) exercising counterrevolutionary influences. The possibilities were all the greater in that Malay, as an "interethnic" language, had ipso facto an almost statusless character. It had thus a free, "democratic" feel from the outset, which had its own attractions for an intellectual class that at one level (the desire to be on equal terms with the colonial elite) aspired to egalitarian norms.[7] It has often been said (mainly by Javanese of a later day) that the adoption of Indonesian as the national language was a magnanimous concession on the part of the Javanese near-majority. It seems more likely, however, that, since even for the more traditionalist intellectuals nationalism was then still partly seen in terms of breaking out of "Javanism" and the hierarchical modes of Javanese social intercourse, the simple modalities of Indonesian had their own ideological appeal. The language also offered the possibility of relating socially in an essentially Dutch manner, but without the mediation of the Dutch language. The very awkwardness and unfamiliarity of the new language reflected the sense of creativity and exploration involved in a "socialist" and would-be egalitarian lifestyle.

The Adventures of a New Language

The major public function of Indonesian has lain in its role as national unifier. Though it began to play this part in the 1920s, it was not until the Japanese occupation that it formally became the language of state, to be taught in schools and used in offices as a matter of official policy. During the Revolution of 1945–49 it was the language of resistance to the returning Dutch and the language of hope for the future. The Revolution also accelerated the process of filling Indonesian with the emotionally resonant words that give any language its cultural identity and aura, and that seem to express its speakers' most vital experiences. The key words *Rakyat* (the People), *merdéka* (free-

[7]The interethnic character of the language made it all the more successful as an unifier, since it was not tied to the interests of any major ethnic-linguistic group in the struggle for interregional ascendancy.

dom), *perjuangan* (struggle), *Pergerakan* (the Movement), *kebangsaan* (nationality), *kedaulatan* (sovereignty), *semangat* (dynamic spirit), and, of course, *révolusi*: All stem from the seedtime of the Republic, the time of its deepest awareness of itself as the expression of a hopeful new enterprise and solidarity. Virtually all the emotive words in Indonesian are connected to the struggle and violence of a physical revolution, and most have highly political-heroic connotations. They live and vibrate because they are part of the historical memory of a still surviving generation, and were coined within the most important experience of modern Indonesian life. The contrast with Javanese, where the emotive words, sonorous and onomatopoeic, have grown in depth and resonance over generations, and relate to aesthetic and religious sensibility, is striking.

Aside from the key words born of the Revolution and the struggle that preceded it, Indonesian is a language without extensive historical memories and connotations. It looks to the future; as such, it is par excellence the language of youth and rebellion. For the majority of literary artists too, who resent the oppressiveness of the Dutch and Javanese literary traditions, Indonesian offers an attractive medium of expression. Its very flatness and simplicity allow writers to feel that they can mold it in their own image and according to their own aspirations. Nonetheless, even if for the chosen few Indonesian's lack of givenness creates a sense of liberation, both literary and political, there has always been an underlying cultural risk involved. Especially since the Revolution, the language's lack of cultural resonances, of a solid tradition, has led to unexpected transformations, as we shall see below.

Furthermore, precisely because Indonesian represented a project, an aspiration to unity and equality, a generous wager on the future—in the face of some increasingly intractable social facts—the language has since 1950 gradually developed a "formal" character that has up to now scarcely been commented upon. Contemporary Indonesian has something curiously impersonal and neuter about it, which sets up psychological distances between its speakers. This change is the result, not of any social stratification "built into" the language, but of its democratic-egalitarian character in a society still traditionally status oriented in its deepest thinking. The vitality of Indonesian depending less on its historical antecedents than its symbolic character as an expression of the anticolonial project (at once the unification of the whole former Dutch colonial empire into a harmonious nation, the democratization of the national community, and the growth of a free spirit of fraternity), the postrevolutionary fate of this project has had decisive effects on the language. Forming a new and thin topsoil to the cultures of Indonesia, it has proven only too subject to erosion once the winds began to blow.

It is not so much that the language is continuing to acquire new vocabularies as such (though this indeed is happening) as that the older words have acquired a "satanic" reversed meaning, reflecting the transitions from the hopeful years of the Revolution to the harsher years that followed. The most celebrated example of this reversal has been the fate of the word *bung* (brother). During the Revolution it expressed the real fraternity of the national struggle, and was used freely by all active participants in the struggle. Today, with the exception of a few national figures like Sukarno, Hatta, and Sutomo (and their case *bung* is spelt *Bung*), virtually no one of importance is referred to in this way (outside small nostalgic left-wing cliques). While *Bung* has stayed high and honorific, *bung* has slipped lower and lower, and is now generally a peremptory, disdainful means of summoning a pedicab driver, waiter, doorman, or street-side cigarette vendor. Another example is the word *aksi,* which from its popularization by the celebrated early Communist leader Tan Malaka, meant action, revolutionary action, and even now crops up in the names of such organizations as KAMI (Kesatuan Aksi Mahasiswa Indonesia— Indonesian Students' Action Union). More often today, however, it is the satanic meaning of *aksi* that is widespread, in the sense of a "show" (pretentious, fake, artificial). Further examples could readily be provided. The point is not that these words are now used cynically. It is that people use *Bung* and *bung, Aksi* and *aksi,* quite unselfconsciously, in their disassociated meanings.

This fission within some of the most important emotive words of the Indonesian language reflects both sociological and cultural characteristics of postrevolutionary Indonesia. It indicates the restratification of contemporary Indonesian society and the determination to maintain the aspirations and idealism of Indonesian in a changing social context, by a process of dualization. This situation becomes all the more clear if one remembers that even today, twenty years after the Revolution began, Indonesian is by no means the everyday language of more than a tiny segment of the population. One can say with some confidence that in only two cities in all Indonesia is Indonesian the normal medium of communication outside official channels. The major provincial capitals, Makasar, Padang, Palembang, Bandung, Surabaya, Solo, and Semarang, all speak their own regional languages, be it Makassarese, Minangkabau, Sundanese, or Javanese. Only in Medan and Jakarta is Indonesian the real urban language. Even here, Medanese is really, thanks to its close ties to the Malay Peninsula, more Malay than Indonesian, and has much of the character of a provincial dialect.

It is primarily in the metropolitan melting pot of Jakarta that Indonesian has developed and shown its creativity in the post-Revolution years. The energy has come from the immense influx of fortune seekers, especially from Java, but also from all the other islands, into a capital where so much power and wealth is concentrated. Contemporary Indonesian also reflects the peculiar personality of Jakarta, its sense of solidarity vis-à-vis the provinces and the brutal, commercial, power-oriented and cynical character of its everyday life.

The most distinctive aspect of Jakarta's influence on Indonesian has been borrowings from the so-called *bahasa Jakarta* (Jakartan). Bahasa Jakarta or *bahasa Betawi* has long been in existence, developed over the decades by Balinese, Sundanese, Buginese, Javanese, and Chinese settlers there. It is a rough, lower-class urban speech, totally without "high" moral or status pretensions. It is virtually impossible to be pompous in bahasa Jakarta, so brutally earthy and humorous is its feel. By an unexpected turn of history, however, this lumpen-language has increasingly become the "in" language of the younger Jakarta elite, especially in the later fifties and sixties. Particularly for politicians, newsmen, and students, bahasa Jakarta, in slightly dressed-up form, has become a normal vehicle of social intercourse. Its popularity clearly derives from its intimate, jazzy, cynical character, which forms a satisfying counterpoint to the formal, official Indonesian of public communication. It expresses the danger, excitement, humor, and coarseness of post-Revolution Jakarta as no other language could do. Its acrid onomatopoeia parallels the flavor of ngoko in Javanese, while bahasa Indonesia grows more and more into an analogue of krama.

The most interesting external manifestation of this change is the metropolitan newspaper, which, for our purposes, can be divided into two quite clearly separable portions: first, the portion in bahasa Indonesia, which covers all news items, all features, all advertisements and all editorials (about 95 percent of the newsprint); second, the portion in bahasa Jakarta, which covers only the *pojok* (corner-columns). Though the pojok rarely run more than half a column, they are the first thing in the paper to which the Jakarta reader turns. The essence of the pojok is biting, anonymous comment on the latest news or the general political or economic situation. Often pojok will refer indirectly to events that are open secrets, though censorship will not permit them to be mentioned in the newspaper. Frequently they take the form of brief dialogues between two (supposed) proletarians or petty traders: Bang Dul, Pak Otong, and so forth. The art of pojok writing is one of allusion, innuendo, sarcasm, and mock surprise. For example, a pojok may quote a senior minister or army officer making an uplifting speech in Indonesian about the need to live simply, work hard, and avoid corruption. On a separate line comes the rejoinder: *Bener dèh*! (Absolutely!) Evidently a simple agreement with what the great man has said. But the metropolitan reader immediately notes that the pojok writer has used not the Indonesian *benar* but the Jakartan *bener,* which has strong "come off it" connotations, and has added the untranslatable but salty Jakartan particle *dèh* (something like "indeed"), which pithily expresses ridicule and disbelief. In just two words, then, the pojok formally praises the minister or officer while at the same time implying that he is hypocritical, lazy, corrupt, and pompous. Or again, the pojok may say: *Hasilnjé adé juga. Ikan gedé ketangkap. Alhamdulillah*! (It finally worked. They got a big fish. Praise be!) From the sarcastic Arabic "Praise be!" and the Jakartan suffixes, the reader will immediately know that an important political figure has been arrested for corruption, though the case itself, and even the arrest, may never be made public.

The contrast between the Indonesian and Jakartan sections of the newspapers is complete and immediate. The Indonesian parts are high-minded, serious, and moralizing, usually sermons by the president, generals, ministers, or editors. They are doubtless very improving, but also official, ideological, patronizing, and authoritarian. All are directed down the social-political hierarchy from the great to the small, from the *pemimpin* (leader) or *tokoh* (bigshot) to the rakyat (people), the *wong cilik* (little man) or the *massa* (the masses). The Jakartan parts are malicious, democratic, humorous, and above all intimate. The empty distances of Indonesia are scaled down to the knowing intimacy of Jakarta. As Jakartan-speakers put it, the pojok convey a pervasive atmosphere of "TST" (*tahu sama tahu*—we understand each other only too well).

In addition to the inflections, the vocabulary of Indonesian and Jakartan are in striking contrast. Editorials love words like *imperialisme, pembangunan* (upbuilding), *kemajuan* (progress), *amanat penderitaan rakyat* (message of the people's suffering), *kontra-révolusionèr* (counterrevolutionary) and perjuangan. The pojok speak in terms of *masuk kantong* (filling one's pockets), *sépak ke atas* (kick upstairs), *nyatut* (to chisel), *jatuh ke kasur* (fall on a mattress—i.e., be removed from office but receive a fat sinecure as consolation prize), *main kayu* (play rough and dirty) and *ngakunyé* (so he claims). The editorial may speak of *démokratis* (democratic)—the pojok echoes it as *dia mau gratis* (he wants it for free).

How are we to explain this emergence of Jakartan as a key element in the metropolitan language of politics? It is clearly unprecedented in Indonesian history *in its terminology*, which derives from the post independence situation, where Indonesians control their own government and rulers and ruled (higher-level ruled) engage in some form of real dialogue. There is a temptation to regard Jakartan as the "real" language, with Indonesian merely there for show, propaganda, or self-aggrandizement. The cynical wit of the pojok and the metropolitan gossip network are easy enough to take as the "reality" until one recognizes that Jakartan is still the language of one city, with virtually no roots outside, and that for the great mass of Indonesians, Indonesian retains its hold as the symbol and promise of the future. It thus has a reality that transcends the hopes and fears of the present ruling elite.

We are back with the problem of the mask. Public mask, private face, which is real? Why is the mask so important? What is the private face without the public mask? Does the mask mislead, attract, symbolize, or possess?

Javanese Modalities and the Present Cultural Crisis

The deepening crisis that has preoccupied all politically minded Indonesians since at least as far back as 1956, while many-faceted, centers on the petering out of revolutionary impulse within the post revolutionary elite. Sociologically it is manifested in the growing stratification of Indonesian society, the increasing isolation of the elite from the masses, and the development of parasitic bureaucratic structures in all fields of social activity. Politically, the slow narrowing of the regime's political base, the uncreative conservatism of its policies, and the ever more frantic effort to protect its varied vested interests reflect the same condition. The economic situation is in no way more promising. The impact of these changes on the language of Indonesian politics has been of great importance. Part of what has been happening has been an inevitable process of Javanization of Indonesian, in terms of both vocabulary and modalities. Part has been the drying up of

Indonesian (revolutionary Malay) as a wellspring for renewed creativity. Very probably the most important development has been this last: the slowdown of the revolutionary *essor* at the center of Indonesian politics. But the two are intertwined; the relationship between Indonesian and Javanese is in itself an indicator of the psychological and political state of the nation and of the general road down which the Indonesian elite has been heading. Given the growing paralysis of the revolutionary impulse, revolutionary Malay has been increasingly felt as out of touch, almost dysfunctional to communication within the emerging system. The most convenient way of grappling linguistically with this change has been to fall back on older traditions. The problem is not, as has been so often claimed, the cultural imperialism of the Javanese, but rather the impending defeat of Indonesian (for the nonce, at least) not as a *language,* but as an autonomous vehicle of thought.

The Javanization of Indonesian has a number of facets, all of which are closely connected to the actual social and political situation.

1. *The kramanization of public Indonesian.* As the "reality" of revolutionary Malay has increasingly been undercut by events it has tended to become a language of political politeness, in which any educated modern priyayi should be fluent, and which distinguishes him from the *rakyat yang bodoh.*[8] This etiquette helps to disassociate the priyayi from the rawer aspects of contemporary politics, and to associate him with the more idealistic. Acquisition of the vocabulary of krama Indonesian in itself involves a form of initiation into a higher level of political sophistication. It implies a certain discipline to become fully aware of the nuances and subtleties of the public language.

Just as Javanese krama originally represented a glorifying and archaizing of the basic ngoko vocabulary, so the kramanization of bahasa Indonesia has moved in the same direction, since glorification and archaism, as always, are meant to identify the present with a heroic past. The archaisms and honorifics tend to come from Javanese and Sanskritized Old Javanese, since both for sonority and for glorious historical resonances these sources offer the richest treasury. Thus Pancasila, independent Indonesia's political ideology, was originally a

---

[8]The newcomer is often struck by the unselfconsciousness with which the *priyayi* (even "leftist" priyayi) refer to the masses as *bodoh,* since this word is usually translated as "stupid." It seems intolerable snobbery, and indeed often is. But when one hears the same man talking about the people as *masih bodoh* (still stupid), things become clearer. In the West stupidity is determined, and is a trait of a fixed personality. We never talk of people "still" being "stupid." For the Javanese "stupidity" is the reverse of being "educated" or "awakened." It is therefore a failing that can, in theory, always be remedied.

set of Buddhist principles, mentioned in one of the oldest preserved Javanese literary texts, the *Nagarakrtagama.* The modern krama name for the Mobile Brigade of the Police, Bhayangkari, is the same as that used in Old Javanese for "Palace Guard." The Sapta Marga, ideological charter of the Indonesian army, is Old Javanese for the "Seven Principles." Dozens of these archaisms became current under later Guided Democracy: Tri Ubaya Sakti, Pancatunggal, Pancaward-hana, Mandala, Satya Lencana, Pramuka, and so on. Many of them are true krama words in that there are ordinary or ngoko everyday equivalents (e.g., Mobrig for Bhayangkari). All of them tend to be used most on occasions of high ceremonial importance and to be applied to objects and institutions of the highest political prestige. While almost none of these words are fully comprehended in their original sense, the fact that they are of Sanskritic or Old Javanese origin is well understood, and therefore the modern institutions can be seen as inheriting the prestige and majesty of the originals.

2. *The new ngoko.* I have already suggested that bahasa Jakarta has at least partially been absorbed into political Indonesian to perform the role of ngoko, as revolutionary Malay has gradually moved up to krama status. This movement shows how Javanese modalities have penetrated Indonesian even more than Javanese as a language. But it is also true that there has been a steady influx of ngoko Javanese words into Indonesian at all levels (almost none from contemporary Javanese krama). This influx partly reflects the growing power of the Javanese, and especially President Sukarno, at the center of Indonesian politics since 1956. Since Sukarno and the heavily Javanese PKI (Indonesian Communist Party) have been the only two consciously innovative forces in developing the language of Indonesian politics, this *verbal* Javanization (which is now even quite fashionable) shows its ancestry rather clearly. The most well-known Javanese imports—words like *ganyang* (eat up), *krumus* (chew up), *gontok-gontokan* (brawling), *nggrogoti* (undermine by gnawing), *bobrok* (hopelessly rotten), *plin-tat-plintut* (half-hearted, insincere) *berkiprah* (strut in victory)—not only have the typical Javanese sensual immediacy (by onomatopoeia), but are almost invariably words implying danger, disaster, and violence. This feature is in turn unmistakably a sign of the deepening social conflicts and tensions of the past decade as the economic and social plight of the Indonesians has become markedly worse and as hatreds have been turned inward on the society itself rather than on the outside world.

3. *The neutralization or capture of revolutionary symbols.* This process can be described as the assimilation of these symbols to an

unrevolutionary, or even counterrevolutionary, traditionalism. It is done in two ways:

(a) By burying words of great symbolic power, such as *révolusi, sosialisme,* and *démokrasi,* which have real historic roots, within hermetic acronyms like Jarèk, Resopim, and Usdèk.[9] These combination words are not "functional" in the sense that Nep or Sovkhoz once were in the Soviet Union—convenient shorthands for specific policies and concrete institutions. Rather, they are what one could half-paradoxically call synthetic syntheses of ideas that refer to no concrete reality but that by verbal manipulation may be thought to acquire a life of their own. Jalan Révolusi Kita is still an attempt to use words syntactically to convey an idea or an appeal. Jarèk, however, is not a word at all, but simply a *thing,* into which the ingredient *révolusi* has been stirred. It has become a mantra, of which any overt meaning is of no importance. Hence, it could pop up as one of what Sukarno, quite unselfconsciously, called the Amulets (Azimat) of the Revolution. Looked at somewhat differently, it also represents a transformation of foreign symbols and messages, parallel to what we have observed happening to Arabic and Islam in older times. As with Arabic, the formal language of revolutionary socialism has been appropriated and given an esoteric sense. The acquisition by rote of the newer political acronyms thus forms an analogue to the learning of incomprehensible *ayat* (verses) of the Koran in the pesantrèn: Both represent access to a mystery. This is why we can attribute quite similar functions to Jarèk and the traditional Arabo-Islamic formula *bismillahirochmanirochim* (in the name of Allah the Merciful, the Compassionate).

(b) By reifying action and process into essence and quality. Sukarno has constantly been accused by his Western judges of "betraying" socialism, democracy, and revolution. What is not recognized is that these words today are no longer dictionary equivalents of *sosialisme, démokrasi,* and *révolusi,* which have acquired free-floating meanings of their own. When Lieutenant-General Suharto talks quite seriously of "the hierarchy of the revolution being disturbed," or refers to the Communists as "counterrevolutionary," it is clear that these terms have an esoteric local sense. Revolution is no longer a social process but a mentality or a combat record. One may "be" revolutionary ex officio, by having participated in the nationalist struggle) or "become" revolutionary (by "mental retooling," as former defense minister Gen-

[9]These are Sukarno coinages for *Ja*lan *Ré*volusi *Ki*ta (the Path of Our Revolution); *Ré*vo-lusi-*So*sialisme-*Pim*pinan (Revolution-Socialism-Leadership) ; and *U*ndang-undang *D*asar 1945, *Sosialisme* à la Indonesia, Démokrasi Terpimpin, Ékonomi Terpimpin, Kepribadian Nasional (the 1945 Constitution, Indonesian Socialism, Guided Democracy, Guided Economy, and National Identity).

eral Nasution put it so elegantly), but one does not "act" revolutionary. What is socially approved is a state of mind, not a series of deeds.
Similarly, an official can simultaneously loudly applaud the slogan-
phrase *gotong-royong* (mutual help and cooperation) and denounce
the slogan-phrase *sama rata sama rasa* (all equal in status, all feeling
equal), because the latter (popular in leftist circles) still retains something of its original meaning, while the former has been fossilized into
the-word-for-the-present-mode-of-government. Ipso facto, then, *gotong-royong* is both desirable and in practice.

A similar process is at work in the transformation of words like
démokrasi and *sosialisme*. We fall into nominalism when we identify
socialism and democracy as things that Are—they are only what we
make them. If we were to imagine the adventures of the Indonesian
idea of *musyawarah* (consultation?) or the Javanese idea of gotong-
rotong, once taken over by the American educational establishment
and inculcated into the younger generation of Americans, we can
come to a more serious understanding of the whole process whereby
Western concepts of politics are being absorbed and transformed
within Indonesian-Javanese mental structures. In any such cross-cultural transfer, the inevitable thrust is to appropriate the foreign concept and try to anchor it provisionally to traditional ways of thinking
and modes of behavior. Depending on the conceptions of the elite and
its determination, either the imported ideas and modalities or the
traditional ones assume general ascendancy: In most large and non-
Communist societies it is almost inevitable that, at least in the short
run, the traditional modalities tend to prevail.

4. *Javanese images of politics.* It has frequently been argued that the
Javanese sense of history is cyclical and not linear; my own feeling is
that in general this is true. At the very least, where we tend to look for
parallels, many Javanese look for reiterations or reflections. The subject is a complicated one, which cannot be dealt with satisfactorily in
this essay; nevertheless it is worth considering, for example, what is
the fate of the idea of revolution within a cyclical intuition of history.
Does it not really end up in former Foreign minister Dr. Subandrio's
curious formula, "Revolution is continuity"?[10] In the classical cycles
of Javanese historiography, the golden age of the distant past gradually
disintegrated into successively lower and more miserable eras, culminating in the era of disaster, the Kaliyuga or Jaman Edan (Age of
Madness) in which all values are transvalued, all social institutions
are turned upside down, and society breaks apart. But the wheel of

---

[10]As cited in Lance Castles, "Notes on the Islamic School at Gontor," *Indonesia* 1 (April
1966); 30–45, at 33.

time continues to revolve, and out of the darkness of the Jaman Edan a new Golden Age begins again under a new Ratu Adil (Just King). Here is "revolution is continuity" with a vengeance! The metaphors of cycle and revolution come together without too great a shock within this perspective. Sukarno's Sosialisme à la Indonesia is much closer in every way to the Jaman Mas (Golden Age) than it is to Marx's classless society. It is above all a *restoration*: the old order reemerging in technical, modern dress; the Golden Age at a much higher level of average per capita income, but with the older verities and structures scarcely altered.

The Javanese image of the components of Javanese society is another case in point. The dominant division is undoubtedly felt to be between the *aliran* (cultural-religious communities), not between classes or even *political* persuasions. The aliran are basically discontinuous mental universes and ways of life, which cross class lines and cannot be simply subsumed under the rubric "ideology." They lie under the political parties but are not of them. The Muslim parties NU, PSII, and Perti can all be seen as part of the Islamic aliran, for example, but that aliran includes quite nonpolitical peasants, teachers, and traders. There is (still) a Communist sub-aliran and a priyayi-led nationalist sub-aliran (both within the larger abangan aliran). The division of society by aliran is a peculiarly Javanese conception, which nonetheless is increasingly imposed upon Indonesia's own view of her politics. Yet these aliran are (despite the present brutal massacres perpetrated against the Communists) "givens" in the Javanese political landscape. There is no real expectation that they are anything but permanent aspects of society, sometimes up, sometimes down.

Finally there is the image of the mask and the puppet, to which we have alluded at intervals throughout this discussion. The vocabulary of Indonesian political language has increasingly been dominated by words that explicitly or implicitly evoke these images: *dhalang, mendalangi, wayangnya, lakon, gara-gara, prang tanding, jejer,* Bratayuda, Durna, are all political words drawn from the universe of the shadow play.[11] *Kedok* (mask), as used in phrases like *terbuka kedoknya* (he was unmasked) and *dengan kedok* (under the mask of), refer to the images of the mask, both in the *topèng* mask-dance and in the

---

[11]Puppet-master; manipulate like a puppet; his or their puppet; puppet play or story; turmoil in the cosmos (in wayang), hence political crisis; duel (in wayang), hence rivalrous conflict; opening scene (in wayang), hence opening act in a political drama; the final war between brothers in the Mahabharata, hence any bloody showdown; the cunning teacher and advisor of the Kurawa brothers, hence a cunning political intellectual (especially Dr. Subandrio).

dualistic structures of Javanese social relationships. All are terms that have a special resonance for the Javanese, indeed, the words themselves are almost all Javanese in origin. So deeply imbedded are these images in the Javanese mind that conceptions of the "game of politics" are invariably colored by them. It is very hard for Javanese, and increasingly for all metropolitan Indonesians, to believe in any form of political spontaneity—in the accidental, or the fortuitous. Something is always going on "behind the screen," where unseen dhalang are at work. The public "appearance" of the great is always regarded, less with cynicism, than with the faith that to some extent at least it is a mask. The obsession with intrigue, with the *sandiwara* (stage play) of politics, even with the aesthetic side of political behavior (the art of playing politics) are characteristic of a view of politics in which *virtù* in sudden transformations and role reversals is an accepted political value. Politics as elaborate and magnificent drama, rather than as a process for the attainment of specific ends and the satisfaction of concrete interests—this is a viewpoint that at least in its symbolism derives from the central role of traditional drama (wayang) in the Javanese experience.[12]

But here we can also see that Indonesian (and perhaps modernity) is having its revenge. For although the image of the mask is as powerful as ever, its ambiguity appears to be declining, as a result of the buffeting that traditional conceptions of opposites—as complementarities and as expressions of an underlying unity—are receiving in contemporary Indonesian conditions. There is a growing uncertainty about the relationship between the seen and the unseen, the real and the Real. The idea of the mask thus increasingly becomes the idea of a disguise for a hidden purpose, worn to deceive or to conceal a truth. The growing popularity of words to describe hypocrisy—*munafik, gadungan, sok, palsu, bermukadua*—is thus significant. All these words imply betrayal of a single Real reality. The language and imagery of Javanese tradition here survive, but within an Indonesian-Western modality that has largely stripped it of its metaphysical richness.

To conclude, then, it seems that the languages of Indonesian politics are approaching a fusing point, which will be all the more rapidly attained when the old Dutch-speaking elite dies out. The radical gaps between Javanese and its traditions and revolutionary Indonesian and

---

[12]For further discussion of the pictures of politics developed through a wayang education, see my *Mythology and the Tolerance of the Javanese,* Cornell Modern Indonesia Project Monograph Series (Ithaca, N.Y.: Cornell University, 1965).

its aspirations seems destined to disappear, by assimilation and the changing character of Indonesian experience. The structural Javanization of Indonesian and the imposition of Javanese modalities does not alter the fact that the national language remains Indonesian, and that the aspirations contained in the Indonesian project are inerasable within Indonesian society. The whole process is obscure, complex, and immensely significant—for it symbolizes and expresses the conquest of modernity via a new language that at the same time is becoming anchored in traditional conceptions of the world.

CHAPTER *5*

Cartoons and Monuments: The Evolution of Political Communication under the New Order

With the appearance in 1970 of *Indonesian Political Thinking,* students of Indonesian society and politics were for the first time presented with a wide-ranging collection of writings and speeches by important Indonesian politicians and intellectuals in the post-1945 period.[1] The timing of its publication was not fortuitous: It clearly reflected a growing scholarly interest in Indonesian ideology and political discourse.[2] Work by Dahm, Legge, Mrázek, Mortimer, and

First published in 1973 as "Notes on Contemporary Political Communication in Indonesia," *Indonesia* 16 (October 1973); updated and reprinted 1978, in Karl D. Jackson and Lucian W. Pye, ed., *Political Power and Communications in Indonesia* (Berkeley: University of California Press, 1978), pp. 282–31. Reprinted with permission.

[1]Herbert Feith and Lance Castles, ed., *Indonesian Political Thinking, 1945–1965* (Ithaca, N.Y.: Cornell University Press, 1970). For a useful critique, see Alfian, "'Indonesian Political Thinking': A Review," *Indonesia* 11 (April 1971):193–200.

[2]In addition, a number of translations of important individual texts by Indonesian political leaders have been published. These include: Sutan Sjahrir, *Out of Exile,* trans. Charles Wolf, Jr. (New York: John Day, 1949); Mohammad Hatta, *Past and Future,* Cornell Modern Indonesia Project Translation Series (Ithaca, N.Y.: Cornell University, 1960); Sukarno, *Marhaen and Proletarian,* trans. Claire Holt, Cornell Modern Indonesia Project Translation Series (Ithaca, N.Y.: Cornell University, 1960); Dipa Nusantara Aidit, *The Selected Works of D. N. Aidit,* 2 vols. (Washington, D.C.: U.S. Joint Publications Research Service, 1961); Abdul Haris Nasution, *Toward a People's Army* (Jakarta: Delegasi, 1964); Fundamentals of Guerrilla Warfare (New York: Praeger, 1965); Sutan Sjahrir, *Our Struggle,* trans. Benedict Anderson, Cornell Modern Indonesia Project Translation Series (Ithaca, N.Y.: Cornell University, 1968); Sukarno, *Nationalism, Islam, and Marxism,* trans. Karel Warouw and Peter Weldon, Cornell Modern Indonesia Project Translation Series (Ithaca, N.Y.: Cornell University, 1970); and Tahi Bonar Simatupang, *Report from Banaran,* trans. Benedict Anderson and Elizabeth Graves, Cornell Modern Indonesia Project Translation Series (Ithaca, N.Y.: Cornell University, 1972).

Weatherbee has been devoted to thoughtful, pioneering analysis of important segments of Indonesian political thought.[3] Their studies show not only how rich this field of enquiry is, but also how much more research still needs to be done.

At the same time it is useful to recognize that the materials used in this genre of research have a specialized character. In general, they take the form of more or less studied, quasi-literary, *printed* statements of positions—whether they reach the scholar as printed speeches, printed articles, or printed books. Almost invariably they are exegetic in character, addressed to particular audiences to combat alternative exegeses, arguments, and appeals. In such circumstances, it is understandable that in his introduction to *Indonesian Political Thinking* Herbert Feith tentatively characterized the overall body of Indonesian political thought as "diffusely moral," "optimistic," and marked by "a tendency to see society as undifferentiated."[4] Yet while these traits may well be characteristic of the political communications with which he was concerned, it could be argued that they are less "typically Indonesian" (or typically "Asian" or "Third World," as Feith proposed) than typical of a certain genre of utterance. In such a perspective these traits may seem no more surprising than moralism in sermons or irony in satire. One could also suggest that scholars have focused their attention so exclusively on one particular type of political communication that by unconscious synecdoche the part has been taken for the whole. Other important modes of political communication and expression have been neglected, which, if analyzed, would throw a rather different light on Indonesians' conceptions of their politics. Two such modes, which for convenience I call "direct speech" and "symbolic speech," are discussed below. Owing to the nature of the material at hand, only the second is analyzed at length.

Direct Speech

"Direct speech" in reality forms the overwhelming bulk of political communication in any society: gossip, rumors, discussions, argu-

[3]Bernhard Dahm, *Sukarno and the Struggle for Indonesian Independence* (Ithaca, N.Y.: Cornell University Press, 1969); John D. Legge, *Sukarno: A Political Biography* (New York: Praeger, 1972); Rudolf Mrázek, "Tan Malaka: A Political Personality's Structure of Experience," *Indonesia* 14 (October 1972):1–48; Rex Alfred Mortimer, *Indonesian Communism under Sukarno: Ideology and Politics, 1959–1965* (Ithaca, N.Y.: Cornell University Press, 1974); Donald Weatherbee, *Ideology in Indonesia: Sukarno's Indonesian Revolution*, Southeast Asia Studies Monograph Series no. 8 (New Haven: Yale University, 1966).

[4]Feith and Castles, *Indonesian Political Thinking*, p. 18.

ments, interrogations, intrigues. Yet despite its vast quantity, almost all such communication escapes the scholarly eye. What is observed is seldom reported directly, but rather is congealed into indirect speech: "rumors circulated in Jakarta that . . . ," "the interviewee told the author that at the party conference . . ." and so forth. In the process, the live, ephemeral communication is transmuted into an illustration or symbolic representation. Only rarely is it accorded the status of speech qua speech, capable *in itself* of speaking directly to Indonesian political concerns. Yet even the most marginal observation of or participation in Indonesian political life shows that such utterance is simply another mode of political communication—as it were, playing *ngoko* to the *krama* of *Indonesian Political Thinking*.[5] As might be expected from a ngoko mode, this type of speech is rarely "moralistic" or "optimistic"; nor does it present Indonesian society as an "undifferentiated whole."

In part, neglect of this type of communication has its roots in scholarly convention. Krama communication, organized and printed, appears more permanent, more replicable, and thus more credible, for if they can rarely hear the same argument or witness the same conference or intrigue, different scholars can at least read the same texts. Analysis based on unreplicable interviews or overheard chat seems tenuous and problematic. Unless checked by krama sources, therefore, ngoko messages are of dubious value. Most often, they are either aggregated and used to describe a political force or reality ("rumors circulated that . . . ") or introduced raw into the analysis as "quotations from field notes"—colorful illustrations of themes derived from the study of krama documents.

The problem is more than one of etiquette. Scholars, particularly if they are foreigners, are disadvantaged in gaining effective access to many types of ngoko communication. The spoken word is ephemeral, and this fact in itself imposes high linguistic and mnemonic demands on the observer-analyst. Beyond that, much ngoko speech cannot take place if the foreigner is looking on—he tends to kramanize things with his alien presence. Even in the intimacy of the private interview, the "subject" usually suspects that what he says will end up as printed exegesis, and thus confides in krama to his recording angel.

Yet some ngoko discourses clearly are available in more or less untransmuted form. In them aliens can observe, *at any time,* Indone-

[5]*Krama* and *ngoko* are respectively the "high" (polite, formal) and "low" (intimate, informal) levels of Javanese speech. For further discussion of krama and ngoko forms in relation to Indonesian political discourse, see chap. 4, above.

sians talking, not to the world or to the faithful, but to and against each other, sometimes even to themselves. Rare as they may be, by taking printed form these utterances have lost their ephemerality and come to assume documentary status. Some notable examples are the stenographic records of the discussions of the Sanyō-Kaigi (Council of Advisers), the Badan Penyelidik (Investigating Committee) and the Panitia Persiapan Kemerdékaan Indonesia (Committee for the Preparation of Indonesian Independence) in the Japanese period;[6] and the records of the DPR (Parliament) and Konstituante (Constituent Assembly) in the period after independence.[7] In all these texts ngoko and krama speech are mixed—the talk varying widely in spontaneity and informality—but the ngoko element is important and often even preponderant. (In most of these cases, Indonesians are in real dialogue with one another and foreigners are not present as sympathetic censors.) Most voluminous of all are the stenographic proceedings of the Extraordinary Military Tribunals which, since 1966, have judged and condemned some dozens of left-wing military officers and civilian politicians.[8] Although many of these documents have long been available, the tendency has been to mine them for content (historical fact) rather than for form and meaning (political thought).

Symbolic Speech

If direct speech often eludes the academic eye because of its fluid and ephemeral nature, symbolic speech escapes attention for rather different reasons. We understand that public monuments and rituals, cartoons, films, and advertisements represent a mode of political communication. But the grammar may be perplexing, the relation of form and content at once more salient and more ambiguous. More than printed speech, these visual condensations of significance find their meanings shift, deepen, invert, or drain away with time. Since their audiences are necessarily fleeting and anonymous, context is all

[6]A partial translation of one extended Sanyō-Kaigi discussion is contained in "The Problem of Rice," *Indonesia* 2 (October 1966): 77–123. A somewhat tampered-with version of the debates of the other two bodies is contained in Muhammad Yamin, ed., *Naskah persiapan Undang-Undang Dasar 1945* (Jakarta: Jajasan Prapantja, 1959–60), vol. 1.
[7]See *Ichtisar Parlemen; Risalah Perundingan Dewan Perwakilan Rakjat; Tentang Dasar Negara Republik Indonesia dalam Konstituante* (Jakarta?: n.p. n.d. [1958?]).
[8]It is sad that it should be such records of judicial interrogations, where the stakes, at least for the accused, are so high, and where all parties, for their own reasons, are deeply concerned to question, justify, and accuse, that bring the alien his keenest sense of ngoko exchange.

important, yet singularly problematic to the would-be interpreter. For example, on August 17, 1945, a new-made Red-White national flag was flown at Sukarno's side as he read the historic Proclamation of Indonesian Independence. Twenty-three years later, on August 17, 1968, the same flag was flown again, for the last time. In the meantime it had become a *pusaka* (magical heirloom). The red had faded to the color of dried blood, the white to ashen gray. On all sides fluttered hundreds of newly made flags, brilliant in the morning sun. In 1945—can one doubt it?—the flag had expressed an extraordinary hope and promise. In 1968, who could be sure what its flying meant, amidst the myriad replicas, either to those who flew it or to those who watched it fly?

In what follows, I will try to explore some of the meanings of different elements in the symbolic speech of the New Order era, both to illustrate, however tentatively, a method of interpretation and to suggest how such interpretation throws light on the "political thinking" of the period. In a number of instances I will be making explicit contrasts with the symbolic speech of the pre-1965 era, not only to highlight certain characteristic features of New Order symbolic speech, but also to show how the latter in many ways developed out of, or against, the former.

Cartoons

Of all the forms of visual political communications, cartoons are perhaps the most readily decipherable. Since they frequently make use of written words, they seem closest to conventional printed documents. As they are usually responses to particular historical events, they can, on one level at least, be mined for their "factual" content.[9] A book of Herblock cartoons, for example, tells the reader a great deal that is concrete and specific about American politics in various phases of the post–World War II era. But one would miss something, I think, if one were to study the cartoons from this perspective alone. Form may tell as much as content. To demonstrate this point, let us look at the work of two very successful Indonesian cartoonists and observe not only the targets of their attacks, but also the way in which the form of their cartoons communicates another type of meaning altogether.

The elder of the two cartoonists is Sibarani, who made his reputation as editorial cartoonist for the sensationalist left-wing daily *Bin-*

[9] A good example of this approach is Ernest F. Henderson, *Symbol and Satire in the French Revolution* (London: Putnam's Sons, 1912).

tang Timur in the late 1950s and early 1960s. The younger is Johnny Hidajat, perhaps the most popular of New Order cartoonists, working for *Pos Kota,* a sensationalist right-wing paper sponsored by the Jakarta municipal authorities, and for a variety of weeklies, particularly the very successful *Stop* (partly modeled on *Mad* magazine).[10] Before I attempt to analyze some of the two artists' typical cartoons, a brief explanation of each example may be useful.

Figure 1*a.* John Foster Dulles is flying a political kite—Sjafrudin Prawiranegara, the prime minister of the PRRI, the CIA-backed rebel government in Sumatra in 1958–59. But the kite is immobile, hopelessly entangled in the Rakyat (People) Tree.

Figure 1*b.* As the dollar sun shines, Foreign Capital greedily swallows up the produce of Indonesian soil, digests it, and excretes. Indonesian capitalists feed on the excrement, digest it, and excrete in turn. An unnamed figure, presumably representing the common people, feeds on what is left.

Figure 1*c.* The caption tells us that the sinister sneezing face labeled Anti-Communist is that of former vice-president Hatta. In the brain bubble the following ideas: Defend Dutch Capital! Smash the PKI! Overthrow the Sukarno regime! Join SEATO! Bring down the government! Irian *niet nodig!* (Dutch for "isn't necessary!"). Hatta's teeth are caricatures of leading PRRI figures. One can identify (top row): Major Somba, Des Alwi, Lieutenant Colonel Saleh Lahade, Colonel Zulkifli Lubis, Colonel Dahlan Djambek, and Runturambi; (bottom row): Lieutenant Colonel Achmad Husein (as a pig), Colonel Simbolon, Lieutenant Colonel Ventje Sumual, Sjafrudin Prawiranegara, Sumitro Djojohadikusumo (?), and Burhanuddin Harahap.

Figure 1*d.* Outside the concentration camp at Ladang Lawas (in West Sumatra, where the PRRI forces held many left-wing militants prisoner in 1958), the Masyumi leader, Mohammad Natsir (identified as Himmler/Natzir), goosesteps. Both his body and the Masyumi emblem (the Islamic crescent moon and star) have been turned into swastikas. His sword is labeled "Holy War."

Figure 1*e.* The Statue of Liberty, in the guise of President Eisenhower, brandishes the severed head of Jimmy Wilson, a young black executed in the late 1950s for stealing $1.95. The torch of freedom has become a bleeding head, the aura glitters with dollars, and the book has been replaced by a blood-stained sword.

[10]I have found no written studies of Sibarani or his work, but there is an informative article on Hidajat in *Tempo,* January 31, 1976. It is a curious fact that both men belong to Indonesia's small Protestant minority.

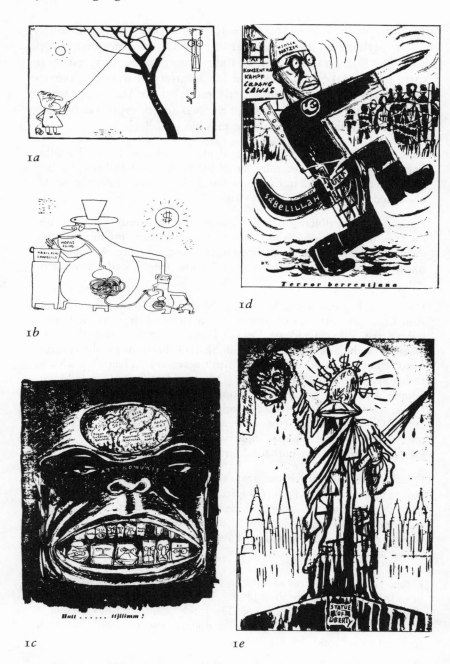

1a

1b

1c

1d

1e

Figure 1. Sibarani cartoons

1*f*

1*g*

Figure 1*f*. The PRRI cart is drawn by a donkey named Sjafrudin Prawiranegara. On it ride Allan Pope (the CIA operative and pilot shot down by central government forces near Ambon in May 1958), Tasrif (alleged mastermind of the attempted assassination of President Sukarno in November 1957) and the executioners of Situjuh and Ladang Lawas (two prison camps in West Sumatra).

Figure 1*g*. A memorial to the left-wing militants who died at the hands of the PRRI. The caption reads: "Arise!"

Figure 2*a*. Djon Domino sings *pantun* (folk quatrains) at an expensive restaurant to earn money. The lyrics read:

In Krawang market work the pickpockets—
They take the train, alight at Bekasi.
The people starve, they cannot pay their debts—
Big shots enrich themselves illegally!

With a sour expression, the company director turns and says: "That's enough! Here's a dime!" Djon accepts with a grin.

Figure 2. Johnny Hidajat cartoons

2d

2e

2f

Figure 2*b*. Djon and his friends are playing cards. Friend: "Arbitrary officials . . . ?" Djon: "We crush!" Friend: "Lazy officials . . . ?" Djon: "We dismiss!" Friend: "Corrupt officials . . . ?" Djon: "We get friendly with, they're well heeled!" Friend: "Shhh!"

Figure 2*c*. Djon calls on a prospective father-in-law. Father-in-law: "Djon! Are you serious about Ida?" Djon: "Of course I'm serious, *pak!* Only I need three years first to finish my studies!" Father-in-law: "In that case, give me a down payment of half-a-million, so I don't give her to someone else!"

Figure 2*d*. Djon and his friend watch a luxurious official limousine roar by. Djon: "Hey there, big shot, have a thought for the fate of the people! Don't just think of 'commissions' and young concubines!" Friend: "How can he possibly hear you, Djon?" Djon: "Think I'm crazy? If he could hear me, he'd clout me a good one! After all, I'm a relative of his!"

Figure 2*e*. Djon and his girl friend Ida are out riding on his motorbike. Ida: "Do you really love me, Djon?" Djon: "One hundred percent, Ida!" Ida: "Suppose I sold myself, Djon?" Djon: "Then I'd be your pimp, so long as I got a cut!"

Figure 2*f*. Djon is teaching some children about the meaning of Sanskritized words. Djon: "Bina Marga?" First boy: "Bina means erect, build; marga means road, so *bina marga* means roadbuilding." Djon: "Bina Ria?" Second boy: "Bina means erect, make; ria means happy, so *bina ria* means something that makes you happy!"[11] Djon: "Binatu?"[12] Third boy: "Bina means erect; 'tu means you-know-what, so *binatu* means you-know-what is erect!"

While satirical or comic art is very old in Indonesia, it would be a mistake not to recognize the novelty of the cartoon form. The cartoon, as we know it, is dependent on a sophisticated printing technology as well as on a partly monetarized economy creating a public able and willing to purchase this type of industrial commodity. But beyond that, the cartoon appears to correspond historically to the development of a certain type of consciousness—one that conceives of politics secularly as a separate, half-autonomous realm of human interaction, and one in which mass publics share. It seems plausible that the normally oppositionist aspect of the cartooning tradition derives less

[11]The reference is to the Bina Ria amusement park in Jakarta, much patronized by lovers and prostitutes.

[12]*Binatu* (launderer) is an ordinary Malay word, not a Sanskritized honorific—but it happens to begin with the syllables *bina,* so is exploited here for comic effect.

from the lampooning instinct than from the historical fact that mass publics had access to modern types of political communication long before they had access to power. Cartoons were a way of creating collective consciences by people without access to bureaucratic or other institutionalized forms of political muscle.[13] In Indonesia, the conditions outlined above did not come into being until the early part of the twentieth century, and therefore, while I have no data on the dates of the first Indonesian cartoons or comic strips, it would seem unlikely that they appeared much earlier than the 1930s.

In formal terms, then, Sibarani and Hidajat have a common ancestry in the great eighteenth-century British cartoonists James Gillray and Thomas Rowlandson and in the fertile caricaturists of the French Revolution, mediated through the tradition of Dutch cartooning and the later corpus of the American comic strip.[14] But while this tells us something about the adoption of the cartoon/comic strip *format,* it tells us little about the individual artists' personal style and message.

It would not be hard to find an indigenous ancestry for Sibarani's powerful and rough-hewn style. In the immediate past one thinks of the cartoon and poster art that developed so rapidly under official sponsorship during the Japanese occupation, and less officially in the subsequent national revolution.[15] Farther back in time, the sharply humorous and eerily monumental art of Sibarani's Batak ancestors

[13]This may account for the relative rarity and late appearance of cartoons as instruments of official political propaganda. Perhaps the best-known example of this minority group is the Soviet official humor magazine *Krokodil.* A nice collection of *Krokodil* cartoons is contained in Roger Swearingen, *What's So Funny, Comrade?* (New York: Praeger, 1961).

[14]For some interesting material on the history of cartooning, see Reinhold Reitberger and Wolfgang Fuchs, *Comics, Anatomy of a Mass Medium* (Boston: Little, Brown, 1971), especially at pp. 7, 11, 29, 174–75. Though the authors declare that "from political caricature to comic strip was but a short step," they point out that "comics have [only] existed for the last seventy-five years." They note, too, that historically the prime audience for comic strips has been the lower middle class. The first "indigenous" comic strips (i.e., not American imports) did not appear even in Europe until the 1920s, and only really flourished after World War II. The first strips to appear in Indonesian newspapers were also American imports.

[15]For some examples, see various issues of *Djawa Baroe;* Anonymous, *Marilah membela tanah air kita dengan darah daging kita!* (Jakarta: n.p., 1945), and Departemen Penerangan, *Lukisan Revolusi, 1945–1950* (Jakarta: n.p., n.d. [1954?]). Some distinctions need to be made here, though their interpretation will be left to later in this essay. Under the occupation, cartoons and posters were widely used, but they appeared exclusively under the aegis of the military authorities. The targets of the cartoons were typically outside society— the Dutch, the British, and the Americans. During the Revolution, posters and graffiti were the most common and most popular forms of visual speech, while cartoons became a relative rarity. Of forty newspapers and magazines I have checked from that period, only eight carried cartoons at all; even these cartoons appeared irregularly, and at rare intervals. Doubtless part of the explanation lies in the technical problems caused by the shortages and disorder of those years. But the fact that the great bulk of these cartoons were printed in papers published in Dutch-occupied Jakarta, not in towns held by the Republic, suggests that the full answer lies as much in the political-cultural as in the technical realm.

comes to mind.[16] For many Indonesians the Batak have a reputation for being *serem* (sinister, frightening) in physiognomy and character, and Sibarani's cartoons could well be described this way. But indigenous tradition in itself sheds little light on the historical meaning of an artist's work; to explore this more coherently we must turn to the specifics of his style.

Many of Sibarani's best cartoons depend for their emotional effect on a stark chiaroscuro. Executioners, embezzlers, imperialists, and spies appear as somber figures in a twilight landscape. Moral and pictorial darkness complement each other. The artist does not simply label Natsir or Tasrif a butcher, but reinforces the judgment with a simple element of design. At first glance Sibarani seems merely to be exploiting a standard cartooning technique for "blackening" the objects of his enmity. Yet by looking at the landscape of the cartoons, as well as the central figures, one can learn something more about the meaning of this lighting. Sibarani's readers lived and read his cartoons in a physical landscape drenched in sunlight, dust, and color. The actions he describes and condemns took place in daylight, more or less in public, often in the crowded rough-and-tumble of urban politics. Yet one sees none of this in his designs. This suggests that the chiaroscuro is less political expressionism used as a pillorying device than a means of political education. Sunlight in the world and darkness within the image is a contrast that shows Sibarani's readers something about the everyday opacity of social-political order and the reality of the forces that move it. Sibarani's chiaroscuro is thus a tool for political demystification.[17]

Another key element in Sibarani's style is its iconographic density, exemplified by the conscious layering of symbolic elements. In itself, this layering is a traditional aspect of a certain type of editorial cartooning.[18] But it is instructive to see how Sibarani employs the device,

[16]See, for example, the varied illustrations in Abraham Johannes de Lorm and Gerard Louwrens Tichelman, *Beeldende Kunst der Bataks* (Leiden: Brill, 1941); also Gerard Louwrens Tichelman, "Toenggal Panaloean, de Bataksche Tooverstaf," *Tijdschrift voor Indische taal-, land- en volkenkunde* 77 (1937):611–35; and D. W. N. de Boer, *Het Toba Bataksche huis* (Batavia: Kolff, 1920).

[17]One could argue that even the personal caricatures are deployed to the same ends. If Husein becomes a pig and Sjafrudin a donkey, it is less because their physiognomies lend themselves to "animalization" (note that in cartoon 1c only Husein is so transformed, and in cartoon 1f only Sjafrudin), than that the particular animals are chosen and used because of a *verbal* association with particular moral qualities. Put crudely, it is as if Sibarani were saying: "Sjafrudin may have a law degree, but he is an ass; Husein may be an army officer, but he is a dirty pig."

[18]The caricaturists of the French Revolution were particularly ingenious builders of elaborate cartoon emblems. See Henderson, *Symbol and Satire,* passim.

and for what purposes. Cartoon 1*d* is a good example of his method. Sibarani seizes on the fortuitous assonance of Natsir and Nazi as the basis for an intricately constructed icon.[19] The point made explicitly on Natsir's cap—Himmler-Natzir—is picked up in the swastikaed Masyumi crescent moon and star and the very shape of Natsir's goose-stepping body. The sign at the entrance to the Ladang Lawas camp identifies it with Nazism by the use of German rather than Indonesian words; and as a final emblematic detail, instead of the "correct" ending to Konzentrationslager (concentration camp), Sibarani ingeniously substitutes not *kamp,* but *kampf,* a deft reference to Hitler's *Mein Kampf.* In cartoon 1*e* the same method is employed to dismantle the formal iconography of the Statue of Liberty and reassemble it for educational purposes. We have already observed that the torch has become a severed head, the book a bloody sword, the aura a dollar glow, and the placid female face a caricature of Eisenhower. Again one finds Sibarani's characteristic use of language for iconographic point. The Indonesian words on the label attached to the head, "Jimmy Wilson, pentjuri \$1.95 [Jimmy Wilson, stealer of \$1.95]" stand outside the icon, acting as an explanatory footnote. But "Statue of Liberty" remains in English, inside the icon. American "liberty" is being pilloried, not *merdéka* or *kemerdékaan:* indeed, merdéka and liberty are implicitly contrasted by this device. In cartoon 1*g,* too, the significance of the death of left-wing militants is condensed onto the image of the Crucifixion, while the caption alludes to the Resurrection.

In all these instances, the dense, meticulous iconography serves the same purpose as the chiaroscuro: by distortion and designing artifice to reveal the artificial nature of perceived, received reality and thereby to demonstrate the really real. (The contrast is between the violently emblematic and "artificial" style of Sibarani and the naturalism of Hidajat. Where Hidajat says, "Look, my pictures are like life," Sib-

[19]I have found no satisfactory explanation of the Indonesian fascination with the Third Reich. In the early 1960s bookshops did a flourishing trade in cheap and lurid booklets on Nazi atrocities, espionage, and terror. One finds quite frequent references to Nazism, by no means always horrorstricken, in the writings of the political elite. A notable example is Soekarno, *Ilmu Pengetahuan Sekadar Alat Mentjapai Sesuatu* (Jakarta: Departemen Penerangan Republic Indonesia, Penerbitan Chusus no. 253, 1963). Cf. also Mangaradja Onggang Parlindungan, *Pongkinangolngolan Sinambela gelar Tuanku Rao; terror agama Islam mazhab Hambali di tanah Batak, 1816–1833* (Jakarta: Tandjung Pengharapan, 1964). One of the most effective instruments of the psychological warfare campaign waged against the left after the 1965 "coup" was the coining of the acronym Gestapu (from Gerakan Tiga Puluh Septémbér—September 30th Movement), which linked the coup conspirators with the cruelty of the Gestapo.

arani says, "Only my cartoons will show you what everyday appearances conceal.")

A third notable element in Sibarani's style is the use of foreign languages and symbols. In some cases the point is clear. For example, in cartoon 1*c*, Sibarani deliberately uses the hybrid *Irian niet nodig* rather than the Indonesian *Irian tidak perlu* or the Dutch *Nieuw-Guinea niet nodig* to pillory the mestizo Dutch-mindedness of ex-vice-president Hatta and his anti-Communist associates. In other cases, the meaning is more obscure. In cartoon 1*f*, for example, Sjafrudin is depicted as a donkey. To understand the point of the cartoon, one almost has to know the European stereotype of the donkey and the use in Dutch and English of *ezel* or *ass* to describe stupidity and obstinacy. For the animal itself is rarely found in Indonesia, and the Indonesian word for donkey, *keledai,* seems only recently, under Dutch influence, to have acquired such connotations, preponderantly in urban centers. How far is Sibarani aware of how European this cartoon's point has become? In cartoon 1*e*, he clearly uses the imagery of the Crucifixion in a quite unselfconscious manner: Christian symbols have become fully assimilated into the contemporary style and identity of Toba Batak like himself. On the other hand, in numerous cartoons not reproduced here, Sibarani deftly uses scenes from American Westerns playing in Jakarta movie houses to satirize Western imperialist intrigues and menaces. One gets the strong impression that this ambiguous jousting with foreign signs and symbols shows Sibarani precisely as a "nationalist"—a man who sees the nation as an *enterprise.* For such men, defining what is national can only be a complex project of juxtapositions and separations between the "foreign" and the "indigenous."[20]

This judgment is reinforced by the "national" quality of Sibarani's work. If the landscape of his cartoons is dark and threatening, it is nonetheless a national landscape, peopled by national figures. Murder is done in Ladang Lawas in rural West Sumatra, but Ladang Lawas appears as a place in the moral-political geography of Indonesia, not of Sumatra and not of the Alam Minangkabau. Eisenhower stands at the gates of both New York and Jakarta. Dulles's mishap is caused by the tree of the entire Indonesian people. Irian is "nodig." And names are named—men who, if they acted on provincial and local stages, nonetheless drew their significance, for Sibarani, from the parts they

[20]This was a central theme in the intellectual tradition of the prewar *pergerakan* (anti-colonial movement). For a sophisticated treatment, see Ruth Thomas McVey, "Taman Siswa and the Indonesian National Awakening," *Indonesia* 4 (October 1967): 128–49.

played in the national drama. They are named not simply because Sibarani wanted, and dared, to do so, but because names assign responsibility, reveal reality, and place cartoonist, reader, and target in a clear relationship in political space. This trait is in turn linked to the presence of the cartoonist himself. He never appears in his own cartoons; it is as if he stood beside or behind them, proffering them to his readers with index finger pointed. The significance of this posture only becomes clear, however, when contrasted with the role that Hidajat plays with respect to his cartoons.

If Hidajat's work seems so different from Sibarani's, it may be tempting to attribute this to differences in ancestry and genre. Hidajat's forms appear to derive from a comic-strip tradition going back at least as far as the Japanese occupation. The comic-strip genre has its own conventions, to which Hidajat strictly adheres: The strip explores situations and actions, the cartoon sums up a condition.[21] Rather than elaborating on space to explore meaning, the strip moves rapidly through time toward a denouement. The printed word is "in the picture" and carries the movement of the strip, only rarely performing an iconographic function. In part, then, one might account for the rudimentary drawing, the absence of landscape, and the symbolic poverty in terms of genre conventions—though this does not tell us why the conventions are adopted in the first place. Nor do the conventions help to explain Hidajat's popularity. Even the jokes themselves, good as they usually are, do not adequately account for the strip's success. The interpreter is inclined, therefore, to turn to style and, ultimately, context.

It may be useful to start with the central figure of Hidajat's cartoons—the long-nosed, canvas-capped, T-shirted Djon Domino. The long nose, a physiognomical rarity among Indonesians, suggests at once an iconographic allusion to Pétruk, the long-nosed clown (*punakawan*) of the wayang shadow-puppet theater (figure 3).[22] Why Pétruk should have been selected from the wide variety of such punakawan is a question that will be taken up later on. For the moment, what is important is that, qua punakawan, Pétruk has a dual role to play. In wayang of whatever sort, the punakawan appear both as comic characters *within the line* of the drama, embedded in its space and time, and as mouthpieces for satire and criticism directed straight at the audience, so to speak *at right angles* to the drama and

---

[21]There is probably an analogy here with the relationship between editorials and *pojok* (corner-columns) on the front pages of Indonesian newspapers.

[22]This connection is explicitly made in the *Tempo* article cited in n. 10, above.

Figure 3. Pétruk

outside its space and time.[23] So here one sees Pétruk playing his part *in the strips,* but there is also, as it were, a *dhalang* (puppeteer) behind the paper screen, or a player behind the mask. Djon Domino, as Pétruk here is termed, is readily deciphered: Djon = Johnny (Hidajat), Domino = mask, or better, half-mask.[24] Djon Domino is Hidajat behind his mask.

Yet there are further ambiguities, as befits the relationship between player and mask. Djon Domino appears in the strips dressed identically (it is an iconographically conventionalized *costume* one observes) as: singer in a restaurant, roadside layabout, student, motorcyclist, teacher, and relative of a high government official. These roles have no connection with each other—in "real life" they would be, in many cases, mutually exclusive. In an obvious way they are created in

[23]This applies to both of the most popular contemporary forms of wayang—*wayang wong* and *wayang kulit.* In the older wayang kulit shadow play, highly stylized and iconographically specialized leather puppets are deployed and vocally animated by a single puppeteer (*dhalang*) seated behind a lighted screen. For much of the audience the dhalang is invisible, yet his personal presence is manifested through all the puppets, above all through the sallies of the punakawan. In the newer wayang wong, a stage drama in which the older puppet roles are taken by human actors, the punakawan players wear heavily stylized facial makeup modeled on wayang kulit iconography. From behind these "masks" the players—very often the stars of the troupe—direct their sardonic anachronistic asides to the delighted audience.

[24]"Domino" may of course refer to the game of dominoes, very popular with street vendors and other poor people with a lot of time of their hands. In any case, the validity of my interpretation is marginal to the main argument developed here.

the service of particular jokes and satirical observations. But one notes that Djon Domino not only has no clear-cut social role or status, he has no friends or enemies, no family or identifiable associates, unlike many stock characters in American strips. Only his mask links Djon Domino's protean and elusive appearances. It becomes evident that the mast mediates its creator's dhalang consciousness.

This feature relates directly to another half-hidden element of order and continuity in the strips. Almost all of them reveal a symmetrical relationship between Djon Domino and the target of his creator's satire. Thus, in cartoon 2*a*, Djon is cadger—petty blackmailer to the embezzling director; in 2*b* he is would-be accomplice to a corrupt official; in 2*c* he is the loser in a cynical game of wits with a prospective father-in-law; in 2*d* he is "masih famili" with the opulent minister; in 2*e* he plays pimp to his girlfriend's prostitute; in 2*f* he pretends shock while egging on the sexually precocious and knowing children. In effect, in almost every strip, Djon appears as a less successful version of the target pilloried, as an accomplice, almost as a hanger-on. The key phrase is *masih famili*—which implies a kin relationship, but also a subordinate or dependent form of that relationship. This status in turn is connected to both the traditional and contemporary meanings of the Pétruk-Djon Domino figure.

The punakawan in the wayang drama are servants, followers, and dependents; they follow where their *satria* (knightly) or other masters lead them. They are closely intimate with their masters (as it were "masih famili"), and yet permanently consigned to their subordination. Their jokes are often sly digs at their masters' pretensions, but these digs are without subversive intent: The nature of the wayang world—a world of masters and servants—is not called into question. As we have seen, however, the punakawan also play a direct role vis-à-vis the audience. In traditional milieux, it is precisely subordinate elements among the audience to whom they appeal and who appreciate them most: servants, children, women. Indeed, responding to the jokes at all involves, for any member of the audience, an identification, if only temporary, with the subordinate and dominated. Thus, in the performance of wayang, a complex net of intimacies, dependencies, and solidarities is created. And it is the punakawan's iconography that links them all.

Hidajat's domino serves largely the same function. Yet there is one key difference from the wayang world: In even modern forms of the ancient drama, subordination is not complicity. The satria may be laughed at—at the appropriate time—but his moral universe is separate, autonomous, and recognized by punakawan and audiences as such.[25] The satria is a different order of man, not just a man of higher power and status. The punakawan are not and cannot be satria. When they on occasion try, the result is chaos. The best-known play (*lakon*) on this theme is the *Pétruk Dadi Ratu* (Petruk Becomes King), a wild farce in which Pétruk "masks" himself as a king, holds temporary sway, causes tremendous comic disorder, and is finally "unmasked" (resumes his mask)—at which point the drama closes in renewed serenity and order. But in modern times the words *Pétruk Dadi Ratu* have become a proverbial commonplace to describe real social and political conditions of disorder, corruption, and black farce.[26] One might be inclined to view Hidajat's strips as a variation on this theme: Each authority figure that appears could be seen as a Pétruk playing a role that is not in him. But a closer look at the universe of the cartoons suggests that their theme may rather be Ratu Dadi Pétruk, an idea inconceivable in the traditional world. Moral statuses are indistinct, everyone is a clown, and subordinate and master are linked not in complementarity but complicity. Pétruk is not unmasked in each denouement; rather, it is the king.

Another stylistic element in Hidajat's strips that relates both to the Javanese past and the Indonesian present is the use of obscenity. Again, the contrast with Sibarani is instructive. Many of Hidajat's cartoons are sexually explicit in a manner inconceivable a few years earlier. In part this novelty reflects the fact that in contemporary Jakarta sex and sexual jokes are much more publicly acceptable than hitherto. The nightclub and the massage parlor are well-established institutions of metropolitan life. In Sukarno's day, the one arena where sex and sexual jokes were publicly permissible was in the popular traditional theater, whether wayang, *ludruk,* or *kethoprak.* In wayang, at least, they were above all the province of the punakawan.[27] It is therefore not surprising, if we accept Djon Domino as Pétruk, to find Hidajat's strips a natural outlet for such jokes. But the style of the

[25]See the analysis of autonomous "status" moralities in the Javanese tradition contained in my *Mythology and the Tolerance of the Javanese,* Cornell Modern Indonesia Project Monograph Series (Ithaca, N.Y.: Cornell University, 1965).

[26]There are comparable *lakon* about other punakawan becoming kings—all in the same vein. But none has the popularity of Pétruk's temporary elevation. One suspects that the answer to the question of why Hidajat picked Pétruk as the model for Djon Domino lies precisely in his peculiar proverbial association with disorder and reversal.

[27]To the digest of some traditionalists this has been slowly changing in the commercial wayang wong (where human actors rather than puppets play the parts). One finds satria-class women, such as Banowati and Srikandhi, occasionally engaging in sexual banter and risqué jokes.

jokes and the context in which they are made suggests that they have a new meaning.

One of the odd yet logical aspects of sexuality in wayang is its rigid social stratification. Though sexual gossip in traditionalist areas of Java focuses continually on cross-status sex (masters sleeping with servants, aristocrats with prostitutes, officials with actors), on-stage sexual relations are confined within status groups—or at least the servant (punakawan)—master (satria) separation is rigidly maintained. Aristocrats mate with aristocrats, servants with servants. Demons and giants are often shown lusting after aristocratic women, to the audience's great amusement, but with a few very special exceptions, they never succeed in getting them. This *sexual invulnerability* is an important element in the prestige of the satria group, both in itself and because in some respects it is a sign of self-control and thus of power.[28] In Hidajat's strips, by contrast, no one is "invulnerable." In 2c, sex is a matter of commercial bargaining between Djon and his prospective father-in-law; in 2d Djon and Ida are both lovers and pimp and whore in the making; in 2f teacher Djon eggs on his pupils to answer questions with sexual repartee. It seems clear that sex is being used here not to make separations, or to show the complementarity of opposites, but to reveal vulnerabilities and complicities. Lovers, teachers, and fathers-in-law are "just like everyone else." Gossip has become form.

Sex as such is largely absent from Sibarani's cartoons, but he uses obscenity for his own very different purposes. Cartoon 1b is a good example. It has none of Sibarani's typical chiaroscuro, perhaps because the artist is here dealing not with the nature of particular men or specific events, but rather with a basic social condition. The plain penlines have almost the character of a diagram or equation rather than an emblem or icon. The second half of the cartoon's theme is well described by *New York Times* correspondent James Sterba:

The people in the kampong . . . along the canal . . . make their living by picking through the trash bins of the wealthy residents of Menteng, Jakarta's prosperous residential section, which begins on the other side of the railroad tracks. Everything of value is taken from the bins, mostly at night or in the early morning hours, just after the trash is thrown away by maids and houseboys. The salvage is carted in baskets back to the canal for sorting and sale. Most of the dirt-floor shacks are made of cardboard picked from trash. Five soft-drink or beer cans are worth a

[28]For further comment on the relationship between Javanese views of power and sexuality, see chap. 1, above, at pp. 29, 32, 40–41.

penny. Broken glass and broken dishes bring a cent a kilogram . . . as do old bones. Assorted broken plastic sells for four cents a kilogram. Unbroken bottles, all reusable, can bring from half a cent to a nickel, depending on the size and color; clear white glass is worth more than green or brown. A quart beer bottle, a small treasure, is worth a nickel. An average trash picker makes about 100 Rupiahs, or 25 cents a day.[29]

The first half depicts a symmetrical relationship between powerful foreign capitalists (wealthy foreigners in general) and a dependent, parasitic Indonesian urban middle class. The metaphor of coprophagy is used to bring out the humiliation Sibarani saw in the political and economic relationships prevailing in Indonesia at the time. Obscenity is a way of talking about domination and subordination. Thus, whereas Hidajat uses sexual imagery to describe intimacy and complicity, Sibarani employs excrement to depict alienation and degradation. (Only the foreign capitalists "eat no shit.")

Lastly, the question of locale. There is no landscape in Hidajat's pictures. The empty white space recalls the cotton *kelir* (screen) against which the wayang plays are performed. Just as the kelir encloses and delimits a world, that of wayang, so Hidajat's strips define a particular milieu, that of Jakarta in the early 1970s. This is not Old Jakarta-Batavia, the colonial city whose population was largely composed of pious Moslem *orang Betawi* (Batavians), but the new city that grew up after independence, dominated by migrants from all over Indonesia, and particularly from the Javanese hinterland. Language and costume make this clear. The speech in Hidajat's balloons is bahasa Jakarta, laced with the Javanisms that the flood of migrants brought to the old metropolitan argot. Djon Domino's prospective father-in-law, with his *surjan* (*lurik* jacket), *jarik* (wraparound skirt) and particularly his "egg"-tailed *blangkon* (headcloth) is unmistakably from Yogyakarta, but he speaks in the same bahasa Jakarta as Djon himself. This fact points up one of the most interesting aspects of Hidajat's strips—their linguistic homogeneity. Whereas Sibarani uses different languages quite self-consciously to build his iconography and to talk in different ways about the national project, Hidajat is consistently monoglot—foreign words almost never appear and all parties use the same "level" of language, the ngoko of bahasa Jakarta. Why this should be so is not altogether clear. It could be argued that Hidajat, a younger man than Sibarani, grew to maturity within what Hildred Geertz has called the "metropolitan superculture of Indo-

[29]*New York Times*, March 20, 1973.

nesia";[30] and that accordingly language is simply less problematic and political a matter than it was for Sibarani.[31] Or, in different words, that nationalness for Hidajat is no longer a self-conscious project but a received reality. While this may well be true, it also seems plausible to see the use of bahasa Jakarta in the strips as analogous to the use of sex. Both are devices for talking about the contemporary relationship between ruler and ruled (or at least a certain segment of the ruled). Just as no one is sexually invulnerable, so no one is linguistically impregnable. Like sexual innuendo, resolute use of the vulgar and familiar bahasa Jakarta points to an acknowledgment of power combined with a refusal of any moral status. This stance in turn is tied to something to which I shall return at the end of this essay—why it is that, though Hidajat's Jakarta is being deluged with foreign influences (far more than that of Sibarani) and foreigners are in constant contact with Djon Domino's world of prostitutes, cabdrivers, hawkers, students, and so forth, they are absolutely excluded from the cartoons.

Monuments

In the days of Sukarno's ascendancy under Guided Democracy, Indonesia saw a great deal of monumental construction. Visitors to Jakarta since the early 1960s would find it difficult to overlook the National Monument, the Gelora Stadium, the Istiqlal Mosque, and other, more utilitarian structures that have come to dominate the skyline in the city's center. It would be an error, however, to imagine that monument building was a peculiarity of the Sukarno years. As we shall see, the New Order has in some ways been even more monument minded, though the type and style of the monuments have changed and their locations are more widely dispersed. While the political intent of Sukarno's constructions has often been noted by journalists

[30]See Hildred Geertz, "Indonesian Cultures and Communities," in Ruth Thomas McVey, ed., rev. ed., *Indonesia* (New Haven: HRAF Press, 1967), pp. 24–96, at 35–37: "The Indonesian metropolitan superculture is still in the process of formation, and is at most only two or three generations old. . . . It is in the areas of political ideology, artistic styles, and material culture that the content of the metropolitan superculture has been most elaborated. The foremost characteristic of the superculture is the colloquial everyday use of the Indonesian language. . . . The prime external symbols of adherence to the superculture are the acquisition of higher education, facility with foreign languages, travel experience abroad, and Western luxury goods such as automobiles. . . . It is the intellectual and political elite and the wealthy of the great cities who are bearers of the full metropolitan superculture."

[31]For a different type of analysis of the cultural linguistic movement to which Hildred Geertz is referring, see chap. 4, above, at pp. 125–26, 132–40.

and scholars, analysis has rarely gone further than formulations of the type: "X was a prestige project, designed to impress Indonesians and foreigners with Sukarno's domestic and international political successes," or "Y" was essentially a "monument symbolizing Indonesia's new-found self-confidence" (or lack of confidence). In effect, the monuments were treated as manipulative devices or as psychological symptoms: Either way, the approach was purely diagnostic. Few observers have recognized that monuments are a type of speech, or tried to discern concretely what is being said, why form and content are specifically what they are.

It may be useful to begin a discussion of monumental styles by drawing a schematic contrast between the periods of Guided Democracy and the New Order—in part because the politics of the two periods were very different, but also because certain themes quite apparent in New Order building were there in embryo under the previous regime, and these themes have something to do with the longer-term transformation of "Indonesian political thinking." In what follows I discuss above all nonutilitarian monuments, that is, those in which iconography clearly prevails over functionality.

It is a peculiarity of monuments of this type that, by and large, they face two ways in time. Normally they commemorate events or experiences in the past, but at the same time they are intended, in their all-weather durability, for posterity. Most are expected to outlive their constructors, and so partly take on the aspect of a bequest or testament. This means that monuments are really ways of mediating between particular types of pasts and futures.

Two of the best-known monuments of the Sukarno era stand in the center of Jakarta: the Liberation of West Irian Monument in Lapangan Bantèng and the National Monument in Médan Merdéka. The first consists of a rugged human figure, standing on top of two vertical concrete steles, his arms flung up to the sky, and broken chains at his feet. The style of the figure is realist, or better, Yogyakarta socialist realist.[32] The National Monument is conceived more abstractly: a tall stele, crowned with a golden "flame," implanted in a flat-topped base large enough to contain within it chambers for the exhibition of patriotic reliefs and tableaux as well as certain "national heirlooms." The style of the Irian Monument is both modern and, as it were, "individual." It does not obviously evoke traditional Indonesian monumental art, and the form itself has evidently been created for a

[32]For a good discussion of modern artistic schools in Indonesia, see Claire Holt, *Art in Indonesia, Continuities and Change* (Ithaca, N.Y.: Cornell University Press, 1967), chap. 9.

specific historical event. The statue symbolizes directly the liberation of the Irianese from Dutch colonial rule.[33] Innovation and uniqueness remind the observer of the final completion of a historic task—the reunification of Indonesia under Indonesian rule—launched more than half a century before. Paradoxically, therefore, novelty of form emphasizes the achievements of the past, but at the same time commemorates a project in which the constructor and his audience in different ways participated directly (and thus points back to the future they once shared). Even if the modern statuary is mediocre, it nonetheless is a *traditional* monument in the sense that it is part of the real movement of Indonesian history, not a gloss upon it.[34]

The National Monument is more ambiguous in character and seems to foreshadow the monuments of the New Order in some interesting respects. In terms of formal style the monument is mestizo: it borrows from the conventions of European patriotic obelisks, while at the same time evoking the *lingga-yoni* of ancient Javanese art.[35] The lingga-yoni motif was quite consciously chosen (Sukarno reportedly joked that the monument testified both to his own and to Indonesia's inexhaustible virility): it was to be national because it was traditional, not, as it were, traditional because it was national. The monument, in fact, commemorates no specific event or achievement, but is rather in the nature of a summary of or commentary on the Indonesian past. Thus, the implicit movement of the form lies in the opposite direction to that of the Irian Monument: conventional iconography appears to use the past to express Indonesia's triumphant modernity, but in fact it points backward in that it is no more than a gloss on that past. To put it another way, whereas the ancient Javanese built lingga-yoni monuments because they meant something (Kempers says they stood for "the Duality . . . which is dissolved into the Supreme Unity or Totality of all existence") *in themselves,* and were part of the ancient present and future, Sukarno built his to show that the present Indonesia is connected to the past. The National Monument is thus less part of

---

[33]It is thus analogous to the fine, melancholy statue of General Sudirman on Malioboro Boulevard in Yogyakarta, which commemorates the last heroic years of his life as guerrilla leader in the Revolution.

[34]In this respect it resembles the first national monument of the newborn Republic: the stele cum plaque erected in 1946 at Pegangsaan Timur 56, Jakarta, to commemorate the proclamation of independence there a year earlier (see *Ra'jat*, August 19–20, 1946 for a picture with a descriptive article). What is noticeable about both monuments is that their construction followed very closely in time the events or circumstances that they commemorated. The contrast with the monuments now to be discussed is striking.

[35]Compare, for example, August Johan Bernet Kempers, *Ancient Indonesian Art* (Amsterdam: van der Peet, 1959), p. 19 and plate 166; and Holt, *Art in Indonesia,* plate 18.

tradition than a way of claiming it. The lingga-yoni in Médan Merdéka means nothing in itself, but is a sign for "continuity."

The monuments of the New Order exhibit this pattern far more clearly. Oddly enough, the most celebrated of the New Order's monuments is one still unbuilt: the so-called Proyèk Miniatur Indonesia Indah (Beautiful Indonesia in Miniature Project), popularly known as "Mini," which is to be constructed by the Our Hope Foundation (Yayasan Harapan Kita), chaired by President Suharto's wife. Whether the initial inspiration for the project came from her March 1970 visit to Bangkok (where an analogous project, Timland, has been completed)[36] or from the vogue for beautification work by presidential wives, as described to the public in the fall of 1971 Mini was to consist of a fenced-in one hundred-hectare compound containing an eight-hectare artificial lake, in which little islands representing the archipelago would be placed. In addition, there would be twenty-six *adat* (traditional) houses from each of Indonesia's provinces (one hectare apiece), a one thousand-room tourist hotel, an imitation waterfall, a cable car, a revolving and an outdoor theater, and so forth.[37] The adat houses would contain appropriate handicrafts from the various regions.

For reasons that need not detain us here, Mini was unpopular from the start, prompting a wave of student protests in a number of cities and some strongly critical editorials in the metropolitan press.[38] The controversy, however, did have the effect of goading the project's sponsors into clarifying the purposes of their undertaking. Speaking to the Working Conference of Provincial Governors on December 1, 1971, Mrs. Suharto urged them to contribute financially to the project on the ground that it would serve to "project" their regional cultures onto the Jakarta stage for the international tourist. But she also went on to say: "If, in the olden days, our ancestors worked cooperatively together [*bergotong-royong*] to create the Borobudur, which now commands the attention of the whole world [it is not clear whether this reference was to the Borobudur's beauty or its disastrous state of disrepair], today we too can work cooperatively to build the Beautiful

[36] *Tempo*, June 5, 1971.

[37] *Tempo*, November 27, 1971.

[38] As early as May 1971 some of the people who had been evicted to make room for the project complained to the Lembaga Bantuan Hukum (Legal Aid Institute) that they were being compelled to sell their land to Harapan Kita at prices less than half their real market value, and that the land they were being given in compensation was of much lower quality. (For details see *Tempo*, May 20, 1971.) The student protests began on December 16, 1971, in Jakarta, spread to Bandung by December 23, and to Yogyakarta by December 28. (For details, see *Sinar Harapan*, December 16, 22, 28, 1971.)

Indonesia in Miniature Project."³⁹ In response to what she felt was intemperate criticism, the president's wife told reporters on December 15:

> Whatever happens, I won't retreat an inch! This project must go through! Its implementation won't retreat a single step! For this project is not a prestige project—some of its purposes are to be of service to the People. The timing of its construction is also just right—so long as I'm alive. For someone's conception cannot possibly be carried out by someone else, only by the conceiver herself—unless I am summoned by God in the meantime!"⁴⁰

The opposition continued, however, and the head of state was finally forced to take matters in hand. In the well-known "Pertamina" speech of January 6, 1972, he said: "Quite frankly, I'll deal with them! No matter who they are! Anyone who refuses to understand this warning, frankly I'll deal with them! If they go on making trouble, it's no problem for me! I'll use Supersemar!"⁴¹ The project, he went on, was intended to make Indonesia known to tourists and to raise national consciousness. As he put it, since there were so few remains of Majapahit and Sriwijaya, new things were needed to raise national consciousness and pride.

To get a fuller sense of the significance of Mini it may be useful to look at some other New Order monuments, noting for the moment only the way the president and his wife linked Mini to the glories of the ancient Indonesian past. The traveler returning to East Java in recent years will have been struck by the extraordinary proliferation of public monuments in that region, which, not wholly coincidentally, contains the surviving ruins of Majapahit. These constructions take a variety of shapes. One finds, for example, on the outskirts of Ponorogo, a large concrete replica of a major temple in the Panataran complex near Blitar.⁴² The main entranceways to the town of Tulung-

---

³⁹*Sinar Harapan*, December 1, 1971.

⁴⁰*Harian Kami*, December 16, 1971. It was in this context that Mrs. Suharto used the Javanese term *mumpung*, which has subsequently become something of a byword in Indonesian political parlance. *Mumpung* means, more or less, "so long as I have the opportunity." For more on mumpung, see below, at pp. 187–88.

⁴¹*Harian Kami*, January 7, 1972. Supersemar is an acronym for Surat Perintah Sebelas Maret (Order of March 11), the document signed by Sukarno on March 11, 1966, transferring all executive authority to the then general Suharto. The acronym is also a wayang rebus: super = super, Semar is the all-powerful senior punakawan and elder brother of Bathara Guru (Shiva).

⁴²For the original, see Kempers, *Ancient Indonesian Art*, plates 271, 274; and Holt, *Art in Indonesia*, plate 65.

Figure 4. Roadside village between Malang and Selecta

agung are flanked by yellow-painted guardian *raseksa,* reduced versions of the great giant-ogre statues that guard the gateway to Candhi Singhasari, and similar to the little giant-demons found at the entrance of the royal palaces of Central Java.[43] Across the main road leading into the mountain resort of Selecta a permanent archway has been constructed, consisting of two "East Java"-style *méru* linked over motorists' heads by a horizontal cat's cradle of metal trelliswork.[44] And in countless villages along the highways through the province the eye is caught by strange new portals at village entrances and in front of the doors of the more prosperous wayside houses: strange, because they consist of man-sized concrete numbers, painted red—1 and 9 to the left, 4 and 5 to the right (figure 4).

[43]Kempers, *Ancient Indonesian Art,* plate 239.

[44]Compare Holt, *Art in Indonesia,* plate 47, showing a Majapahit-period *méru* portal (at Trawulan). The emblem of East Java's Brawijaya Army Division consists of this type of méru with a star on top. (Most of the East Java construction has been done under its auspices.)

The cumulative effect of these innumerable constructions is impressive: They represent a sustained program of monument construction and distribution far surpassing the efforts of the Sukarno years, and possibly without precedent in Indonesian history since precolonial times. Yet, why these forms? one asks oneself. What is being said? One notes, first of all, that many of the monuments appear at first sight to be replicas of ancient ruins. But closer inspection shows that the ruins are at once copied and not copied. What is typically replicated is the "general shape" of the ruin, so that the passerby immediately understands the *reference*. ("Of course, the temple at Panataran!") At the same time, though funds were clearly not lacking for the program of construction and East Java has no lack of talented artisans, little attempt has been made to reproduce the gracefully executed reliefs and ornamentation of the ancient models. The workmanship seems clumsy and hurried. The replicas begin to look more like signposts than reproductions. And, in a way, they are.

Another interesting monument, in the same vein, is the Tegalrejo complex under construction outside Yogyakarta. The site is believed to have been that of Pangéran Diponegoro's *puri* (palace/quarters) during the Java War (1825–30), although all that survives seems to be a blasted mangosteen tree. Inaugurated by General Surono in August 1969 and financed by the Rumpun Diponegoro ("family" of the Diponegoro Army Division of Central Java), the monument consists of a large 150-by-60-meter fenced-in compound containing a roomy *pendhapa* (Javanese traditional audience hall) decorated with reliefs of Diponegoro's exploits, two *gamelan* from the Yogyakarta palace and some antique Jepara chairs; a museum; a library; an administrative office; and a mosque. The shape of the structures is traditional—"to stir people's memories of ancient days." A special inscription (*prasasti*) has been put up, which reads: "All the members of the Diponegoro Division Family, Inheritors of the Heroic Fighting Spirit of Pangéran Diponegoro, have built this Diponegoro Monument on the site of the Pangéran's former puri in order to venerate and record the Fighting Spirit of the Hero Pangéran Diponegoro for eternity."[45]

---

[45]For details, see *Tempo*, February 26, 1972. For all the self-conscious archaism of this inscription, the Rumpun Diponegoro is very much aware of the needs of the times. A guest house is to be built behind the *pendhapa* for tourists wishing to see performances or to meditate (*nyepi*). Plans are afoot for the later construction of a proper modern tourist hotel and a shopping plaza.

There is an interesting comparison to be made with a curious painting done in the mid-1950s by the artist Oesman Effendi, a painting that was part of a series commissioned for reproduction in Indonesian classrooms to give schoolchildren a picture of the progress of

Figure 5. Borobudur by Oesman Effendi (Photo: Claire Holt)

their history. The work shows the Borobudur "as it might once have looked," plastered gleaming white, undamaged, upright, symmetrical, and grand (figure 5). There are two odd things, however, about the picture. First, the immediate glory of the Borobudur, its incomparable reliefs, are not even blurredly represented. Second, *there are no people at the shrine,* though the painting is supposed to convey the actuality of the glorious Shailéndra age. All that one sees, then, is a brilliant, deserted shape: not a representation of the past, but a sign for it. That the weird character of this painting is not accidental is demonstrated by others in the series that were not painted by Oesman Effendi. The greatness of the seventeenth-century kingdom of Mataram, for example, is depicted in two works by Trisno Sumardjo and Zaini: one shows the deserted tomb of Sénapati in Kutha Gedhé, the other the equally deserted mausoleum of his grandson Sultan Agung at Imogiri. It is strange enough that glory should be represented by tombs; but these tombs are neither shown as they appear to tourists and pilgrims today nor depicted in any historically plausible manner. The simplicity, emptiness, and sheen show that what we have here is a sign. Perhaps it is not coincidental that all three of these "mortuary artists" of the 1950s ended as strong adherents of the New Order in the 1960s and 1970s.

One is reminded of the curious episode in which Prince Norodom Sihanouk had a sizable (and hideous) miniature replica of the great Bayon at Angkor constructed and put on display in the national sports stadium at Phnom Penh as part of the celebrations commemorating the fifteenth anniversary of Cambodia's independence, November 9, 1968. The replica was used for that particular part of the celebrations in which the Royal Khmer Socialist Youth "paid tribute to Samdech 'Father of Independence.' "[46] The Cambodian leader's construction is particularly apposite in this context, for the Bayon was constructed by Jayavarman VII to be the center of the city of Angkor, a city that was in its own way a Mini of the abode of the gods.[47] But Jayavarman, his sculptors, and his architects built their Mini from the mind's eye, creating a monument of awesome grandeur and beauty, as it were, "on the model" of an unseen heavenly city. Sihanouk's portable Bayon, then, was not only a mini of a Mini, but meant something quite different from its model; it was a claim to the national past, not a creative elaboration of it. As in the case of the Indonesian monuments we have been looking at, Bayon II is a gloss, produced by a changed consciousness; and in a secondary sense, like the Indonesian monuments, it is an advertisement for the legitimacy of the ruler: a legitimacy, however, conceived less in terms of legal-biological than of cultural genealogy.[48]

We can now return to the Proyèk Mini and interpret it as in many ways analogous to Bayon II, Tegalrejo, and the rest. Traditional Javanese, Batak, Minangkabau, or Toraja houses, like Jayavarman's masterpiece, drew their authentic power from their generation in contemporary and living cultures. All were, in a sense, built for the present and the future. Even when they are constructed today, in the landscapes that gave their forms birth, many continue to embody longstanding meanings. The general forms are firmly established, but there are always countless small, personal variations of ornament, texture, and proportion. For their inhabitants and their neighbors they are

---

[46]See *Kambuja* 45 (December 15, 1968). I am indebted to Dieter Bartels for this reference.

[47]On the royal Southeast Asian city as a planned microcosm of the divine macrocosm, see Robert Heine-Geldern, *Conceptions of State and Kingship in Southeast Asia*, Southeast Asia Program Data Paper no. 18 (Ithaca, N.Y.: Cornell University), especially pp. 3–4.

[48]On the Javanese way of using a special type of "cultural" genealogy as a sign of power, see chap. 1, above, pp. 38–41. In contrast to Western emphasis on genealogical descent as a legal concept, the Javanese stress is on "cultural" linkage. The contemporary variation on this tradition is that aside from claiming power on the basis of possession of, say, a *kris* that once belonged to Sultan Agung, one constructs a replica of the kris, as a "power-less" sign of power.

unproblematic and represent nothing beyond themselves. In other cases, however, these houses are becoming monuments, in the sense that they are no longer lived in, have become museums, or are mechanically reconstructed to advertise the essence of tradition. In Jakarta, Surabaya, Médan, and Makasar, new urban dwellings are being built that provide a clear stylistic link between the *rumah adat* (adat house) and Mini's "rumah adat." One may find, for example, a successful Minangkabau businessman erecting for himself not a real Minangkabau adat house but rather a "Minangkabau-style" house, identified as such by an adventitious agglomeration of Minangkabau decoration or by an abstracted motif (the typical winged roof, for example). These formal elements enable the owner to signal to his neighbors and passersby that here lives a successful Minangkabau: Minangkabau by the winged roof, successful by the Dutch colonial, Singapore modern, or otherwise up-to-date living space.[49] Motif in such cases has been wholly separated from function and serves only to communicate a message of Minangkabauity. In the completed Mini all this has gone one step further, since the houses are "pure adat" and *no one lives in them*. Warehouses of regional artifacts, they are in effect icons of ethnicity, and Mini as a whole an icon of "Indonesian-ness" generated by the formal juxtaposition of these ethnicities. Indeed, its significance is all the more salient to the extent that concrete and immediate life is drained from its architectural components. Nothing more poignant, in a way, than that this sign-for-Indonesia should be located in the living heart of the metropolis where Indonesia is so much in becoming; indeed, that living Indonesians should be required to make way for Indonesian-ness.

To sum up, then, it seems that a common element in many of the New Order's public monuments lies in a style of replication, designed to reveal essence and continuity rather than record existence and change. But to show that this idea need not express itself solely in archaism, one very different monument may perhaps usefully be mentioned. This is the Yani Museum, which has been established in memory of the former commander of the Indonesian army who was murdered during the October 1, 1965 affair. It can hardly be said that the museum is housed in General Yani's well-appointed home, for the

---

[49]Compare the discussion of Basque architectural motifs in Parisian suburban housing in Roland Barthes's elegant *Mythologies* (New York: Hill and Wang, 1972), pp. 124–25. The difference between Paris and Jakarta, however, seems to be that whereas Parisians may affect Basqueness without being in any way Basque, in Jakarta it is unlikely that any but Minangkabau would build "Minangkabau" houses or any but Batak "Batak."

museum really is the home, which has been turned into a monument by two contrary types of alterations. First, a few specific mementos have been lodged in it: the gun with which the Communist leader, D. N. Aidit, was executed lies in a glass cabinet above Yani's bed; the site where Yani fell has a plaque embedded in the marble flooring; and so forth. Second, almost anything that might have been peculiarly and personally Yani's has been removed. The walls of the house are lined with signed photographs of visiting dignitaries, gifts conferred on Yani on his trips abroad, tokens and insignia of various Indonesian military units, army uniforms, a few conventional Indisch landscapes, some trophies, and so forth. The house is Yani's house, and yet it already has the feeling of a "rumah adat." Yani's life has been completely drained away. One would guess nothing of his reputed charm and intelligence, his meteoric career, his conspicuous life-style, even his habits and beliefs. Though the events commemorated are less than a decade old, and the monument is in every way "untraditional" in form, one sees the link with the archaism of Tegalrejo: Both are *signs for tradition.* One could easily imagine the museum being decorated with a prasasti of its own: "All the members of the Family of the Indonesian army, Inheritors of the Heroic Fighting spirit of Achmad Yani, have built this Yani Museum on the site of Yani's former puri in order to venerate and record the fighting Spirit of the Hero General Yani for eternity."

Bequests and Inheritances: Questions of Tradition

Finally, we turn to the immediate historical interpretation of the style we have been trying to identify. On March 2, 1972, General Djamin Gintings announced to the public, after conferring with the president, that he had received from Suharto some guidelines on how "the spirit and soul of '45 [i.e. the Revolution of 1945–49] might be passed on to the younger generation."[50] A week later, General Jasin, deputy army chief of staff, revealed that the forthcoming Army Seminar would discuss the integration of the Army Younger Generation and the Ordinary (i.e., civilian) Younger Generation, to achieve harmony between them and to implant in both a love of country. The object of "drawing society closer to the Armed Forces" would thereby

[50]*Harian Kami*, March 3, 1972. Gintings was a prominent leader of the so-called Musyawarah Angkatan '45 (Consultative Council of the 1945 Generation), formed in the Guided Democracy period to bring together veterans of the Revolution of 1945.

be achieved.[51] Opening the seminar on March 13, President Suharto observed that while scientific and technological knowledge could be acquired from abroad, "the source of leadership, character and determination as a people building its future must continue to be drawn from the history of our own struggle and our own identity." The present grave danger was "indications of an estrangement of the younger generation precisely from the history of the national struggle and the national identity. . . . The consequence is that they tend to orient themselves towards an alien culture, not their own." If this process were not halted, in one generation their own culture and identity would be irretrievably lost. He warned the members of the 1945 generation to take cognizance of their own actions and style of life and see how far they themselves lived up to their own values. Otherwise, their example would only alienate the young still further.

> We need to arm ourselves with the philosophy of devoted service to state and nation taught by Mangkunegoro I in his *Tri Darma*. The first Darma is *rumongso handuwèni*—to feel that one has a share of something which is the property or interest, the property or interest of the state and nation. From this feeling there arises the second Darma— *wajib mèlu hangrukebi*—meaning to share responsibility for defending and sustaining this common property or interest. To carry out this first and second Darma, a third is needed, in other words, *mulat sariro hangrosowani*, meaning to have the courage constantly to examine ourselves to see how far we have really acted to defend the common property or interest.[52]

Other officers expressed themselves in less philosophical terms. The "army intellectual," General Sajidiman, remarked: "The problem is how to convince the younger generation of the truth of the values of '45 as the Generation of '45 is itself convinced." Only during the Revolution, fighting and suffering with the People, realizing that if one deviated from the Pancasila one was destroyed, did his generation truly understand the truth of these values. General Darjatmo observed that the values of Forty-five were "steadfastness of heart to struggle for the interests of the People, an unconquerable spirit, the basic principles contained in the Prologue to the 1945 Constitution and the

---

[51]*Harian Kami*, March 10, 1972. It was specified that the seminar would be attended by about five hundred people, including army chiefs, alumni of the Army Staff and Command College, some civilian intellectuals, but no *"pejuang diluar ABRI* [freedom-fighters outside the Indonesian Armed Forces]."

[52]*Ibid.*, March 14, 1972.

Pancasila. . . . All of these values infuse the New Order at the present time." Finally, General Sumitro spoke directly to the younger generation: "There is no good reason why the younger generation should not have full confidence in the older generation, for the older generation *has bequeathed to them its doctrines,* which are the products of its experience, although the younger generation will always have the right to test the truth of these doctrines in institutions of education."[53]

Old themes undoubtedly, at least at first sight. Suharto is not the first leader to quote Javanese adages, or Sumitro a pioneer in transforming values into *doktrin.* One recalls Sukarno appealing to Indonesians to "return to our Revolution," to go back to the "track of our Revolution, and "never abandon history." But there is also an obvious difference. Sukarno made his appeals to people who had been "in the Revolution," had once been on its "track" and had "made history." He spoke to the memories and conscience of a community that had *shared* a climactic historical experience, but that, as he saw it, had allowed itself to become divided, corrupted, and demoralized. Suharto and his generals, however, are more and more speaking to groups who do not share that experience, except in the most tangential way. The links are now less those of a shared political enterprise than those of kinship, in all its ambiguity. Hence a new language of "inheritance" and "bequest."

Kinship, however, is thought of and used in two different ways. In one sense, it is a metaphor for the overall relationship between generations in Indonesian history, and for what links the present to the Revolution.[54] Whatever conflicts may exist between old and young in

[53]Ibid., March 16, 1972. Italics added. Not all of the seminar participants seem to have shared Sumitro's self-satisfaction. Shortly afterward, General A. H. Nasution was quoted as saying that at the Bandung Commanders' Call (meeting of territorial commanders that immediately preceded the seminar) he had observed many generals whose bellies protruded above the tables at which they were sitting. "When I was Army Chief of Staff, this sort of thing never occurred" (*Indonesia Raya,* March 28, 1972). Nasution was chief of staff in 1950–52 and 1955–62.

[54]It has long been a tradition to periodize Indonesian political and cultural history by generation. There is a rough correspondence between the political sequence Angkatan '28 (the year of the celebrated Oath of Youth), Angkatan '45 (the year of the Proclamation of Independence), Angkatan '66 (the year of Sukarno's overthrow) and Pujangga Baru (writers of the 1930s), Angkatan' 45 (writers of the Japanese occupation and revolutionary years), Angkatan' 66 (writers of the postrevolutionary years). There are a number of interesting polemical pieces on this theme, particularly in the literary field (where divisions by generation are especially problematic). For some articles on the controversy surrounding the concept of the Generation of '66, for example, see: Hans Baguë Jassin, "Angkatan 66, Bangkitnja satu generasi," *Horison* 1 (Aug. 1966): 36–41; Satyagraha Hoerip, "Angkatan 66 dalam kesusasteraan kita," *Horison* 1 (Dec. 1966): 188–89; Aoh Karta Hamidjaja, "Daerah dan Angkatan 66," *Horison* 2 (Feb. 1967): 58–60; and Rachmat Djoko Pradopo, "Penggolongan angkatan dan Angkatan 66 dalam sastra," *Horison* 2 (June 1967): 165–68.

Indonesia, they are conflicts "within the family," as the concept of generation in itself implies. Young and old, rulers and opposition, are "masih famili," as Djon Domino would put it. In another sense, kinship has a more direct sociological significance. Only a very small urban, privileged minority of Indonesian youth can reasonably be regarded as so oriented to foreign culture as to be in danger of losing "its culture and identity." And this minority is largely composed of the extended families of Indonesia's contemporary power holders. In many ways, then, the generals are speaking to their own children within an all-Indonesian rhetoric.

For there is a real and painful paradox in the position of Indonesia's rulers. They wield vast power over the political life of the nation, but find the culture, morals, and values of their younger kinfolk increasingly out of their control.[55] There is a prevailing feeling that established values are rapidly disappearing in certain youth circles. This is less a matter of such *causes célèbres* as the Sum Kuning gang-rape case (which involved sons of the Yogyakarta elite and was therefore never properly cleared up) than of general style. Two scandalous episodes may serve to illustrate this concern. In Surabaya the 1972 New Year celebrations were the occasion for holding a contest to select a king and a queen of freaks (*orang ékséntrik*). The competition seems to have been fierce. All kinds of outré clothes were displayed; some youths simulated sexual intercourse with a group of young transvestites; and a certain Udjang went so far as to strip nude and exhibit himself before the crowd. The irony of the episode lay in the choice of the arena for the contest: Tambaksari Stadium, entitled Flaming Spirit of November 10, in memory of the tragic and heroic battle of the Surabayans against the British, which opened on November 10, 1945.[56] The second scandal occurred in May 1972 in Yogyakarta, traditionally a conservative and respectable center of Javanese culture, the revolutionary capital between 1946 and 1949 and President Suharto's place of provenance. The authorities had given permission for eight bands to perform on a local football field. When these bands finally wished to pack up and go home, the audi-

---

[55]People in Jakarta frequently comment on how few children of well-known pejuang have "*jadi orang* [made respectable careers for themselves]." They shake their heads at the number who have become bandleaders, fashion models, criminals, tourist agents, PR men, callgirls, and whatnot. The facts are usually attributed to parental spoiling or to the great opportunities for social mobility which independence has offered, such that "outsiders" have been able to reach the positions that these children would have inherited automatically in an earlier age. There is probably an element of truth in both suggestions.

[56]For details see *Tempo*, January 29, 1972.

ence protested violently. As the national weekly *Tempo* described the scene:

> Buttons were torn open. People pushed forward to the dais. One boy climbed the collapsible ladder by the stage, exposed his genitals and rubbed them against the metal. Another opened his underpants and caressed "himself" openly before the public. Another leapt onto the dais and began kissing the drummer who was wearing half-female costume. It was then that the police made their appearance on the stage. On the orders [of the police commander], the performance was then closed.[57]

What was scandalous here, of course, was the public display of sexuality by upper- or middle-class people, not their private sexual behavior (about which traditional Java has generally been tolerant).

Such events suggest to Indonesia's rulers that the future threatens to elude them, and so the past is summoned to their aid. Most of them are deeply aware of the far journey they have made in their lives from the rural townships of late colonial Java to the metropolitan pomp of the "cosmopolitan" Jakarta they now enjoy. Given this abrupt, almost fortuitous transition, it is not surprising that their present power at times feels adventitious. In part, this is the basis for that *mumpung* psychology to which I have previously referred.[58] (Another part, as can be seen from Mrs. Suharto's remarks, is middle-aged intimations of mortality.) But there is more to it than adventitiousness of power. Their past has also not prepared them morally for the lives that they now lead. Most of them grew up in the sphere of provincial Javanese society, and the norms and values of that society have left powerful residues at the core of their consciousness. For such provincials, tags drawn from the *Tri Darma* or from Mangkunegara IV's *Tripama* do represent the real and solid basis of Javanese tradition. When Suharto quotes Mangkunegara I, his words are not a gloss on tradition, like Mini, but a real expression of it. Furthermore, for most of the men and women of Suharto's political generation, the Revolution of 1945 *was* a

[57]Ibid., May 20, 1972.
[58]It is instructive to read a section of the defense speech of senior PKI leader Sudisman before the Extraordinary Military Tribunal on July 21, 1967: "To make us conscious of our limitations and to keep our feet on the ground, we Javanese use the phrase *odjo dumèh*—a phrase I find very hard to translate exactly into Indonesian. If one analyzes why this should be so, it is because people who *dumèh kuasa* or 'let power go to their heads' are usually politely warned with the words *odjo dumèh*." Sudisman, *Analysis of Responsibility*, trans. Benedict Anderson (Melbourne: The Works Cooperative, 1975), p. 14. *Dumèh* is very close to *mumpung*: thus, *dumèh kuasa* means "just because [I] happen to have the power"; and *odjo dumèh* is "don't, just because you happen to [have the power]."

profound moral experience and a creative act of fundamental value. The egalitarian solidarity to which General Sajidiman referred at the Army Seminar was not a rhetorical fiction, but was a basic element of the revolutionary ethos.[59] Yet that experience is now a quarter of a century in the past; General Sajidiman and his colleagues now live in opulence far away from the common people. At the same time, little in their postrevolutionary experience has allowed for the creation of a new moral stance that would permit them to deal with their present circumstances with inner tranquility. *Pembangunan* (development) has no more than instrumental implications, and derives whatever moral thrust it has from the revolutionary ethos of the past. Accordingly, the contrast between circumstances and ethos has led to the congealing of the values of 1945 into the Doktrin of the Values of 1945; Pancasila Democracy and Pancasila Economy, phrases that evoke the memory of Sukarno's historic 1945 speech proclaiming the moral basis of an independent Indonesian state, are doktrin too, icons attesting to the coherence of present and past, or the life of the past in the present, though they are experienced by many as their fundamental negation—military authoritarianism and an economy subjected to foreign capital.

Their children, however, have grown up in the sphere where their fathers' journeys ended. They are not provincials come to the metropolis, but natural denizens of the new urban centers. The lives they observe and lead themselves are not clearly linked to the ethos either of the Revolution or of *Tri Darma*. For them the moral tensions that underlie their parents' lives—Pancasila live vs. Pancasila Doktrin, wajib mèlu hangrukebi vs. mumpung—have little meaning. Their link to their parents' generation is less moral or political (they have their own city-bred ethos of competition, individualism, self-expression, and so forth) than one of kinship. They are, after all, masih famili. One begins to see part of the meaning of that multitude of scarlet numbers scattered across the East Java countryside. The numbers, in their own way, are like Tegalrejo, the National Monument, and even Mini— attenuated glosses on historical experience. By a flattening of time, it is almost as if 1945 were as remote as 1830. As the Diponegoro Family is "heir" to Diponegoro, so the younger generation family is to be "heir" to the Revolution. The numbers are signs for continuity with tradition.

The motifs outlined here are well delineated in a curious film that

[59]See my *Java in a Time of Revolution* (Ithaca, N.Y.: Cornell University Press, 1972), especially chaps. 2, 3, 7, 8, 15.

had its Jakarta première a few weeks after the Army Seminar closed. *Léwat Tengah Malam* (Past Midnight) is the story of a former *pejuang* (freedom fighter) of the revolutionary period, who, disgusted with the corruption and opportunism he sees around him in contemporary Jakarta, becomes a skilled professional burglar. Exploiting the entrée that his revolutionary experience gives him to the fashionable homes of the capital's new rich—he is, as Jakartans say, *binnen* ("in")—he robs their safes and jewelry boxes. Together with faithful comrades from the old days, he uses the loot to establish a productive factory in a poverty-stricken area of rural Java, treating the workers with paternal solicitude and care. Under his managerial alias he wins the loyalty and admiration of the local population by his unselfish efforts to involve them in genuine development. His downfall comes when he falls in love with a beautiful policewoman employed as an undercover agent by his elder brother, an incorruptible commissioner of the metropolitan police. The brothers finally confront one another. Each recognizes the sincerity of the other's motives, and the hero agrees to surrender and serve his legally ordained prison term, with the policewoman promising to wait for him.

What is most striking about the film is the counterpoint between its ethos and the movement of the plot. The moral leitmotiv is commitment to pejuang ideals, the ideals of 1945; but the plot *requires* the hero—who is frequently referred to early in the film as a mysterious *bandit intelèk* (intellectual [educated] bandit)—to pretend to be a member of the corrupt and wealthy ruling class by dressing, drinking, driving, and holidaying in a suitably ostentatious and luxurious manner. (If the hero pretends to be decadently corrupt in order to fool his victims, the policewoman also pretends to be a liberated woman of high fashion in order to fool the hero!) The hero's basic concern for the welfare of the people is thus consistently juxtaposed to his flashy clothes and sleek sports cars. Only his melancholy expression signifies his real values, and is thereby a genuine mask of the traditional sort. On the other hand, if the contemporary situation makes the product of the bandit's robberies a development project, the moral impulse is not so much a drive to achieve "accelerated modernization" as a continuation of the spirit of Forty-five. The characters in the bandit's group even ruminate on the Sajidiman theme of the pejuang's dependence on the People in the Revolution and the need to repay the moral debt thereby incurred. Beyond that, another typical "traditional" theme is sounded in a romantic flashback in which the hero recalls his village boyhood, splashing carefree in the ponds and running through the shimmering rice fields. It is no coincidence that this flashback occurs to him while he is on holiday in Bali, staying at a luxurious beach hotel with the undercover policewoman.

Finally, one notes the recurrence of the kinship motif. Burglar and police commissioner are, after all, brothers. The tie that links them is that of family. But the hero's success in his criminal profession depends on his close social ties with Jakarta's nouveaux riches. He can steal from them with impunity because he is invited to their parties. So to speak, he is masih famili.[60] Paradoxically, the link between kinship and 1945 is crime cum development. It is as if the film were saying: "Yes, indeed, there are many rich and ostentatious ex-pejuang in Jakarta, and yes, there is a lot of crime in high places, but don't be misled! The old revolutionary and traditional values are still there. Just look at the mask! Watch the development! In any case, be patient, wait and see how it all turns out!"

Conclusion

In a way, all the different visual political communications that we have been examining are related to the career and history of what can broadly be termed the "revolutionary generation." In Indonesia today, a major social and cultural turning point is approaching: the gradual passing of this generation. Scarcely a month goes by without the newspapers recording the death of yet another well-known pejuang. The proximate eclipse of this generation, in conjunction with the present absence of dramatic political conflict in Indonesia, makes one reflect on the vast changes that have taken place in the twenty-five years that this generation has dominated the scene. On the social level, one observes the articulation of a fully Indonesian class structure both in the countryside (with the abandonment of land reform and agrarian redistribution since 1965, landlordism and debt bondage have notably increased) and in the larger cities (where a weak but visibly prosperous indigenous middle class has emerged).[61] On the political

---

[60]Yet the hero has no children, though he must be close to middle age, and has little immediate prospect of having them. The issue of legacies therefore does not arise, perhaps not accidentally.

[61]Classes are in part defined over time by marriages. The consolidation of a ruling class is typically marked by endogamy. The society pages of the Indonesian press make interesting reading in this regard. "Family" power seems to function socially as economic and bureaucratic power do in the economic and political realms. For indications of increasing class differentiation and oppression in rural areas, especially since 1965, see, e.g., Mubyarto,

level, power has been concentrated and stabilized in the hands of a moderately unified military elite.[62] On the cultural level, a mestizo metropolitan culture has developed and spread, which is no longer adopted but grown up in. This is the reality of what the successors of the "revolutionary generation" will inherit. At the same time, as the 1972 Army Seminar shows, this is far from what the "revolutionary generation" sees (publicly, at any rate) as its bequests.

The evident discrepancy between such bequests and such inheritances, between history as conceived by legators and history as experienced by legatees, brings us back to the cartoonists with whom we started. Sibarani belonged (perhaps still belongs) to the "revolutionary generation." Partly because of his left-wing sympathies, partly because of the period in which he did his best-known work, there is no question in his cartoons of legacies and bequests. Though the drawings are often full of darkness and horror, paradoxically they have an optimistic base. Real conflict was taking place in Indonesian society, and the future was not foreclosed. The promise of 1945, in other words its continuity, was real, although it remained to be fulfilled. The Revolution was by no means "over." His cartoons were directly political, indeed educational, precisely for this reason. They showed intellectuals who were "really" bandits, not bandits who were "really" intellectuals. The spirit and values of Forty-five were things to be acted on, not encoded and bequeathed. If his cartoons' impulses came from the past, they pointed directly into the future. They were, to put it another way, quite traditional, in that they were submerged in history rather than glosses on it.

By the middle years of Guided Democracy things had begun to change, and after 1965 the direction of that change was finally determined for the "revolutionary generation." With Sukarno it was still a question of "returning to" the Revolution as a real political act and possibility. Under the New Order there is nothing to return to, and the "Spirit of '45" is less to be acted on than to be bequeathed. Monu-

---

"The Sugar Industry," *Bulletin of Indonesian Economic Studies* 5 (July 1969):37–59; Paul R. Duester, "Rural Consequences of Indonesian Inflation: A Case Study of the Jogjakarta Region" (Ph.D. thesis, University of Wisconsin, 1971); Richard William Franke, "The Javanese Kangen Family" (draft paper, 1971); Richard William Franke, "The Green Revolution in a Javanese Village" (Ph.D. thesis, Harvard University, 1972); David Harry Penny and Masri Singarimbun, "A Case Study of Rural Poverty," *Bulletin of Indonesian Economic Studies* 8 (March 1972):79–98; Roger Dee Montgomery, "Employment and Unemployment in Jogjakarta" (Ph.D. thesis, Cornell University, 1974).

[62]On this topic, see Ruth Thomas McVey, "The Post-Revolutionary Transformation of the Indonesian Army," pt. 1, *Indonesia* 11 (April 1971): 131–76; pt. 2, *Indonesia* 13 (April 1972): 147–82.

ments, films, and doktrin attest to this changing consciousness. *Léwat Tengah Malam* is a form for showing that whatever the present is, it is really the past. And the archaism of Mini, Tegalrejo, and the East Java monuments communicates the same message in different ways; essentially, nothing has changed: Diponegoro's spirit, the 1945 spirit, Majapahit's spirit are always with us. There is no need to return to them, because they are, by definition, here.

In Hidajat, we see the lineaments of the revolutionary generation's legatees. The white light of his cartoons reveals a fundamental pessimism under the comedy and farce. Nothing in his drawings suggests the possibility of change. The world it encloses is without real conflict, and thus without a force within it that could alter it at all. If older characters appear one would not guess that they are pejuang or even ex-pejuang. The generations are linked together in a homogeneous moral bond. Though there is no explicit conflict or argument between generations in his strips, this should not conceal the fact that "no argument" itself distills a fundamental argument. The Revolution, the national struggle, the spirit of Forty-five are not part of real experience or lived tradition, and so must now appear as gleaming, depopulated Borobudur at best, or riddling doktrin at worst.

This brings us to a question raised earlier: How is one to explain the absence of foreigners in Hidajat's cartoons, when Hidajat's Jakarta is so conspicuously filled with their dominating presence? The answer, I think, is that at bottom the foreigners make no difference. Including them in the world of the cartoons would not change its character, but merely extend it farther into space. Sibarani drew his Americans because their presence and actions were major contributing elements to the conflict he saw working itself out in his generation in his society. Dulles and Allan Pope were counterposed to the Rakyat; together they represented two fundamentally antagonistic political forces and moral universes. In Hidajat's work, Johnson, Nixon, Kissinger—or better, in keeping with his Jakarta style, local American diplomats and businessmen—can be counterposed to nothing: They would merely be a further ramification of an indefinitely extended "famili."[63] For there are no more kings, only a world of Pétruk. What Jakarta is like today

[63]Lest it be thought that this absence is simply a matter of discretion, given the present intimate relationship between Indonesia's rulers and the United States, it should be pointed out that even the enemies of the state—the Communists (domestic, Russian, Chinese, or whatever)—also never appear in the strips, whether in their own form or in the guise of saboteurs and spies. If the inhabitants of Hidajat's cartoons are aware of the Indonesian government's constant warnings of subversive threats to the world they inhabit, they give no sign of it.

is in reality what the world is like: The city is in its own way an authentic Mini. One discerns here a new perspective—pragmatism it has often been called, though it seems, in Hidajat's work, to be a more complex blend of irony and resignation. What one observes, however, is that with Hidajat, we are back in the flow of history. His work has, in its own way, all of Sibarani's immediacy, and in style and content is thereby just as traditional.

CHAPTER **6**

Sembah-Sumpah: The Politics of Language and Javanese Culture

What I sensed to be a longish object was being gently rapped upon my bowed, bared head. How insolent this creature I was forced to honor! For I had to welcome each soft blow with a respectful *sembah* [gesture of respect performed by placing the palms together in front of, and at right angles to, the face]. God damn it!

After five of these blows, he withdrew the object, which now hung down by the side of his chair: it was a riding-crop made from a bull's pizzle, the haft wrapped in fine, thin leather.

"You!" he addressed me in a soft, hoarse voice. "Your humble servant, My Honored Lord," said my mouth; and like a machine my hands moved up to make yet another sembah, while my heart swore [*sumpah*] for the umpteenth time.

Pramoedya Ananta Toer, *Bumi Manusia*
(Man's Earth), p. 109

I used to think of it as a black hole. Here was a literary tradition going back over a thousand years—as old as French and English literature, older than Russian. Here was a sophisticated corpus of writing produced by and for a few hundreds, or perhaps thousands, of men and women, over centuries in which 90 percent of a population numbering no more than two or three million was probably illiterate. Here was a vocabulary of untold richness: Pigeaud's

First published in 1984. Roger Long and Damaris Kirchhofer, ed., *Change and Continuity in Southeast Asia,* Center for Asian and Pacific Studies, Southeast Asia Paper no. 17 (Honolulu: University of Hawaii at Manoa, 1984), pp. 15–57. Reprinted with permission.

Javanese-Dutch dictionary contains more than 40,000 headings (Echols's Indonesian-English dictionary has a mere 12,000 or so, and even Poerwadarminta's Indonesian-Indonesian lexicon has only about 27,000).[1] And here was a language that in our own time flourishes in countless homes, offices, markets, and schools, in *wayang* performances, on the radio, in song, in ritual. Yet today, when the population has passed 60 million and the percentage of illiterates has surely fallen below 40 percent, why have such cultural descendants of Prapanca and Tantular, the two Jasadipuras and Ronggawarsita, as Pramoedya Ananta Toer, Sapardi Djoko Damono, Marco Kartodikromo, Rendra, Semaun, Goenawan Mohamad, and so many others *not* been writing in Javanese? Surely for most of them it has been the language of their childhood homes, youthful love affairs, close friendships, and marriages? Surely in the memories of most linger wayang stories and fragments of *tembang* (a type of Javanese song)? The old nationalist leader Dr. Soetomo had said, *kacang mangsa ninggal lanjaran*—"how could the bean leave the bean-pole?"[2] But if they had not left their bean-poles, these beans certainly did not seem to be twining their way straight up them. Into what black hole, then, had Javanese literature disappeared?[3] Why? And indeed, when? After all, Sundanese literature seemed to have survived. After all, *Buiten Het Gareel* (Out of Harness), one of the half-dozen best novels ever written by an Indonesian, was originally penned in Sundanese.[4]

The most obvious explanations for the black hole are political and economic. While I do not find them adequate in themselves, they are of sufficient interest for it to be worth discussing them briefly before turning to what I hope will be a useful alternative line of analysis.

The first kind of explanation emphasizes the nexus between the character and thrust of Dutch imperialism, the development of print-capitalism, and the availability of an indigenous, interinsular lingua franca (what some Dutchmen nastily called *brabbel-Maleisch*, gib-

[1] These are my own rough calculations.

[2] Radèn Soetomo, *Kenang-Kenangan* (Surabaya: n.p., 1934), p. 4.

[3] I do not want to be misunderstood. Up to the present a steady, if not voluminous, stream of Javanese-language poetry, short stories, novels, and other writings has continued to be produced. But how many people believe that these works are either of abiding quality or seriously engage the attention of Javanese society? One is George Quinn, who makes a vigorous defense of modern Javanese literature, and a bracing attack on the prejudices of most Javanologists, in "The Case of the Invisible Literature: Power, Scholarship, and Contemporary Javanese Writing," *Indonesia* 35 (April 1983):1–36. I find the attack more convincing than the defense.

[4] I concur with Teeuw, who wrote: "I would not hesitate to call Mrs. Soewarsih [Djojopoespito]'s novel . . . the best novel written by an Indonesian before the war." Andries Teeuw, *Modern Indonesian Literature* (The Hague: Nijhoff, 1967), p. 64.

berish Malay). The argument goes more or less as follows: In being
able not merely to hang on to their small eighteenth-century possessions in Southeast Asia but to expand them enormously in the period
from 1830 to 1910, the Dutch were extremely lucky, for by then
Holland had become a fourth-rate European power, on the order of
Portugal and Belgium.[5] Her luck (like that of Belgium and Portugal)
lay in her strategic importance to Britain, the superpower of the nineteenth century. To maintain its own military security, further its bal-
ance-of-power politique in northern Europe, and safeguard its domination of the Mediterranean, Britain had every interest in protecting
these small, weak states, which either faced it across the Channel and
controlled the riverine gateways to central Europe (the Rhine, the
Meuse, and the Scheldt) or commanded access to the Straits of Gibral-
tar. In East Asia, Holland was a useful subordinate ally against Britain's main rival, France. Such were the considerations that lay behind
the Anglo-Dutch Treaty of 1824, whereby London restored to The
Hague much of the Asian empire it had captured with such utter ease
during the Napoleonic Wars.[6] Nor did the British seriously attempt to
block the Dutch as the latter expanded their control over Sumatra,
Kalimantan, Sulawesi, and Indonesia Timur between 1830 and
1910.[7] Had Dutch power in the nineteenth century been confined to
Java, as it easily might have been, the language of a twentieth-century,

[5]In the age of steam Holland had neither an army nor a navy capable of taking on any
significant European rival—or Japan. In fact, she did not really become an industrialized
country until the twentieth century. The weakness of Dutch capitalism is sufficiently indicated by the fact that it was unable to break the royal business monopoly in the Indies,
represented by the Nederlandsche Handelmaatschappij, until the 1870s.

[6]"In 1860, Lord Wodehouse, then Under-Secretary at the Foreign Office—no doubt
influenced by recent French exploits in Vietnam—praised the treaty in 1824: 'It seems to me
in many respects very advantageous that the Dutch should possess this Archipelago. If it was
not in the hands of the Dutch, it would fall under the sway of some other maritime power,
presumably the French, unless we took it ourselves. The French might, if they possessed such
an eastern empire, be really dangerous to India and Australia, but the Dutch are and must
remain too weak to cause us any alarm.' The Dutch exclusive policy, he also noted, had been
relaxed. There were thus not merely no serious reasons for opposing, but real reasons for
accepting Dutch extension in the Archipelago." Nicholas Tarling, *A Concise History of
Southeast Asia* (New York: Praeger, 1966), p. 125.

[7]The basic nature of the Anglo-Dutch relationship is indicated by the facts that: (1) the
Dutch had to ask London for a release from their obligation to respect Acèh's independence
when they decided to conquer it in 1873, and (2) British capital had to be permitted a major
role in the Indies economy (as Wodehouse smugly noted). Aside from the large British share
in the huge Shell petroleum combine, we may note that by 1912 nearly half the capital
invested in the Indies rubber industry, and a sizable part of that invested in tea cultivation,
was British. See Malcolm Caldwell, *Indonesia* (London: Oxford University Press, 1968), p.
54. John S. Furnivall, *Colonial Policy and Practice* (New York: New York University Press,
1956), p. 254, observed that by 1940 the British had about 450 million guilders' worth of
investments in the Indies, while the Dutch total was about 2,500 million.

ex-colonial Javanese nation-state would probably have been Javanese. But by 1910, the now huge Dutch empire in the East covered so many important ethnolinguistic groups that the "Javanese option" was essentially eliminated. As Hoffman has ably shown, the Dutch colonial regime was both the earliest and the most energetic promoter of what later became *bahasa Indonesia,* partly because it had no serious intention of making Dutch the language of interracial colonial life, partly because it needed a single vehicle of communication for its heterogeneous empire.[8] Thus, already in the nineteenth century Javanese had become simply a convenience for administering one part—even if still perhaps the most important part—of the colony. In other words, the status of Javanese had dropped to that of a provincial language by the end of the Cultuurstelsel era (1830–70). In the expanding school system of the early twentieth century, "Maleisch" became increasingly important for generating the subordinate native cadres needed to man the rapidly expanding state and corporate bureaucracies, both of which required their staffs to handle matters of interisland importance and often to serve in areas well outside their ethnolinguistic homelands. Finally—so the argument goes—print-capitalism contributed to this process, since the actual and potential markets for printed texts in "Maleisch" were obviously larger than those for Javanese.

The first part of this argument has some plausibility. Can we doubt that if Java had remained a British colony from 1811 to 1945 (perhaps

---

[8]John Hoffman, "A Colonial Investment: Indies Malay to 1901," *Indonesia* 27 (April 1979):65–92. In his *The Portuguese Seaborne Empire, 1415–1825* (Harmondsworth, Middlesex: Pelican Books, 1973), pp. 128–29, Charles Boxer offers the interesting suggestion that Dutch was defeated already in the seventeenth century, less by "Malay" than by Portuguese, which was already deeply rooted as the language of Asian maritime trade:

In Asia the Portuguese language, or rather the Creole forms thereof, resisted Dutch official pressure and legislation with . . . remarkable success. . . . The contemporary Muslim rulers of Macassar were likewise fluent in Portuguese. . . . In April 1645 Gerrit Demmer, the governor of the Moluccas, observed that Portuguese, "or even English," seemed to be an easier language for the Ambonese to learn, and more attractive to them than Dutch. The most striking evidence of the victory of the language of Camoes over that of Vondel was provided by the Dutch colonial capital of Batavia, "Queen of the Eastern Seas." The Portuguese never set foot there, save as prisoners of war or else as occasional and fleeting visitors. Yet a Creole form of their language was introduced by slaves and household servants from the region of the Bay of Bengal, and it was spoken by the Dutch and half-caste women born and bred at Batavia, sometimes to the exclusion of their own mother tongue. There was much official criticism of this practice, but, as . . . Governor-General Johan Maetsuyker and his council at Batavia explained to the directors of the Dutch East India Company in 1659: "The Portuguese language is an easy language to speak and to learn. That is the reason why we cannot prevent the slaves brought here from Arakan who have never heard a word of Portuguese (and indeed even our own children) from taking to that language in preference to all other languages and making it their own."

united administratively with Malaya and Sumatra) much of the modern literature produced there would, as in Ghana, Nigeria, India, and other British imperial possessions, have been written in English? Or that if the Dutch empire had been confined to Java Javanese would be a national language today? Of its final component I am less convinced. Was the market really of that importance? On this question the work of Nidhi Aeusrivongse is very illuminating.⁹ After emphasizing the central role played by the colonial regime's Balai Pustaka (formally set up in 1917) in the printing and dissemination of indigenous works of literature, he nonetheless points out that, even in 1938, no more than 400,000 people, out of a total population of about 70 million, checked out books from the three thousand or so reading-room libraries it had set up—that is, less than 0.6 percent of the population. The annual turnover of books in these libraries in 1940 was only 3 million volumes, about seven and a half books per person per year. Thus, the consumption even of "free" books was very low. At the same time, the usual commercial edition of literary works was about fifteen hundred.¹⁰ If this was the size of the market—very comparable to the vernacular print-markets in Europe in the eighteenth century¹¹—it is hard to believe that Malay language books were likely to be much more profitable than Javanese: in both cases the market was tiny.¹² The argument is much stronger in the case of the press.¹³ But here the anomaly is that the ascendancy of Malay over Javanese (clear well before World War I and long before the Sumpah Pemuda [Oath of Youth] of 1928) was certainly largely due to the fact that a key element in this market—both as producers and as consumers—was the Chinese-less *peranakan* (Indonesia-born) Chinese community in the larger towns and cities.¹⁴

⁹Nidhi Aeusrivongse, "Fiction as History: A Study of Pre-War Indonesian Novels and Novelists (1920–1942)" (Ph.D. thesis, University of Michigan, 1975), pp. 43–45.

¹⁰Ibid., p. 127. Balai Pustaka usually printed about five thousand copies—three thousand for its reading-rooms, two thousand for the open market.

¹¹See Lucien Fèbvre and Henri-Jean Martin, *The Coming of the Book* (London: New Left Books, 1976), pp. 218–20.

¹²Balai Pustaka published works in both "Malay" and Javanese and there is no reason to think that one line was much more profitable than the other.

¹³Nidhi Aeusrivongse, "Fiction as History," pp. 32–33. Ahmat Adam, "The Vernacular Press and the Emergence of Modern Indonesian Consciousness (1855–1913)" (Ph.D. thesis, University of London, 1984), is instructive on this point.

¹⁴The important role of the peranakan Chinese in the development of the Indonesian language and literature, long virtually ignored, has recently been the subject of valuable studies, e.g., Claudine Salmon, *Literature in Malay by the Chinese of Indonesia: A Provisional Bibliography* (Paris: Editions de la Maison de l'Homme, 1981); and John B. Kwee,

Another important line of argument stresses the rise of Indonesian nationalism, and goes somewhat like this: The first generation of modern Indonesian nationalists were determined not to let themselves be "divided and ruled" any longer and therefore very early saw the need for a national language that was also not the colonial language. *Bahasa Melayu* was a centuries-old interisland lingua franca ideally suited to this purpose. Indonesian nationalists of Javanese origin, aside from recognizing the "difficulty" of Javanese, were farsighted and generous enough not to press their native language's claims on Indonesia's other ethnolinguistic groups. Hence the Sumpah Pemuda. There is some truth in this, but what it ignores is the fact that the Sumpah was actually not the start of a new era but rather the logical culmination of at least three decades of linguistic transformation, whereby even in Javanese-speaking areas Javanese steadily lost ground to bahasa Melayu in the worlds of commerce, politics, and literature. Indeed, it was only *because* of this long transformation that anyone was in a position by 1928 to swear the Sumpah with a calm sembah. In other words, it was less nationalism that created a common language than that a common language helped create nationalism. And, in any case, this argument does not really explain the rush of Javanese to write outside their own language *for their fellow Javanese.*

I am inclined therefore to seek an explanation *internal* to Javanese society and culture, arguing that Javanese writers have turned to bahasa Indonesia partly, no doubt, to reach non-Javanese readers but more deeply as a way of, shall we say, wrestling with the power of Javanese. I would propose the paradox that it has been precisely the weight of Javanese tradition and traditional culture, and its menacing sociocultural implications, that have sent gifted Javanese writers into what is, from one point of view, a sort of internal exile. In this sense, the whole literary and paraliterary tradition with which the body of this essay deals can be thought of as *karya pulau Buru,* a "product of Buru [the island where Pramoedya was incarcerated for ten years by the Suharto regime, and where he composed his great tetralogy of novels on the origins of Indonesia as a nation]."

The backdrop to my argument is a double crisis in Javanese culture already clearly evident before "modern times." One of these crises the Javanese shared with other colonized peoples; the other strikes me as possibly sui generis.

"Chinese Malay Literature of the Peranakan Chinese in Indonesia, 1880–1942" (Ph.D. thesis, University of Auckland, 1977).

The Politico-cultural Crisis

There was always a painful, even morbid, undertone to Sukarno's endless insistence on his Indonesia having endured 350 years of colonialism. It was not merely almost as though he were claiming some world record (alas, in this regard Indonesia was easily outdistanced by the Philippines and Latin America, not to speak of East Timor). Sukarno, and surely a great many of his listeners, knew very well that, as stated, the claim was false. Many parts of Indonesia only experienced colonial rule in the twentieth century; many parts even of Java only seriously encountered colonialism in the eighteenth century. Yet it is possible to make sense of the proud pain in Sukarno's voice if we think of him not simply as a Javanese, or as an Indonesian, but as a Javanese *ruler*. For, in fact, beginning in the early seventeenth century, Javanese rulers had indeed experienced an almost unbroken series of defeats, humiliations, and catastrophes.[15] By the end of the eighteenth century Pakubuwanas, Hamengkubuwanas, and Mangkunegaras had all become petty princelings "ruling" on Dutch sufferance and surviving economically on Dutch subsidies. Even the collapse of the East India Company did them no good. Where the nationalists of 1945 were able to take advantage of the collapse of the Japanese empire, the Javanese rulers of 1800 could do, and did, little to throw off the Dutch yoke. Prince Diponegoro's insurrection itself was less an anti-Dutch affair than a Javanese civil war in which the Dutch supported the prince's enemies.[16] After 1830, the only Javanese who clashed physically with

---

[15]A simplified list: 1629—Sultan Agung's rout by the VOC (Vereenigde Oost-Indische Compagnie) before Batavia. 1674—Mataram sacked by Trunajaya. For the first time in its history Java overrun militarily by *wong Sabrang* (people from overseas): Buginese, Balinese, Madurese, Dutch. 1677—Amangkurat II put on the new throne of Kartasura by the VOC, who defeat Trunajaya. 1707—Amangkurat III deposed by the VOC and exiled to Ceylon. Puppet Pakubuwana I makes large concessions to the VOC. 1740–43—Gègèr Pacina. Kartasura sacked by Chinese and Javanese rebels. Pakubuwana II cedes the entire northern *pasisir* (littoral) to the VOC in exchange for a new throne in Surakarta. 1755 and 1757— VOC-imposed division of the realm into Sunanate, Sultanate, and Mangkunegaran. 1809— Hamengkubuwana II deposed by Daendels. 1812—Hamengkubuwana II exiled to Penang by Raffles. c. 1814—Sultanate split by Raffles's creation of the Pakualaman. 1830—defeat and exile of Diponegoro. And so on.

[16]Nowhere in his "memoirs" (the *Babad Dipanegara*), I think, does the prince speak of getting rid of the Dutch; indeed, it is not clear that he thinks of "the Dutch" as a collectivity at all. Harry J. Benda and John A. Larkin, ed., *The World of Southeast Asia: Selected Historical Readings* (New York: Harper & Row, 1967), p. 158, quote him as reporting a voice saying: "I tell you, in three years' time the realm of Jogjakarta [*not* Batavia] will have been brought to perdition." Later on, the Ratu Adil (Just King) tells Diponegoro that he "must lead my whole army into battle. Conquer [*not* liberate] Java with it." A slightly different version of all this is given in Ann Kumar, "Diponegoro (1787?–1855)," *Indonesia* 13 (April 1972):69–118, at 77, 103.

the colonialists were small clusters of *haji* (returned pilgrims from Mecca), local toughs, peasants, and other elements of the common people.[17] The Javanese upper class became the pliant tool of the Dutch in erecting the ruthlessly exploitative Cultuurstelsel, in facilitating the depredations of private agrarian capitalism in the Liberal era, and so on till the close of the colonial age. From this perspective, Sukarno can be seen as the first Javanese ruler in almost 350 years to have some real independence.

But the fact that the Dutch ended up by coopting the Javanese ruling class, rather than eliminating it as the British did in Burma, meant a particularly grave fossilization of the Javanese social system, in which ever greater pomp was displayed by the ruling class to conceal the reality of increasing impotence. To borrow a phrase from Breton de Nijs, the sunans and sultans had become *levende wayangpoppen* (living wayang puppets); we may recall the famous photo of Pakubuwana X looking like a bewildered young wife on the arm of a huge, fat, ugly Dutch Resident of Surakarta.[18] The growing sense of impotence and impasse is evident in some of the court literature of that era. In his discussion of the extraordinary mid-century *Babad Ambon* (Chronicle of Ambon) Day demonstrates this very well.[19] Written very much in the traditional heroic style, this chronicle nonetheless is an account of Pakubuwana VI's painful exile in Ambon. All the traditional tropes of regal magnificence are there in the poem, but they have a peculiar inverted quality, since they describe for the first time a lonely Javanese king longing for his palace and wives thousands of miles away—a king who has Dutch guards for his bungalow prison, not a huge royal retinue.

But surely the most telling expression of the impotence of the ruling class is the famous passage in Ronggawarsita's last poem, *Serat Kala Tidha* (Poem of a Time of Darkness), composed shortly before his death in 1873:

> Ratuné ratu utama
> Patihé patih linuwih
> Pra nayaka tyas raharja
> Panekaré becik-becik

[17]Sartono Kartodirdjo, "Agrarian Radicalism in Java," in Claire Holt et al., ed., *Culture and Politics in Indonesia* (Ithaca, N.Y.: Cornell University Press, 1972), pp. 71–125.
[18]E. Breton de Nijs (pseudonym of Robert Nieuwenhuys), *Tempo Doeloe* (Amsterdam: E. M. Querido, 1961), p. 101.
[19]John Anthony Day, "Meanings of Change in the Poetry of Nineteenth Century Java" (Ph.D. thesis, Cornell University, 1981), chap. 3.

Parandéné tan dadi
Paliyasing kalabendu.

The King kingly perfection
The Chief Minister chiefly in truth
The *bupati* constant of heart
The lower officials excellent
Yet none can serve to stay
The time of doom.[20]

These lines are unimaginable in any earlier period of Javanese history. For they mean that even a perfect traditional monarchy was now incapable of fulfilling its ancient self-defined task precisely of preventing the *kalabendu*. As I have written elsewhere, "The single terrible word *parandéné* (yet) expresses Ronggawarsita's desperate, and quite untraditional, sense that the old conception of the world was no longer valid, the cosmic rhythm had come unsprung, and Javanese 'power' was impotence."[21] Nor was this sense of uselessness and stagnation confined to court circles. There is much fictional truth in Pramoedya's description of "Minke" and his Dutch teacher in a Hoogere Burgerschool (elite high-school) classroom at the turn of the century:

[Tuan Lastendienst] bilang: di bidang ilmu Jepang juga mengalami kebangkitan. Kitisato telah menemukan kuman pès, Shiga menemukan kuman dysenteri—dan dengan demikian Jepang telah juga berjasa pada ummat manusia. . . . Melihat aku mempunyai perhatian penuh dan membikin catatan Meneer Lastendienst bertanya padaku dengan nada mendakwa: Eh, Minke, wakil bangsa Jawa dalam ruangan ini, apa sudah disumbangkan bangsamu pada ummat manusia? Bukan saja aku menggeragap mendapat pertanyaan dadakan itu, boleh jadi *seluruh déwa dalam kotak wayang ki dalang akan hilang semangat hanya untuk menjawab.*[22]

[Mr. Lastendienst] said: "In the field of science Japan too has experienced a resurgence. Kitisato has discovered the plague microbe, Shiga the germ of dysentery—so the Japanese too have rendered service to mankind. . . ." Then, noticing that I was listening with the utmost atten-

[20]Radèn Ngabèhi Ronggawarsita, *Serat Kala Tida* (Surakarta?: Persatuan, 1933?). My translation.
[21]See chapter 7, below.
[22]Pramoedya Ananta Toer, *Bumi Manusia* (Jakarta: Hasta Mitra, 1980), p. 99. Italics added.

tion and taking notes, Mr. Lastendienst asked me in an accusing tone: "Well, Minke, you represent the Javanese in this classroom—what have your people contributed to mankind?" It was not merely that I was utterly nonplussed by this sudden question: most likely the entire pantheon of gods in the dhalang [puppeteer]'s wayang-chest would have despaired of making any answer.

The Literature and Language Crisis

If the politico-cultural crisis outlined above was one that ruling-class Javanese shared with coopted ruling classes in many other parts of the colonial world—if Meneer Lastendienst's query could easily have been posed to representatives of many other peoples than the Javanese—the crisis of Javanese language and literature strikes me as a special one. To see why, we must turn to the peculiar character and history of the Javanese language and its literature, and to print-capitalism's revolutionary impact on literary production from the 1880s onward. The crisis had, I think, three distinct causes, which began to interact painfully in the course of the nineteenth century.

The first was the profound break in the ancient literary tradition caused first by the fall of Hindu-Buddhist Majapahit (mid-fifteenth century) and then by the smashing of the succeeding Islamo-Javanese *pasisir* civilization by two different kinds of barbarians: the VOC and that Genghis Khan of Java Sultan Agung.23 One can think of the period from 1500 to 1750 as a kind of deepening Javanese Dark Ages, scarred by incessant wars, deportations, rapine, massacres, and famine.24 How catastrophic the period of destruction was can be judged

23Daniel George Edward Hall, in *A History of Southeast Asia* (London: Macmillan, 1968), wrote that in 1617 "Pajang, which was foolish enough to rebel, became Agung's next victim, and for her presumption was horribly devastated." During the 1620–25 siege of Surabaya "every year after harvest [sic] the Mataram forces systematically ravaged the surrounding countryside" (p. 284). "In 1639 he conquered Balambangan and deported much of its population" (p. 310). Agung's deification by modern Javanese politicians and historians, however understandable, shows how little read even the masterpieces of New Javanese literature have become. The hero of the greatest of these, the *Serat Centhini*, one Sèh Amongraga, is a refugee in flight after the destruction of Surabaya by Agung's armies. (It is notable that no scene in this very long poem takes place in the royal court.) At the same time, Reid rightly reminds us of R. Mohammad Ali's honorable dissent on Agung in his *Pengantar Ilmu Sedjarah Indonesia* (Jakarta: Bhratara, 1963). See Anthony Reid, "The Nationalist Quest for an Indonesian Past," in Anthony Reid and David Marr, ed., *Perceptions of the Past in Southeast Asia* (Singapore: Heinemann, 1979), pp. 281–98, at p. 298.

24Seventeen-fifty may be too early a date for the end of the Dark Ages. See Ann Kumar, "Javanese Historiography in and of the 'Colonial Period': A Case Study," in Reid and Marr, *Perceptions of the Past*, pp. 187–206, for an account of the barbaric ferocity of the Dutch

by the extent to which present-day knowledge of Old Javanese civilization depends on manuscripts found not on Java but on Bali and
Lombok.[25] By the time Javanese literary culture began to revive, in the
later eighteenth century, a large part of Old Java's Sanskritic literature
was either lost or had become nearly incomprehensible; it did not
become accessible until the late-nineteenth-century florescence of
Dutch academic philology. In the meantime, a whole tradition of
poetry making among gentlemen-courtiers had essentially disappeared.[26]

One of the most curious illustrations of this cultural break is the
death of *wayang bèbèr,* an ancient type of wayang performed not with
movable puppets but with elaborately painted scrolls.[27] The reason it
died was that after the Dark Ages no one any longer knew how to
perform it, shall we say, Majapahit-style?—that is, with the elaborate
narrations and lyrical descriptions so touchingly depicted by Father
Zoetmulder. Thus, the only "conceivable" possibility was to play wayang bèbèr in wayang purwa style with movable puppets—the one
wayang type that survived, because it was rooted in popular-oral, not
court-literary, culture. But for this performing style, the beautiful, still,
painted scrolls of wayang bèbèr were completely unsuited. And so an
old art form died.

The break in the tradition—a sort of cultural amnesia—was not
mitigated by the survival of an alternative linguistic link to the past
(compare the role of medieval Latin vis-à-vis Anglo-Saxon literature
and English). In this sense, Javanese culture lost a mandarin court
culture and literature analogous to what peoples such as the Vietnamese, Chinese, and Japanese possessed up until modern times.
While some manuscripts continued to be copied and studied, the old

---

conquest of Balambangan between 1767 and 1781. On p. 192 she quotes C. J. Bosch,
writing from Bondowoso in 1848, as saying that "this region is perhaps the only one in Java
where a once numerous population was *entirely* wiped out" (italics added).

[25]Cf. S. Supomo, "The Image of Majapahit in Later Javanese and Indonesian Writing," in
:bid., pp. 171–85. At p. 182 he reminds us that Georges Coedès's article "Le Royaume de
Çrīvijaya," *Bulletin de l'Ecole Française d'Extrême Orient* 18 (1918):1–34, not only proved
the existence of Sriwijaya long before the emergence of Majapahit, but brought to light "a
whole great kingdom of the past that had been completely forgotten by later generations."

[26]A loving monument to this sensuous, sophisticated Old Javanese literary culture is
Petrus Josephus Zoetmulder, S. J., *Kalangwan, A Survey of Old Javanese Literature* (The
Hague: Nijhoff, 1974).

[27]For fuller details, see my "The Last Picture Show: Wayang Bèbèr," in Jean Taylor et al.,
eds., *Proceedings, Conference on Modern Indonesian Literature, 1974* (Madison: Center
for Southeast Asian Studies, University of Wisconsin, 1976), pp. 33–81.

literature was largely inaccessible, physically and linguistically, to nineteenth-century Javanese.

The second cause of crisis was in some ways a consequence of the first. When Javanese literary culture began to revive in the eighteenth century[28] it had lost its grip on the older, esoteric court language, and had, if you like, to re-create its mystery, or power, on an essentially vernacular base. In other words, the elevation of New Javanese court language and literature over ordinary speech had to be, and was, not the consequence of a cosmopolitan elite's familiarity with a foreign language and literature (Sanskrit), but of artificial, archaizing variations on a language that all Javanese more or less had in common. In this process nothing is more striking than the development of *krama* and *krama inggil,* the high-polite and very-high-polite levels of Javanese speech, which, so far as we can tell, occurred toward the end of the Dark Ages. It is, of course, likely that something of the sort would have occurred anyway, given the hierarchical structures of premodern Javanese society.[29] But there are good reasons for thinking that the extreme character of linguistic development in Java was above all a function of the increasing impotence of the Javanese upper class—and indirectly of Dutch colonial encouragement, in other words were a sort of compensation for a loss of real authority.[30] One can think of

[28]See Soebardi, "Radèn Ngabèhi Jasadipura I, Court Poet of Surakarta: His Life and Works," *Indonesia* 8 (October 1969):81–102. After the signing of the Treaty of Gianti in 1755, he wrote, "Surakarta appeared to come to life. It entered a period of order and tranquility [rust en orde?]; the kingdom was consolidated; the damage left in the wake of the struggle of several years before was repaired. At the same time, there was a marked revival in Javanese cultural life. Great efforts were made to produce new works in Javanese literature and to replace books which had been destroyed during the Chinese rebellion and the Mangkubumi war" (83). My own view is that the destruction had been going on for two centuries, not merely "several years."

[29]Compare the development of the elevated ceremonial speech style *rajasap* in Thai culture in the same era.

[30]The mania of the nineteenth-century Javanese *priyayi* (administrative literati, hence Javanese ruling class) for *hormat* (respect, deference, status), certainly accentuated by the colonial regime's introduction of European-style hereditary rights to rank and office, is well known. It is mordantly satirized in Pramoedya Ananta Toer's description of the thoughts of "Sastro Kassier" (Cashier Sastro) as he prepares to sell his daughter to the Dutch planter Plikemboh:

Tapi jabatan: dia segala dan semua bagi Pribumi bukan tani dan bukan tukang. Harta-benda bolèh punah, keluarga bolèh hancur, nama bolèh rusak, jabatan harus selamat. Dia bukan hanya penghidupan, di dalamnya juga kehormatan, kebenaran, hargadiri, penghidupan sekaligus. Orang berkelahi, berdoa, bertirakat, memfitnah, membohong, membanting tulang, mencelakakan sesama, demi sang jabatan. . . . Semakin jabatan mendekatkan orang pada lingkungan orang Eropa, semakin terhormatlah orang. Sekali pun bolèh jadi penghasilan tidak seberapa dan yang ada padanya hanya satu belangkon belaka. Orang Eropa adalah lambang kekuasaan tanpa batas. Dan kekuasaan mendatangkan uang. Meréka telah kalahkan raja-raja, para sultan dan susuhunan, para ulama dan para jawara.

the immense, high walls around the *kraton* (palaces) in Solo and Yogyakarta in the same light: These walls were absolutely no military protection against the Dutch but served as a sort of material krama, separating, elevating, and mystifying the courts—high above Javanese society. We would not be wrong, therefore, to adopt in large measure the view of Brandes: "Scientific research . . . makes it clear . . . that, no matter how many traditional elements may be found in krama, krama is nonetheless, when one considers it closely, a pathological phenomenon, an excrescence on the actual stems of the Javanese language, frequently a considerable deformation, that krama is only superficially attached to Javanese, that it is highly affected."[31]

For my argument, however, the key point is that colonial krama was *not* a privileged *literary* language, like Old Javanese, but, more than anything else, an oral and social language. Thus, it became much more deeply embedded in everyday Javanese life than Old Javanese ever was. Its spread and development owe everything to the long period (say 1680–1940) in which Dutch power simultaneously fossilized the Javanese ruling class and "feudalized" their relations with the rest of society. New heights of *hormat* (respect, deference, status) could be demanded because the ruling class had the alien and invincible Dutch behind them and depended less and less on the norms of Javanese society as a whole.[32] The pseudofeudalism of colonial Javanese society thus deeply affected the language of Java, and oral com-

---

But Office! It was everything and all for those Natives who were neither peasants nor artisans. Goods and chattels could vanish, the family be destroyed, and honor ruined— but Office had to be kept safe at all costs.

Office was not merely a source of livelihood. It meant respect, value, and also self esteem. Men would quarrel, pray, meditate, slander, lie, slave, and ruin one another— all for Office. The more that Office brought a man into contact with Europeans, the more respect he commanded. No matter if his salary was minimal, and he had only one headcloth to his pate! The Europeans were symbols of a limitless power. And in its train power brought them wealth. They had defeated the kings, the sultans and susuhunans, the *ulama* [religious scholars], and the *jawara* [village toughs].

Pramoedya Ananta Toer, *Anak Semua Bangsa* (Jakarta: Hasta Mitra, 1980), p. 130.

[31] Jan Laurens Andries Brandes, "Een Jayapattra of acte van eene Rechterlijke Uitspraak van Çaka 849," *Tijdschrift voor Indische taal-, land- en volkenkunde* 32 (1889):98–149, at 134. I owe the citation to Eugenius Marius Uhlenbeck, *Studies in Javanese Morphology* (The Hague: Nijhoff, 1968), p. 294 (though Uhlenbeck mistakenly gives as his source another Brandes article in the same journal). Brandes curtly adds: "This is partly the result of a schoolmarmish pedantry to which all Javanese are more or less subjected: to the point that all, high and low, regard krama, the language of politeness, as more beautiful, and much to be preferred to, their own thoroughly healthy ngoko."

[32] This may help account for the great change in atmosphere from the robust, self-confident sensuousness of the Kalangwan literature to the melancholy, omen-fraught, turgid introspectiveness of much post-1800 court literature.

munication was just as fossilized as other parts of the culture. This in turn meant that the great vernacularization movements of the nine- teenth and twentieth centuries, in places as far apart as Finland and China, Vietnam and Czechoslovakia, were really out of the ques- tion.[33] In these societies the ruling classes either spoke and wrote in a foreign language—German, Swedish, Chinese—or at least (as in China) maintained a mandarinal administrative language sharply dis- tinct from the rest of society. The forces that came to be identified with popular nationalism and social reform could quite easily turn to a relatively uncontaminated "native language" or vernacular to over- throw the cultural supremacy of the ruling class (all the easier, of course, when the ruling class's language could be branded as foreign). For Javanese such a liberating vernacularization movement was ex- tremely difficult because the language of the ruling class, both oral and literary, *was* native, and because its power, with Dutch help, had penetrated so deep. Almost every Javanese knew, *had* to know, some krama for survival.[34]

It is likely that the energy put into "kramanizing" Javanese culture was heightened by the quarter from which some resistance came. The point is made nicely by Uhlenbeck:

> Despite the fact that it has played a major role in Javanese life for over four centuries, there is one field in which practically no ceremonial [i.e., krama] words occur at all, and that is the Moslem religion. This lacuna cannot be explained by the fact that this area makes heavy use of loan- words because—as is well known—loanwords as such are by no means excluded from the ceremonial opposition.[35]

This insulation of the vocabulary of Islam from the pressures of kra- manization certainly has a great deal to do with the internal values of Islam itself, which contain strong egalitarian elements.[36] Islam also has, in the Arabic-derived word *ummat* (community of believers), a self-conscious conception of horizontal solidarity.[37] But the essential point is that this linguistic insulation indicates clearly the stubborn

---

[33]On these vernacularization movements see Hugh Seton-Waton, *Nations and States* (Boulder: Westview Press, 1977); and Aira Kemiläinen, *Nationalism* (Jyväskylä: Kustanta- jat Publishers, 1964), esp. pp. 208–15.

[34]Two interesting exceptions are noted below.

[35]Uhlenbeck, *Studies*, p. 284.

[36]This is not to deny that within the ummat written Arabic sometimes played an esoteric role, rather like Sanskrit in an earlier era. See chapter 4, pp. 127, 129–30.

[37]Until recently there was no word in Javanese for *society*.

refusal of an important part of Javanese society to be fully absorbed into the pseudofeudal social system; this sector remained a large, indigestible lump in the mouth of the dominant culture, which could neither swallow it nor spit it out. It is very instructive that the most violent Javanese literary polemics of the pre-1900 era, texts such as the *Serat Dermagandhul,* the *Suluk Gatholoco,* and even the *Wulangrèh,* were aimed at "un-Javanese" Javanese Islam, *not* against the Dutch. (Indeed, to my limited knowledge, there is not a single pre-twentieth-century Javanese literary text fundamentally and openly antagonistic to the Dutch). In other words, *this* part of the crisis in Javanese society was perceived by Javanese literati as *internal* to that society, and this created a profound sense of anxiety and anger. (This anxiety and anger have by no means disappeared today.) Seen from another angle, the insulation of the Islamic vocabulary from kramanization meant that there was already in premodern times a linguistic foundation for a critique of the existing culture from within. Yet this foundation was both quite narrow and strongly identified with a social sector that tended, perhaps as a matter of survival, to be exclusive and inward-looking.

Before proceeding to the final element in the language and literature crisis—the impact of print-capitalism—it is necessary to make a few preliminary comments about krama. It is well known that the krama vocabulary is not very large, perhaps little more than a thousand words in all.[38] In this sense it is no match for *ngoko,* the "low"-familiar level of Javanese speech: There are no words in krama that lack a ngoko equivalent, while there are thousands of ngoko words that stand on their own—already a sufficient indication of krama's political origins. But there are three peculiarities about krama that deserve special attention. The first is that its vocabulary includes verbs as well as nouns and pronouns, that is, it covers not just the names of things but the motor relations between them. Second, krama words and their ngoko equivalents are in many cases different from a lexical point of view (thus, one cannot derive the ngoko, krama, and krama inggil words for *horse—jaran, kapal,* and *turangga*—from one another). Third, the use of, say, *jaran, kapal,* or *turangga* has nothing to do with *what* is being said but rather indicates the relationship between speaker and interlocutor. *Aku arep mangan* and *kula badhé nedha* both "mean" "I'm going to eat," but the first can only be said

---

[38]Soepomo Poedjosoedarmo, "Wordlist of Javanese Non-Ngoko Vocabularies," *Indonesia* 7 (April 1969):165–90, gives about 1,000 krama and 300 krama inggil items.

between intimates and social near-equals or by a high-status person to someone lower down; the second can only be used to strangers or someone of higher status. The lexical estrangement of the two vocabularies, combined with the implications of dyadic hierarchy between speaker and interlocutor, produce the following: In English, which has long had its own linguistic hierarchies, one can say: "Please give me something to eat, sir"; "Please give me something to eat"; "Give me something to eat"; and "Give me something to eat, you idiot!" "Give me something to eat" remains lexically stable throughout. Minor adjustments allow for the expression of different relations between speaker and interlocutor. No such lexical stability exists in Javanese. A change in any one of the words in *aku arep mangan* requires changes in the others. To say *kula sampun mangan, aku wis nedha, kula wis nedha,* and so forth *mean nothing.*[39] They are just mistakes, or bad Javanese. They are neither insulting, obsequious, satirical, nor innovative—simply embarrassing. In effect, krama's sociopolitical implications are so powerful and deep that "play" between the levels is virtually ruled out.

Both the formal rigidity and the inherently dyadic, hierarchical implications of the ngoko-krama system were brought into question by the advent of print-capitalism, in ways that have a great deal to do, I think, with the appearance of the black hole. To get a sense of why, one has first to consider the social and cultural context in which Javanese literature was produced and disseminated prior to the print revolution. In the older culture, literature was still to a high degree an intimate, social art. While prose works existed and gradually became more common as time passed, poetry was the dominant literary mode. And although a certain amount of "private" reading went on, most literature was meant to be performed, face to face, among small groups of people. For this was a poetry that was always *sung*. The various meters in which poems were composed were much more indicators of the melody or key in which the poems were to be sung than disciplines exerted on the rhythms of ordinary speech. I have performed the experiment of asking Javanese friends to *say* the words of Mangkunegara IV's famous poem *Tripama*. In every instance they found it impossible. They would forget and have to remind themselves by starting to sing. (English-speakers might try to "say" the words of "God Save the Queen" or "Waltzing Matilda," Japanese-speakers

[39]This is not in fact 100-percent true in all circumstances, but the exceptions are rare enough, I think, that they can be ignored for the sake of the argument.

those of "Kimigayo.") The intimacy of the milieux within which sung poems were performed meant that the dyadic core of New Javanese was not seriously violated. Whether *ingsun* (I) or *sira* (you) was heard by the small group, each member would "hear" such pronouns as extensions of everyday dyadic speech. Finally, in a context where poetry and song were inseparable, and both were tied to music in a wider sense (as well as dance), it is not surprising that artists in these fields mingled easily, exchanged ideas, and often had equivalent ranks and emoluments calibrated within the palace ranking system—for example, Nyai Lurah Bedhaya (dancer), Nyai Bèi Madusari (singer), Radèn Tumenggung Warsodiningrat (musician).

The coing of the printed book, followed much later by the arrival of the record and the cassette, changed all this dramatically. To the literary world, print-capitalism brought a sudden, enormous silence. Thousands of identical copies of an author's words were distributed through the market to thousands of private, separate, unknown readers. For the first time Javanese writers were confronted with an invisible, atomized public. Silent prose rather than sung poetry quickly became the norm. But the central problem for anyone writing now in Javanese was what one might call the "problem of pronouns." For it became more and more difficult to sustain the old pronominal forms in the world of the market. One can see this on both sides of the I-you divide. The old ingsun-I might be the singer, the composer, the sovereign praised, or a particular character in a poem's narrative, but the identity of this "I" was clear to everyone listening. In the silence of the market, however, *who* was ingsun (or aku or kula)? No one could be sure except as this "I" imposed himself through his own words, that is, personalized his voice and style, and, if successful, eventually imposed the persona of "I, Author X," whom most readers would never encounter except on the printed page. So with "you," for the market created a multiplicity of "yous"—aristocrats, busboys, hairdressers, officials, schoolgirls, and even Dutchmen. For this social multiplicity the Javanese language offers no obvious answer; there is really no word for a homogeneous, collective, public (thus equal-before-the-author) "you," perhaps even no real second person plural. The print-market thus created speakers and interlocutors wholly outside the existing conventions of the language. What was the right "you" for all these collections of putative social superiors, equals, and inferiors? With the market came also the breakup of other old connections. Gifted authors became famous as authors; good singers fell steadily in status until the coming of the cassette; good Javanese musicians rapidly lost caste; talented painters moved into the bourgeois market and vied with authors as figured personae. (It is perhaps not coincidental that the *gamelan* ensemble appears rarely in modern prose literature, whereas the piano and violin are very visible.)

In turn, all of this was tied to the question of the *subject* of literature. For much of the old court literature had been concerned with the glories, especially the martial glories, of rulers, as well as the mysteries of religion. But after 1830 Javanese rulers never went to war again, and their putative glories were obviously hollow. The persuasiveness of the old-time religion was called into question as Islam assumed a more orthodox and iconoclastic character, as Christian missions made their inroads, and as the skepticism of European secular culture spread its ravages. What was one seriously to write about? And for whom? In what voice? From these questions arose this one: In what language?

The answer proved to be bahasa Indonesia. It turned out to be a God-send to Javanese writers, not so much because it offered an escape from a stagnant Javanese world but rather because it provided a citadel from which to pursue a sort of Javanese cultural civil war. I would like to try to demonstrate this by sketching out a sort of "tradition"—with its byways, naturally, as well as its thoroughfares—which, for convenience, I will define as stretching from Ronggawarsita to Yudhistira Ardi Noegraha.

I pick Ronggawarsita to begin with because he is nowadays, with some justification, regarded as the *pujangga panutup* (last court poet)—a man who, though he was acquainted with Dutch and Eurasian Javanologists and at least bits of their work, was still fully a figure of the old Javanese court world. I pick him because only by bearing him in mind can one think usefully about the career of an able Javanese boy, Lesya, born in 1884, eleven years after the pujangga's death, who later became famous as Prof. Dr. R. M. Ng. Poerbatjaraka. I pick him, finally, because, as I have tried to show earlier in this essay, he was possibly the first writer to say something "impossible" in Javanese: *Ratuné ratu utama. . . . Parandéné tan dadi paliyasing kalabendu.* This "impossibility" meant closing the book on a tradition of writing about ratu utama that went back centuries. For if the modern ratu utama could not stave off the kalabendu, why bother writing about him and his kind ever again? What could *utama* mean in such circumstances? Certainly nothing self-evidently embedded in the very nature of the world. Perhaps *utama* inside quotation marks? But the idea of putting anything in ironical quotation marks (how

does one sing them?) was wholly foreign to Javanese tradition, implying as it does a reading culture and a subtle connivance between
author and reader at the subject's expense.

Ronggawarsita's oxymoron was in fact a spontaneous expression of
cultural pain. Is it a mistake to think that its harshness is accentuated
by the contrast between the despair of the dying poet's words and the
sensuous beauty of the sung *macapat* meter Sinom (Youth!)? I think
not, since at least this sort of oxymoron had its nineteenth-century
precedents. Compare this stanza of the *Suluk Gatholoco,* also composed in Sinom, which is quite typical of the poem's style:

> Santri tiga duk miyarsa
> Sareng misuh silitbabi
> Ki Gatholoco angucap
> Apa ta silité babi
> Digawa kang darbèni
> Nora gepuk raganingsun
> Santri tiga angucap
> Biyangamu silitbabi
> Gatholoco mojar iku ora kaprah

> On hearing this, the santri three
> Abused him, shouting: "Pig's asshole!"
> Said Gatholoco in response:
> "Why speak you of a pig's asshole?
> Its owner bears it, thus
> On me it has no bearing!" Cried
> The santri three in turn:
> "Your mother is a pig's asshole!"
> Said Gatholoco: "That is very odd indeed."[40]

One might perhaps say that there is no macapat meter designed to
express feelings of anger, hatred, or despair, and thus the author of this
suluk was "stuck" with Sinom. But did he have no conscious idea of
the eerie opposition of sound and meaning in a stanza such as this?

Ronggawarsita is also important to the tradition I am inventing in
that he was a self-conscious revivalist, making his own studies of Old
Javanese literature, perhaps in a search for an ancient source of

---

[40]My doggerel translation of section 5, stanza 58, the original to be found on p. 79 of
Philippus van Akkeren, *Een Gedrocht en toch de Volmaakte Mens, De Javaanse Suluk
Gatoloco* (The Hague: Excelsior, 1951). A translation of the full text has appeared in two
parts, in *Indonesia* 32 (October 1981):109–50, and 33 (April 1982):31–88.

strength in a Jaman Édan (Age of Madness).[41] But self-consciously reviving the old meant juxtaposing it with the present and thus distancing the old in a way that backhandedly foreshadowed the work of his great successor.

There can be little doubt that had he been born a century earlier, Poerbatjaraka would have become a notable pujangga: he had great linguistic gifts, enormous intellectual energy, a retentive memory, and a thorough knowledge of Javanese culture. But, being born in 1884 to a high official of the Sunanate, he attended the HIS (Dutch-Native School) attached to the royal palace, learned Malay and Dutch, chatted regularly with the Sunan's Dutch bodyguards, and came to read a study of a classical Javanese text by Hendrik Kern.[42] Exploiting what he found in Kern to confound his palace seniors in literary matters, he got into political hot water. Increasingly dissatisfied with the ossification of palace intellectual life, he began to pester certain Dutch officials to help him proceed with his studies of Old Javanese. In 1910, his ability and persistence won him an appointment in Batavia (at the age of twenty-six). His success there later brought him to Leiden University, where he assisted Professor Hazeu in the teaching of Javanese. In 1926, at the age of forty-two, he won his doctorate with a thesis entitled "Agastya in den Archipel" (Agastya in the archipelago).

The most interesting thing about this thesis, the first academic philological study of the Javanese past by a Javanese, is that it was written in Dutch. The choice of language was not principally imposed on him by Leiden. As early as 1914 he had begun publishing scholarly articles in Dutch, and a steady stream of Dutch-language publications followed throughout the colonial era. He only began to write in Indonesian and Javanese after independence and in his old age. Was his choice of language a matter of audience—Dutch academics and antiquarian civil servants? No doubt, in part. But I am confident there was more to it than that. Poerbatjaraka was violently hostile to Ronggawarsita, whom he considered a pretentious fraud and an ignorant, superstitious dabbler in Old Javanese literature. By contrast, he

---

[41]This revivalist spirit is already evident with the Jasadipuras (and has parallels in mainland Southeast Asia, particularly nineteenth-century Siam). But it is something new. The poets of the Kalangwan era loved decaying ruins and overgrown shrines, but they loved them *as* ruins, without nostalgia or any desire to restore their past splendor. Nothing could be more foreign to the nineteenth-century Javanese spirit.

[42]Most of the biographical material in this paragraph is drawn from Theodoor Pigeaud, "In Memoriam Professor Poerbatjaraka," *Bijdrage tot de taal-, land- en volkenkunde* (henceforth *Bijdrage*) 122 (1966): 405–12, which includes a full bibliography of Poerbatjaraka's works. There is useful additional information in Gerardus Willebrordus Joannes Drewes, "De 'Ontdekking' van Poerbatjaraka," in ibid. 129 (1973): 482–91.

thought of himself as a professional and an enlightened twentieth-century man but also in some sense the true heir of Old Java. (Though he would make fun of various Dutch scholars, especially Professor Berg, he was always, as I remember him, very grateful for and respectful of the philological education he had received. He was also contemptuous of much of the palace sphere in which he had been brought up.)[43]

I believe that for Poerbatjaraka the beauty of Dutch was its invulnerability to Javanese: In it one could say anything about Java and Javanese culture, no matter how sacred the subject. In a Dutch sentence "Sinuhun" ("Royal Majesty") was no more than a lexical specimen. In a Javanese sentence it was an obeisance. One can see this Dutch beauty in the title of one of his very first scholarly publications: "Een pseudo-Padjadjaransche kroniek" (A pseudo-Pajajaran-ese chronicle).[44] Notice how a putative sacred heirloom is distanced and demystified by the mordant "pseudo-" in front of, and "-sche" behind, the glory of Pajajaran. The violence of the disjuncture between Dutch language and indigenous subject allowed the scholar (and, he must have hoped, his Javanese readers) to keep a continuously critical stance vis-à-vis the received tradition. (Try to imagine a [Javanese] "Agastya wonten ing Nusantara"!)

Nonetheless, Poerbatjaraka remains a byway to our tradition in that what he used against Javanese was Dutch. He did so because he came to maturity before the great wave of Indonesian nationalism got under way, which increasingly made Dutch a political pariah; and his life was devoted to scholarship, not politics, in an academic world where Dutch survived longer than almost anywhere else in Indonesia.

Yet the impulse at work in Poerbatjaraka's writing affected significant sections of Javanese society, and not only at the cultivated top. We can only note briefly here the fact that the members of the Saminist movement, roughly contemporaneous with Poerbatjaraka's youth,[45] insisted on using only ngoko in addressing other Javanese, no matter how high their social or official positions. Unsurprisingly, nothing

---

[43]I think he would have enjoyed Minke's apostrophe: "Ya Allah . . . nènèk moyang yang keterlaluan!" ("My God, ancestors . . . you're too much!") Pramoedya Ananta Toer, *Bumi Manusia*, p. 108.

[44]This article, written in collaboration with Cornelis Marinus Pleyte, appeared in *Tijdschrift voor Indische taal-, land- en volkenkunde* 56 (1914): 257–80.

[45]The movement seems to have got under way near Blora around 1890. In 1907, an alarmed colonial regime exiled its putative leader, Surontiko Samin. See George McT. Kahin, *Nationalism and Revolution in Indonesia* (Ithaca, N.Y.: Cornell University Press, 1952), p. 43.

enraged Javanese aristocratic officials more than this linguistic refusal (the Dutch, behind the wall of Dutch, were much less upset). Indeed, on occasion they reacted with physical violence to Saminist "impertinence."[46]

The Saminists were, of course, a small group of lowly peasants in the remote interior of Java. But after 1910, there was growing controversy in the wider Javanese society over the whole krama issue. The first impulse for change took the form of hesitant, individual attempts to democratize "up." Dr. Soetomo recalled that his father, a *wedana* (district officer) in the Binnenlandsch Bestuur (Territorial Administrative Service) and thus a native of very high rank, insisted on speaking to "almost everyone" in krama.[47] According to his biographer, Soetomo followed suit, habitually using krama to his driver.[48] There was, however, much more organized social force behind a movement called Djawa Dipo (formed in 1918), which urged the abolition of krama, that is, a leveling "down."

Djawa Dipo's leading figure was a young Javanese of minor aristocratic origins called Radèn Tjokrosoedarmo, who as early as 1913 had been a top leader of the Sarékat Islam and its chief representative in Surabaya.[49] Zürcher gives a nice vignette of the young rebel and of the political implications of ngoko and krama in that era. He records that when at one point Tjokrosoedarmo was summoned to court on some charge or other:

> On entering the courtroom he immediately committed an offence. He remained standing before the Jaksa [public prosecutor]. The latter, a man of the old stamp, reminded Tjokro that according to adat a person brought before the court had to squat (silo). But the defendant refused on grounds of principle. The hearing thus opened according to the will of the defendant. But Tjokro Soedarmo went still further. When the first questions were directed to him, he answered. Not, however, in high-Javanese, Kromo, but in common Ngoko, the language in which superiors are pleased to address inferiors. At this point the Jaksa's astonishment reached its peak, and he asked defendant if he did not know that he had to speak to him in Kromo. Soedarmo knew this perfectly well, but

[46]See Harry J. Benda and Lance Castles, "The Samin Movement," *Bijdrage* 125 (1969): 207–40, which remains much the most sensitive and vivid account of the movement in English.

[47]Soetomo, *Kenang-Kenangan,* p. 42. His father died unexpectedly in 1907.

[48]Imam Supardi, *Dr. Soetomo—Riwajat Hidup dan Perdjuangannja* (Jakarta: Djambatan, 1951), pp. 36, 38.

[49]For this information, and the materials cited in the next five notes, I am grateful to Takashi Shiraishi.

once again appealing to his principles, he declared that he would not speak in Kromo, a decision he based on the fact that in this venue the Jaksa's status was not that of a Javanese, but of a Government official. Accordingly, it was impossible for him to tender a form of respect that only had meaning for Javanese. To this the Jaksa found no reply, though he became extremely annoyed. He immediately summoned the opas [messenger, office-boy] and asked him: "If I ask you something, in what language do you answer me?" "In Kromo," replied mas opas. "Good," said the Jaksa, "then translate into Kromo what the defendant says to me in Ngoko."[50]

Unlike the Saminists, Tjokrosoedarmo did not get slapped in the face for "impertinence." But the painful comedy of this vignette shows clearly the deep-rooted power of the colonial-feudal culture.

Early in 1918 Tjokrosoedarmo launched his Djawa Dipo movement at a meeting in Surabaya, which he addressed in ngoko to the following effect:[51] Now that the Creator has brought light to the slumbering Orient, it is no longer appropriate to continue living under intolerable conditions of irrelevant inequality. From the point of view of equality and to make things easier for foreigners, it is not only desirable but even necessary to jettison krama. Ngoko is the *bahasa asli* (original language; language of origin?) in which a Javanese thinks and in which he speaks to his children. Ngoko has to become the language of the "future reborn Javanese people."

Djawa Dipo soon won the official support of the leadership of the Sarékat Islam and its newspaper, *Oetoesan Hindia*. Members of the movement committed themselves always to speak in ngoko (it was recommended, but not insisted upon, that they have others speak to them in ngoko, too). Logically enough, it was thought necessary also to democratize the Javanese system of titles: Henceforth all males were to be addressed as Wiro, married women as Wara, and unmarried girls as Rara. Thus Sarékat Islam leader Tjokroaminoto and his wife appeared for a time in the pages of *Oetoesan Hindia* as Wiro and Wara Tjokroaminoto.[52]

Unsurprisingly, the movement met with abusive opposition from

---

[50]P. J. Zürcher, Jr., "Djawa Dipo," *De Indische Gids* 42 (1920): 691–95, at 692–93.
[51]Pawitrohadinoto, "De Djowodipo-Beweging," *De Indische Gids* 41 (1919): 220–23. The name derived from the magical weapon Aji Dipo, said to belong to Prince Wibisana in the Ramayana. During the war between the forces of Rahwana and Rama's army of apes, Rahwana's son Indrajit used his magical weapon Warnabara to put the apes to sleep by darkening their hearts and minds. But then Wibisana used the Aji Dipo to revive them by bringing light to their spirits (221).
[52]Ibid., p. 222.

much of Javanese officialdom, which found in this instance an unlikely but vociferous champion in Dr. Tjipto Mangoenkoesoemo.[53] Although a Javanese commentator friendly to the movement pointed out the complete absence of krama among the Tenggerese of East Java (often regarded as the most faithful repositories of ancient Javanese culture), and its rarity in certain very old Javanese villages in East Priangan—not to mention the fact that the great wayang hero Bima speaks ngoko even to Sang Hyang Jagadnata, ruler of the cosmos[54]—officialdom insisted publicly that the abolition of krama would mean the "destruction of literature [*sic*],"[55] for krama was the language of literature and ngoko was generally unsuited for it.[56] Less publicly, "Kings, Princes, Regents, Jaksas, Demangs, Wedonos, etc., all fear the future undermining of their power *which depends so much on the two languages and the 'hormat'* "[57] Zürcher concluded his analysis on an optimistic note: "The fact is that all this hormat and kromo comes

[53]Ibid. Zürcher, "Djawa Dipo," p. 692, attributed this to "a kind of conservatism" originating from his "childhood years." Some Dutch reports claimed that Djawa Dipo had no influence outside the Sarékat Islam and the newspapers *Oetoesan Hindia* and *Sinar Djawa;* and that even in the S.I. itself and the Muslim "Kaumkringen" of Solo there was fierce opposition to it. State Archives, The Hague, "Algemeene beschouwingen over de Inlandsche pers in 1918" (January to mid-March; April to July), *Mailrapport* 264x/18 (Secret).

[54]Pawitrohadinoto, "De Djowodipo-Beweging," p. 222. The case of the Tenggerese is sufficiently well known, that of the Priangan villages less so. The writer gave as his source Rudolf Aernoud Kern, "Een Javaansch sprekende bevolking in de Preanger Regentschappen." (No place of publication cited.)

[55]Ibid., "de afschaffing van het 'kromo' de vernietiging beteekent van de Javaansche letterkunde."

[56]Not only literature, of course. The belief among genteel Javanese that krama expresses the very essence of Javanese civilization—and thus should be a source of pride for Javanese patriots—is amusingly depicted in this exchange between Minke and his kindly, conservative mother:
"Itu tanda kau bukan Jawa lagi, tak mengindahkan siapa lebih tua, lebih berhak akan kehormatan, siapa yang lebih berkuasa."
"Ah, Bunda, jangan hukum sahaya. Saya hormati yang lebih benar."
"Orang Jawa sujud berbakti kepada yang lebih tua, lebih berkuasa, satu jalan pada penghujung keluhuran. Orang harus berani mengalah, Gus."

"That's a sign that you're no longer Javanese, that you don't care about who is the older, who has a right to respect, and who has greater power."
"Oh, Mother, don't condemn me out of hand. I do respect . . . those who are in the right."
"We Javanese serve reverently those who are older and more powerful—that is the one and only path to the heights of glory. One has to have the courage to give way, my child."
Pramoedya Ananta Toer, *Bumi Manusia*, p. 116. Elsewhere (p. 53), Minke comments that he does not wish to "menganiaya" (torment) his girlfriend, the Eurasian beauty Annelies, "with a language that forces her to situate herself socially within the peculiar intricacy of the Javanese way of life."

[57]Zürcher, "Djawa Dipo," p. 692 (italics added).

from another age when the little man crouched in the dust before the nobility and gave them hormat. But these times are long past. The Javan has awakened, he has become a human being [*is mensch geworden*], and this consciousness is likely not to be consonant with continued respect for the slavish tradition of strict hormat. But traditions die slowly and change will come slowly, led by men who no longer know the words 'tida brani [I don't dare].' "[58]

In fact, within a few years Djawa Dipo was dead, though some of its spirit continued to live in the early PKI (Partai Komunis Indonesia— Indonesian Communist party), which, nonetheless, often adopted the Poerbatjarakan device of resorting to Dutch, rather than insisting on ngoko, to create an atmosphere of equality.[59] And we are all aware that krama is very much alive and well today, more than sixty years after Tjokrosoedarmo's spirited address. The reasons for Djawa Dipo's failure surely lie in the continuing power of Java's pseudofeudal culture. Yet I believe that a much more sustained assault would have come had the language choices remained Javanese or Dutch. It was the successful spread of Indonesian that unexpectedly produced a third option, a language as "democratic" as ngoko, and as non-Javanese as Dutch, but with the further inestimable advantage that it could become an indigenous national language. It seems to me that many of the impulses behind Djawa Dipo simply transferred themselves to the movement for the propagation of bahasa Indonesia. (I vividly remember from the 1960s the rage of a senior Javanese bureaucrat when one of his younger Javanese subordinates had the Tjokrosoedarmian insolence to respond to a question asked in ngoko in the "new ngoko" of bahasa Indonesia—straight back!)

The year before Poerbatjaraka received his doctorate at Leiden, a baby was born in Blora who would grow up to be Indonesia's—or should I say Indonesian's?—greatest writer. Like Poerbatjaraka, though in a very different style, Pramoedya Ananta Toer was, and is, a rebel against the Javanese culture he imbibed as a child and young man. So far as I know, he has never published a page in the language of his childhood home; but this does not mean that Java and its culture are ever very far from his mind. I would argue in fact that, like

---

[58]Ibid., pp. 694–95.

[59]In the entertaining account of an early *vergadering* (political meeting) contained in Soemantri's radical novel *Rasa Merdika, Hikajat: Soedjanmo* (Semarang: Drukkerij V.S.T.P., 1924), pp. 92–93, we find, at the collective level, the use of *saudara-saudara* (brothers and sisters in Indonesian) and at the "intercomrade" level, *broer* and *zus* (brother and sister in Dutch).

Poerbatjaraka's Dutch, Pramoedya's bahasa Indonesia is a cultural fortress from which to cross swords with his heritage.

It may be useful to begin our discussion of Pramoedya with two exemplary passages from his short story "Machluk Dibelakang Rumah" (Creatures behind houses), which is concerned with the *babu* (maids) who do the dirty work behind the houses of arriviste Javanese come to Jakarta after independence:

> Barangkali patut pula kutjeritakan, bahwa rumahku tergolong pada petak jang terdiri atas duapuluhtiga pintu—duapuluhtiga keluarga! Dapat dikatakan semua petak mempunjai babunja masing-masing. Dan para prijaji dari udik ini tak djarang datang kekota ini setelah lebih dulu mendjadi babu atau djongos. Didaérah petak ini! Untuk mengabdi! Sedjalan dengan adjaran paraprijaji tua didjaman beheula: Berendah-rendah akan luhur achirnja. Djuga prijaji-prijaji udik jang datang ke Djakarta ini dahulu mengabdi. Pengabdiannja mémang membawanja keharkat jang lebih tinggi: djadi prijaji dikota. Tetapi kadang-kadang meréka lupa pada pengabdiannja dulu. Karena itu sering terdengar teriakan histéris didaérahku ini: Sekali lagi, gua seterika perut luh!
> [Of the fate of the babu] Djiwanja mengembara kemana-mana sewaktu tubuhnja mentjutji, berdjalan, atau makan, atau tidur. Dapat dipastikan tiap minggu sekali ia kena bentjana: terpelését disumur, paku terbenam dalam kakinja, terseterika lengan, terbalik menumpuk bangku, bahkan sekali waktu sedang beristirahat disebuah kursi rotan jang telah péot, ia kedjatuhan sepéda, kursi mendjatuhi dérétan piring, dan setelah itu ia kedjatuhan pulung diatas kepalanja dari djuragan.

Perhaps I should also say that my home was located in a single row of partitioned dwellings—23 frontdoors . . . 23 families! One could say that every such row had its own maids. And these priyayi [gentleman officials] from the sticks quite often had come to the city after previous service as maids or houseboys. In this neighborhood of partitioned-dwellings! To serve! In full accord with the teachings of the old priyayi in times gone by: bow down now, and you'll rise high in the end. Yes, these priyayi who had come to Jakarta from the sticks had previously been in service. And their service had indeed raised them to a higher status: that of city priyayi. But sometimes they forgot their previous service. And so in my neighborhood one often heard this hysterical shriek:

Next time, I'll put the iron to your belly!

Her spirit would rove far and wide while her body laundered, ironed, walked, or ate, or slept. You could be sure that once every week some disaster would strike: she'd slip and fall by the well, she'd get a nail in the sole of her foot, she'd burn her arm with the iron, or she'd stumble headlong over a bench . . . in fact once, while she was resting in a dilapidated rattan chair, a bicycle fell over on her, the chair sent a row of dishes crashing, and in due course a *pulung* from her master landed on her head.[60]

It would be difficult to overemphasize the grief and anger in these passages, but we are a long way from the *Suluk Gatholoco*'s silit babi or Ronggawarsita's parandéné. The first passage is perfectly intelligible to any reasonably educated Indonesian reader. It appears to be a satire on upstart nouveaux riches and "new" civil servants who, forgetting their humble pasts as babu and *jongos* (houseboys)[61] to the former colonial rulers, are brutal to their own servants. But the full vengefulness of the author will only be felt by *Javanese* readers (though the word *jawa* is never mentioned in the story). For the term *priyayi* epitomizes the nineteenth-century pseudofeudal ideal of the refined, cultivated, leisured, upper-class Javanese.[62] Thus "prijaji dari udik" (priyayi from the sticks) is just as "impossible" as Ronggawarsita's helplessly perfect king, but now the oxymoron is utterly self-aware and venomous (still more "impossible"—priyayi who used to be babu and jongos!). Notice also the subtle Javanism of "paraprijaji"; the parodic Indonesianization of a standard Javanese motto in "berendah-rendah akan luhur achirnja";[63] the sardonic use of the Jakarta-Sundanese *baheula* for the normal *dulu* or *lama;* and finally the brutality, next to all of this, of "Next time, I'll put the iron to your belly!" in bahasa Jakarta. The whole force of the passage comes from the sophisticated play between different languages within the medium of Indonesian. It is absolutely untranslatable into Javanese—yet it de-

---

[60]Both passages occur on p. 121 of Pramoedya Ananta Toer, *Tjerita dari Djakarta, Sekumpulan Karikatur Keadaan dan Manusianja* (Jakarta: Grafica, 1957).

[61]These are, par excellence, the colonial words for household servants. The creation of jongos is sociologically very instructive. In traditional upper-class Javanese homes adult males were almost never employed as servants inside the house: the danger of cross-class sex with noble wives and daughters was too great. It was the Dutch who created the implicitly "castrated" adult male household servant, with whom their daughters would be quite safe. One is reminded of Richard Wright's famous story about the black husband who, when his wife falls sick, puts on her clothes and does her work as a maid in a white household—and the whites never notice.

[62]I say "nineteenth-century" advisedly. In a splendid article on the Mangkunegaran court of the 1790s, Ann Kumar has shown how *priyayi* was there used in contemptuous contrast to (Djawa Dipo's!) *wira* (man, male). See Ann Kumar, "Javanese Court Society and Politics in the Late Eighteenth Century: The Record of a Lady Soldier" [pt. 2: "Political Developments: The Courts and the Company, 1784–1791"], *Indonesia* 30 (October 1980):67–111, at 108.

[63]Cf. Minke's mother (as quoted above): "We Javanese serve reverently those who are older and more powerful—that is the one and only path to the heights of glory."

pends no less absolutely on the existence of Javanese, and a readership of Javanese.

I would guess that most of Pramoedya's non-Javanese readers will miss the point of the second passage, even though in some editions the words *kedjatuhan pulung* are italicized, and in others *kedjatuhan* is replaced by the explicitly Javanese *ketiban*. Since *pulung* in Indonesian means "pellet," they may even frown in puzzlement. But every Javanese reader will see at once that Pramoedya is quoting the classical Javanese *topos* describing the mysterious ball of radiance that descends on the head of the man destined to be the new king: such a hero is said to be *ketiban pulung*.[64] The lash flails in all directions: A bicycle equals a pulung, and a babu replaces a heroic future king. One can use the same words for the rise of a new dynasty and the brutal mistreatment of a household servant. I would emphasize again that the sentence is written in Indonesian; only in non-Javanese can one speak to Javanese this way out of the side of one's mouth. And how Javanese in its own way all this is! One can almost see the smile on the writer's face as one foot flies back to kick Javanese traditional culture in the teeth.

Another famous passage is the opening of the mordant tale *Djongos + Babu* (Houseboy + housemaid) (*not Djongos dan [and] Babu,* and *not* easily translatable into Javanese). It goes like this:

Sedjak Jan Pietersz. Coen turun-temurun keluarga itu memang berdarah hamba. Hamba jang tak tanggung-tanggung—setia sampai bulu-bulunja. Mungkin djuga bukan sedjak Coen sadja. Besar kemungkinan sudah sedjak Pieter Both atau disaat-saat Houtman mengelana disemua samudera. Orang tak ada jang tahu dengan pasti. Jang sudah njata, keluarga itu dikenal dikala Coen belum djadi artja jang diusir Djepang dari depan gedung Financiën.

Keluarga pertama ini dikenal karena tertjatat dibuku besar dengan huruf latin, inlandsch sergeant . . . stb. no. . . . . Pangkat sersan waktu itu sangat tinggi. Dengan pangkat itu orang bisa berbiak. Dan keluarga itu menurunkan empatpuluh anak. Entah berapa biangnja. Orang tak ada jang tahu. Soal ini tak boléh masuk buku besar.
Turunan kedua—hamba djuga, serdadu tak berkelas!
Kemudian dari turunan keturunan, derdjat hambanja turun djuga. Kian ketjil kian ketjil. Achirnja sampai tahun 1949 sampailah keluarga itu pada Sobi dan Inah—titik derdjat hamba jang penghabisan. Setahun

64See Soemarsaid Moertono, *State and Statecraft in Old Java,* Cornell Modern Indonesia Project Monograph Series (Ithaca, N.Y.: Cornell University, 1968), pp. 56–57.

jang lalu mereka masih hamba-hamba negeri. Keduanja tak tahu: Baha-
ja mengawang diatas kepala. Derdjat hambanja akan turun satu derdjat
lagi—hamba-hamba distrik-fédéral-Batavia! Sobi djongos, Inah babu.

Sekiranja Tuhan masih bermurahhati seperti didjaman dulu, sudi
memandjangkan keturunan hamba itu, pasti keturunan jang ke-
tigapuluh bukan manusia lagi, tapi—tjatjing jang mendjulurdjulur didalam tanah.[65]

From the days of Jan Pietersz. Coen, generation after generation, the
family had always had true servile blood. Servile to the nth degree—
faithful from top to toe. Maybe not merely since the days of Coen.
There's a good chance as far back as the time of Pieter Both, or when
Houtman sailed the seven seas. No one knows for sure. What's certain is
that the family was already known at a time when Coen had not yet
become the statue kicked out by the Japanese from in front of the
Financiën Building.

The original family is known because it was recorded in a big book
with Latin letters. . . Native Sergeant . . . Gazette No. . . . In those
days the rank of sergeant was a very high one. With such a rank, a man
could breed abundantly. And the lineage produced forty children in that
generation. Who knows from how many dams. No one has any idea.
Such things were not permitted to be recorded in the big book.

The second generation—servant once again: soldier, without rank!
Then, from generation to generation, their servile status sank down
and down. Lower and lower. Until, in 1949, the family line descended to
Sobi and Inah—the ultimate in servanthood. A year before they had still
been servants of their own country. Neither had any idea of the peril
looming over their heads: that their servanthood would sink down one
further step. They would become servants of the Federalist Municipality
of Batavia! Sobi as houseboy, Inah as housemaid.

If only God were as merciful as in olden times, and were prepared to
prolong this servile lineage, unquestionably the thirtieth generation

---

[65]Pramoedya Ananta Toer, *Tjerita dari Djakarta*, p. 7. J. P. Coen was the founder of the
Dutch East India Company stronghold of Batavia (Jakarta) in 1619. Pieter Both was the first
governor-general in the Indies (1609–14). Cornelis de Houtman led the first Dutch naval
expedition to the Indies, 1595–97. During the Japanese occupation of Java (1942–45),
prominent symbols of Dutch colonialism, including Coen's statue, were removed and often
destroyed. The Financiën Building, headquarters of the colonial Department of Finance, was
located on the eastern side of today's Merdéka Square. Between 1946 and 1949 Batavia
(Jakarta) was under restored Dutch colonial control, and was the capital of the "Federalist"
state that the Dutch attempted to build to compete with the Indonesian Republic in the
interior.

would no longer be human beings, but rather maggots squirming in the earth.

Much of the force of this splendid tirade comes from the fact that it is written in Indonesian, cannot be written in Javanese, and can be fully experienced (painfully) only by Javanese readers. For it is a sardonic parody (*karikatur!*) of the classical chronicles, with their elaborate genealogies of famous heroes. Here is a *silsilah* (family tree) of servants, who "if only God were as merciful as in olden times," would be permitted to decline (notice the play on *turun* [descend] and *turunan* [descendant]) eventually from being human beings to being maggots. Here is a comic version of classic dating systems, now marked, not by great Javanese dynasts, but by various Dutch adventurers of the late sixteenth and early seventeenth centuries—the era of Panembahan Sénapati and Sultan Agung! (And the typical allusiveness of classical references to period is marvelously parodied in my favorite Pramoedya sentence: "At a time when Coen had not yet become the statue kicked out by the Japanese from in front of the gedung Financiën"—at each turn of phrase one is promised a "date," but at the next that promise is undermined).⁶⁶ The classical polyphiloprogenitiveness of great Javanese rulers is satirized in the figure of the "founding father" sergeant who likewise can "berbiak," with who knows how many "bijang" (words of the coarsest animallike overtones: we may recall the three santri's *biyangamu silit babi*). Notice also the special typographical features of the passage: "Pietersz." and "stb. no." are Dutch, and "huruf latin," conventions, which not only make their own mocking point, but cannot be intelligibly rendered in the ancestral script.

For another style in which Pramoedya uses Indonesian against Javanese, let us turn to the famous tale *Dendam* (Revenge).⁶⁷ The setting of this story is the Revolution, and its central drama is the arrest, interrogation, torture, and eventual death of a haji who appears to be a spy for the Dutch. The strange power of the tale, and its almost unbearable suspense, come from the fact that until the last moment the haji is invulnerable to the tortures inflicted on him and continues to smile "presis seperti gadis mendapat mimpi bagus" (exactly like a girl who is having a beautiful dream).⁶⁸ Tied to an electric pole, he is

---

⁶⁶(1) *Di kala Coen;* (2) *Belum djadi artja;* (3) *(Achirnja) djadi artja;* (4) *Artja diusir Djepang*—that is, any date between 1619 and 1942. Notice the difference between the hybrid *gedung Financiën* and, say, *Departemen Keuangan.*

⁶⁷Contained in *Subuh* (Jakarta: Balai Pustaka, 1950), pp. 38–61.

⁶⁸Ibid., p. 55. The two following quotations also come from p. 55.

stabbed in the belly with a *bambu runcing* (a bamboo pole sharpened at one end to make a spear):

> Udjung tombaknja mengedjap hilang, menjelinap kedalam perut hadji itu. . . . Bambu itu ditarik tjepat. . . . Udjung bambu itu meliuk sedikit dan tetap kering. . . . Kunantikan isi perutnja keluar. Tak keluar. Ia tetap tersenjum sabar. Dan ia tak luka.

> The tip of the spear flashed and disappeared, slipping into the haji's belly. . . . The bamboo was quickly pulled out. . . . The tip was slightly bent and still quite dry. . . . I waited for his guts to gush out. But they didn't. He continued to smile patiently. And he was not wounded at all.

Shortly afterward the haji is stabbed in the eye:

> Aku lihat udjung tombak bambu masuk kedalam matanja dan lari pula dengan tiada meninggalkan bekas.

> I saw the tip of a bamboo spear pierce his eye and flee without leaving a trace.

Then suddenly:

> Aku melihat senjum hadji itu tiba-tiba hilang. Kedua tangannja jang terikat kebelakang bergerak-gerak. Dan tali pengikat, jang telah rantas-rantas kena samurai, putus. Orang-orang jang mabok itu tiba-tiba djadi insaf akan keselamatannja. Ketjemasan tergambar pada muka meréka. Pelan-pelan orang mundur kebelakang. Kedua tangan kurban itu telah bebas.[69]

> I saw the haji's smile suddenly vanish. The two hands tied behind his back stirred. And the rope that bound him, which had been half cut through in places by the samurai-sword, broke apart. The intoxicated suddenly took thought for their own safety. On their faces fear was etched. Slowly people edged backward. The victim's two hands now were free.

But the haji's feet are still attached by a rope to the back of a truck, and someone yells for the truck to start up. The haji is yanked off his feet and dragged along behind the accelerating truck—"ia masih nampak tenang djua. Dan ia belum lagi mendapat luka berat oleh

[69]Ibid., p. 56.

asahan batu dan aspal djalan raja" (Yet he still appeared completely calm. And he still had suffered no serious injury from the scraping of stones and asphalt of the highway).[70] His invulnerability is only destroyed when a soldier with a particular samurai sword stabs him, crying out the strange words "Kembali djadi tanah!" (Become earth once more!)[71] With the utterance of this *mantra* (magic spell) the haji immediately dies.

There is nothing in this tale to suggest that either the haji or the mob of would-be torturers and executioners are Javanese. The presumable locale is Cikampèk, in northern West Java, which was an important railway junction, supply depot, and military base for the Republican forces facing the Dutch in Batavia; and when the soldiers speak, they use a stylized form of the Jakarta dialect. Nonetheless, the story is incomprehensible unless one bears in mind a series of famous tableaux from traditional Javanese wayang culture: Bisma, riddled with wounds, lying on a bed of up-pointing arrows; Abimanyu's shredded flesh in a howling circle of Kurawa enemies; Suyudana in his final proud, despairing battle with Bima;[72] Niwatakawaca, who cannot be killed even by the gods till he is tricked by Supraba's soft voice into revealing the secret of his invulnerability; above all, perhaps, the well-loved scenes where Arjuna is mobbed by *raseksa* or *buta* (giants), especially the fang-toothed Buta Cakil: he stands quite still, apparently defenseless, a calm smile on his face. His shrieking enemies attempt to stab, slash, and maim him, but the smooth film of his invulnerability foils their every effort. Finally, the hero "loses his smile" and goes on the attack—at which point the mob "tiba-tiba djadi insaf akan keselamatannja."

Non-Javanese readers can take *Dendam* pretty much on its obvious terms as describing a grim episode in the Revolution. Javanese readers, however, will feel the peculiar linguistic violence of the veiled allusions and ironic parallels: soldiers of the Republic/mob of buta; haji-spy/Arjuna. Yet for such Javanese readers the violence of the tale comes precisely from its being written in Indonesian, not Javanese. If translated into Javanese, it becomes embedded in a Javanese world in which invulnerable haji are not at all foreign, and can readily be assimilated to the genre of Javanese-style *cerita silat* (penny dreadfuls). It is only the matter-of-fact *alienness* of Indonesian that allows Pra-

---

[70]Ibid., p. 57.
[71]Ibid., p. 58.
[72]He knows he will die; but Bima cannot overcome his *kasektèn* (magical power) except by using dishonorable methods.

moedya to exploit the abyss between two worlds and languages, and to "quote" Javanese culture rather than speak from within it.

Before leaving Pramoedya, it may be worth touching on one more important element in the odd relationship between Indonesian and Javanese—what one can think of as "the weight of words," or the link between language and reality. Both the felt antiquity and the hierachical rigidities of Javanese make it a language tied tightly to the immediacy of experience and the very nature of the world. Conversely, the modernity of bahasa Indonesia and its astonishing absorptive capacities distance it from immediate experience and loosen it from the grip of the world. *Dendam* offers some illustrations of this point. What strikes me as the one flaw in the tale (though one sees why Pramoedya made the decision he did) is that the mantra that dissolves the haji's invulnerability is in bahasa Indonesia. I hope I am not far wrong in thinking that Indonesian mantra cannot really be mantra, for the conception behind a mantra is that certain words, in certain prescribed orders, have active "power" in the world—beyond their evident semantic thrust lie secret and dangerous meanings. This sense of the "power" of words seems to be utterly foreign to Indonesian, whose charm for us, and its speakers, is that nothing in it is secret or dangerous, for the language slips lightly along the world. The bite of sacrilege is remote from this language, which has so few sacred cows of its own.

The solemn rigidity of Javanese, in its later life at least, which makes "aku sampun mangan" meaningless, can be contrasted with all the subtle possibilities of authorial play that Indonesian affords. (For example, each of the following has its own connotations: "saya sudah makan," "aku sudah makan," "saya sih sudah mangan," "gua udah makan," and so on. Almost all the terms are interchangeable in a way that Javanese virtually excludes.) Among the subtle glories of Pramoedya's prose are his inventions of new words, adaptations of old words, distortions of old meanings, and such things as the heightening-by-distance effect achieved by putting Indonesian words into the mouths of his utterly Javanese peasants. He is always keenly aware that Indonesian is a language that by its very freedom and inventiveness pulls into the future rather than reverberates with the past. Here are some reflections of the anonymous "I" of *Dendam:*

Aku berangkat kesetasiun dengan uniform pradjurit. . . . Dan aku bangga pada uniform-hidjauku buatan pendjara Tjipinang itu. Akupun bangga pada pangkatku: pradjurit belum berkelas dan berpangkat. . . .[73] Karena itu akupun pergi kesetasiun. Mengapa 'kan tidak? Selalu dan selalu manusia suka memperlihatkan kelebihannja. Apalagi kalau kenjataan jang telandjang itu diberi fantasi sedikit: aku pemuda revolusionèr. . . . Dan bila hati ini mulut pasti akan terdengar teriak fantasi itu: "Lihatlah—aku djuga seorang patriot."[74]

I left for the station in my soldier's uniform. . . . And I was proud of my green uniform made in Cipinang Prison. I was also proud of my rank: private, without stripes or rank. . . . And so I went to the station . . . and why not? Forever and always men love to show off their superiority. Specially if the reality is dressed up in a bit of fantasy: I am a revolutionary pemuda. . . . And if this heart were lips, without question this fantasy could be heard shouting: "Look! I too am a patriot!"

"Patriot," "pemuda revolusionèr" (revolutionary youth)—these fantasies are also linguistic inventions. In this sense, they are the exact opposite of mantra: not syllables resonating with the secrets of the universe but rather words that, like the words of a gifted, marketed author, draw on themselves for what power they can exert. They are what Pramoedya in so many of his stories calls *istilah*, human inventions in historical time and circumstances, that, by their very novelty and unanchoredness in the world, draw men and women into action through the imagination. One might say, perhaps exaggerating, that it was because so many youngsters had the *fantasi* that they were or could be "pemuda revolusionèr" and "patriot" that the Revolution broke out and had what success it did.

Half a century after Poerbatjaraka's Leiden doctorate, and Pramoedya's birth, a novel was published in Jakarta which opened with the following words:

Disebuah pagi yang merangsang, Arjuna bertolak pinggang. Hatinya gundah dan penasaran. Semalam papinya marah-marah karena melihat anaknya yang satu itu berciuman dengan seorang perempuan didalam mobil dinasnya.

"Anak tak tahu aturan! Siapa perempuan itu?" hardiknya.

"Salah seorang pacar saya," jawab Arjuna dengan hati kesal karena merasa diusik urusan pribadinya.

---

[73]Recall Sobi's and Inah's distinguished ancestors: "The second generation—servant once again: soldier, without rank!" *Tjerita dari Djakarta*, p. 7.

[74]Pramoedya Aranta Toer, "Dendam," pp. 42–43.

"Salah seorang pacarmu? Salah seorang?!" Papinya mendelik. Tadi malam. Dan Arjuna bertambah tak senang pada sikap Papi itu.[75]

One maddening morning Arjuna stood with his arms akimbo. He felt depressed and pissed off. The previous evening his daddy had flown into a rage when he spotted that kid of his necking with a girl in *his* official limo.

"You little hooligan! Who is that girl!" he had scolded.

"Oh, one of my girlfriends," answered Arjuna resentfully, feeling that his personal life was being meddled with.

"One of your girlfriends? One of . . . ?" Daddy's eyeballs bulged. Last night. And Arjuna got more and more fed up with Daddy's attitude.

This is the unmistakable voice of Yudhistira Ardi Noegraha (*né* Mulyana), in 1977 still in his early twenties (as Pramoedya had been when he began publishing in 1947): a voice of marvelously supple and nonchalant impudence. The key word of course is the fifth: for if we were to substitute Hassan, or Henk, or Sumardi for Arjuna, all the malice would disappear and we would have nothing but an ordinary scene between a boring, middle-aged Indonesian official and his childishly rebellious son. But by stealing Arjuna from the Javanese classics and plunging him into the *borné* bourgeois world of contemporary Jakarta, Yudhistira in his own way picks up from his ancestors and continues their civil war. The words in the paragraph are carefully chosen: "bertolak pinggang" (to have one's arms akimbo) is a thoroughly "kurangajar" (insolent) body posture which the Arjuna of wayang (henceforth Arjuna I) never assumes. The last thing that Arjuna I's heart should be is "gundah dan penasaran." The splendor of "salah seorang pacar saya" lies in Arjuna II's and his father's deadpan unawareness of what the writer and all Javanese readers know only too well: that Arjuna I is much admired for his countless sexual conquests.

The rest of the novel proceeds along essentially the same lines: a series of rather chaste love affairs between Arjuna II, his friends and rivals (Kreshna, that is, Kreshna II, Abimanyu II, and Palgunadi II), and their schoolmates Setyowati II, Arimbi II, and Anggraeni II, punctuated with quarrels with their parents and other older relatives.[76]

[75] Yudhistira Ardi Noegraha, *Arjuna Mencari Cinta* (Jakarta: Cypress, 1977), p. 7. My analysis in the following pages owes much to Savitri Scherer, "Introducing Yudhistira Ardi Noegraha," *Indonesia* 31 (April 1981):31–52.

[76] As we learn from *Arjuna Mencari Cinta* and its sequel *Arjuna Drop Out* (Jakarta:

The malicious exploitation of wayang names (from both the Mahabharata and the Ramayana) is done in two different ways. First, these sacred names are, on the telephone and in casual conversations, impudently abbreviated to "Ar," "Kresh," and "Set." Second, though superficially selected at random, the names are in fact organized in such a way as to show (Javanese) wayang-lovers that no mistakes of the "aku sampun mangan" type are being made. Everything is "wrong," but in a calculated manner. For example, there are only a small number of wayang-women with whom Arjuna I is *not* sexually involved, but the names of *all* Arjuna II's girls fall into this category. "Bad" Kurawa names rarely occur, and when they do, they mainly denote exemplary or at least neutral characters (see below). And Yudhistira is careful to give the name Palgunadi (II) to Arjuna II's rival in love (whom he cheats shamefully) because it recalls the relations between Arjuna I and Palgunadi I—though the wayang-play *Palgunadi* is not among the most popular or best known. (Thus wayang-loving readers will know that Yudhistira knows his wayang very well.)

Throughout, the brio of the novel comes from the doubleness of the writing, in which Yudhistira pokes his readers in the ribs, while the characters go their bourgeois way completely oblivious of the overtones of what they say. A nice example is the following exchange: When Burisrawa II, the father of Arimbi II, finds out that Arjuna II has escorted her home, though he has strictly forbidden her to see the young playboy, he draws a pistol and threatens to shoot the lad:

"Kalau tembakan Oom barusan menghancurkan kepala saya, pasti Oom pun akan menghancurkan kepala sendiri setelah Oom tahu siapa saya!" begitu kata Arjuna.

Mendengar itu, si Oom mengerutkan kening.

"Memangnya, kamu siapa?" suara si Oom mengandung semacam sesal dan kecemasan.

"Saya Arjuna. Pacar Arimbi!" sahut Arjuna sambil meneruskan langkahnya dan menghilang dari rumah itu.[77]

Cypress, 1980), Arjuna II's father is Brataséna II (Brataséna I is Arjuna I's elder brother); his mother is Banowati II (Banowati I is Arjuna I's mistress, married to his cousin Suyudana I); his uncle is Sangkuni II (Sangkuni I is the evil chief minister to Suyudana I); his grandmother is Draupadi II, or Padi ("tapi bukan Dewi Sri" [but not Dewi Sri—i.e., the goddess of *padi*, rice], jokes Yudhistira on p. 9 of *Arjuna Drop Out*), while Draupadi I is no blood relation to Arjuna I at all; his grandfather is called Walmiki (Valmiki is the legendary author of the *Ramayana*). A further nice touch is that when Arjuna II enrolls briefly at Gajah Mada University, one of his "kawan sefakultas" (friend in the same department/faculty) is called Cakil (cf. above, p. 225).

[77] Yudhistira Ardi Noegraha, *Arjuna Mencari Cinta*, p. 113.

"I warn you, Unc, if you shoot and blow my head off, you'll be blowing your own head off too the minute you find out who I am!" Thus Arjuna.

On hearing this, 'Unc' knitted his brows.

"Well, who are you, anyway?" In Unc's voice there were now traces of a certain regret and alarm.

"I am Arjuna. Arimbi's boyfriend!" replied Arjuna, continuing on his way and vanishing out through the front door.

Here the doubleness comes from the contrast between Burisrawa II's Indonesian worry that this insolent boy's father may be someone important and powerful in the Jakarta elite and all those wayang scenes where a giant, ogre, or someone from Sabrang (overseas) encounters the great Arjuna I and ignorantly demands to know who he is.

The novel's conclusion complicates the sardonic play of allusion further. Arjuna II has been violently dressed down by his father for kissing the latter's secretary, Pergiwati II.[78] Now he finds his father himself in Pergiwati II's arms:

> Kemarahannya kian memuncak ketika ternyata kedua orang yang meléngkét jadi satu bagai kéong racun di hadapannya itu tidak juga menyadari kehadirannya. Sehingga, dengan geram ia lalu menendang pintu dibelakangnya sampai menimbulkan ledakan keras.
>
> Kedua orang itu terlonjak, dan seketika meréka melepaskan pelukan masing-masing dan menghadap ke pintu. Dan ketika meréka melihat Arjuna yang tampangnya sudah tidak mirip Arjuna lagi, melainkan mirip raksasa itu, meréka tambah kagèt, sehingga mata meréka terbuka lébar-lébar dan mulut meréka ternganga-nganga.
>
> Sementara itu, dengan geram Arjuna lantas mengambil anak panah dan busurnya. Memasangnya dan membidikkannya ke dada Papinya yang terkutuk itu. Anak panah melesat dan tepat menembus jantung. Crap!
>
> Tapi panah dan busur itu hanya ada di dalam angan-angan Arjuna saja, sehingga Papinya dan Pergiwati yang menyaksikan kelakuan Arjuna yang ganjil itu, mengerutkan kening masing-masing. Tapi Arjuna tak mau menghiraukan semua itu. Dengan suara keras, ia lalu berteriak. Menghardikkan makian yang pernah keluar dari mulut Papinya setelah ia mencium mulut Pergiwati di tempat itu juga.
>
> "Kamu ini betul-betul kurang-ajar! Bréngsèk! Tidak tahu aturan!

---

[78]Ibid., p. 152.

Sétan! Kambing! Kuda! Sapi! Kerbau dan kawan-kawannya!!!" kutuk-
nya. Arjuna lalu meludah.
Fuih!![79]

His fury continued to mount when it became obvious that the pair
before him, glued together like poisonous snails, were still oblivious of
his presence. At that, he angrily kicked the door behind him to, making
a loud bang.
The couple leapt to their feet, abandoning their embraces, and swung
around to face the door. And when they observed an Arjuna whose face
no longer resembled Arjuna's, but rather that of a giant, they were even
more astounded; their eyes bulged and their mouths gaped.
Meanwhile, Arjuna furiously picked up his bow and arrow, fitted the
arrow, and aimed it at the breast of his damned Daddy. The arrow flew
off and pierced straight through Daddy's heart. Bzzzt!
But arrow and bow existed only in Arjuna's imagination—so that his
Daddy and Pergiwati, watching his weird behavior, simply frowned in
puzzlement. But Arjuna refused to heed any of this. He started shouting
at the top of his voice. Bellowing out the curses that had earlier exploded
from Daddy's mouth when he'd caught Arjuna kissing Pergiwati's lips in
this very same room
"You hooligan! Louse! Lout! Devil! Goat! Ox! Water-buffalo! Etc.!
Etc.!!!" he cursed. Then Arjuna spat.
Fuih!!

For the first and last time in the novel, Yudhistira, for malicious fun,
makes Arjuna II seem aware of his namesake.[80] We are to imagine
him going emptily through the motions of Arjuna I drawing his bow
and letting fly his invincible arrow Pasopati. "Papi" and Pergiwati II
have not the faintest idea what is going on. Neither Arjuna II, nor
"Papi," nor Pergiwati II really thinks that Arjuna II's face now "looks
like a giant's"; the phrase is inserted by the author simply to tease his
wayang-loving Javanese readers, who will recognize at once a parody
of the occasional terrible transformations of heroes like Kreshna I and
Yudhistira I into colossal, fire-breathing, multiheaded giants (*tiwi-
krama*). Finally, Yudhistira has the fun of writing "Then Arjuna spat.
Fuih!!" in which the "fuih" certainly flies up off the page into some
readers' faces. Note that the entire passage, not to speak of the book,

---

[79]Ibid., pp. 185–86.
[80]This is entirely "out of character," and thus a nice example of secret dialogue between
author and reader at right angles to the text.

depends for its effect on the invisible presence of Javanese alongside Indonesian, or rather its visible encapsulation within it.

Yudhistira can only have been delighted when the authorities were goaded into banning a projected film based on *Arjuna Mencari Cinta*—not because it satirized elite Jakarta life, but because it would "damage the wayang world."[81] For, of course, there is nothing in the novel, except countless deadpan allusions, the final four paragraphs, and the names, that is about wayang at all. But it was precisely the insouciant *lèse-majesté* of the names that really angered an establishment still deeply sunk in the residues of colonial Javanese culture.

Yudhistira made fun of the ban in *Arjuna Drop Out*, the sequel to *Arjuna Mencari Cinta*, in the following dialogue between Arjuna and a former girlfriend, Jeng Sum (Sumbadra I was Arjuna I's main wife and greatest love), who is described as happily married to an absurdly honest bank clerk called Aswatama (II) and blessed with a young baby whom she has named Pancawala (II).[82] Says Arjuna II:

"Siapa namanya?"
"Pancawala."
"Wah, seperti nama anak Prabu Yudhistira saja." Jeng Sum tersenyum. "Mémangnya Jeng Sum sering nonton wayang?" Jeng Sum cuma senyum. "Tapi hati-hati lho, jeng. Salah-salah anak itu nanti mendapat kesulitan karena namanya."
"Lho, mémangnya kenapa?"
"Memakai nama wayang itu dilarang. Dianggap menghancurkan kebudayaan."[83]

"What's his name?"
"Pancawala."
"Wow! Just the same as Prabu Yudhistira's kid." Jeng Sum smiles. "I guess you often watch wayang, huh?" Jeng Sum merely smiles. "Well, be

[81]A spokesman for the Direktorat Pembinaan Film told *Sinar Harapan* on August 14, 1979, that "all wayang names in this story must be replaced: by names 'yang bukan [*sic*] berasal dari dunia pewayangan, termasuk judul ceritanya' (which do not originate from the wayang world, including the title of the story) so that it would not 'merugikan dunia pewayangan' (damage the wayang world)." See *Tempo*, September 1, 1979, for this, and for a witty editorial comment by Goenawan Mohamad.

[82]Aswatama I, among the worst of the Kurawa, treacherously murders Pancawala I, as well as Banowati I and Srikandhi I, after the Bratayuda War is over. Aswatama II, however, is simply a bank clerk who is "segan mencuri uang negara. Betapa ia telah menyia-nyiakan kesempatan yang ada! Betapa bodohnya ia mau berjujur-jujur di tengah lingkungan dan masyarakatnya yang korup!" (reluctant to steal the public's money. *How* he has wasted the opportunities before him! *How* stupid he is to want to be an "honest Joe" in the midst of a corrupt environment and a corrupt society!) *Arjuna Drop Out*, p. 113.

[83]Ibid., p. 28.

real careful now. Otherwise the kid'll have a lot of trouble later on because of his name."

"Really? How come?"

"Using wayang names is banned. It's supposed to be 'destructive to culture.'"

Here again, the bile comes not so much from the obvious gibe at the film censors, but from every Javanese reader's awareness that the traditional reason for being "hati-hati, lho" is that wayang names are so "heavy" and "power-full" that small children, unless they come from the highest aristocratic circles (and not always then), do not have the strength to bear them, and thus may "nanti mendapat kesulitan."[84]

Let me conclude these quotations from Yudhistira's work with a passage from *Arjuna Drop Out* where the Javanese civil war is pursued from quite another rampart. Frustrated by life in Jakarta, Arjuna II takes the train to Yogyakarta, where he arrives early in the morning:

Yogyakarta, sekarang ternyata telah banyak berubah. Tampak sedang mencoba bersolèk, dengan gincu yang tak cocok, dengan bedak tanpa selera. Padahal jiwanya tetap saja jiwa yang dulu. Jiwa priyayi yang selalu hadir dengan ironi: blangkon di kepala, dasi di léhèr, keris di pinggang, samsonite di tangan. Selalu bicara tentang kejayaan Mataram, sambil memimpikan Amsterdam.

Arjuna menghirup udara, mencoba menikmati rasa Jawa. Rasa menjadi orang Jawa kembali setelah bercerai dengan induknya sekian lama. Setelah kebudayaan campur-baur kota Jakarta mengasemblingnya menjadi sebuah produk baru yang kosmopolit-universal—tanpa ciri kedaérahan sama sekali. Bahkan hampir tanpa tulang punggung. Apa artinya itu, kurang jelas.

Bécak melewati tugu perempatan yang sangat terkenal dan menjadi ciri kota itu, di samping Jalan Malioboro. Tapi tugu itu kini, di tengah perubahan yang terjadi, betul-betul menjadi hanya fosil.[85] Tata-kota yang ngawur membuatnya menjadi amat lucu.[86]

These days, Jogja's obviously changed a lot. Blatantly trying to be stylish, with the wrong color lipstick, and vulgar face powder. In spirit, however, the same as always. The priyayi soul always ironically present: *blangkon* on the head, tie at the neck, kris at the waist, and samsonite

---

[84]Yudhistira, himself of humble origins, has assumed one of the most power-full wayang names. Yudhistira Ardi Noegraha is an "expansion" of Yan, the nickname derived from his "real" name Mul-yan-a.

[85]In less than two generations this stone monument to the revolutionary dead in the former revolutionary capital has become a "fossil."

[86]*Arjuna Drop Out*, p. 23.

briefcase in hand. Always talking about the glory of Mataram, while dreaming of Amsterdam.

Arjuna breathes in the air, trying to enjoy the feeling of Java. The feeling of becoming Javanese once again, after so long a separation from his roots. After the jumbled culture of Jakarta has assembled him into a new, cosmopolitan-universal product—without the slight trace of provincial character. In fact, virtually without backbone. Meaning what? Not too clear.

The pedicabs fly past the famous obelisk at the intersection—the city's trade-mark, along with Malioboro Boulevard. But these days, in the midst of all the changes taking place, the obelisk is really just a fossil. The senseless ordering of the city has turned it into something ludicrous.

The malice of this passage has few equals in modern Indonesian literature. No doubt some of this malice is apparent to any reader of Indonesian, but its full bite is only felt by the Javanese reader caught between Arjuna II and his creator. For example, many non-Javanese readers may take "dengan gincu yang tak cocok, dengan bedak tanpa selera" Indonesian-style, as evoking images of prostitutes, coarse market vendors, or nouveau riche, vulgarian women, and they will not be wrong. But Javanese (especially Yogyakarta Javanese) will know that it was (perhaps still is) common for Jogjanese male aristocrats to use lipstick and powder to heighten their *halus* (refined) prettiness. And the malice of the pairings of Javanese headcloth (blangkon) with Indonesian tie (dasi), Javanese kris with Americo-Indonesian samsonite (briefcase) requires an understanding of the multilingual referents to have its effect. "Mencoba menikmati rasa Jawa" can be read in Indonesian as "tried to enjoy the feeling of being Javanese," but it can also be read *à la javanaise* as "tried to enjoy the Javanese *Rasa,*" in mocking reference to a fundamental concept in traditional Javanese religio-mystical thought.[87] The construction of "mengasemblingnya," with its casual, misspelled verbification of an American gerund, reminds us of the special freedom that Indonesian offers its users. Lastly, we may note not merely the cynical quotation of the standard conservative

[87]This kind of mockery is more brutally expressed in a passage where Setyowati II, the first of Arjuna II's jilted girlfriends (she eventually becomes the lover of his younger sister), quarrels with her father, a captain in the navy: "ingin saja rasanya ia menceburkan sang Papi ke samudra luas biar ditelan Naga Taksaka atau Hyang Antaboga. Syukur-syukur kalau tenggelam ke dalam telinga Déwaruci dan tak bisa kembali" (she felt like hurling Dad into the wide ocean so he could be devoured by the sea-monsters Taksaka or Antaboga. Not bad too if he were to be swallowed up in Déwa Ruci's ear and never reappear) (ibid., p. 51). Nothing is more sacred to the wayang world than Bima's finding the ultimate *kawruh* (mystical knowledge) by entering the ear of Déwa Ruci (a god in miniature form of Bima himself) at the bottom of the ocean.

Javanese (again, especially Jogjanese) criticism of Jakarta and its culture (does any other ethnic group talk about Jakartans as being "tanpa ciri kedaérahan sama sekali"?), and the amused nod to the fact that the phrase "tanpa tulang punggung," expressing Jogjanese/Javanese pride, is a translation from the English (and Dutch?)—while "apa artinya itu, kurang jelas," which underlines this point, is directed straight at the reader in a style perfectly adapted to the silent complicity of the print-market. A passage so soaked with quotations and allusions to different languages and cultures is virtually impossible in Javanese; and, besides, the whole point of using Indonesian here is precisely to put Java in its place.

I have tried to argue that the invisible presence of Javanese language and literature has been very important for the creativity of Javanese writing in Indonesian. In this sense, it is like a black hole—something one knows is there even if one cannot see it. "Javanese literature" has in one sense "disappeared," yet its ghost is very much around—a curious, backhanded tribute to its power. Can the argument be used to illumine the very different attitude of, say, Sundanese writers toward their mother tongue—and their periodic enthusiasm for writing in it? Possibly. It strikes me that Sundanese writers may fear that their language is, not dangerous, but in danger: danger of dying out by neglect, danger of becoming irrelevant, danger of being crowded out by Indonesian, even perhaps by Javanese. Such fears breed tender solicitude, not anger and malice. If we ask ourselves why in the Indonesian context the language and culture of Java are sui generis, I do not believe that the answer is simply that the Javanese are far the largest ethnic group, that Javanese culture is somehow "superior" to its competitors, or that the Javanese run the country—though all these propositions have some elements of truth. For the fact is that the Javanese language and Javanese culture have for almost a century now been much more of a problem to the Javanese themselves than to anyone else: a problem that cannot be resolved by any obvious or easy means, since it involves and implicates almost all sectors of Javanese society.

In Soemantri's sweetly leftist novel *Rasa Merdika* (1924) the protagonists are, naturally, two young Javanese "socialisten." The handsome hero Soedjanmo, with his "roman moeka jang berkoelit hitem manis" (attractive brown-skinned face) is the son of an Assistant Wedana who flees a secure career in the colonial bureaucracy to learn about the modern world and the *rasa merdika* (feeling of freedom) by working as a bookkeeper with a Dutch trading company in P[e-kalongan]. His sweetheart, Roro (shades of Djawa Dipo!) Soepini, is:

> seorang gadis jang dapet peladjaran dari M.U.L.O. . . . meskipoen ia tergolong pada kaoem pertengahan, lantaran tertarik oleh pamilienja, tetapi ia boekannja sebagai kebanjakan temen-temennja; ia soeka sekali mendengerken voordracht-voordracht jang bergoena dan baik bagi oemoem.[88]

> a girl with a MULO education, who, though she belongs to the middle class by family background, still very much enjoys—unlike most of her friends—listening to lectures that are good and useful for the public.

They first meet at a radical vergadering and quickly fall in love. Here is a vignette of our radical, middle-class heroine preparing for a romantic tryst:

> Semantara lama dari pada ia berpakaian itoe, maka kita lihat dia soedah keloear dari kamarnja dengen berbadjoe soetera woengoe berserta memakai centuur soetera koening moeda ber-streep merah dipaloetken diléhèrnja. Kain pandjang batik Pekalongan jang di pakai dimana ada gambarnja boeroeng merak hinggap di atas dahan pohon, menambahken poela ketjantikan roro Soepini, bisa menarik hati siapa jang memandangnja.
>
> Ia memakai poela sepatoe sandal koening dari kalfleer dengen haknja jang tinggi, menambahken djalannja bisa djadi rapi, dan sedikit berlagak.
>
> Satoe tasch ketjil terbikin dari koelit binatang berboeloe jang dipegang di tangan kanan, menoendjoekken poela bahasa ia ada seorang gadis jang termasoek dalem djaman peroebahan.
>
> "Mi," panggil ia pada hambanja perempoean.
>
> Mi lekas dateng padanja.
>
> "Tjariken deeleman sebentar!" soeroeh ia pada Mi.[89]

> After some time at her toilette, she now appears to us emerging from her room. She's dressed in a purple silk blouse, and has a bright yellow silk slendang with a red stripe swathed around her shoulders. The Pekalongan batik *kain* [skirt] she's wearing, with its pattern of peacocks

---

[88]Soemantri, *Rasa Merdika*, p. 75.

[89]Ibid., p. 101. Is it wholly unfair to see in the following description of Soepini an early version of Yudhistira Ardi Noegraha's *blangkon* cum samsonite Yogyakarta priyayi? Wouldn't substituting *pembangunan* (development) for the more modest *peroebahan* (change) do the trick? But Soemantri writes wholly without *ironi*.

perched on branches, accentuates Soepini's beauty, which attracts all who see her.

She is also wearing high-heeled sandals of yellow calf-leather, which bring out the elegance of her gait, and even make it slightly sway.

The small *tasch* [Dutch for handbag], made from the skin of some furry animal, which she holds in her right hand, also shows that she is a young woman who belongs in this era of change.

"Mi!" she summons her maid.

Mi quickly appears before her.

"Go hail me a carriage!" she orders Mi.

And this "machluk dibelakang rumah," of whom we are told neither the age, looks, character, feelings, history, or experience, continues for the rest of the story to be the faithful emissary of, and intermediary between, the middle-class radical lovers.

These things run very deep, and change very slowly. Half a century later, it appears that even in the suffering and humiliation of prison, some former PKI (Communist party) leaders still managed to find among their party followers what one can think of as "houseboys" to attend to their personal needs. One cannot help wondering what language was used when dirty clothes passed down, and clean clothes moved back up, such prison hierarchies. For "mendengarkan orang bicara kromo padaku, aku merasa sebagai manusia pilihan, bertempat disuatu ketinggian, déwa dalam tubuh manusia, dan keénakan warisan ini membelai-belai" (hearing someone address me in kromo, I felt like one of the elect, high on a pedestal, a god in a human body . . . and the voluptuousness of this inheritance caressed me).[90]

[90]Pramoedya Ananta Toer, *Anak Semua Bangsa*, pp. 183–84.

PART III

CONSCIOUSNESS

CHAPTER 7

A Time of Darkness and a Time of Light: Transposition in Early Indonesian Nationalist Thought

Just before his death in 1873, in the old royal capital of Surakarta, R. Ng. Ronggawarsita, the last of the great Javanese *pujangga* (court poets), wrote a despairing poem that he called *Serat Kala Tidha* (Poem of a time of darkness).[1] Something of the tone of this poem may be gleaned from the following lines:

> The lustre of the realm
> Is now vanished to the eye
> In ruins the teaching of good ways
> For there is no example left
> The heart of the learned poet
> So coiled about with care
> Seeing all the wretchedness
> That everything is darkened
> The world immersed in misery
>
> The King kingly perfection
> The Chief Minister chiefly in truth
> The *bupati* constant of heart
> The lower officials excellent
> Yet none can serve to stay
> The time of doom. . . .

First published in 1979. Anthony Reid and David Marr, ed., *Perceptions of the Past in Southeast Asia* (Hong Kong: Heinemann, 1979), pp. 219–48. Reprinted with permission.
[1]Radèn Ngabèhi Ronggawarsita, *Serat Kala Tida* ([Surakarta]: Persatuan, [1933]).

> In this time of madness
> To join the mad is unbearable
> Anguish to the suffering heart
> Yet not to join
> Means losing all
> Starvation at the end.[2]

Taken one by one, most of these lines are unremarkable variations on classical *topoi* in Javanese culture. Both Javanese folklore and court literature contain highly conventionalized descriptions of *jaman kala-bendu*—times of flood, earthquake, and volcanic eruption in the natural order and famine, violence, and immorality in the social. Both traditions also present time-honored images of golden ages—periods of cosmic order and social well-being, in which each person plays out his appointed role, hierarchies are maintained, and harmony prevails. The explanation for the primordial oscillations between such epochs lay, according to traditional Javanese thought,[3] in the success or failure of the ruler to concentrate around and in himself the immanent power of the universe, through ascesis, selfless devotion to duty, and the capacity to attract or absorb other power-full persons or objects. The more perfect the ruler, the more brilliant and happy the society.

If the lines I have cited are in themselves so unremarkable, what accounts for the strange and painful sensations they arouse? Simply their extraordinary *juxtaposition*. For stanzas 2 and 8 belong to the topos "time of darkness," while the first four lines of stanza 3 are a central part of the classical imagery of a "time of light." According to traditional Javanese logic, *if* "the king [were] kingly perfection, the Chief Minister chiefly in truth," then cosmos and society should *necessarily* be in order. But the next two lines show precisely the opposite. The single terrible word *parandéné* (yet) expresses Ronggawarsita's desperate, and quite untraditional, sense that the old conception of

---

[2]I have translated freely, and rather coarsely, from stanzas 2, 3 and 8. The Javanese text runs as follows: *Mangkya darajating praja / Kawuryan wus sunya ruri / Rurah pangrèhing ngukara / Karana tanpa palupi / Ponang para mengkawi / Kawileting tyas maladkung / Kungas kasudranira / Tidhem tandhaning dumadi / Ardayèng rat déning karoban rubéda / / Ratuné ratu utama / Patihé patih linuwih / Pra nayaka tyas raharja / Panekaré becik-becik / Parandéné tan dadi / Paliyasing kalabendu . . . / / Amenengi jaman édan / Éwuh ayahing pambudi / Mèlu édan nora tahan / Yèn tan mèlu anglakoni / Boya kaduman melik / Kaliren wekasanipun.* Here *bupati* refers to high-ranking court officials not of royal blood. My attention was first drawn to this poem by Tony Day.

[3]A more extensive treatment of traditional Javanese conceptions and images of power is given in chap. 1, above.

the world was no longer valid, the cosmic rhythm had come unsprung and Javanese Power was impotence. In their history the Javanese had gone through many "times of darkness," but always with the sure expectation that eventually a ruler would come to reconcentrate the Power and inaugurate a new "time of light." In 1873, however, the dying poet spoke his fear that now was a "time of darkness" that might never end.[4]

Thirty-five years later, on May 20, 1908, a small group of teenage Javanese students in the colonial capital of Batavia formed an organization that they called Budi Utomo. May 20 is now celebrated annually in Indonesia as the Day of National Awakening. Akira Nagazumi's fine study on the early years of this organization is fittingly entitled *The Dawn of Indonesian Nationalism*[5]—for dawn marks the passage from darkness of light, from sleep to wakefulness. And if both Nagazumi and contemporary Indonesians speak of May 20, 1908 in these figurative terms, they are not being willfully anachronistic. How many of the newspapers and periodicals from the early years of this century contain, in their very names, images of radiant light![6] Kartini's famous collected letters, *Door Duisternis tot Licht* (Through darkness to light), bear the same symbolic stamp.[7]

What are we to make of this metamorphosis of imagery? Some scholars have tended to read it as signifying the passage from tradition

[4]Ronggawarsita's words may be the sharpest and most explicit expression of the general crisis of the nineteenth-century Javanese spirit, as Dutch colonial rule steadily consolidated itself. But many other texts convey the same feeling in more oblique form. It is instructive to compare style and subject matter in a major pre-nineteenth-century text, such as the *Babad Tanah Jawi* and the strange but typically nineteenth-century poem *Suluk Gatholoco*. The *Babad Tanah Jawi* recounts the bloody events of precolonial Javanese history in plain and matter-of-fact language. In the *Suluk Gatholoco*, which deals mainly with an imaginary theological debate between some "Arabized" Javanese Muslims and a champion of "Javanese" Islam in the form of an ambulatory, philosophizing penis (*gatho* = penis, *ngloco* = masturbate), no violence occurs. But the language employed is unforgettable in its ornate ferocity.

[5]Akira Nagazumi, *The Dawn of Indonesian Nationalism: The Early Years of Budi Utomo, 1908–1918*, Institute of Developing Economies, Occasional Papers Series no. 10 (Tokyo, 1972).

[6]About 25 percent of the Indonesian newspapers for the period 1900–1925 listed in Godfrey Raymond Nunn, *Indonesian Newspapers: An International Union List*, Chinese Materials Research Aids Service Center, Occasional Series no. 14 (Taipeh, 1971), include in their titles one or more of the following words: *matahari* (sun), *surya* (sun), *bintang* (star), *nyala* (flame), *suluh* (torch), *pelita* (lamp), *sinar* (ray), *cahaya* (radiance), *api* (fire), and *fajar* (dawn). Others contain such words as *muda* (young), *baru* (new), and *gugah* (awakened).

[7]The title was actually given by Kartini's editor, Jacques Henry Abendanon, when he published her letters posthumously in 1911. But he was closely involved with, and sympathetic to, the "awakening" movement, and his choice of title fitted well with that milieu. See Hildred Geertz's introduction to Radèn Adjeng Kartini, *Letters of a Javanese Princess* (New York: Norton, 1964), especially pp. 15–16, 23.

to modernity, as though they "who walked in darkness [had] seen a great light." Robert Van Niel, for example, writes that "in the atmosphere of the Westernized school . . . young Javanese found a life that differed from what they had known in their home environment. Not only was the difference one of physical environment, but what was far more important, one of mental environment: perhaps only slightly inaccurately generalized as the difference between a scientific-rational attitude and a mystical-animistic attitude."[8] In this perspective, Budi Utomo represents simply the earliest Indonesian attempt to cope with the colonial condition in Western (modern) ways. Even though Budi Utomo's very name was more Javanese than Indonesian; though its membership was restricted ethnically to what Clifford Geertz has called "Inner Indonesia" and socially to *priyayi* students and officials;[9] and though its formal aims did not encompass political independence;[10] yet its *structural* novelty seemed to mark a clear break with the past. As Van Niel puts it, "Budi Utomo appears on the Indonesian scene as an *organization* based upon a *free and conscious* united effort by *individuals*."[11] With its programs, branches, subscriptions, reports, and congresses, Budi Utomo seemed to have no indigenous ancestry, but rather to be the wind-borne seed from which the Indonesian nationalist movement grew.[12]

If Indonesian writers have usually been unwilling to accept Van Niel's psychological and pedagogical dichotomies, they have developed dichotomies of their own, conceived in moral, political, and generational terms, as is evidenced by the pervasive pairing of *maju/ kolot* (progressive/backward), *muda/tua* (young/old), and *sadar/ masih bodoh* (aware/still ignorant).[13] In both perspectives Budi Utomo has come to seem the locus of a fundamental transformation of con-

[8]Robert Van Niel, *The Emergence of the Modern Indonesian Elite* (The Hague: van Hoeve, 1950), p. 173.

[9]"Inner Indonesia" refers to the islands of Java, Bali, and Madura and their "Hinduized" populations. *Priyayi* refers to the traditional Javanese upper class of officials and literati. In fact, the founding members of Budi Utomo were exclusively ethnic Javanese. See Nagazumi, *Dawn*, p. 39.

[10]For details on these aims, see ibid., pp. 157–60.

[11]Van Niel, *Emergence*, p. 57. Italics added.

[12]It is this organizational novelty, clearly derived from the West, that has encouraged some Western scholars to interpret Indonesian (and Southeast Asian) nationalism as a Western import and to date the beginnings of this nationalism to the formation of Western-style organizations. (For example, the founding of the Young Men's Buddhist Association in Rangoon in 1906 is often taken to mark the onset of the Burmese nationalist movement.) Cf. Brian Harrison, *Southeast Asia, A Short History* (London: Macmillan, 1954), pp. 236–37.

[13]For example, Lintong Mulia Sitorus, in his *Sedjarah Pergerakan Kebangsaan Indonesia* (Jakarta: Pustaka Rakjat, 1951), writes: "Till the end of the 19th century, the colored peoples still slept soundly, while the whites were busily at work in every field" (p. 6).

sciousness. Yet much about this transformation remains obscure. What follows below is a preliminary attempt to illumine that obscurity.

Budi Utomo was founded by students at the STOVIA[14] medical school in Batavia, led by a nineteen-year-old East Javanese boy called Soetomo, who eventually became one of the most prominent nationalist leaders of his generation. Van Niel may be exaggerating a little when he writes that "it is doubtful if any one man was of greater importance in shaping Indonesian life in the 1920s."[15] But as founder of the Surabaya-based Indonesian Study Club in 1924, of Partai Bangsa Indonesia (Party of the Indonesian Nation) in 1930, and a Parindra (Great Indonesia Party) in 1935, Soetomo was certainly a central figure in preindependence Indonesian politics.[16] On his death in 1938 he was mourned by thousands as a devoted servant of his people.[17] A successful graduate of the most advanced Western-style school in the Netherlands Indies, he could, in the first two decades of the century, be regarded as the epitome of all that was maju, muda, and sadar.[18] By chance, Soetomo was also the first prominent Indonesian to write something like an autobiography, the well-known *Kenang-Kenangan*—a title that can be translated as Memoirs, but is really better rendered as Memories. It seems reasonable, therefore, that the study of this "autobiography" may offer clues as to what it meant to be a member of the generation of the "awakened," and, more generally, of the way in which past, present, and future were conceived of and linked together in the mind of that generation's most enduring political personality.[19]

[14]*School tot Opleiding van Inlandsche Artsen*—School for the Training of Native Doctors.

[15]Van Niel, *Emergence*, p. 224.

[16]For details on these parties, see Jan Meinhard Pluvier, *Overzicht van de ontwikkeling der nationalistische beweging in Indonesië in der jaren 1930 tot 1942* (The Hague: van Hoeve, 1953).

[17]"Fifty thousand people followed his bier; the image of this man of the people lived in the hearts of the masses who had so much to thank him for. Soetomo was indeed an extraordinary figure, one of the noblest leaders of the nationalist movement in its decades-old history" (Daniel Marcellus Georg Koch, *Batig Slot: Figuren uit het oude Indië* [Amsterdam: De Brug/Djambatan, 1960], p. 145). The standard general account of Soetomo's life is Imam Supardi, *Dr. Soetomo—Riwajat Hidup dan Perdjuangannja* (Jakarta: Djambatan, 1951).

[18]This is the judgment of Nagazumi, *Dawn*, p. 34. For details on the evolution of the STOVIA, and the character of its curriculum and student body, see Van Niel, *Emergence*, p. 16.

[19]For some discussion of Indonesian autobiography, see Savitri Scherer, "Harmony and Dissonance: Early Nationalist Thought in Java" (M.A. thesis, Cornell University, 1975), pp. 188–89. For specific studies in Indonesian biography and autobiography, see Scherer's

Before exploring *Kenang-Kenangan,* however, we may remind ourselves of the main facts of Soetomo's life. He was born in the village of
Ngepèh, near Nganjuk, East Java, on July 30, 1888.[20] His maternal
grandfather was a well-to-do *kepalang* (superior village headman)
who had earlier served in the Binnenlandsch Bestuur (territorial native
administration). His father was a very able teacher and administrator
who rose to the rank of *wedana,* then the highest bureaucratic rank
normally open to Javanese not born to aristocratic bupati families.[21]
Up to the age of six, Soetomo was brought up by his maternal grandparents. Then he was sent to a Dutch-language primary school (ELS)
in Bangil. It is an indication of his privileged educational background
that in 1895, probably the year he was enrolled, there were no more
than 1,135 Indonesians enrolled in such primary schools throughout
the Netherlands Indies.[22] In 1903, largely at his father's insistence, he
entered the STOVIA. He was then fourteen. He graduated in 1911, at
twenty-two, and subsequently, by the contractual terms of his initial
enrollment, worked as a government doctor in various parts of Java
and Sumatra. In 1917, while stationed in Blora, he met a widowed
Dutch nurse and married her. Two years later he was given the opportunity to continue his medical studies in Holland, returning home
only in 1923. He was by then prominent enough to be selected as a
member of the Surabaya Municipal Council. But shortly thereafter he
resigned from this position and formed the first and most famous of
the political "study clubs" of the 1920s. From that time until his death
in 1938, he was immersed in nationalist politics.[23]

Such is the skeletal outline of Soetomo's life, following in abbreviated form the fuller picture presented in Imam Supardi's quiet hagio-
graphy. In what ways does Soetomo's "autobiography" correspond to
this silhouette? Scarcely at all. There is, for example, virtually no
mention of his political successes or failures in the thirty years that
followed the founding of Budi Utomo. We learn of his political activities only in passing—as, for instance, when he compassionately

---

treatment of Soetomo, Tjipto Mangoenkoesoemo, and Ki Hadjar Dewantara; Taufik Ab-
dullah, "Modernization in the Minangkabau World: West Sumatra in the Early Decades of
the Twentieth Century," in Claire Holt, ed., *Culture and Politics in Indonesia* (Ithaca, N.Y.:
Cornell University Press, 1972), pp. 179–245; Rudolf Mrázek, "Tan Malaka: A Political
Personality's Structure of Experience," *Indonesia* 14 (October 1972): 1–48; and John D.
Legge, *Sukarno: A Political Biography* (New York: Praeger, 1972).

[20]He was thus an almost exact contemporary of Ho Chi Minh and Burma's first prime
minister, Dr. Ba Maw.

[21]See Scherer, "Harmony," pp. 191–200, for further detail. Here *bupati* refers to Java's
traditional provincial nobility.

[22]Ibid., p. 30.

[23]Supardi, *Dr. Soetomo,* pp. 2–8.

describes his wife having to cook constantly for the stream of student visitors to their house in Holland.[24] The very structure of the auto-biography is rather strange and hardly follows what we imagine as the contours of Soetomo's historical life. The first 48 pages are devoted to his parents and grandparents, and the last 57 to his schoolfellows (and political comrades), his wife, and some family retainers. Only the central 30 pages deal substantively with his own life—and they close with his schooldays in Batavia.

In a notice to his readers, and in a brief preface, Soetomo gives some accounting of this shape:

As mentioned in the introduction to his book, the purpose of the writer in writing this book of memories is the desire to accede to the requests of various people who would like to understand the story [*riwayat*] of my life. In this book I do not set down the story of my life[25] in the plainest terms, because, as mentioned in the introduction, it is inappropriate for me to be the one to write my story. I [therefore] only depict various excerpts [*pungutan*] from the stories of various people who were connected with my life, so that, from the excerpts of the stories of these people, my story can be envisaged. . . .[26] For a long time now, and from various quarters, I have received requests to write the history of my life (*biografie*). Above all from my own group there have been not a few requests of this type. In addition, several journalists have made the same request. But I rejected them all, for I am of the opinion that it is inappropriate for a man to make a history of the life of some-one who has not yet returned to eternity [*belum pulang ke zaman yang baka*], in other words the picture of his life is not yet completed. . . .[27]
So I have taken another way, whereby I can have the fullest oppor-tunity to pay my respects to my forefathers and whoever else has helped me,[28] so that as a result my own *lelakon* can be thereby revealed.[29] Mindful of the Javanese saying *kacang mangsa ninggal lanjaran*, which

---

[24]Radèn Soetomo, *Kenang-Kenangan* (Surabaya: n.p., 1934), pp. 118–19.

[25]Although in modern Indonesian the terms *penghidupan* and *kehidupan* have rather different meanings (perhaps "style of life" and "life"), Soetomo seems to use them inter-changeably in this passage.

[26]Ibid., inside of cover.

[27]Ibid., p. 3. Soetomo adds the Dutch word *biografie* in parentheses, as if he were uncertain that his Indonesian readers would understand the phrase "history of my life."

[28]Compare the words of another very Javanese Indonesian leader, Communist party secretary-general Sudisman, in his defense speech before the Extraordinary Military Tri-bunal that sentenced him to death in 1967: "I am a Communist who was born in Java, and therefore it is my duty, in accordance with the custom of the Javanese, to take my leave by saying: First, *matur nuwun*, I thank all those who have helped me in the course of the struggle" (Sudisman, *Analysis of Responsibility*, trans. Benedict Anderson [Melbourne: The Works Cooperative, 1975], p. 24).

[29]*Lelakon* is a Javanese term that is notoriously impossible to translate. It is something like a mixture of "destiny," "role," "life aim," and "moral responsibility."

means that a man's descendants will never abandon his qualities, from my describing the qualities and character of my forefathers the reader will easily be able to understand my true character.[30]

The writer's hope is that . . . this book of memories . . . can be used as a means for comparing conditions in the former time [*zaman dahulu*] with the present [*masa sekarang*].[31]

Some of the more important themes of "Memories" are already laid out in these modest explanatory words, which deserve some comment before we proceed further with the text.

First of all, it is striking that, although Western scholars have habitually referred to Memories as an autobiography, Soetomo himself never uses the word, or any Indonesian-language version of it: He notes that he had long rejected requests to write his *biography*. Yet "Memories" is not a biography in any ordinary sense. Even when he writes at length about his forefathers, we are not given their biographies, but simply excerpts or "pluckings" from their "stories." Soetomo makes no attempt to place these ancestral figures in a maturing personal or historical context. They loom up in episodes to which no clear time can be assigned, except, as we shall see, for the significant markers zaman dahulu and masa sekarang.

I think we will not begin to make sense of this method of writing if we are not clear about the nature and assumptions of modern Western-style biography and autobiography. These literary forms are essentially about the interplay between "person" and "history." "History" is a global and linear framework for comprehending the evolution of man and society. "Person" is the individual subjectivity that experiences this "history" and takes part in it. The study of a man's life is therefore usually a study of his progress toward and absorption into his historical role. If parents and grandparents appear in such works, they serve to illuminate a social, economic, and psychological context out of which the "person" emerges—or a sort of starting line from which to judge his performance in the race to come. The fundamental movement of such texts is therefore *away* from ancestry toward the "individual." They are analogous to paintings built up on canvas and easel by the constant addition of small new dabs of color until an unexpected whole—the work of art—appears.

In Memories we find, I think, a method that is more analogous to

[30]Soetomo, *Kenang-Kenangan*, p. 4. The saying literally means: "How could the bean abandon the bean-pole?" The word *tabi'at*, translated here as "character," could also be rendered as "nature."
[31]Ibid., p. 6.

that of classical sculpture—the discovery of essential form in the contingency of stone or other raw materials. The homely folk saying "kacang mangsa ninggal lanjaran" implies a very different sense of person and time from those typical in Western biography or autobiography. For, as we shall see, here history appears not as the painter who gives a life its essential meaning but as contingency, the raw stone through which the search for an essential nature is pursued. Soetomo's pages about his parents are not meant to show the social and psychological environment out of which the nationalist leader goes to meet his destiny, but look rather to reveal the lanjaran toward which the kacang seeks its homeward-wending way. We are, in effect, being shown the character (nature) of his ancestry, *toward* which his life's movement tends. The quest is not for individual fulfillment or historical uniqueness, but for reunion and identification. It is in this sense, by showing the nature of his ancestors, that Soetomo can invite his readers, who know his historical role, to see what his nature really is.[32] In a context where historical time is so adventitious, chronology is necessarily of minor importance; this is why, I believe, Soetomo's own life and those of his forefathers appear to us in the pages of Memories so fragmented, episodic and unanchored.[33]

In the second place, the generally melancholy tone of Memories is set from the start. Soon after the basic draft was written, his beloved wife died, and the last-minute addition that Soetomo devotes to her is marked by some spare, anguished language. He records also the deaths of the two other people whom he most admired: Goenawan Mangoenkoesoemo, a friend so close that Dr. Tjipto Mangoenkoesoemo, Goenawan's elder brother, referred to their relationship as that of *wayang* (puppet) and *dhalang* (puppeteer);[34] and his father—an

---

[32]This is no less true of all the other personages who appear in Memories. There are a few occasions when some of them seem to change—for example, Soetomo's ambitious mother learns the hard way that official position does not always bring happiness. But Soetomo makes it clear that the real "she" has not changed at all. She has simply lost some illusions about the nature of the world. Ibid., p. 25.

[33]Nothing could be more striking in this regard than the fact that *Kenang-Kenangan* makes no mention of the three most "world-shaking" events experienced by Southeast Asians in the early years of the twentieth century: Asian Japan's stunning defeat of European Russia in 1905; the outbreak of World War I in 1914; and the Bolshevik Revolution in 1917. By contrast, almost all later Indonesian memoirs are tightly linked to the ongoing march of world history. See, for example, Sutan Sjahrir, *Out of Exile,* trans. Charles Wolf, Jr. (New York: John Day, 1949); Cindy Adams, *Sukarno: An Autobiography as Told to Cindy Adams* (Indianapolis: Bobbs-Merrill, 1965); and Ali Sastroamidjojo, *Tonggak-tonggak di Perjalananku* (Jakarta: Kinta, 1974).

[34]When Goenawan died, Tjipto is said to have remarked: "Now Soetomo has lost his dhalang." Soetomo, *Kenang-Kenangan,* p. 95.

event that, as he observes himself, was crucial to his sudden emergence as the leading spirit of Budi Utomo. But the tone of melancholy has deeper causes than these personal losses. It derives, I think, from what we have seen in the last quoted passage from Soetomo's preface, signaled there and throughout Memories by the repeated contrast between zaman dahulu and masa sekarang. There are times when one seems to get a clear idea of the nature of the contrast between these "times," if not of the point of transition between them. Soetomo records asking villagers in Ngepèh what it was like in the zaman dahulu: "The villagers answered: "Tuan, there was nothing to equal conditions in the zaman of Lurah Kadji [Soetomo's grandfather]." What was the difference? "*In that time,* the time of Lurah Kadji, people were absolutely forbidden [by Lurah Kadji] to rent their land to the [sugar] factories."35 He describes his grandfather's education in the following terms:

> He was the son of a rich man who used to be headman there. For that reason, *if one looks at his time,* he received an adequate education. He was sent from *pesantrèn* to *pesantrèn,*36 wherever there were famous teachers. Because of his travels my grandfather had a rather broad perspective. According to what people say, it was only in the *pesantrèn* of Sepanjang (near Surabaya) that he got a broad and adequate *ilmu.*37 *At that time,* there was no *sekolahan* yet.38 Aside from studying Koranic recitation, he also learned to read and write Javanese and Malay, and studied *ilmu falak* [astronomy], which explains the course of the stars and moon. He also studied *ilmu kebatinan*39 and *ilmu kedotan* (the knowledge whereby one is not wounded if stabbed and if struck feels no pain)40. . . . In the time of my grandfather, youngsters were very fond of *sport* [sic] and art (*kunst*). One was not a man if one could not ride a saddleless horse and did not dare to stand up on the horse's back. One

35Ibid., p. 13. Italics added.

36*Pesantrèn*—traditional Javanese Islamic school. Here, as elsewhere, Soetomo first gives the Javanese word and then translates it into Indonesian for his non-Javanese readers.

37The semantics of this passage are significant. Soetomo always uses the highly respectful "deep" word *ilmu* (clearly a translation of the Javanese *ngèlmu*) for "traditional" Javanese and Islamic studies. The sense is always knowledge of what is "real" or ontologically true. So far as I have been able to discover he never uses this word for things learned in Dutch schools.

38*Sekolahan,* an indigenization of the Dutch word for school, has no particular resonances. Soetomo's laconic reference here leaves one in doubt about his stance toward these Westernized schools. One might imagine that the sentence should be understood to run parallel to "no one yet rented their land to the sugar factories."

39*Ilmu kebatinan*—knowledge of the inward—is the highest form of traditional Javanese religious learning, commonly referred to by Westerners as "Javanese mysticism."

40Soetomo, *Kenang-Kenangan*, pp. 10–11. Italics added.

was also not a man if one could not use bow and arrow and handle a lance. Dancing and *nembang* [classical Javanese singing] were a part of art which self-respecting youngsters had to know, while *rampok harimau* was a sport widely popular among the People.[41]

And here is Soetomo's description of his grandfather offering his guests refreshments: "If one looks *at the time*, it is not surprising that my grandfather gave his laborers genever [Dutch gin]. *At that time*, too, even though people were already beginning to be aware [sadar] and ashamed [malu], there were many occasions when my grandfather would offer his guests opium. . . . In olden times [*zaman kuno*], smoking opium was regarded as a sign and instrument of high status and luxury."[42]

The ambiguity of these descriptions undermines any initial confidence that the two "times" correspond either to two historical periods or to "tradition" and "modernity."[43] At no point does Soetomo express either nostalgia or contempt for the education of his grandfather. All we get is the enigmatic "if one looks at the time." Genever was a Dutch import into Java, and probably opium too, at least on a large scale, but here both appear as emblems of the zaman kuno.[44] There is no clear indication of the relationship between sadar and malu (this is one of the rare occasions when these words occur in Memories). Social evolution? Political development? Cultural enlightenment? Or the transformation Hildred Geertz describes from *durung Jawa* (not yet Javanese, unaware, not knowing shame) to *wis Jawa* (Javanese, aware, knowing shame), transposed from Javanese children to Javanese society as a whole?[45]

The ambiguous relationship of past and present is nowhere better expressed than in the vivid episode where Soetomo describes his discomfort at the kind of village justice his grandfather meted out. The old man would tie village offenders to the pillars of his *pendhapa* (a sort of wall-less front pavilion to the headman's house) for several days at a time. "When I was adult, I had already been influenced by

[41]Ibid., p. 12. Italics added. *Rampok harimau* is an Indonesian translation of the Javanese *rampog macan*, a gladiatorial battle between a panther or tiger and a group of armed men.

[42]Ibid., p. 17. Italics added. The word translated as "high status" is *kebangsaan*, which usually means "nationality" or "race." I suspect that it may be a misprint for *kebangsawanan* (noble rank).

[43]Yet note that, from our historical perspective, the zaman kuno must roughly coincide with Ronggawarsita's Time of Darkness.

[44]The phallic hero of the *Suluk Gatholoco* is described as a dedicated opium user.

[45]Hildred Geertz, *The Javanese Family: A Study of Kinship and Socialization* (Glencoe: The Free Press, 1961), p. 105.

the writings of Multatuli[46]—the foremost champion of seizing and protecting the rights of our people—and I asked my grandfather what power [*kekuasaan*] gave him the right to be so bold as to sentence villagers in this way."[47] Here one might expect a conventional contrast of traditional and modern, old and new. But the story proceeds in an unexpected way, for the grandfather explains that his punishments are actually a *reform*—previously, criminals were sent away to jails in towns. Since, in his view, they typically returned as hardened characters, he created a new, local system of justice that would keep them within the village community. Soetomo concludes with these words. "So, though I could not agree with his stance, I could understand the reasons why my grandfather established these rules. And therefore, although I was already influenced by the new current [*aliran baru*], my respect for him did not diminish in the least, *especially if one looks at his time.*"[48]

Soetomo's reference here to being influenced by Multatuli and the rather obscure "new current" is one of the very rare instances where "new thinking" is mentioned in Memories. But one does not get a strong feeling that the implications are developmental or progressive at all. The adult Soetomo simply did not initially understand his grandfather's reforms. There is neither an endorsement of his grandfather's actions nor an insistence on the correctness of the "new current." One merely senses a certain asymmetrical separation in moral stance. Soetomo, standing on his own moral ground, has learned to understand and to retain respect for his grandfather. But the old man, calmly confident of his good judgment, does not reciprocate.[49]

Over and over again in Memories this picture of connection and separation occurs. The ancestors remain "achieved," self-contained figures, fully manifesting and representing their ancestral qualities. When they quarrel, as Soetomo's grandfather and father are described as doing, they quarrel in a wholly unironical and representational

---

[46]The reference is to the famous colonial iconoclast Eduard Douwes Dekker (1820–87), who under the pen name Multatuli ("I have suffered much") published a largely autobiographical novel called *Max Havelaar* in 1859. A vitriolic attack on the injustices of nineteenth-century colonial administration and the cruelty and corruption of the coopted Javanese ruling class, it created a sensation, and helped to arouse a movement for reform in the Indies.

[47]Soetomo, *Kenang-Kenangan,* p. 13.

[48]Ibid., p. 14. Italics added.

[49]Soetomo presents a vivid contrast to Multatuli. One of the things that most outraged the Dutchman was the personalized (i.e., arbitrary) "justice" meted out by powerful native officials.

way.[50] The father objects to the views of his father-in-law on the proper career for his son, but on the matter-of-fact grounds that they are practically and morally wrong. The two men are separated by their quarrel but united in the solid way they fill up their skins. Soetomo, their descendant, is not only bound to their "qualities" and "character," but sees this "bondedness" in a strange, new, detached way. He does not say that his ancestors' views are "wrong," precisely because he sees them as bathed in "time." Soetomo's separation from his forefathers is located exactly at this conceptual level: that he perceives himself and them encased in different times. Yet the *connection* is at the level of that pluralized perception. Here are signs of a new "watching self," of a distancing between person and culture. It looks very much, too, as if Soetomo is embarking on the construction of an *idea of a tradition*. For what, in the end, is a Tradition, so understood, but a way of making connections in separation, of acknowledging by not repeating? The distinction between *zaman dahulu* and *masa sekarang*, then, is probably less one of historical epochs than of altered states of consciousness.

At the same time, we shall not exhaust the meaning of the term *zaman dahulu* if we do not juxtapose it to other uses of the word *zaman*. For example, we find Soetomo writing that it would be better for others to write the story of his life "after I have escaped from this fleeting time [*zaman yang fana*]";[51] or that it is inappropriate for a man's history to be written before he returns to "eternal time [*zaman yang baka*]."[52] Repeatedly, he says that in this zaman yang fana "no happiness or suffering lasts for ever."[53] In another passage he uses the old image of the "turning world."[54] In these figures there is, of course, something quite traditionally Javanese, but it would be inadequate to stress this point alone: What is more significant is their new relation to the other uses of *zaman*. In traditional Javanese thought there was, as it were, a natural consonance between the movement of a man's life and the movement of the cosmos. The turning wheel is an image of motion and stillness, departure and return. The form of universal time is one of creation and destruction, and again creation and destruction.[55] Man is born into this zaman yang fana, lives his life, and then,

---

[50]See below, p. 259. The relevant passages in *Kenang-Kenangan* are at pp. 66–68.
[51]Ibid., p. 4.
[52]Ibid., p. 3.
[53]Ibid., p. 7.
[54]Ibid., p. 22.
[55]See chap. 1, above, especially pp. 33–35.

254 / *Language and Power*

as Soetomo puts it, "returns" to the zaman yang baka. The circle is
completed and another generation starts a new cycle. So, for traditional Javanese man, death was the point toward which life moved,
and in some sense becoming Javanese was learning to live in rhythm
with this movement.[56]

It is clear that Soetomo understood and accepted an idea of time
that could be either fleeting or eternal, an idea in which, indeed, that
distinction overrode all others. In this sense he was a traditional Javanese. But he was also a man who had been educated in a Western-
style medical school, of which Darwinism was the cosmological un-
derpinning, and for which death was defeat.[57] In this mode of consciousness the cosmos no longer turned but moved on, up, ahead, and
death was not "return" but the real end of a man. Soetomo was thus
fully exposed to the fundamental disjunction of progressive Western
thought—history as species development and life as individual decay.
Memories shows that he was not only influenced by the "new current"
(with all the ironies sprung tight within the phrase) but saw it within
two quite different conceptions of time—and thereby found a recording self within.

In the central part of Memories, the life of Soetomo moves to its
intersection with what today is taken as national history—the founding of Budi Utomo. Soetomo begins his account of his own life with
six years of great happiness spent at the home of his grandfather in
Ngepèh. The section is characterized by two contrasting themes: the
basic harmony of village life and Soetomo's own unpleasant and destructive behavior in it. The harmony of village life is not conveyed in
the way that many later Indonesian nationalist leaders would figure it,
in statements *about* that harmony and its ideological and cultural
basis. Rather, it emerges in a way that is both typically Javanese and
strongly reminiscent of the writing of Indonesia's greatest author, Pramoedya Ananta Toer. Here is Soetomo's description of a major village
occasion:

> When the time came for *sambatan*—a request for help in carrying out
> some project that required many hands—a very big reception took place

[56]I well remember how my former music teacher in Jakarta, one of the most distinguished
classical musicians of his generation, gradually divested himself of all his possessions and
family responsibilities as he saw his end approaching. Nothing more gently determined
could be imagined.

[57]On the impact of Darwinian conceptions in Java in the early twentieth century, see, for
example, Bernhard Dahm, *History of Indonesia in the Twentieth Century* (New York:
Praeger, 1971), p. 30; Nagazumi, *Dawn*, pp. 45, 53, 185 (n. 80).

in the pendhapa of my grandfather's house. Dozens were given food there, so that the big pendhapa was full of people. The kitchen too was full of people working and serving those who were eating. Sambatan was usually performed when people were working the rice-fields. During the sambatan the rice-fields were bustling with villagers full of joy. Dozens of people were ploughing or harrowing side by side. "Hèr, hèr, hèr" or "Giak, giak, giak," signal-words to oxen or water-buffalo, could constantly be heard here and there. Tembang and *uran-uran*,[58] sung by those at work, made the hearts of those who saw and heard them filled with joy.

It was not only humankind that was drawn to and could experience the atmosphere, from the influence of this joy and happiness. It was as though the oxen and water buffalo also shared this joy of heart, shared in the seductive sound of that melodious and exalted tembang and uran-uran. Slowly, with steady pace, step by step, the oxen and water-buffalo walked on, dragging ploughs and harrows and chewing their cud. Sometimes, goaded by the flies that settled on and crawled over their bodies, they swung their horned heads from left to right, fanning their tails as well. Hearing the crack of the whip—though pestered by the flies—the oxen and water-buffalo walked on, walked on, mindful of and fulfilling their duty. Seeing such a peaceful scene, who would not share the fresh coolness in his heart, when everything was so tranquil and pleasing to the heart? What more could be hoped or asked for on this earth? Perhaps because of this feeling, because of the peace and unity of nature and living creatures, farmers find it hard to change their nature, a nature that loves this calm and peace. When work ceased about 11 o'clock, in the pendhapa plates of rice, dishes and pitchers were laid out in rows, awaiting the arrival of those who were coming to eat. Clamorous was the sound of the people heading for the pendhapa. . . . Very often I was seated in the lap of one of the people in the pendhapa, facing the various bamboo plates and wooden trays filled with betel and tobacco, with a joyful heart because I was listening to the jokes of those who were filling their bellies. One by one, after each had eaten his fill, they came to where I was, to accept their share—a roll of betel with its accompanying ingredients and with tobacco. Anyone who knew me or who was rather bold, with kindly face and much laughter would play with me by caressing that part of my body which is not fit to be mentioned here. Who would not feel happy, who would not feel the desire to be at one, with the fullest love, with those farmers?[59]

My playmates were Sadimin and Tjengèk, who at that time were youngsters. They shared in looking after me by playing their flutes. Tjengèk was a young blind boy, but it was as though he was never sad,

---

[58] *Tembang*—classical Javanese songs; *uran-uran*—folk songs.
[59] Soetomo, *Kenang-Kenangan*, pp. 15–16.

always gay and joking. Only the voice of his flute, when it was blown, made a sound that was terrifying and moved the heart, as though hoping for some hope that could never be attained.[60]

The most striking thing about these descriptions is the way they are filled with sound, not words. Words may be alluded to, as in the case of Tjengèk's jokes, but we know nothing of their content. No need to give words, except those without signification,[61] for the sense of happiness (and of Tjengèk's anguish) comes from sheer sound. The image of harmony is conveyed precisely by the absence of any separation between sound and meaning. (The harmony is only "spoiled" by the adult Soetomo, who, by writing words, tries to catch what to be caught cannot be spoken.)

By contrast, Soetomo describes his childhood self in the most unflattering terms. He was very spoiled, could twist his grandparents around his little finger, enjoyed whining to them about his uncles and aunts and seeing the latter reduced to tears.[62] "I felt myself extremely naughty, acted like a king and treated the people connected with me . . . in a quite arbitrary way."[63] Later, when he went to school, he was "spendthrift, arrogant, and proud if I could deceive my parents by asking for extra money on the pretext of needing books or a jacket, but actually for treat my friends or anyone else, if I happened to be going for snacks."[64] He liked to fight, was lazy about his studies, and regularly used to cheat on his examinations.[65] He was jealous of his younger brother, who he felt was favored by his parents. On one occasion he felt so mortified by this discrimination that he rode off into the woods and burst into tears of anger and self-pity.[66] He used to steal as well.[67] There is only one aspect of his childhood character that he admires in retrospect—his rage at injustice and willingness to fight it.[68] But generally we are given a clear picture of a person with the traits least approved of by Javanese, and least like his forefathers, who in different ways are described as serious, hardworking, farsighted, responsible, and "deep" people. One need not doubt that

[60]Ibid., p. 58. Compare Pramoedya Ananta Toer's beautiful story "Anak Haram," in his *Tjerita dari Blora* (Jakarta: Balai Pustaka, 1952), pp. 227–62.
[61]For example, *hèr* and *giak*, sounds used to turn the oxen to the right and left.
[62]Soetomo, *Kenang-Kenangan*, p. 55.
[63]Ibid., p. 56.
[64]Ibid., p. 68.
[65]Ibid., pp. 65, 68.
[66]Ibid., p. 64.
[67]Ibid., pp. 61–62.
[68]Ibid., p. 65. For more on this, see below, p. 258.

some of this is true and that Soetomo was indeed a spoiled and troublesome child. What is interesting, however, is that he makes so much of his bad behavior.[69] As will become apparent later, the point is certainly *not* that the "person" Soetomo developed forward from naughty child to respected national leader.

As mentioned earlier, before being enrolled in the STOVIA Soetomo was sent to a Dutch-language elementary school in Bangil. While in Bangil, he stayed with a maternal uncle. He gives us two main memories from this time in his life. The first is what he learned from this uncle, who is introduced to the reader in a rather curious way. Soetomo writes:

> [He] was an individual who was very strange in his manner of eating and drinking, let alone of sleeping. . . . [He] rarely ate like ordinary people, and he mainly slept in the middle of the floor, on a chair. So too, after I had been Islamized [*diselamkan*—circumcized], as a result of his teaching I was ashamed to eat to the point my belly felt full. At that time I usually ate just once a day, and took care not to feel full and satisfied. If one found oneself in the midst of eating something extremely tasty, went my uncle's teachings, one should stop and not continue eating. Also, every evening I had to step outside the house, at least twice a night, and he required me to study how to have power over [*berkuasa*] the course of my thoughts. They had to be given direction, just like the desires of my own heart. To this end, every night I had to gaze with a calm mind to the West, East, North and South, while Heaven and Earth too were not to be neglected. At that time, I did not fully understand the purpose of all this. But if I did not carry out this kind of obligation, my thoughts seemed impure and confused; while the act of gazing ahead, behind, left, and right, above and below would bring cool freshness to my heart.[70]

What is remarkable about this passage is not the behavior of the uncle, which is quite normal for a Javanese priyayi steeped in the meditative practices of kebatinan culture. Rather, it is that Soetomo should describe it as strange—and then go on to show that it became

---

[69]The full point of this emphasis will be brought out below at pp. 261–63. To all this there is a remarkable parallel in the autobiography of the Burmese leader U Nu, *Saturday's Son,* trans. U Law Yone (New Haven: Yale University Press, 1975). In chap. 1, "Flaming Youth," Nu cheerfully describes himself as a youthful liar, cheat, thief, brothel frequenter, and dabbler in cocaine and opium. In this case, however, I am convinced that a systematic correspondence with the structure of the Gautama Buddha's life is intended.

[70]Soetomo, *Kenang-Kenangan,* p. 65. It is hard to know how to translate the latter part of this quotation, since the Indonesian has no indicator of tense. It may be that Soetomo is here referring simultaneously to past and present.

second nature to him. I suspect that we are to understand the word "strange" in two ways: the strangeness of the uncle's behavior as it appeared to the child Soetomo, who was still "not yet Javanese"; and the strangeness felt by the new "watching self" in recording the long-past experiences of the inner self (*batin*).

The second interesting aspect of Soetomo's years in Bangil is what he tells of his activities in the elite sekolahan of his primary school: "My teachers and Dutch schoolmates never humiliated me—*quite the opposite.* But if I heard insulting words addressed to other Javanese students, like *penthol*[71] or 'Javanese'—my listening ears burned. And if there was any situation that was unjust [*tidak adil*] I also acted, so that quite often I fought with the children at that school. I never won, for the Dutch pupils were bigger and stronger than my friends, and they could easily beat me down."[72] The description is quite matter-of-fact. But it is the first time in Memories that Soetomo speaks of himself favorably, even if wryly. The reader has learned in earlier passages that one essential aspect of Soetomo's father's nature was precisely his concern for justice (*keadilan*).[73] One could say, then, that the young Soetomo is starting to grow closer to the ancestral qualities. But he also goes out of his way to show that he was not ill treated by his Dutch teachers or fellow pupils; "quite the opposite." It is important to see this not as a boast of his social acceptability to the Dutch,[74] but as a way of showing that the struggle for justice must involve an absence of personal interest (*pamrih*).[75] For in the Javanese tradition one does not seek justice for oneself, but out of commitment to one's *darma* (duty). The story thus has a double significance: It shows both a growing (sociological) consciousness of the racial injustices of colonial society, from which an intensifying nationalist movement was to grow, and a "deep" Javanese in the process of formation.

[71]*Penthol*—coarse Javanese for "idiot" or "dummy." Even today one can hear this phrase on non-Javanese lips.

[72]Soetomo, *Kenang-Kenangan*, p. 65. Italics added.

[73]Among many vivid examples perhaps the most affecting is Soetomo's account of his father's "hypermodern" (*sic*) attitude toward women. He was so "progressive" in wanting to give his daughters a good Dutch education that his neighbors suspected that he had become a Christian! "Very often in the evening, after work, he would take his daughters on his lap, one by one, or would support them with slow, quiet singing of tembang. And very often he would let fall some words on the injustice (*ketidakadilan*) of our people towards women." Ibid., pp. 48–49.

[74]Compare the smug, colonial way in which Abu Hanifah, a leader of the political generation after Soetomo's, describes how he was fully accepted by the Dutch, unlike his friends and classmates, because of his superior understanding of the Dutch language and Western ways. Abu Hanifah, *Tales of a Revolution* (Sydney: Angus and Robertson, 1972), pp. 39–40.

[75]On pamrih in Javanese thinking, see chap. 1, pp. 51–53.

Following his account of his clashes with Dutch schoolchildren, Soetomo describes his holidays back at Ngepèh. Returning to his grandfather's home was "living in freedom with respect to naughtiness and pleasure. There I was spoiled and praised till I felt myself a truly extraordinary child."[76] Yet the very next thing he records is his very ordinary fear of lightning and thunder. When storms came he would run and hide his head in his grandmother's lap. But then his grandfather would take him by the hand and say to him "sweetly and gently": *Lé, kowé aja wedi karo bledhèg. Kowé rak turunan Ki Ageng Séla, mengko bledhèg rak wedi dhéwé.* Soetomo translates this for his non-Javanese readers thus: "Child,[77] do not fear the lightning. Are you not the descendant of Ki Ageng Séla? Surely the lightning will come to be afraid of you." Soetomo concludes: "And because of the conviction in his words, gradually I lost my fear of thunder and lightning, however terrible their voice."[78]

It is difficult not to see in this passage, coming directly after Soetomo's defeats at the hands of the Dutch children, a veiled allusion to the struggle of Indonesians generally against the Dutch, "however terrible their voice." But in addition, we may note that courage here comes from memory—memory of one's origins. One grows up by growing back.

Next, in a section entitled "Why I followed my father's wishes,"[79] Soetomo turns to the reasons he became a student in the STOVIA. Here he describes the bitter conflict between his father and grandfather on the subject of his future. His grandfather desperately wanted Soetomo to become a high official. He used to urge the boy to refuse if his father tried to send him to medical school. His father, overwhelmed by the frustrations and humiliations of native official life, would have none of it for his son. Soetomo gives us two reasons why he followed his father's wishes and, somewhat surprisingly, tells us at what age each reason took effect. At the age of eight, he was childishly impressed by the white

[76]Soetomo, *Kenang-Kenangan*, p. 66. Note the interesting negative use of *kemerdékaan* (freedom), jewel word to a later generation of Indonesians, in this moral context.

[77]*Lé* is probably untranslatable. A short form of *konthol é* (his penis), it is the usual affectionate Javanese term of address to a small boy. Javanese folklore has it that when the lightning attempted to strike the magically powerful Ki Ageng Séla, the sage seized it and tied it firmly to a nearby tree. The sobbing lightning was only released when it promised never to strike a descendant of its captor. These descendants—the people of Java—would be identified by the leaves of the poison-tree worn on their hats. To this day, some Javanese villagers wear these leaves if they are out in the open in thundery weather.

[78]Soetomo, *Kenang-Kenangan*, p. 66. Note again, what is impressive to Soetomo is the conviction *in* the words, i.e., the *sound* more than the meaning.

[79]Ibid., pp. 66–68.

uniforms of the STOVIA students, which seemed much grander than the black garments worn by government officials. The second reason "happened" when he was about thirteen:

> At that time my father was an Assistant Wedana in Glodok, and once it so happened that I was at home. Very early in the morning my father had to go to Magetan in a *bèndi*.[80] About 4 a.m., my mother was already seated before the charcoal fire, toasting bread for breakfast, and I and my little brother were already awake. We saw father coming out of his room, already dressed in his official clothes, standing before us and grumbling about the status [*derajat*] of anyone who worked as a priyayi of the Binnenlandsch Bestuur. . . . Because my father went on and on grumbling, I asked him: "Father, why do you do this work then?" My question was immediately answered: "If I did not do this work, would all of you be able to eat bread and butter?"[81] The word *korban* and the meaning of this word I did not yet understand, but hearing it in my inmost self [batin] I revered my father deeply. "I have only one request to make of you," so my father continued, "I ask that none of my children grow up to be priyayi B[innenlandsch] B[estuur]."[82]

In this passage we still see Soetomo as a child who "does not yet understand [*belum mengerti*]"—a phrase, it may be noted, that he never uses for any Western-style teaching that he later receives. But the narration here is really more remarkable than the event. For while we can be sure that "historically" Soetomo's father spoke to his son in Javanese, his words here are given in Indonesian.[83] And we observe that Soetomo is caught by the word *korban*—which does not occur in the sentences his father utters! In one sense, it is clear what has happened. In his memory Soetomo must be recalling his father's words in Javanese, among them, very probably, *ngurban*. *Ngurban* is one of the deep moral and emotional words of Javanese, meaning to do without in order to achieve some great goal, or to help someone in need. It precisely echoes the teachings of Soetomo's uncle in Bangil.[84] The child Soetomo was thus struck by a word he did not yet understand, of

---

[80]*Bèndi*—two-wheeled horse-drawn carriage. In parts of rural Java even today the bèndi is a status symbol.

[81]It is curious that Soetomo makes no particular point of this European-style breakfast, which must have been something of a rarity in the Javanese world of Madiun at the turn of the century.

[82]Soetomo, *Kenang-Kenangan*, pp. 67–68.

[83]This is true of all Soetomo's quotations from his father, whereas his grandfather's words are always first given in Javanese and then translated into Indonesian.

[84]See the account of how his grandfather won his higher-status wife by prolonged ascetic self-denial. Ibid., p. 11. Cf. also chap. 1, above, pp. 24–25.

which he was not yet "aware," but the understanding of which would later allow him to "become Javanese." The strange thing here, however, is the interlingual slippage. For the Indonesian sentence gives little sense of the moral exchange alluded to—which indeed has meaning primarily in a Javanese context. If Soetomo earlier translated his grandfather's words into Indonesian, now, perhaps involuntarily, he reverses course, moving from Indonesian back to Javanese. This is perhaps why he is not explicit about the lesson he learned. It may be that Soetomo, understanding something of his father's sacrifice, agreed to go to medical school, rather than become a "priyayi B.B.," out of gratitude and respect. Or, possibly, intimations of the idea of ngurban—giving direction to thoughts and desires for some greater purpose—led him to will his entry into an institution that would keep him permanently out of the old Javanese official elite and the traditional status hierarchy.

The following section brings us to the STOVIA. The picture of the author as a dirty, naughty, lazy, and spendthrift character is further elaborated. He takes nothing seriously, since if he is expelled his grandfather will be pleased and his parents will support him anyway.[85] We learn almost nothing of what happens in the Westernized classroom, only of childish pranks. But the section closes with these significant words: "Even though I was still spendthrift, obstinate and naughty, yet about one year before my father left for eternal time [zaman yang baka]—it was only then that I understood that I too could work without copying (*nurun*) and thereby came the awareness [*kesadaran*] that working by copying is work in degradation."[86]

At first sight, this seems quite straightforward: A lazy boy comes to see that cheating is bad and childish. Yet I think there is more involved. Soetomo's language, particularly the terms *nurun* and *kesadaran,* suggests complexities of two different kinds. He gives us a hint by first using the Indonesian word *meniru* (to imitate, copy) and then adding the Javanese-derived *nurun* in parentheses.[87] On the one hand, this seems a clear allusion to the whole issue of modernization as "imitation" of the West, which haunted Soetomo's generation of

[85]Soetomo, *Kenang-Kenangan,* p. 69.
[86]Ibid.
[87]This is one of the very rare cases in Memories where Soetomo first uses an Indonesian term and then "explains" it in Javanese, rather than the other way round. *Nurun,* in the sense of cheating by copying, seems to have entered the Indonesian language from Javanese quite recently. For instance, it is not found in this sense in Welfridus Joseph Sabarija Poerwadarminta's standard *Kamus Umum Bahasa Indonesia* (Jakarta: Perpustakaan Perguruan Kementerian P.P. dan K., 1954).

Indonesian leaders.[88] Soetomo's readers in the 1930s would certainly have seen the words "working by copying is work in degradation" in the context of the whole colonial experience. That *kesadaran*—the key word of early nationalist thought—is used in this small classroom episode suggests the larger meaning of the narration. On the other hand, we should remember the significance of the idea of *turun* in Javanese culture. Being a true *turunan* (descendant) means not abandoning the nature or qualities of one's forefathers. Imitation, in the sense of drawing close to this nature, is central to the genealogy of Javanese morals.[89] We have already seen that the most important parts of Soetomo's education so far have been the occasions when he learned to imitate, following his grandfather, his uncle, or his father. So the passage quoted above gives us a pregnant image of the contrary directions of his dual education, symbolized by the antagonistic Dutch and Javanese meanings of imitation. "Without copying" in the Dutch classroom means "copying" Dutch culture, in other words, absorbing its values seriously; this however, implies not imitating Javanese tradition, which extols imitation. But is also foreshadows the nationalist solution—imitating one's forefathers by not imitating them. Being a good Javanese by becoming a good Indonesian.

We come finally to the moral center of Soetomo's Memories, the section that he calls "Change of nature" [*Perobahan Perangai*].[90] Its content is simple but surprising, and in effect, perhaps for extra emphasis, it is told twice over. Soetomo has been accustomed to copying the work of his more industrious classmates. Then one day a teacher asks the class a pair of questions—one on algebra and the other on physics. Seeing no one else prepared to answer, even the brightest, Soetomo raises his hand just for fun and discovers "to my own astonishment" that he somehow knows the correct answer. This sudden ability is put in an interesting context: "The Director of the school had established a new system in my class, insisting that mathematics be taught over, so that the pupils could continually make use of their intellects. . . . The reader should understand that our class had hitherto been given lessons that could be followed with very little *intellect*, provided one's memory [*geheugen*] was sufficient."[91] In the narrative

---

[88]This view is supported, I think, by the placing of the passage in the text—immediately *before* Soetomo's "change of nature." See below, pp. 263–65.

[89]Imitation was, and is, a central tool of traditional Javanese pedagogy, whether in dance schools or pesantrèn.

[90]Soetomo, *Kenang-Kenangan*, pp. 69–73.

[91]Ibid., p. 70. Note the use of Dutch terminology here—*intellect* and *geheugen*. It is suggestive of the wide divergence between Western and Javanese ideas of the components of personhood. Compare the earlier references to batin, and the remarks on budi below, p. 269.

the change in pedagogy is tied to Soetomo's discovery: "'Hey,' I thought, 'in this case I too have a brain'". In other words, once the Dutch lessons stop being rote learning and imitation, Soetomo comes to perceive his own quality and capacity.[92] "From that time on, I grew ashamed to copy [nurun] any more."[93] It is with this awareness of shame—as it were, "becoming Javanese," but in the setting of a Western classroom—that Soetomo shows his nature as having changed, so that he now can write: "It was only about two years before my father left me that it appeared from the expression on his face that he had some hopes for me. This is understandable because at that time my nature began to change. From childhood up till then, my life had always depended on others."[94]

About that time the character of his relations with his father also began to change. He no longer wrote home only to ask for money, but exchanged letters with his father about the proper education for his younger brothers and sisters. "My father began to have some esteem for me, whereas I had *drawn close to his batin*. In this happy condition, full of good hope for the flourishing of my family, in a time [zaman] of glorious ideals, suddenly and quite unexpectedly, on July 28, 1907, came a telegram telling of my father's death."[95]

Considering Soetomo's earlier account of his emotional relationship with his father as none too close,[96] the description of his feelings on the morrow of his bereavement may seem rather odd.

Who can feel for the trouble that then assailed me?[97] No one in this world but those in a situation like my own. Even at that time, let alone now, I could not describe the trouble and the darkness that were in my heart; and my closest friends, even though they shared my sorrow, could not console me. I though of the lot of my mother, I thought of that of my little brothers and sisters with the death of my father. It was as though they had lost the umbrella that protected them, lost the staff on which

[92]A further involution of the paradox of imitation.
[93]Soetomo, *Kenang-Kenangan*, p. 71. But Soetomo adds that, because he understood so well the misery of those pupils regarded as "stupid," he began regularly to help them with their work and to allow them to copy from him (p. 72). It is as if cheating is legitimate provided it is done without pamrih.
[94]Ibid., p. 69.
[95]Ibid., p. 74. Italics added.
[96]"My relationship to and love for my parents, up till the day of my father's death, was not very close and intimate. I was not much at ease with my father and mother, so that to them I used high Javanese [bahasa kromo]. In addition I felt not so much love as simply respect (eerbied). At that time, my love was directed only to my grandfather and grandmother" (ibid., p. 63).
[97]This sentence seems grammatically confused. Soetomo has *tiada merasai* (cannot feel) when the sense requires simply *merasai*.

they leaned, lost everything, every promise and foundation that they needed for their development. What had we done wrong? Was God just? . . . My father's death at that time contained this meaning for me: it was as though I had received a punishment, quite unexpectedly and of immeasurable severity, meaning the loss of dignity, humiliation and the rest. . . . I felt that people had changed their attitudes towards me and my family. The respectful words, the generosity, the sweetness of their talk and the kindliness of some of our acquaintances appeared not to be genuine, but only an external veneer—and this was because of the influence of my father's death.[98]

The people who came to console the family often stole his father's belongings, gossiped about his debts, and speculated about how much property he had left his children. "So I felt troubled and anguished, I felt humiliated, I felt deprived of honor, I felt that I lived like someone stripped stark naked in public. . . . At this time of great grief, when it seemed as if the sun no longer showed his rays, at this time it was only my grandfather and my uncle who eased my burden."[99] In school he completely changed his behavior: He stopped being spendthrift, naughty and lazy—to the point that a gulf opened between him and his friends. "And so my life changed. At night it was the stars and the moon that became my friends, to help me concentrate [*menghening-kan cipta*], so that I could succeed, as eldest son, in fulfilling my responsibilities. . . .[100] My thoughts and feelings became separated from their environment, seeking another course for their life, heading in another direction which would bring them an opportunity to flower."[101]

Soetomo now became the head of the stricken family and had to assume the responsibilities involved. What is interesting in his description of that time, however, is his new perception of exterior and interior (*lahir* and batin) and the separation he records himself experiencing from the world.[102] This separation prepares the way for a denouement that is not depicted as such in Memories but is prefigured in the passages cited above. For Soetomo now seeks to "meet" his

[98]Ibid., pp. 74–75.
[99]Ibid., p. 75.
[100]Ibid., p. 76. *Mengheningkan cipta* (Javanese, *ngeningaken cipta*) means the practice of meditation for the concentration of one's inner being. Here Soetomo applies the teachings of his uncle in Bangil.
[101]Ibid., p. 78.
[102]This is figured in the disjuncture depicted between the sounds of the neighbors' words and their meaning. Contrast this disjuncture with the deep correspondence shown in Soetomo's accounts of the sambatan in Ngepèh (above) and of his feelings about Dr. Wahidin (below).

father and to live up to the moral responsibilities of family and tradition.[103] But he will do this by "finding *another* direction."

Five months later, at the onset of the rains at the end of 1907, Dr. Wahidin Soedirohoesodo arrived in Batavia to rest from his long search for funds to help intelligent young Javanese pursue Western education. During his stay, he came to speak to the STOVIA students. Here is how Soetomo describes that meeting, from which Budi Utomo was to be born a few months later:

> The meeting with Dr. Wahidin Soedirohoesodo, with his tranquil features, his wise manner and tone, and his conviction in explaining his ideals, left a deep impression on me. His melodious and *rustig* (Jav., *sarèn*) voice opened up my thoughts and spirit, and brought me new ideals and a new world that could, it seemed, console my wounded heart. Speaking with Dr. Wahidin, listening to his aims . . . removed all narrow feelings and goals limited to my own private needs. One became another person, one felt oneself in motion, trembling throughout one's flesh and bones, one's views became broad, one's feelings refined [*halus*], one's ideals beautiful . . . in short, one felt one's most high obligations in this world.[104]

Here the autobiographical part of Memories comes to an end, with Soetomo just nineteen and Budi Utomo still unformed. The rest of the book records the services of Soetomo's friends, retainers, and, above all, his wife. From these pages one can infer something of his later life, but that is not the focus of the writing. From Soetomo's perspective, I think, what is essential has already been said.

Had his life, in his own eyes, had a linear trajectory, had it run in some sense parallel to the movement of the world, the political events of 1907–1908 would have been a mere beginning. But I think that it

[103]There is probably a parallel here with one of the basic themes of the Javanese wayang: a young hero's separation from his father and long search to find him. The moment of maximum separation occurs when the devoted young man, alone in the forest except for a wise guru (Dr. Wahidin?), practices meditation to find the means for completing his quest. The depth of his concentration produces the *gara-gara*, or churning of the cosmos (formation of Budi Utomo?). The play's resolution usually comes when the long-lost father acknowledges the hero as truly his descendant (turunan). On this theme, see K. P. G. A. A. Mangkunagara VII, *On the Wayang Kulit (Purwa) and Its Symbolic and Mystical Elements*, trans. Claire Holt, Southeast Asia Program Data Paper no. 27 (Ithaca, N.Y.: Cornell University, 1957), pp. 11–16.

[104]Soetomo, *Kenang-Kenangan,* pp. 80–81. In this passage, as so often, Soetomo turns from Dutch or Indonesian to Javanese to express the nuances of his feelings. Note that the very syntax of the closing sentence—the shift from "I" to "one" (my poor translation of *orang* here)—conveys the abandonment of egoism and pamrih—and perhaps a movement from Soetomo the individual to the whole audience of Javanese boys.

should now be clear that the perceived movement of his life had another shape, not so much political, in our sense of the word, as moral. To specify this shape more clearly, it may be useful to turn to a term that Soetomo himself elsewhere employs—*lelakon,* appointed course in life, somewhere between darma and destiny. For the events of 1907–1908—losing his father and finding Dr. Wahidin, leaving his family and finding his *guru*—reflect the passage of a Javanese man's life, from *kesenangan* (pleasure) to *kewajiban* (duty), from *kenakalan* (naughtiness) to *kemuliaan* (excellence), from imitation to setting an example.[105]

Nothing could be more striking, in this connection, than the strange link between the enormous, almost physiological surge of emotion, the giddy feeling of immensely expanding horizons that Soetomo records of his meeting with Dr. Wahidin, and the picture he gives of the doctor himself. Not only do we get a glimpse of a most traditional if resolute Javanese gentleman,[106] but we are brought back to a unified world where sight, sound, and meaning again coincide. "Calm," "melodious," "tranquil"—the expressions Soetomo uses for the sound and sight of Dr. Wahidin he had used earlier to describe the village life of Ngepèh, the circle of zaman kuno. "Not yet Javanese," he had then been a disruptive element. Now Javanese, he rejoins his forefathers.

Yet if he has found his *asal* (origins), we are not being treated to the simple story of a Javanese growing up. For the traditional Dr. Wahidin brings the young Soetomo "new ideals and a new world." What were these new ideals, this new world? The Western science and rationalism of which Van Niel writes? In such matters Soetomo was already far better educated than the old doctor had ever been. With his years in the

[105]Compare the last two portions of Ronggawarsita's *Kala Tidha,* entitled *Sabda Tama* and *Sabda Jati.*

[106]In a passage immediately antecedent (p. 80) Soetomo transmits a story that Wahidin told about himself. In a certain place where he hoped to call a meeting to raise scholarship funds, the Dutch Assistant Resident was antagonistic. Accordingly, the local priyayi, who secretly wished to attend, did not dare go. So Wahidin entered the Dutchman's office (here the syntax changes and Soetomo takes over the narration from Wahidin) and stood there quite still—until the Assistant Resident looked at him. Acting as though in awe, he prostrated himself below the Dutchman's table, offering the respectful *sembah* gesture and speaking in the humblest language: "Tuan Assistant Resident became *sabar* [got control of himself], and at that very moment his face became sweet and smiling. Tuan Assistant Resident said to him: 'Doctor, your purpose deserves the strongest support. It would be well if you spoke before a meeting, so that all my officials can hear you.' Thus by the aid of Tuan Assistant Resident, who had originally intended to block his purpose, [Dr. Wahidin] won extraordinary attention." The gentle irony of this episode, no less than the acceptance of submission to achieve a high aim, is characteristically Javanese.

ELS and the STOVIA, with his excellent command of Dutch, Soetomo was much closer to the "new world" conceived by Westerners than was his enlightener. I believe rather than Soetomo, and probably others in the STOVIA milieu, sensed in Wahidin an example of how to proceed into the colonial Western world without imitation; at a deeper level, how to imitate one's forebears without imitating them, how not to abandon Javanese tradition when one no longer lived imbedded in it, and how to match the watching self with the batin. Ronggawarsita had imaged the Time of Darkness with the harsh oxymoron of impotent kingly perfection. The ratu utama, sign for Glorious Java, was no longer believable. Wahidin, however, showed that it was possible, even essential, to detach adjective from noun. Once detached, the weight of its meaning shifted from what we might call political efficacy to ethical commitment: in a word, to a perfected moral faculty (*budi utama*). And this ethical commitment was a burden that anyone might assume—not excluding Javanese teenagers, especially one whose own name compounded *su* (excellent) with *utama* (perfected).[107]

But commitment to what? In the old Javanese tradition, kingly perfection meant commitment to kingly power. Concentrated power produced fertility, prosperity, and harmony in the community. Social well-being was a by-product of power's commitment of itself.[108] But once kingly power had proven impotent, the by-product could readily become central goal.

If one looks at the ideas that Soetomo worked with all his life, one finds a vocabulary and an idiom of a very consistent kind. There is, for example, almost no utilization of political notions based in Western sociology.[109] The Marxian categories central to the political language of Sukarno's entire generation, from its conservative to its radical members, are totally absent. Where Sukarno and his contemporaries talked of Indonesia Merdéka (Free Indonesia), Soetomo typically spoke of his ideal as Indonesia Mulia (Glorious, or Perfected Indonesia). *Merdéka*, liberation, implied, of course, much more radical and *political* aims. It is a word that is the peculiar glory of Indonesian, or "revolutionary Malay,"[110] but has few resonances in Javanese. *Mulia* is just the reverse. In the passage of Memories quoted above (p.

[107]Koch, *Batig Slot*, writes: "The struggle for social betterment attracted him [Soetomo] more than politics. He radiated love for his country and his people" (p. 139).

[108]See chap. 1, above.

[109]See Scherer, "Harmony," pp. 212–13. For a full discussion of Soetomo's political thinking, see also pp. 207–47.

[110]See chap. 1, above.

243) we can see what mulia naturally goes with, and it seems the very opposite of kemerdékaan: kewajiban, or obligation.

As Savitri Scherer has sensitively shown, Soetomo compared Indonesia Mulia to a gamelan orchestra in which each person plays the instrument allotted to him as best he can. From the intertwining of fulfilled musical obligations comes the glory (kemuliaan) of the gamelan sound.[111] Playing one's instrument is performing one's lelakon, living up to the responsibilities one has inherited or that have fallen to one's lot. Soetomo's idea of uplifting his society was to make it feasible for all the instruments to be played as perfectly as possible. Peasants and workers had to be fed, cared for, and educated to become good peasants and good workers, mindful of their obligations and capable of fulfilling them.[112] When in the 1930s—to the disgust of some of his younger nationalist colleagues—Soetomo appealed to the collaborationist aristocracy and priyayi for their support, he did so by way of urging them to "remember their origins," in other words, to accept the moral obligations of their tradition.[113]

We can perhaps then think of Soetomo's nationalist mission in terms of a musical simile, involving the systematic transposition of old melodies into new keys, different scales, and changed orchestrations. Memories offers some conspicuous examples of this. His uncle meditated in his Javanese home, Soetomo in the Western STOVIA. His grandfather created a system of "useful justice" in Ngepèh, and Soetomo spent his life in search of a useful justice for the Indonesia being born.[114] His father tried to live with dignity in the chains of the

[111]Compare the overwhelmingly *aural* depiction of the harmony pervading the sambatan in Ngepèh (above).

[112]Scherer, "Harmony," pp. 218–39. This association of gamelan and politics is not merely an eccentricity of Soetomo's. I have heard from elderly court musicians in Surakarta that there is a special gamelan composition called "Dendha Séwu," traditionally played when the ruling dynasty was in grave trouble. The composition itself is not technically difficult, so that if the court's master musicians could not play it perfectly, this was taken as a confirming omen of impending disaster.

[113]Soetomo said of his party, Parindra, that it "makes the best effort to woo them [the upper priyayi] so that their dedication to the land and the people could be accelerated according to their own darma, that is, the darma of a true ksatrya according to their aristocratic blood." Taken from Soetomo's address to Parindra's opening congress, December 25, 1935, titled "Bekerdja dengan tiada mengenal buahnja," and cited in Scherer, "Harmony," p. 235.

[114]In *Kenang-Kenangan*, p. 20, Soetomo notes that his grandfather, bitterly disappointed that the boy was not going to enter the native administration, requested that at the very least he keep a horse for riding, as a sign of priyayi-dom. "Quite unexpectedly, there came a time when I could fulfil my grandfather's longing. When as a doctor I had to care for the health of the people in the region of Mt. Lawu, I kept two horses which, every day, turn and turn about, bore me to the villagers." A nice image of transposition: rural doctor as the new priyayi. Soetomo also recalls (p. 42) that his father insisted on speaking in high Javanese to

colonial bureaucracy, Soetomo did so as an alien-trained doctor. His forefathers, as he described them, saw marriage as a cementing of solidarity in the Javanese world; and Soetomo, in his touching description of his Dutch wife, appears to have seen his own marriage in the same light.[115] But the central image of transposition is the organization that Soetomo made history by founding: Budi Utomo. For Budi Utomo is fully recognizable in both Javanese and Indonesian tonalities.[116] Situated across the two languages, it looked both forward and back, signifying committed endeavor—a later generation would say struggle[117]—to live up to something long there in the memory and imagination.

The images of light, dawn, and sun suffusing the publications of the Budi Utomo years are both specific to the course of Javanese and Indonesian history and larger symbols of revival and regeneration.[118]

---

almost everyone and in this was among the first to spread "democratic ways." Supardi (*Dr. Soetomo*, pp. 36, 38) notes that Soetomo did exactly the same thing, and habitually addressed his driver, Pak Soemo, in *krama*. It is perhaps characteristic, nonetheless, that between *ngoko* (low, familiar Javanese) and krama, Soetomo and his father chose to "abolish" ngoko (as it were, leveling *up*). Nagazumi (*Dawn*, p. 193 n. 26) mentions the appearance of a movement, not long after the birth of Budi Utomo, called Jawa Dwipa (Dipo), which advocated the abolition of krama (as it were, leveling *down*). The roughly contemporaneous Saminist movement also resolutely refused to use krama to officialdom. See Harry J. Benda and Lance Castles, "The Samin Movement," *Bijdrage tot de taal-, land- en volkenkunde* 125 (1969):234.

[115] "Here it is only fitting that I express my immeasurable gratitude to her. My wife was someone who truly loved her country. And so she understood and was aware, and constantly urged and prodded me to make my love for my land and people still deeper, and to give that love real expression. My wife was also someone who loved her people. And so she understood my obligation to my people, and constantly urged me to prove my love for my people. My wife stood, not above her people, but amongst them. And so her love was truly alive. As a true Dutchwoman, my wife loved freedom, justice and equality; and so she could not endure a situation full of discrimination, and hated to see behavior that could stain the good name of her nation. It was because of these feelings that she continually urged me to keep on fighting, to join the struggle to abolish this discrimination" (Soetomo, *Kenang-Kenangan*, pp. 127–28).

[116] *Budi utama* is perfectly good, if stilted, Indonesian.

[117] Compare Sudisman, *Analysis:* "We live in order to struggle, and we struggle in order to live. We live not just for the sake of life alone; we live to defend that life with courage till our hearts cease to beat. From the moment that a human being is born, from his first whimper as a baby to his last breath, life is a struggle. Sometimes he will face a struggle that is very difficult, sometimes he will face a hard-fought battle. Not every such contest is crowned with victory. But the aim of life is to have the courage to enter this hard-fought battle and at the same time win the victory. This is the dream of everyone who struggles, not excluding the communists. This too is my dream of life. For without dreams, without ideals, life is barren and empty" (p. 24).

[118] See Taufik Abdullah, "Modernization in the Minangkabau World," pp. 215–18. He speaks of one of the early modernizers in West Sumatra, Datuk Sutan Maharadja, the "father of Malay journalism," who from 1891 to 1913 was successively involved in newspapers entitled *Palita Ketjil* [Little lamp], *Warta Berita* [News report], *Tjaja Soematera* [Light of Sumatra], *Oetoesan Melajoe* [Malay messenger], *Al-Moenir* [Enlightenment] and

They are images conjured up at moments when men's lives appear to run in tandem with the world. When they appear under conditions in which progressive conceptions of time are influential, one would expect them to be linked to images of youth. This is clearly true of the early years of Budi Utomo. How close the nexus between life-moment and linear history was can be judged from the observation of Goenawan Mangoenkoesoemo, Soetomo's closest friend, that the aim of the boys in Budi Utomo was to "remain a motor in order to propel their seniors from behind."[119] The phrase not only employs a distinctly twentieth-century industrial metaphor but, in the Javanese context, sharply reverses the hoary pedagogic apophthegm *tut wuri andayani*—perfection comes when old people guide the young from behind.[120] It is a mordant, excited expression that belongs to youth.

We find nothing comparable in the Memories of Soetomo. Images of light and dawn are quite rare in it. The tone of the book is somber and centers on death rather than birth. If we ask ourselves why this should be so, I think the answer is quite straightforward. By 1934, Soetomo, for all his political successes,[121] was no longer in the vanguard of the nationalist movement. As a man of his time, as well as a Javanese, he could see that the movement's progress and the trajectory of his own life were diverging. His wife had returned to the zaman yang baka and he was preparing in due course to follow her. It was time to think about bequests (*warisan*), and a warisan is really what Memories represents.

Ronggawarsita had lamented that there was "no example left." What he meant was that the old models no longer worked, and so could not be handed down. It was Soetomo's (and his generation's) quiet triumph to have reclaimed their ancestry and to have found thereby an example to bequeath to their posterity.

Soeloeh Melajoe [Malay torch]. Compare the splendid discussion of comparable imagery in China during more or less the same period, in Maurice Meisner, *Li Ta-Chao and the Origins of Chinese Marxism* (Cambridge, Mass.: Harvard University Press, 1967), especially pp. 21–28.

[119]Cited in Nagazumi, *Dawn*, p. 42.

[120]It became a central theme in the educational philosophy of the Taman Siswa school system created by Soetomo's famous contemporary Ki Hadjar Dewantara.

[121]For example, Rukun Tani, the peasant organization he formed in East Java, had more than 20,000 members in 125 branches in 1933, making it easily the largest rural organization affiliated with the nationalist movement. See John Edward Ingleson, "The Secular and Non-Cooperating Nationalist Movement in Indonesia, 1923–1934" (Ph.D. thesis, Monash University, 1974), p. 419. On the successful growth of Parindra, see Susan Abeyasekere, "Relations between the Indonesian Cooperating Nationalists and the Dutch, 1935–1942" (Ph.D. thesis, Monash University, 1972), pp. 127–31.

CHAPTER 8

Professional Dreams: Reflections
on Two Javanese Classics

Mark Twain put it characteristically: "A classic is something that everybody wants to have read and nobody wants to read." Few major works of the later era of traditional Javanese literature fit his words better than the *Serat Centhini*.[1] Ritually described as a masterpiece and, more interestingly (as we shall see), as an encyclopedia of Javanese culture, it has never been printed in its entirety. The only substantial published version, an eight-volume Romanized edition, appeared seventy-five years ago.[2] With a few notable exceptions, it has been neglected by both Western and modern Javanese scholars.[3]

Based on a paper presented in 1984 to the Southeast Asian Summer Studies Institute.

[1]According to Behrend, 98 variant manuscripts of this poem, in eight major recensions, can today be found in various public collections in Indonesia and The Netherlands. The oldest known version originates from a Cirebon manuscript of 1616. The fullest *Centhini*, a colossal work of almost a quarter of a million lines, was completed, he argues, in 1814. It is thought to have been prepared by a committee of poets in the entourage of the then crown prince of Surakarta, who later became Pakubuwana V. Tradition has it that the prince sent emissaries all over Java and Madura to gather every possible form of Javanese knowledge for inclusion in the final text. See Timothy E. Behrend, "The Serat Jatiswara: Structure and Change in a Javanese Poem, 1600–1930" (Ph.D. thesis, Australian National University, 1988), pp. 79–84.

[2]*Serat Tjentini,* ed. R. Ng. Soeradipoera, R. Poerwasoewignja, and R. Wirawangsa (Batavia [Jakarta]: Ruygrok, 1912–15). Behrend believes that the initiative was taken by the scholar-bureaucrat Douwe Rinkes, then director of the Bataviaasch Genootschap van Kunsten en Wetenschappen (Batavian Society of Arts and Sciences), who had the text prepared in Leiden, then sent to Surakarta for checking by Soeradipoera and his aides, and finally printed in Batavia at the society's expense. Behrend, "Serat Jatiswara," p. 89. The only other substantial Romanized version, appearing in four volumes sixty years later, covered barely half the material in the 1912–15 edition: viz., *Serat Centhini,* ed. Tardjan Hadidjaja (Yogyakarta: U.P. Indonesia, 1976–77).

[3]The most substantial mining of the *Centhini*'s vast resources is in Theodoor Gautier Thomas Pigeaud's encyclopedic work on the traditional performing arts of Java and

271

Where not ignored, it has been mined primarily for the copious information it provides on Javanese artistic and religious traditions. But the
text also marks an important milestone in the historical development
of Javanese political culture.

If the *Serat Centhini* can be said to have a story, it amounts to the
following: After the bloody sack in 1625 of the prosperous Islamic,
East Javanese port kingdom of Giri by the armies of Sultan Agung of
the Central Javanese kingdom of Mataram, the three children of the
vanquished ruler (two male, one female) are forced to flee for their
lives. Hunted by the spies of Mataram, they are separated: the elder
son, Jayèngresmi (later known as Sèh Amongraga) escapes to the west,
while the younger son and the daughter (Jayèngsari and Rancangkapti) try to elude their pursuers to the southeast. The text describes their
adventurous wanderings in a vain search to be reunited. They are,
however, linked by the odd figure of Cebolang, who first appears
attached to the small retinue of Amongraga and ends up marrying
Rancangkapti. Cebolang is described as the only child of a revered
sage living on Mount Sokayasa, who, however, disowns the youth on
account of his inveterate gambling, thieving, and adulteries. Forced to
survive by his wits, Cebolang earns his bread as a wandering musician, dancer, and what for want of a better word I shall call conjuror.
    The fact that its leading characters are fugitives or outcasts perma-
nently on the move means that the *mise en scène* of the *Centhini* is
very different from that usually associated with traditional Javanese
literature. There are no episodes on battlefields or in royal courts and
capitals. The ruler of Mataram is merely an ominous, gloomy presence off stage. For the most part, the text's settings are a series of
villages and rural Islamic schools (*pesantrèn*), while the cast of characters, male and female, are *kyai* (traditional Islamic men of learning),
santri (their students), headmen, traders, professional musicians, singers, dancers, prostitutes, and ordinary villagers. The settings, and the
encounters that take place in them, provide opportunities for the
hugely elaborate descriptions of many traditional aspects of Javanese

---

Madura: *Javanese Volksvertoningen* (Batavia: Volkslectuur, 1938). The eminent eth-
nomusicologist Jaap Kunst quoted many short passages dealing with music in his monu-
mental *Music in Java: Its History, Its Theory and Its Technique* [3d, enlarged edition, ed.
Ernst L. Heins] (The Hague: Nijhoff, 1973; originally published by Nijhoff in 1934 as *De
Toonkunst van Java*). See also S. Soebardi, *The Book of Cabolèk: A Critical Edition with
Introduction, Translation, and Notes: a Contribution to the Study of Javanese Mystical
Tradition* (The Hague: Nijhoff, 1975; based on his 1967 Australian National University
Ph.D. thesis).

rural life—folk arts, architecture, cooking, cultivations, ceremonies, fauna and flora, religion, medicine, sexual practices, and so forth— that have earned the *Centhini* its reputation as the encyclopedia of Old Java.

Encyclopedic Politics

Ann Kumar has drawn explicit comparisons between the rural social orders prevailing in Java and France during the eighteenth century. She has thereby signally advanced the conscious incorporation of Old Java's history into the larger history of the modern world.[4] I believe it is possible to extrapolate from her comparisons to reflect on class relations other than those between lords and peasants. An interesting point of departure is suggested by a glance at two encyclopedias—our own *Centhini,* and that of Diderot, d'Alembert, and their associates— composed within half a century of one another.[5] While it is true that the Encyclopédistes foreshadowed the rise to power of the French bourgeoisie, their immediate circle was of quite mixed social origins;[6] moreover, the specific, revolutionary character of their *Encyclopédie* has no exact parallel in the historical rise of other European bourgeoisies. For their project was to marshal a colossal, systematically organized compendium of all the multifarious knowledge accumulated by, and available to, the professional men of learning of their time. The animus behind it was hostility, not merely to reactionary *idées reçues* but also to the ecclesiastical and monarchical authorities behind them. Against the *general* (cultural and political) power of Church and Crown, Diderot and his associates mobilized a formidable coalition of *specific* virtuosities. In effect, the aim was to show that on almost any topic—from the nature of magnetism to the origins of language—the (mostly) commoner, lay cognoscenti "knew more" than their putative social and religious superiors. In this sense, the

[4]Ann Kumar, "The Peasantry and the State on Java: Changes of Relationship, Seventeenth to Nineteenth Centuries," in James Austin Copland Mackie, ed., *Indonesia: Australian Perspectives* (Canberra: Australian National University, Research School of Pacific Studies, 1980), pp. 577–99. For this essay she drew on several of her own earlier monographic studies, and also on the fine research of Robert Elson, Onghokham, Theodoor Pigeaud, and Bertram Schrieke.

[5]I take Behrend's 1814 dating of the full *Centhini* as reasonable, and 1777 as the date of publication of the final supplementary volume of the *Encyclopédie ou Dictionnaire Raisonné des Sciences, des Arts et des Métiers.*

[6]Montesquieu and d'Alembert had aristocratic backgrounds, though the latter was illegitimate. Diderot, Voltaire, and Rousseau were of bourgeois or lower origins.

Encyclopédie can usefully be understood as a weapon in the struggle between a professional, secular clerisy and the whole structure of hegemony of the *ancien régime*.

Now I think it can be argued that the *Centhini* reflects a parallel animus, albeit in a very different political, social, and cultural setting. One might begin the argument by noting three striking general features of this immense poem. The first is that it is thickly strewn with what look very much like entries in an odd sort of encyclopedia.[7] There are, for example, many passages, some several stanzas long, that consist purely of lists: of Javanese sweetmeats, edible freshwater fish, joists and tenons, theological terms, musical compositions, names of mountains, cloths, dances, and so forth. These passages have no syntax—they read like unalphabetized, poetic Yellow Pages. Furthermore, it is very hard to fit them to the traditional aesthetics of Javanese poetry, which was almost always meant to be sung. (An English parallel might be a song consisting, without irony, of the names of forty-five brands of breakfast cereal). Hence, one gets the distinct feeling that such passages are actually meant less to be recited than to be read (consulted?). In other words, if the Javanese reader (not listener) wished to check all the different types of Javanese cookie or gamelan composition, he could go to the *Centhini* and look them up. And the sources of all this knowledge (*ngèlmu*) are not priests, or sages, or noblemen, but virtuoso professionals and compilers.

The second striking feature of the *Centhini* is the way in which the text treats such topics as supernatural entities and sacred objects attached to kings and courts. For they are handled in exactly the same matter-of-fact, encyclopedic way as fish, flora, or food. Canto 85, stanzas 4–5, for example, offers the reader a deadpan catalogue of a score of typical Javanese ghosts and goblins, organized neither alphabetically nor in order of scariness, but simply to fit the prosodic requirements of the meter Wirangrong.

Third is the noticeable absence of any depiction of *kasektèn* (magical Power) being deployed by members of the ruling strata, or indeed by anyone else.[8] The significance of this absence becomes apparent if one compares the *Centhini* with the tales of the *wayang purwa* (traditional shadow-puppet plays), or with such royal chronicles as the

---

[7]The *Encyclopédie* already used the most easily accessed of taxonomic principles—alphabetic order—to order its entries. In the *Centhini* there is no ordering principle beyond the requirements of narrative and prosody. The only way to find an entry is to know the poem very well.

[8]See chap. 1, above, for a discussion of the Javanese idea of Power.

Babad Tanah Jawi. In the wayang stories the aristocratic heroes make the heavens tremble and the seas boil when they meditate; the arrows they shoot in battle turn into thousands of serpents or demons. One hero may fly comfortably through the air; another may simultaneously impregnate a dozen heavenly nymphs; still another penetrates to the depths of the ocean and enters the ear of a deity who is a miniature version of himself. In the chronicles one finds balls of magical radiance descending on the heads of those destined to become kings, mysterious couplings—over successive generations of a dynasty—with Nyai Lara Kidul, the Power-full Goddess of the Southern Seas, and so on. It is hard not to see in the *Centhini*'s refusal of all these marvels a discreetly Gibbonian iconoclasm.

What might be the social basis for the peculiarities that I have briefly adumbrated? Is there anything to be learned from comparison with eighteenth-century France? Two points seem especially worth bearing in mind. First, Diderot and his *confrères* were, in their own view, skilled professionals, men and women devoted to the mastery and development of particular types of knowledge. Second, thanks to the rise of print-capitalism in Europe already from the end of the fifteenth century, the importance of writers within the broader group of professionals was very high.[9] (This is why Diderot and Voltaire exemplify mid-eighteenth-century Europe for us, rather than the professional musicians Mozart and Haydn and the professional painters Tiepolo and Fragonard). By contrast, Java did not encounter print-capitalism until the late nineteenth century. This lateness did not mean that Old Java lacked a substantial professional stratum, but rather that, because print-capitalism did not arrive till the latter half of the nineteenth century, litterateurs had no special prestige or political position within this stratum.[10] Alongside (not above) them were ranged the architects who envisioned, planned, and supervised the construction of Java's myriad mosques, palaces, and fortifications; the puppet masters (*dhalang*) who over generations built the varied traditions of the shadow play; the expert musicians who created the panoply of Javanese musical genres; the adepts of the many branches of Islamic learning; not to speak of dancers, actors, sculptors, smiths, painters, curers, astrologers, magicians, folk botanists, martial-arts

[9]See my *Imagined Communities. Reflections on the Origin and Spread of Nationalism* (London: Verso, 1983), chap. 3.
[10]One notes that the bureaucratic rank titles given to court poets and chroniclers were rarely higher than those bestowed by the rulers on senior dance masters and leaders of court gamelan ensembles.

teachers, burglars, and so on.[11] Such people were almost invariably commoners, but they were certainly not common people. Some were drawn into the service of royal courts and provincial lords, particularly if the exercise of their knowledge and skills required the backup of sizable amounts of manpower and capital (for example, architects), which only such centers of political and economic power could provide. Others preferred the freedom of the road—joining Pigeaud's memorable swarm of *zwervers en trekkers*[12]—peddling their specialities on the broader social market (for example, actors and teachers of martial arts). Still others, such as kyai and *guru ngèlmu* (teachers of mystical lore), would settle in rural retreats, drawing to themselves acolytes and clients by word of respectful or astonished mouth.

There is no satisfactory way to estimate the size of this stratum of experts as a proportion of the Javanese population in the later eighteenth century.[13] But it was certainly much larger than the ruling class. How far different kinds of specialists recognized in one another members of a common stratum is also impossible to guess. What is clear is that, in different degrees, they recognized that they knew things and could do things that the rulers could not. (Born to rule, the Javanese aristocracy had no need to develop specialized knowledges, and assumed, like English gentlemen, an autocratic amateur status).

---

[11]There exist a number of interesting manuscripts that treat the science of housebreaking with encyclopedic thoroughness.

[12]In his *Javanese Volksvertoningen*, pp. 35–36, Pigeaud observes that traveling players "were unquestionably part of the large group of vagabonds and wanderers which must have been a key element in Java's social traffic in olden times." Other elements he mentions are pedlars, merchants, *santri*, and *satria lelana* (banished or masterless 'knights') with their retinues, who were often "hard to distinguish from bandits."

[13]But the remarkable statistics collected by Jaap Kunst in the early 1930s are suggestive (*Music in Java*, pp. 570–71). At that time the population of Java and Madura was just under 41 million. Yet he had counted 17,282 orchestral ensembles, including 12,477 "complete bronze gamelan" in either the *pélog* or *sléndro* tuning, and 6,362 wayang sets of various types, mostly *wayang purwa*. Assuming conservatively that a complete bronze gamelan requires 10–12 skilled players (including reserves and apprentices), we can estimate the number of skilled musicians at about $12 \times 12,000 = 144,000$. (I take it that the same players would handle smaller, non-full gamelan ensembles). If we eliminate women (who in public rarely played gamelan instruments except for the *gendèr*) and children, this means a skill density of about 1 adolescent or adult male in 10. To be sure, most of these musicians were not wanderers but villagers who made their main livelihood from farming. Still, the depth of skill and talent is remarkable. Recognizing that most wayang sets were owned by *dhalang* and "played" only by members of his immediate family, we can estimate the skilled puppeteering population at about 15,000, or 1 in 120 adolescent or adult males. Again, only a minority would have earned their main livelihood from this skill.

To project these figures back to the early nineteenth century is obviously problematic. But I can think of no obvious reason why the proportions should have been lower, and given the rise of primary and secondary education after 1900, which began to take youths out of traditional apprenticeships, it could well have been a bit higher.

But because of the existing distribution of social prestige, economic resources, and political power the specialists were almost always forced to defer to, and often to depend for their livelihood on, such privileged amateurs. This general subordination did not mean that they were not proud of their virtuosities, merely that they were usually prevailed upon to conceal or cloak that pride. (I remember very well from the early 1960s, when I visited the decrepit court of Surakarta, how the elderly court musicians sat poker-faced through a long speech about the nature of Javanese music delivered by a no less elderly prince; only after the prince was out of sight did discreetly mocking smiles and sarcastic comments begin). The only medium that by its very nature would have permitted a conscious, systematically ordered coalition of various, separate, professional mockeries—the mass-produced printed word—did not yet exist.[14]

One might therefore think about this half-veiled class antagonism as a struggle over the "means of production" . . . of knowledge. It was a struggle that pitted gifted commoners with their various particularistic skills and ngèlmu against a royalty cum aristocracy with its generalized claims to sacral authority and kasektèn.

Sodomy and Conjuring

So far we have been dealing with broad and general suppositions. To try to make them plausible and vivid, we now turn to two topics that are almost never mentioned in contemporary discussions of "traditional Javanese culture" but that nonetheless are prominently featured in the *Centhini,* one of that culture's most touted classics. In contrasting ways they offer a peculiarly clear silhouette of the incipient class antagonism referred to above.

One of the characteristic *topoi* in the "anthropological" writings of nineteenth- and twentieth-century colonial officials and missionaries is gloomily pleasurable reference to the natives' incorrigible addiction to pederasty and homosexual sodomy. Dayaks, Acehnese, Balinese, Buginese, Javanese, Batak, Minangkabau, or Chinese—however much these peoples might differ in other ways, they were all said to share a passionate addiction to such vices.[15] This topos served to demon-

---

[14] I use "professional" here to refer both to level of skill and knowledge and to primary source of income and social status.

[15] For example, the noted ethnologist George Alexander Wilken observed that "pederasty [is] a vice universal among the Dayaks" (*Verspreide Geschriften,* ed. Frederik Daniel Eduard

strate either the primitiveness or the degeneracy of the population concerned, and the urgent need for civilizing, Christianizing, and otherwise uplifting them. Pederasty and sodomy also served to draw a drastic moral contrast between "abandoned" natives and good Dutchmen, who naturally regarded such unnatural practices with practised horror. (Needless to say, once Indonesia became an independent nation, the shoe went on the other foot: The repulsive vices were unheard of in the archipelago until depraved Dutchmen arrived on the scene). One of the agreeable things about the *Centhini* is that it shows, by the many examples it offers and its unconditionally Javanese technical vocabulary, that male homosexuality at least was an unproblematic, everyday part of a highly varied traditional Javanese sexual culture. (It includes, inter alia detailed descriptions of sodomy, fellatio, mutual masturbation, multiple-partner intercourse, and transvestitism. Heterosexual sex is described in exactly analogous ways; the *Centhini* is quite catholic—or should one say encyclopedic?—in its coverage).

It is precisely the commonplaceness of male homosexual relations that makes a particular episode of paired sodomies so instructive. The context of the episode can be briefly described as follows: Evicted from home by his father for numerous offences, including many adulteries with married women, Cebolang seeks his livelihood as the leader of a small troupe of traveling performers, the most important of whom is a somewhat effeminate young dancer called Nurwitri. The group plays musics of all kinds (but specializes in an Arabic-influ-

---

van Ossenbruggen [The Hague: van Dorp, 1912] 3:389); the celebrated Islamicist Christiaan Snouck Hurgronje wrote of "the general prevalence of immorality of the worst kind in Acheh," symbolized by the popular *seudati* shows, where the poetry sung was "paederastic in character" (*The Achehnese* [Leiden: Brill, 1906], 2:246, 2:222). The sharptongued physician Julius Jacobs, after visiting Bali in the early 1880s, observed many dance performances by young boys dressed up like women, and commented: "One knows that they are boys, and it is sickening to see men from all strata of Balinese society proffering their *kèpèngs* (Chinese coins) to have the chance to dance with these children, sometimes in the queerest postures; one is still more revolted to discover that these children, sometimes after exercising for hours in a *perpendicular* position, are compelled, utterly exhausted though they may be, to carry out *horizontal* maneuvers with the highest bidders, after being fondled by this man and kissed by that" (*Eenigen tijd onder de Baliërs, eene reisbeschrijving, met aanteekeningen betreffende hygiène, land- en volkenkunde van de eilanden Bali en Lombok* [Batavia: Kolff, 1883], italics in the original).

Discussion assumed a calmer tone by the end of the colonial period: see, e.g., on the Buginese and Makassarese, Hendrik Chabot, *Verwantschap, Stand en Sexe in Zuid-Celebes* (Groningen-Jakarta: Wolters, 1950), pp. 152–58 ("Homosexualiteit"), and C. Nooteboom, "Aantekeningen over de cultuur der Boeginezen en Makassaren," *Indonesië* 2 (1948–49):249–50. On Java and Madura, Pigeaud, *Javaansche Volksvertoningen*, pp. 299–304, 322–24; and J. B. M. de Lyon, "Over de Waroks en Gemblaks van Ponorogo," *Koloniale Tijdschrift* (1941):740–60.

enced ensemble called *terbangan*), puts on dances, and displays a range of *sulapan* (which we might provisionally translate as "conjuring tricks"). In the course of its journeys, the troupe arrives at the *kabupatèn* (provincial administrative center) of Daha and is immediately hired by the local *adipati* (lord) to perform. No less than his many wives, officials, servants, and hangers-on, this lord is enraptured by the skill of the players, particularly of Nurwitri, who dances exquisitely in female dress. After the performance the young star is invited to sleep with the eager adipati, who is described as having "completely forgotten the love of women" (*supé langening wanita*).16 Nurwitri is matter-of-factly complaisant about being sodomized, pleases his patron greatly with his lovemaking, and is rewarded on successive mornings-after with presents of money and expensive clothing. A few nights of revelry later, the adipati's attention shifts to the more masculine Cebolang, whom he orders to dance in female dress. As before, music and dancing arouse the bigwig's sexual desire, and he has no difficulty in getting Cebolang to sleep with him. Canto 4, stanzas 54–60, describe how, and with what pleasure, the adipati sodomizes Cebolang. The troupe's leader is described as "even better in bed than Nurwitri" (*lan Nurwitri kasornèki*) and is rewarded proportionately in the aftermath.17

So far, so normal. The sexual relationship between the males appears closely comparable to that between many males and females. A wealthy, powerful, high-ranking older male enjoys the "passive" favors of a sexually attractive, low-ranking younger person, and rewards that person financially or otherwise. Then something weird happens for which, so far as I know, there is no parallel in any Indonesian literature. The adipati asks Cebolang which partner in the act of sodomy gets the greater pleasure—the penetrator or the penetrated. When Cebolang says "the penetrated, by far" (*mungguh prabédaning rasa / asangat akèh kaoté / mirasa kang jinambu*), the older man allows that he would like to judge for himself.18 Whereupon Cebolang sodomizes the adipati. As it happens, things go very differently than Cebolang has promised. Partly because of the size of Cebolang's penis, the adipati undergoes an agonizing ordeal. His rectum is so torn that he cannot sit down the next day. Cebolang has to

16*Serat Tjentini*, canto 2, stanza 17, through canto 4, stanza 30. The quotation is from canto 4, stanza 29. Here, and in all subsequent quotations, I have modernized the spelling in the source.
17Ibid., canto 4, stanzas 54–60. The quotation is from stanza 57.
18Ibid., stanzas 74–84. The quotation is from stanza 76.

apply a special poultice to the fissure in order to relieve the pain. (This is the only example of painful sexual intercourse in the Centhini, something that may indicate the poem's "politics.")

The most immediately remarkable thing about the second sodomy is that the usual sexual declension is reversed: a young, attractive, low-ranking male is described as dominating an older, less attractive, high-ranking male. But more instructive insights emerge from a careful comparison with the first sodomy.

In that first encounter one notices the following details:[19] the experienced Cebolang has no trouble handling the adipati's penis. He is described as "supple and skilled in all his various movements" (*aluwes awasis ing satata taténing pratingkah*). "His adeptness" (*baudira*) in passive sodomy far exceeds that of his friend Nurwitri. He is in fact shown to be "actively passive." The pair is said to be engaged in a "sweet battle" (*adu manis*). The constant use of reflexive verb forms underscores the mutuality of their activity: "they writhed and wrestled together, thrusting in opposite directions" (*dia-dinia dinaya-daya / dinua-dua*). The adipati's sex organ is "squeezed" (*sinerot*) by Cebolang's practiced sphincter. The younger man's "response" is "no less" (*tan wiwal dènya kiwul*) than his partner's. At one point he advises the older man, in the politest *krama*,[20] to "calm down" (*ingkang sarèh kéwala*)—as if to say "if you want to be good in bed, you have to pace yourself." He is described as "exhausted" (*lempé-lempé*), but his fatigue is that of an accomplished gymnast after a strenuous workout. (The adipati is described as scarcely less tired.) When at dawn Nurwitri walks in on the pair and slyly teases his companion, Cebolang responds with a cheerful grin and wink, and the insouciant claim that "it was the same for both of us" (*aran wong wus padha déné*). Finally, one observes that the author intends a certain complicity between Cebolang and Nurwitri at the expense of the adipati. Cebolang "gives [him] a secret sign" (*ngeblongken*) to indicate that they have succeeded in hoodwinking the aristocrat. While the latter laughs aloud in dull-witted satisfaction at what he regards as his sexual domination of the two young actors, the pair have shrewdly achieved their ends: money, favors, full access to the women's quarters of the kabupatèn, psychological mastery of their employer (he is now set up for Cebolang's role-reversal trap)—and sexual enjoyment to boot.

These details show clearly that (a) Cebolang is (deliberately) de-

[19] The following quotations are taken from ibid., stanzas 56–60.
[20] As noted in previous chapters, krama is the polite respect level of the Javanese language.

picted as a virtuoso sexual professional (in the better sense of the word); (b) he is not lying when he claims that the penetrated partner may get more pleasure than the penetrator—the former simply has to have the right ngèlmu and experience; (c) he retains his masculinity throughout, responding to his partner as might a good boxer, wrestler, or dancer. True, his movements are so supple that the adipati experiences them as if they were a beautiful woman's, but Cebolang never psychologically "yields" to the older man.

The reverse sodomy represents a sharp contrast in almost every respect.[21] The adipati first yields up his social and political preeminence by permitting the young adventurer to address him in *ngoko*, the language level of intimacy and equality (*koko-kinoko kéwala*). Then he asks for knowledge, about which he concedes his ignorance, and in effect asks for instruction from an experience teacher. The text goes out of its way to stress the impressive dimensions of Cebolang's penis (in implicit comparison with the undiscussed size of his partner's). The adipati is described as "yielding utterly" (*anjepluk*). More significantly, he is explicitly said to have "forgotten his manhood" (*supé priané*) and to "feel like a woman" (*lir dyah raosing kalbu*). Recall that when Cebolang was being sodomized, we were told that *in the eyes of his sodomizer* he seemed like, or better than, a woman. In contrast to Cebolang's practiced acceptance of anal penetration, the older man proves incapable of bearing the initial pain. The "tears pour down his face, he whimpers for mercy" (*barebel kang waspa / andruwili sesambaté*). "Oh, stop . . . enough . . . please, no . . . take it out . . . ow . . . ow . . . please stop" (*lah uwis aja-aja / / wurungena baé adhuh uwis*). Indeed, he so loses control of himself that he involuntarily urinates (*kepoyuh*) on the mattress. Cebolang feels "touched" (*ngres tyasira*) and speeds up his thrusts to bring the ordeal to a quicker end. (Contrast this with Cebolang's suggestion that his partner slow down when being himself sodomized earlier on.) Finally, the adipati "collapses in utter exhaustion" (*ngalumpruk marlupa capé*), while the young man merely feels sorry (*sungkawa*) for him, and no mention is made of any fatigue. When he was the sodomizer the adipati was also worn out. Needless to say, Cebolang is also knowledgeable about the right kind of crushed-leaf poultice to heal the aristocrat's anus. And the scene ends with no cheerful jokes.

The paired sodomies, with each partner alternately taking the role of penetrator and penetrated, shows that Cebolang is the master of his

---

[21]The quotations in this paragraph are from *Serat Tjentini*, stanzas 74–84.

master. He is a skilled professional in every aspect of sexual intercourse between males, without ever losing his control or manhood. Indeed, it is precisely because he retains these qualities that he is able, with evident sincerity, to insist that the pleasure obtained from being penetrated is greater than that derived from penetrating. He forces his lord first into linguistic equality, then into sexual submission. On the other hand, the adipati does not even gain the upper hand when he is the sodomizer. And when he is sodomized, he acts like a virgin, or beginning student.

At the same time we should remember that our paired sodomies take up only a dozen or so of the thousands of stanzas of which the *Centhini* is composed. We are not dealing with a sort of Javanese Lord Chatterley's Lover. The adipati experiences no sexual awakening and neither loves nor detests his young partner. Once his rectum has healed and he can again sit comfortably, life in the kabupatèn goes on as before. Cebolang is eventually evicted, but only because he is discovered to be making free with the adipati's concubines. It is therefore difficult to believe that the double-sodomy episode is in any way a statement about sexuality qua sexuality, or for that matter about homosexuality. We may get a better idea of what it is really about if we take a brief, comparative look at conjuring.

As noted earlier, conjuring is a staple of the performance repertoire of many of the *Centhini*'s varied zwervers and trekkers. Cebolang is the first such figure to appear in the text, but his pyrotechnics, impressive as they are, will be topped by other adepts in due course. Regardless of who the particular "master" is, all the conjuring performances share certain generic features. They are always shows (*tontonan*)—in the sense that the conjuror and his associates are hired to display their talents, before audiences, and in the context of a larger set of festivities. They are always accompanied by music, often by specific kinds of dancing and dancers, and usually by ample incense burning. The types of "turn" fall into roughly three categories: (1) Inanimate objects are, for a certain period, made to seem as if they have a life of their own. For example, a rice pounder appears to thump up and down in its container, and a machete and sickle to hack and chop, without human agency.[22] (2) Various objects are temporarily transmogrified. For example, cones of cooked rice (*tumpeng*), or certain leaves, or young coconuts are covered with a *kurungan* (a hemi-

[22]Ibid., canto 3, stanzas 19–23; canto 37, stanza 332.

spheric-shaped wicker cage); when the cage is removed they have turned, respectively, into bouquets of flowers, turtles, and snakes. On the cage being replaced, then removed once again, these objects have resumed their original, true forms.[23] (3) Horrifying events are made to occur, then reversed. This category is of such interest that it is worth offering details of three typical examples.

In the course of some festivities, Cebolang has one of his musicians bound hand and foot, then placed, along with a wheel, inside a kurungan.[24] While the other musicians play the composition Kinanthi Wiratruna, and incense smoke swirls up, Cebolang and his trans-vestite dancers circle the kurungan seven times. When it is removed, the bound musician is free and riding on a tiger's back. The spectators flee in terror, trampling on each other in the process. The adipati stays in place, but he does ask Cebolang whether "the tiger is real" (*apa nora anemeni ingkang sima*). On being assured that it is not, he bids the young conjuror to "terminate it at once" (*yèn mengkono nuli racuten dèn-ènggal*). Tiger and rider are returned to the cage. On its second removal, there are the bound musician and wheel, as before. In another display, the audience-hall where the spectators are sitting is suddenly invaded by huge stilts (*égrang*) of fire, which appear to rush after and do battle with one another.[25] It seems as if the whole build-ing is going up in flames, and almost everyone is thrown into a panic. Then one of the experienced old men present tells the troupe that they have gone too far and must bring the act to an end. A flick of the sash of one of the transvestite dancers makes the blazing stilts immediately vanish. It turns out, however, that in the stampede to escape the illusory flames a small child has been trampled unconscious.[26] The conjurors are now bidden by the same old man to repair the damage. Two of them proceed to lay the child out on a mat and with a big, sharp knife cut his body in half. When the boy's mother, hysterical with grief, collapses over the corpse, the conjurors behead her. The horrified audience, believing that what they are seeing is quite real, terrifying so, conclude that Cebolang's men have been possessed by evil spirits. At this point the two bodies are enshrouded, while the transvestite dancers circle them, strewing flowers from the garlands that form part of their costumes. Immediately mother and son are restored to life and health. The third example has two of the younger

[23]Ibid., canto 3, stanzas 1–18.
[24]Ibid., stanzas 39–48.
[25]Ibid., canto 48, stanzas 28–33.
[26]Ibid., stanzas 42–52.

players in Cebolang's troupe, Jamal and Jamil, performing a duel.[27] In the course of battle, Jamal's forehead is struck with a crowbar. When he collapses, covered in blood, his antagonist rushes up and smashes his head and body with heavy rocks. Again, the audience is frightened witless. Then, at the master conjuror's command, Jamal's corpse is wrapped in a long cloth and transvestite players dance and sing around it, accompanied by a small *angklung* ensemble and billowing clouds of incense.[28] A still-panting Jamal immediately sits up, very much alive and well. And, as always happens even when the most terrifying show has been put on, the audience in the end roars its applause. (Quite often, the combined effect of conjuring and its music is to arouse uncontrolled sexual desire; members of the audience grope one another's breasts and genitals and even engage in public intercourse).

What are we to make of all the conjuring, especially conjuring of the third type? To put it another way, what kind of ngèlmu is being deployed? Is "conjuring" even the appropriate term for these sulapan turns?

That we are dealing with a distinct professional specialization can be confirmed from two directions. First of all, the sulapan are neither supernatural events nor cases of possession. If one thinks of the way-ang repertoire, the chronicles, folk tales—or even whispered gossip in today's Jakarta—the exercise of true Power (kasektèn) always has real effects in the world, and causes irreversible change. Kingdoms fall, princes and ogres are killed, bad village boys turn into permanent monkeys, bloody coups (successful and unsuccessful) actually occur. In contrast, sulapan has no prise on the world; everything always reverts to what it was before. Living people are quickly "killed" and as quickly resurrected. Leaves become turtles, then leaves once again. Nothing really changes. Each "turn" has the same lack of conse-quences as the dramatic sodomies we considered earlier.

But if sulapan and kasektèn are utterly different from one another, can the same be said of conjuring and possession? In one sense, they are obviously distinct. During Cebolang's show, the audience misun-derstood what it was seeing; the horrible illusions created by the conjurors made it seem that they were really possessed. For posses-sion, like kasektèn, does affect the world. On the other hand, a number of the turns performed by Cebolang's men are given specific names by the *Centhini*—*gabus, réog,* and *jaran képang,* for exam-

27Ibid., canto 37, stanzas 256–61.
28An angklung is an instrument made of suspended bamboo tubes which tinkle against each other when struck by the player.

ple—that even today refer to specific ritual performances involving trance possession. Yet if the external look of certain sulapan turns and certain forms of possession may resemble one another, their inner natures are understood as basically different. In sulapan, a commercial show, after all, everything is under immediate human control, whereas in possession human control yields, at least for the nonce, to that of the spirit world.

In the second place, the sulapan conspicuously involve a specific technology and technical vocabulary. The *Centhini* takes a great deal of trouble to tell the reader exactly what combinations of musical instruments, what compositions, what modes of dance, and what costumes are required for each show. The props are virtually unvarying—kurungan, incense, sashes of a certain type. Some of the turns have their own technical names. Perhaps most striking of all is the use of the word *racut,* which might be translated as "to terminate" (an act) or "to dispel" (a phantasm). It is also noticeable, from the examples I have cited, that there are always a few spectators (typically old men) who are not taken in. They may, like the adipati, be amused when the audience scatters in panic, but they make sure that things do not go too far. The players are then told to racut the apparitions back "into the bag." And how simple racut always is (almost like switching off an electric current), compared to the rituals and time usually needed to end possession!

Yet in spite of all that has been said about technique, we are not, in the *Centhini,* in the world of Kinsey or Houdini (though perhaps not far from that of Cagliostro). When Cebolang is being sodomized we are not told which anal muscles he uses to give the adipati such pleasure, or how he acquires his muscular control. Similarly, we are never taken backstage and let in on the actual methods by which sulapan's effects are achieved. Sometimes the reader is left in doubt as to how far they are effects at all. For while Cebolang assures the adipati that his tiger is not real, the text also describes, deadpan, the bisected spectator boy and beheaded mother as dead. Perhaps we should replace the word *conjuror* by *magician.* For the latter blurs two ancient meanings: the virtuoso prestidigitator, who employs ingenious but ordinary means to create uncanny illusions; and the dabbler in the real uncanny, who nonetheless uses his powers pointlessly, for the gratification of an audience. Seen from this angle, the skills of Cebolang and his fellow magicians occupy a distinct site in the cultural landscape of late-eighteenth-century Java. They are not the skills of a faker, but neither are they those of someone with the general, superordinate Power of kasektèn.

A renewed comparison here with eighteenth-century France is valuable. The decisive thing about Diderot's encyclopedia is that it was meant to inform. Its entries are lists with *explanations* about how the world works, and on what principles. Its purpose is to spread enlightenment, to the whole world so far as possible. But the *Centhini*'s lists explain nothing. They refer to knowledges, but these remain more or less esoteric. They can only be properly read by those who already have the necessary ngèlmu. Enlightenment of the ordinary Javanese, let alone the world, is the last thing the text has on its mind.

What then? Sodomy and magicianship may be sources of pleasure, but it would be difficult to argue that either is centrally important to the life of any society, even that of Old Java. I have stressed them here because they so conspicuously set off their master practitioners from other social strata. The sodomies separate the virtuosi from the Powerful, the magic tricks the same virtuosi from the populace: For the latter, the secrets of Cebolang's ngèlmu are as unfathomable as (maybe more unfathomable than) the kasektèn of their lords. The very uselessness, gratuitousness, of sodomy and conjuring helps also to discourage any easy hypostasizing of Old Java as a seamless web of interlocking functional roles or mutually reinforcing patron-client ties. (Other types of ngèlmu, such as puppetmastership or medicine, precisely because they appear useful and socially integrative, may cause the interpreter to let down his guard against *idées reçues*). Their luxuriant secular display in the *Centhini,* alongside so many other knowledges, shows that something new is in the air, a visible, if probably not wholly self-conscious, claim to leadership of the Javanese—so to speak the supersession of kasektèn by a coalition of the ngèlmu. It is significant, too, that Cebolang, like other adepts in the *Centhini,* practices his ngèlmu in exchange for cash.[29] The Old Java of lord and peasant is on its way out.

[29]See Peter Brian Ramsay Carey, "Changing Javanese Perceptions of the Chinese Communities in Central Java, 1755–1825," *Indonesia* 37 (April 1984): 1–47, for a pithy, informed account of the economic and social changes experienced in Central Java during the six decades before the completion of the "full" *Centhini.* The Dutch East India Company's 1740 annexation of Java's northern littoral and its military suppression, in the 1750s, of the endless wars of succession that had racked the island's interior since the 1670s had contradictory consequences. On the one hand, the restoration of peace permitted a rapid rise in agricultural production and commerce; on the other hand, it facilitated the more systematic imposition of taxation. The era was marked by the rapid spread of tax farms, usually managed by Chinese, especially in respect to opium, market taxes, and rural tollgates. Increasingly payments had to be made in cash (typically lead Chinese or copper Company coins). To be able to pay in this form, peasants had to mortgage their crops or sell a larger portion on the market. Hence a significant monetization of the Javanese economy by the turn of the century.

Professional Dreams

So far, so clear. Probably too clear. For I have treated the *Centhini*
as if it were a mirror of society or a quasi-ethnological treatise, permitting us to infer that its pages more or less directly transcribe the life of
late-eighteenth-century Java. Musicians of course really played their
gamelan, dhalang surely puppeteered, and Islamic mystics definitely
instructed youthful santri. But were there really Cebolangs who styl-
ishly sodomized their aristocratic employers and made villagers flee in
terror from the apparitions they conjured up? Who can be sure? Sup-
posing, on the other hand, that the great poem reflects not so much
reality as . . . professional dreams?

The gratuitousness of Cebolang's virtuosities can tempt one into
regarding them as the last, superfluous, elements in a total inventory
of "real" traditional life. But a wider overview of the *Centhini* shows
us very quickly its dreamlike nature. The sexual life so vividly depicted
in its pages already suggests something phantasmagoric. For while
scores of couplings between men and woman of all types and ages
throng its pages, only once, and in casual passing, is mention made of
pregnancy or childbirth. (This is why the text's homosexual and heterosexual episodes can seem so matter-of-factly similar. Its interest is
in sexual virtuosity—including, by the way, female sexual prowess—
not at all in demography or social realism.)

But these are still larger absences than that of procreation. We
observed earlier on the way in which, with the exception of the
adipati, the Javanese ruling class is peripheralized, if not eliminated,
from the reader's field of vision. More striking still is the invisibility of
foreigners. Sèh Amongraga flees his royal home in Giri in 1625, by
which time the Dutch East India Company had already established its
imperial Asian headquarters in Batavia (1619), a mere 450 crow-miles
west along Java's northern shore. By the time of the *Centhini's* final
compilation the Dutch had been in Java for two centuries—but only a
few Dutch loanwords trace their presence in the text. Nothing in its
pages hints at the wars that raged between the 1670s and the 1750s, in
which, for the first time in Java's history, it was ravaged not merely by
Dutch and Javanese, but by Buginese condottieri, Madurese warlords,
and Balinese mercenaries. There is not the slightest acknowledgment
that, since 1740, Java's north-shore ports had all passed "legally" into
Company hands; or that conquering Mataram had long since splin-
tered into three small and feeble interior principalities, all of whose

rulers were on the Company's payroll.[30] No wars, no plagues, no taxation, no corvée, no death.

On the contrary, for most of the *Centhini* Java manifests itself as a phantasmagoric utopia: a proliferation of prosperous, contented, tolerant, politically autonomous, sexually sophisticated rural communities through which professionals are free to roam. As they wander, they display their knowledge to the populace and to each other and are regarded with unrivalrous respect and even cheerful awe. There is no political intrigue, no fear, no kowtowing to noble ignoramuses, and no humiliating dependence on incompetent, venal rulers.[31]

It is just the character of this "perfect Java," benignly coordinated by its specialist virtuosi, that reveals the limits of the *Centhini*'s embryo radicalism. Cebolang may sexually master his master and make free with the latter's wives and concubines, but his mastery is that of the conjuror. As noted earlier, when the adipati's rectum heals, life reverts to what it was before the pair climbed into bed. Nothing changes. The benignity of the professionals is the benignity of men who are masters of *traditional* knowledge. It contrasts powerfully with the agreeable malignity of the *philosophes,* whose knowledge was anything but traditional, was indeed implicitly or explicitly revolutionary. In Java, the perfect society is pre–ancien régime; in France, it will come with the ancien régime's supersession.

---

[30]On the feckless politics of late eighteenth and early nineteenth century Central Java, the best studies are Merle Calvin Ricklefs, *Jogjakarta under Sultan Mangkubumi, 1749–1792* (London: Oxford University Press, 1974); Ann Kumar, "Javanese Court Society and Politics in the Late Eighteenth Century: The Record of a Lady Soldier. Part I: The Religious, Social and Economic Life of the Court," *Indonesia* 29 (April 1980): 1–46; and Peter Brian Ramsay Carey, ed., *Babad Dipanegara: An Account of the Outbreak of the Java War (1825–1830)* (Kuala Lumpur: Art Printers, 1981).

[31]Nothing better reveals the Louis Seize character of Java's surviving dynasts—including the employers of the *Centhini*'s composers—than that they did nothing creative to exploit the disasters that overwhelmed the East India Company and the United Provinces after 1780, when the latter became involved in the wars between England, France, and the young United States. In 1795, French revolutionary armies occupied the Low Countries and established the Batavian Republic under its aegis, and London responded by, inter alia, seizing Ceylon from the Company. In 1798 the Company, already bankrupt for some years, was taken over by the Batavian Republic, which assumed its 143 million guilder debt. (Cf. Clive Day, *The Policy and Administration of the Dutch in Java* [London: Macmillan, 1904], pp. 80–81.) In 1806, Napoleon made his younger brother Louis the first-ever king of the Lowlands, but in 1810 dismissed him for his "manie d'humanité" and peremptorily absorbed the realm into metropolitan France. London retorted by seizing, by 1811, all overseas Dutch possessions, including Java, which fell to Stamford Raffles's men in that year without a struggle. A brief, informative account of these developments can be found in Bernard Hubertus Maria Vlekke, *Nusantara: A History of Indonesia* (Brussels: Editions A. Manteau, 1961), chap. 11. The source for Napoleon's characteristic *mot* is Simon Schama's wonderful *Patriots and Liberators: Revolution in the Netherlands, 1780–1813.* (New York: Knopf, 1977), p. 543.

The very poetics of the *Centhini* underscore its political stance, which, most of the time, wishes away the ruling class and foreign oppressors, rather than assaulting them. Its tone is invariably cool, sweet, smiling—never alienated, furious, or despairing. Its composers display, without false modesty, absolute control of all the stylistic forms, metrical varieties, and sophisticated rhetorical devices then available in Javanese literary culture. But this awesome control is never used ironically; it functions, almost always, to align form and content.

The *Suluk Gatholoco*

If the composition of the full *Centhini* was completed in 1814, as Behrend plausibly argues, then this may have been the last possible historical moment in which such a vast, sweet, and controlled Javanese masterpiece could appear. For in 1812 Stamford Raffles's men marched into Yogyakarta, deposed the sultan, and divided the territory into two microprincipalities, as the East India Company had done in neighboring Surakarta in the 1750s. Moreover, in all four principalities he seized control of the rulers' financial lifeline, the taxfarms, running them henceforth from Batavia.[32] In 1816, as a result of a complex deal emerging from the Congress of Vienna—whereby William of Orange was made the first monarch in his line (succeeding Louis Bonaparte) and was granted the Company's possessions in the Indies by way of compensation for permanent British seizure of Ceylon, the Cape, and other valuable territories—the Dutch took over again from Raffles. Economic and political conditions deteriorated rapidly in Central Java, leading to the outbreak of Prince Diponegoro's rebellion in 1825 and the ensuing five-year Java War, which brought devastation to much of the region. The high cost of the war, and the Netherlands' own near-bankruptcy (the result of the exactions of the Napoleonic era and Belgium's secession in 1830) led to the installation in that year of the brutally exploitative Cultivation System (Cultuurstelsel), which between 1831 and 1877 netted the Dutch treasury as much as 823 million guilders.[33] To ensure no further political trouble, Batavia parked on Central Java's minithrones a series of utterly pliable, mediocre, fainéant princelings. In this long process kasektèn

---

[32]See Carey, "Changing Javanese Perceptions," sections 4, 5.

[33]Far and away the best study of the political and economic aspects of the Cultivation System is Cornelis Fasseur, *Kultuurstelsel en Koloniale Baten, De Nederlandse Exploitatie van Java, 1840–1860* (Leiden: Universitaire Pers, 1975).

and its putative bearers lost more and more credibility, to the point that in 1873 the last court poet of Surakarta, R. Ng. Ronggawarsita, wrote despairingly on his deathbed that there was "no example left."[34]

This background may help to explain the astonishing contrast between the *Centhini* and Javanese culture's next great phantasmagoria, the *Suluk Gatholoco*. Internal evidence makes it clear that this long poem was composed sometime between 1854 and 1873 (most likely in the 1860s)—probably by a single, anonymous author.[35] If the *Suluk Gatholoco* is a classic, it is nonetheless one of the underground kind. When, in 1873, the eminent missionary-scholar Poensen brought a (heavily truncated) version of the poem to the light of printed day, he commented:

> From a literary point of view, the text has very little value. . . . But if we look more carefully at its spirit, then the writer strikes us—with his conceptions of honor and virtue, and his sensible views on such things as what foods are permissible for human beings to eat—as very much a man of the world, wholly lacking in the deep religious strain that characterizes such works as the Wulang Rèh, the Sèh Tékawardi, etc., and thereby also lacking their cultivation and breeding. In fact, he often arouses our disgust, since he does not refrain from committing the most trivial things to paper, and in the grossest way goes into detail about matters which it is not decent to mention.[36]

This sketch of a sort of third-rate Javanese Pantagruel cut no ice with Snouck Hurgronje, grandest of colonial scholar-panjandrums, who denounced the poem as "the heretical dreams of an undoubtedly

---

[34]See chap. 6, above.

[35]At canto 7, stanza 52, the poem mentions what it calls *rispis pérak*. Rispis is clearly a Javanization of *recepis*, a special scrip introduced by Governor-General Rochussen on February 4, 1846, in a desperate attempt to remedy the financial and currency chaos bequeathed by his predecessors. Convertible at a fixed rate with Holland's silver-based coinage, the recepis proved to be the first stable colonial currency in the Indies. By the Currency Law of 1854 it was formally replaced with a silver guilder, though it was not finally withdrawn from circulation until 1861. See "Muntwezen," in *Encyclopaedie van Nederlandsch-Indië* (The Hague/Leiden: Nijhoff/Brill, 1918), 2:793–811, esp. at pp. 803–4. Rispis pérak (silver rispis) must refer to the silver coins replacing the paper recepis between 1854 and 1861. Hence, the *Suluk* cannot have been composed before the late 1850s, and, since a printed version of sorts (see n. 36, below) appeared in 1873, we can assume that it was probably completed in the 1860s. The poem was most likely composed in Kedhiri, East Java, well away from the royal courts, and by a member of the small group of literati not by then in Dutch employ.

[36]Carel Poensen, "Een Javaansch geschrift," *Mededeelingen vanwege het Nederlandsche Zendelinggenootschap* 17 (1873):227. The good missionary here gets in a timely jab at Islam's dietary proscriptions.

opium-besotted Javanese mystic!"[37] Not at all, opined the liberal scholar-bureaucrat Rinkes in 1909, the poem was "a serious satire against all that mystagogic rigmarole."[38] Not until 1951 did Philippus van Akkeren, forced by the arrival of Japanese imperialism and the subsequent national revolution of 1945–49 to abandon his missionary labors in East Java, publish the first full text of the *Suluk,* along with a translation, a full critical apparatus, and a thoughtful, anthropologizing thematic analysis.[39]

Only one version has ever been printed in Java—a limited Surabaya edition of 1889, which attracted little attention at the time.[40] But in 1918 the poem became the center of a Java-wide controversy when an article in *Djawi Hiswara,* organ of the Surakarta branch of the Sarékat Islam (Islamic League—the most popular anticolonial movement of the time) cited passages from it, notably one in which the eponymous hero insists that his frequenting of opium dens is in faithful imitation of the Prophet Muhammad. A rancorous debate ensued in the by-then-lively Indonesian- and Javanese-language press, culminating in a huge protest demonstration in Surabaya organized by a hastily formed Army of the Most Reverend Prophet Muhammad. The army, alas, had no weapons, so was forced to content itself with appeals to the governor-general to have the editor of *Djawi Hiswara* criminally prosecuted.[41] After that, the poem went permanently underground—no Indonesian publisher has dared take the risk of being branded religious apostate, or, for reasons described below, pornographer.[42]

What was all the anger about? The plot of the 397-canto *Suluk* is both simple and strange. The first part, covering the meager 13

[37]Christiaan Snouck Hurgronje, "De betekenis van den Islâm voor zijne belijders in Oost-Indië," *Verspreide Geschriften* (Bonn and Leipzig: Schröder, 1924), 4:15. This essay originally appeared in 1883.

[38]Douwe Adolf Rinkes, *Abdoerraoef van Singkel* (Heerenveen: "Hepkema," 1909), p. 130.

[39]Philippus van Akkeren, *Een gedrocht en toch de volmaakte mens: A Monster, Yet the Perfect Man* (The Hague: "Excelsior," 1951), p. 1. The citations in n. 33–35 above I have taken from p. 1 of van Akkeren's text.

[40]According to Gerardus Willebrordus Joannes Drewes, "The Struggle between Javanese and Islam as Illustrated by the Serat Dermagandul," *Bijdrage tot de taal-, land- en volkenkunde* 122 (1966):309–65, at 314. Van Akkeren wrote that the one printed version he used for his study was a "second printing" of an edition issued by the well-known Javanophile Sino-Javanese publisher Tan Khoen Swie of Kedhiri. But he gave no date for this printing or for that of its antecedent.

[41]For insulting Islam. The above account is taken from Drewes, "The Struggle," pp. 313–15.

[42]For in the meantime the poem's explicit scatological and sexual language (Poensen's "in the grossest way") was becoming an embarrassment to the emerging Western-educated Javanese middle class, which was determined to make "Javanism" Victorianly respectable in their own eyes and those of the Poensens.

stanzas of cantos 1 and 2, introduces the reader to the hero, Gatholoco, described as the only son of King Suksma Wisésa of Jajar, and his
inseparable retainer, Dermagandhul. Appalled by the boy's monstrous
and repulsive appearance, the king bids him spend his first sixteen
years in isolated meditation, accompanied only by Dermagandhul.
Returning home after the sixteen years are up, the lad now has his
head "clipped" by his father. But since this rite only makes him more
hideous he is sent off for another four years of ascesis, hanging upside
down, batlike, in a sacred banyan. This second meditation is rewarded
with the gift of matchless skill in language. The king now gives him his
adult name of Gatholoco and sends him off to see the world, warning
him of a dangerous adversary, the female recluse Perjiwati, who is
meditating in a mountain grotto.

The physical description of Gatholoco and Dermagandhul in canto
2, stanzas 3–5, hints openly at what their names make explicit.[43]
Gatholoco is a compound of *gatho* (penis) and *ngloco* (rub, masturbate); *Dermagandhul* combines *derma* (closely attached) and *gandhul*
(hanging down) to denote testicles; while the root of *Perjiwati* is *parji*
(female genitalia). In other words, the hero and his attendant are a
walking, talking penis-and scrotum, and at one level the poem can be
taken as an allegory of a man's sexual development.[44]

The second part, covering the 191 stanzas of cantos 3 to 6, describes Gatholoco's activity on his travels. Between bouts of gambling
and visits to opium dens, he engages in a long series of vitriolic
debates with "orthodox" Islamic teachers (*guru santri*) on the true
nature of divinity, man, the cosmos, Islam, and much else. In every
case he triumphs by his wit and depth of ngèlmu. One after another,
the guru santri concede defeat and flee his presence in profound
humiliation.

[43]"Shaped unlike a normal man / His body shrivelled, shrunk / And scaly, dry his
wrinkled skin / Without a nose at all / Or eyes, or ears; his pleasure but / To sleep and sleep,
day in, day out, continuously / / Yet once aroused from his deep sleep / Unruly, not to be
appeased. . . . Ugly his body, like a sack / His slumber deep beyond compare / When
sleeping he was like a corpse / He too had neither eyes nor ears / Merely a pair of lips / Nor
thews, nor bones." The Javanese goes: *warnané tan kaprah janmi / wandané apan bungkik /
kulité basisik iku / kelawan tanpa nétra / tanpa irung tanpa kuping / remenané anéndra
sadina-dina / Yèn ngelilir lajeng monthah / tan kena dèn arih. . . . Awon dedegé lir keba /
lèmboné kepati-pati / yèn néndra anglir wong pejah / nora duwé mata kuping / amung ing
lambé iki / nora duwé otot-balung.* The spelling in this and other quotations from the
Suluk has been modernized. The doggerel translation is taken from my English version of
the complete poem, published in *Indonesia* 32 (October 1981):108–50, and 33 (April
1982):31–88.

[44]Taken this way, the first part of the poem describes the growth of a male organ/person
from latency through the ordeal of circumcision (the "clipping") to mature potency and the
prospect of initiation into intercourse.

The third part, covering the 193 stanzas of cantos 7 to 12, depicts Gatholoco's encounter with Perjiwati and her four female attendants. After solving a series of conundrums posed by the five women, he gains entry to Perjiwati's hitherto unpenetrated cave. Dermagandhul attempts to follow, but cannot squeeze in. The motifs of the first part are revived, in that the violent "battles" between Gatholoco and Perjiwati are thinly veiled descriptions of sexual intercourse. After nine months a male child is born, just as hideous as his father, but adored by both parents. The poem then ends with a brief meditation on the meaning of this birth and the nature of life.

The stance and nature of the *Suluk Gatholoco* are best understood in juxtaposition to the *Centhini*. First, one notices the contrast between the two heroes. Sèh Amongraga is a tolerant, gentle paragon of the virtuosi of Old Java.[45] He is handsome, polite, learned, adept in syncretic Javanese (Hindu)-Islamic mysticism, sexually energetic, and cultivated in the traditional arts. He treats the mischievous Cebolang and his troupe with elder-brotherly amusement. Both are solid human beings. Gatholoco is something unique. Not only does he fail to conform to any of the traditional models of Javanese hero (elegant warrior-knight, ascetic sage-priest, Muslim saint, or righteous king), but it is as if he were constructed in deliberate opposition to Amongraga. As canto 2, stanzas 3 and 11, and canto 4, stanzas 1 to 5 reveal, he is a hideous, stinking, foulmouthed, opium-smoking, cantankerous, philosophical, ambulatory penis.

Second, the civilized encyclopedism of the *Centhini* has completely disappeared. Gatholoco and his creator have no interest whatsoever in lists and the multifarious lores that they represent. There is now only one knowledge that matters—the mystical knowledge of the Perfect Male—and Gatholoco expounds and defends it with enraged fanaticism and scabrous, malignant wit. His theological antagonists in the long second part of the poem represent something wholly outside the *Centhini's* dreaming: the oxymoron "false knowledge." The easy syncretism of the previous century, which upheld a flexible mélange of Sufi mysticism and pre-Islamic Hindu-Javanese tradition, has gone up in smoke. It is as if the older culture has broken into violently antagonistic halves: a Mecca-oriented Islamic orthodoxy and what van Akkeren, with some justification, calls a Javanese (cultural) nationalism, back against the wall, fangs bared.

Third, the depiction of sexual life, which is the focus of the poem's

---

[45] Amongraga's title, Sèh, a Javanized version of *sheikh*, suggests how unselfconsciously in those days Islam and older Javanese traditions were harmoniously blended.

final section, emphasizes, at length and in great detail, everything that the *Centhini* passes over in silence: stink, heat, slime, blood, frustration, pregnancy, and childbirth. Gatholoco has only one (and female) sexual partner, and he mates with her in the most coarse, and even brutal, manner.[46] It is also quite clear that this sexual activity has a single purpose: the procreative reproduction of a new Gatholoco, Perfect Male in embryo, ready one day to replace his father in Java's religious war. Nothing could be further from the playful, spendthrift relationship between religion and sexuality of the *Centhini*, as exemplified by the episode where Cebolang, after a sleepless night of fellatio and mutual masturbation with two santri teenagers, nonchalantly rises to lead the pesantrèn's early morning prayers.[47]

Finally, the phantasmagoric mise-en-scène. The *Centhini*'s elisions have been drastically extended and Perfect Java turned into an eerie moonscape. As before, the Dutch are invisible (though the frequency of Dutch loanwords has markedly increased). The kingdom of Jajar is mentioned only once, in the very first stanza, and its "mighty sovereign" disappears for good after the eleventh. Gone are all the actors, conjurors, musicians, artisans, tradesmen, puppeteers, and rowdy villagers who crowd the *Centhini*'s pages. Gatholoco and Dermagandhul pursue their wanderings utterly alone. Stage lit this way, Java appears as a surreal terrain on which the only landmarks are opium dens, grottoes, mountains, and pesantrèn. An imagined, not an idealized, landscape.

But none of this would, in itself, make the *Suluk Gatholoco* a candidate for "classic." What renders the poem exemplary is first hinted at when the reader learns, in canto 2, stanza 8, that, after four years of meditation upside down in a banyan tree, the young hero "gained the *wahyu* and the skill / To best his fellow-man in words / Unschooled in rhetoric, he knew / The varied arts of argument. Not studying to write / He knew all literary arts."[48] For it is exactly the *Suluk*'s angry, subversive exploitation of "all literary arts" that shows

---

[46]It should be noted, however, that Perjiwati is fully Gatholoco's equal in the sexual combat. Indeed, Gatholoco is described as ultimately defeated by her (i.e., after intercourse the penis slips limply out of the vagina).

[47]*Serat Tjenṭini,* canto 37, stanzas 309–28.

[48]The Javanese is: *sinung wahyu bisa nyrékal / iya sesamaning urip / nora sangu ing wicara / sakèhing bicara bangkit / nora sinau nulis / sakèhing sastra pan putus.*

Wahyu is a term usually employed for the mysterious radiance that descends on the head of one destined to be king. That it is used here to signify literary-rhetorical talent suggests the pass to which kingship had fallen in Java by the 1860s, and perhaps hints that Java's only hope lies with its independent literary intelligentsia.

its author as among the desperate last of Old Java's literary professionals.

Take, for example, the opening lines: "The tale to be related here /
Concerns a kingdom celebrated / Both far and wide, called Jajar, and /
Its mighty sovereign, in war / Valiant, invincible / His royal appellation was / Mahraja Suksma Wisésa / / Great was the King's authority
/ Submissive were the outer lands."⁴⁹ The stanza, by itself, is a standard traditional opening to a narrative poem and should introduce a
leisurely, expansive account of the beauties of the royal palace, the
prosperity of the realm, and so on. But all this is eliminated, and
within eighteen lines we are at the description of Gatholoco as a
walking penis. There is an extraordinary insolence in this perfunctori-
ness (as if to say, "you know as well as I do that in Java today there are
no celebrated kingdoms, invincible kings, or submissive outer lands.")

Or take the way in which the author deploys, with easy mastery but
for completely untraditional purposes, the evocative alliterations and
punning assonances of the *Centhini*'s *haute style*. For example, in
canto 5, stanzas 34–35, when his adversaries abuse him as a "tailless
dog," Gatholoco turns the tables on them by exploiting the assonance
between *asu* (dog) and *asal* (origin, source) to interpret the insult as a
deeper truth: that he is in fact the Perfect Male.⁵⁰ Again, in canto 4,
stanzas 32–33, the hero makes a witty theological retort by playing
on the double meaning of *klèlèt* as both "opium-ball" and "turd."⁵¹ It

---

⁴⁹The Javanese is: *Wonten carita winarni / anenggih ingkang negara / Jajar iku ing
naminé / pan wonten ratu digjaya / agagah tur prakosa / jejulukira sang Prabu / Mahraja
Suksma Wisésa / Tuhu ratu kinuwasa / kéringan mancanegari.*

⁵⁰My English version is: "Spitefully Ngabdul Jabar said: / 'I'm utterly fed up / Debating
with a tailless dog!' / Ki Gatholoco said: / 'That name you gave me is correct / For all my
ancestors, through every generation / / Each one of them was tailless, so / That truly none
possessed a tail / Now "dog," interpreted, means "source" / While "tailless" indicates that I
/ Am truly human, with / No tail, unlike your ancestors / You on the other hand / Are who?
With shaven, outplucked heads / Are you from Holland, China, Northwest India / / Or are
you from Bengal?'" The Javanese is: *Ngabdul Jabar ngucap bengis / apegel ati mami /
rembugan lan asu buntung / Gatholoco angucap / bener gonira ngarani / bapa biyung kaki
buyut embah canggah / / ya padha buntung sedaya, tan duwé buntut sayekti / basa asu
makna asal / buntung iku wis ngarani / ulun jinising jalmi / tan buntut kaya bapakmu /
balik sira wong apa / dhasmu gundhul anjedhindhil / apa Landa apa Cina apa Koja / / apa
sira wong Benggala.*

⁵¹"And as for what I eat from day to day / I pick out everything that is most hot / And
what is bitterest alone / For thus each turd I drop / Becomes another mountain high / And
that is why their peaks / All belch forth smoke / The charred remains are what I eat / (What
has become encrusted stone and rock) that is / The *klèlèt* I consume / / In truth, until I drop
my burning turds / These mountain peaks have no reality / They'd disappear immediately /
If I should once refrain / From dropping turds. Check for yourselves / My truthfulness from
what / My anus spouts!" In Javanese: *Kang sun-pangan dhéwé saban ari / ingsun pilih
ingkang luwih panas / sarta ingkang pait dhéwé / déné tetinjaningsun / kabèh iki pan dadya*

is hard to convey in English the peculiar, jarring poetry that erupts from the violent bonding of "turds" and "dogs" with the easy flow of traditional literary artifice: a polytonality quite new to Javanese literature. Yet the reader is always aware that this polytonality is deadly serious—neither an idle playing with styles nor a self-conscious satire on classical tradition. Dogs, truth, God, conundrums, opium, Muhammad, turds—none stands in privileged literary relation to the others. The poem's words remain "within the world," parts of its truth. No irony.

The *Suluk*'s polytonality does not end here. One must remember that the poem, like all Javanese poetry before this century, was composed to be sung, if not always aloud, at least under the breath. Its twelve cantos are distinguished from each other less by subject matter than by shifts between the seven musico-metrical forms in which they are variously composed: Asmarandana, Sinom, Mijil, Dhandhanggula, Gambuh, Kinanthi, and Pangkur. These musico-metric forms have had, at least since the start of the nineteenth century, accepted uses: they are felt, by their music, to arouse and reflect distinct moods and to be appropriate for distinct themes and topics.[52] The author of the *Suluk* proceeds, systematically, to disrupt all these conventional associations. Thus, for example, Asmarandana, the meter in which Jajar and Suksma Wisésa's glory is abruptly polished off, is said variously to be "absorbed, sad, mournful, but sad or mournful in the sense of being lovelorn. Suitable for a tale concerned with the pain of love" and "[arousing] sadness."[53] Dhandhanggula, used for the esoteric discussion of turds and opium balls, is "flexible . . . if used for didactic purposes, very clear; if used for the fever of love, attractive," and "supple, pleasurable . . . good for ending a poem." Mijil, understood as "suitable for moral education, but also for a tale of love," is deployed for the first abusive altercation between Gatholoco and the

---

ardi / milanya kang prawata / kabèh metu kukus / tumusing geni sun-pangan / ingkang dadi padhas watu lawan curi / kalèlèt kang sun-pangan // sadurungé ingsun ngising tai / gunung iku yekti durung ana / ing bésuk iku sirnané / lamun ingsun wus mantun / ngising tai kang metu silit / lah iya nyatakena / kabèh sakandhaku.

"Turd" here refers to the dross left in an opium pipe after a smoke. "Dropping turds" has thus the esoteric meaning of going into a mystical opium trance.

[52]Behrend, "The Serat Jatiswara," pp. 212–16. For a sophisticated and sensitive treatment of the relationship between Javanese song and poetry, see Martin F. Hatch, "Lagu, Laras, Layang: Rethinking Melody in Javanese Music" (Ph.D. thesis, Cornell University, 1980).

[53]Quoted from S. Padmosoekotjo, *Ngèngrèngan Kasusastran-Djawa* (Yogyakarta: Hien Hoo Sing, 1960), 1:22–23; and R. Hardjowirogo, *Patokaning Njekaraken* (Jakarta: Balai Pustaka, 1952), pp. 66–67. The other quotations in this paragraph are drawn from the same two texts.

guru santri. Most striking of all is the fact that canto 5, stanzas 58 and 59, where his adversaries call Gatholoco and his mother "pig's ass-holes" (*silité babi*), and the hero replies in kind, is composed in Sinom, whose character is, we are told, "friendly, clear" and "suitable for moral instruction."[54]

The effect, in each case, is savagely to rub the written words against the smooth grain of the mellifluous singing voice.[55] The peculiar power of the text comes precisely from the wound it slashes open between form and content. Professional skill of this kind makes one think of a solitary ballerina pirouetting on the rim of a precipice.

Epilogue

Not long after the composition of the *Suluk Gatholoco,* change began to accelerate in colonial Java, spurred above all by the deepening of industrialism in Europe (even in backward Holland) and the revolution in communications. In the early 1870s, the monopolistic Cultivation System was liquidated under pressure of liberal reformers and powerful business interests in the Netherlands. In over the rubble came hordes of planters, merchants, lawyers, physicians, and new-style civil servants. The opening of the Suez Canal hastened their passage, while the extension of telegraphic communication kept them in unprecedentedly close touch with the metropole. A local press began to appear in the 1860s, dominated at first by Dutchmen but soon with increasing Eurasian, Chinese, and native participation.[56] In the 1880s came the railways, intended initially to haul exportable sugar from the vast plantations in the interior of Java, but soon carrying millions of Javanese passengers every year.[57] Alongside them appeared the beginnings of a state-sponsored, state-financed schooling system—for the first time in the by then almost 300 years that Dutchmen had been meddling in the archipelago.[58]

[54]For English and Javanese versions of this passage, see chap. 6, above, p. 212.

[55]A few years ago, as an experiment, I asked a young Javanese poet to "read aloud" this passage, blind, at an informal party. He tried twice, but on each occasion had to stop singing because he was laughing so hard.

[56]See Ahmat B. Adam's fine study, "The Vernacular Press and the Emergence of Modern Indonesian Consciousness (1855–1913)" (Ph.D. thesis, University of London, 1984).

[57]See Takashi Shiraishi, *An Age in Motion: Popular Radicalism in Java, 1912–1926* (Ithaca, N.Y.: Cornell University Press, 1990), pp. 8–9.

[58]See George McT. Kahin, *Nationalism and Revolution in Indonesia* (Ithaca, N.Y.: Cornell University Press, 1952), pp. 31–32, for a succinct account of the halting progress of the colonial educational system.

Soon after 1900, signs of a nascent nationalism were clearly visible, fostered by the new types of professionals produced by late colonial capitalism: editors and journalists, mechanics and accountants, school teachers and apothecaries, politicians and surveyors. As the new century wore on, people of this kind became culturally, sociologically, and economically positioned—thanks above all to print and print-capitalism—to undertake the Encyclopédistes' coordination of professional knowledge against the ancien régime in Batavia. The dreams of these professionals, as articulated in the speeches and writings of Sukarno, Dr. Soetomo, Sjahrir, Semaun, and so many others, are familiar enough to us: "Perfect Indonesia"—some short or long way down the yellow brick road.[59] "Perfect Java" and "Perfect Male," however, are today obscure imaginings, all the more so in that the dream of "Perfect Indonesia," like all new forms of consciousness, brought with it its own amnesias. All the more reason, therefore, to take Twain's advice and return to the study of Old Java's ruined maps.

[59]Cf., in this regard, chap. 7, above, p. 267.

Index

Library of Congress Cataloging-in-Publication Data

Anderson, Benedict R. O'G. (Benedict Richard O'Gorman), 1936–
  Language and power : exploring political cultures in Indonesia / Benedict R. O'G.
Anderson.
    p.   cm. — (The Wilder House series in politics, history, and culture)
Includes index.
ISBN 0–8014–2354–6 (alk. paper)
  1. Political culture—Indonesia—History.   2. Indonesia—Politics and
government.   3. Intellectuals—Indonesia—Attitudes—History.   4. Indonesia—
Languages—Political aspects.   I. Title.   II. Series.
JQ776.A64   1990
306.2'09598—dc20

90–55126